ASCENT®
CENTER FOR TECHNICAL KNOWLEDGE

3DEXPERIENCE CATIA 2022x
3D Tolerancing and Annotation

Learning Guide

1st Edition

ASCENT - Center for Technical Knowledge®
3DEXPERIENCE CATIA 2022x
3D Tolerancing and Annotation
1st Edition

Prepared and produced by:

ASCENT Center for Technical Knowledge
630 Peter Jefferson Parkway, Suite 175
Charlottesville, VA 22911

866-527-2368
www.ASCENTed.com

Lead Contributor: Mark Potrzebowski

ASCENT - Center for Technical Knowledge (a division of Rand Worldwide Inc.) is a leading developer of professional learning materials and knowledge products for engineering software applications. ASCENT specializes in designing targeted content that facilitates application-based learning with hands-on software experience. For over 25 years, ASCENT has helped users become more productive through tailored custom learning solutions.

We welcome any comments you may have regarding this guide, or any of our products. To contact us please email: feedback@ASCENTed.com.

AS-3DE22-FTA1-SG // RS-3DE22-FTA1-SG

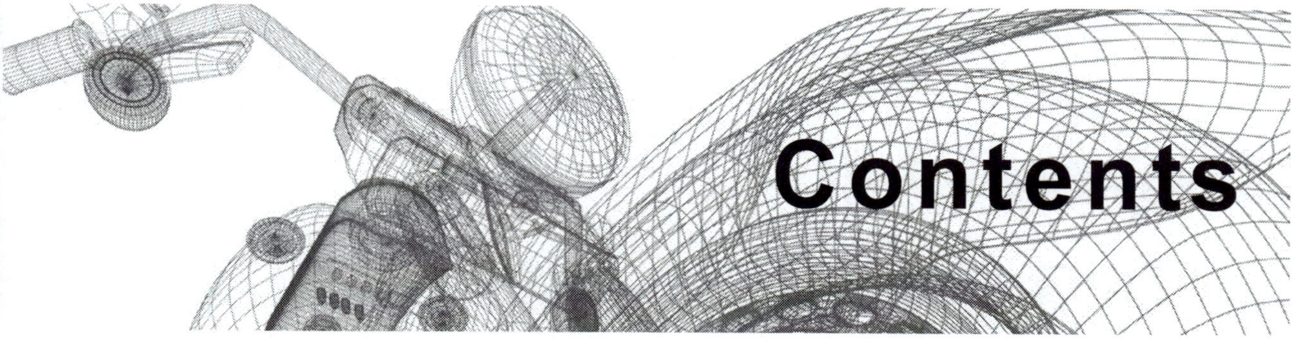

Contents

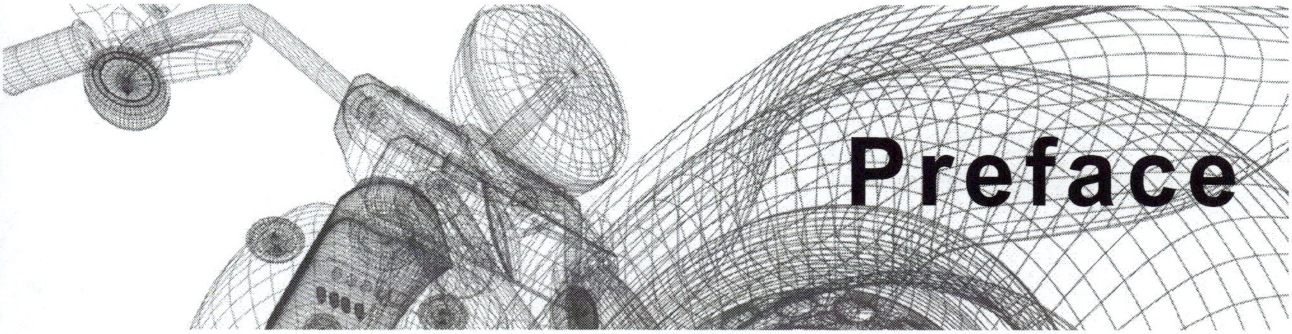

Preface

The *3DEXPERIENCE CATIA 2022x: 3D Tolerancing and Annotation* learning guide has numerous practices that will help you acquire the skills to create and display engineering, manufacturing, and assembly information directly on the 3D part, assembly, or process model. This extensive hands-on guide will provide you with a thorough understanding of geometric tolerances, dimensions, notes, and other annotations critical to the accurate and cost-effective creation of mechanical parts and assemblies. The 3D Tolerancing and Annotation guide complies with the industry and government initiated American Society of Mechanical Engineers' (ASME) Y14.41 3D standards for the creation and submission of model only, paperless design applications.

Topics Covered

- Introduction to 3D tolerancing and annotation
- 3D Tolerancing & Annotation (3D T&A) application overview
- Annotation process
- Extracting 2D views from the 3D model
- Annotation planes and extraction views
- Construction geometry
- Semantic and non-semantic annotations
- Datum reference frames
- Tolerance Advisor
- Basic dimensions
- Annotations: text, flag notes, datum elements, datum targets, surface texture, and dimensions
- Restricted areas
- Threads

- Annotation visualization tools: query, grouping, leader symbols, annotation mirror and transfer, and filters
- Cameras and captures
- Geometry connection management
- 3D T&A analysis and reporting
- Annotation creation at the product level
- 3D Annotation Insight app

Prerequisites

- Access to the 3DEXPERIENCE CATIA 2022x version of the software, to ensure compatibility with this guide. Future software updates that are released by Dassault Systèmes may include changes that are not reflected in this guide. The practices and files included with this guide might not be compatible with prior versions (e.g., 3DEXPERIENCE CATIA 2021x).
- Working knowledge of GD&T application and completion of the *3DEXPERIENCE CATIA 2022x: Introduction to Modeling* course are recommended.

Note on Software Setup

This guide assumes a standard installation of the software using the default preferences during installation. Lectures and practices use the standard software templates and default options for the Content Libraries.

Lead Contributor: Mark Potrzebowski

Mark Potrzebowski has been a trainer and curriculum developer in the PLM industry for over 14 years, with experience on multiple CAD systems, including Pro/ENGINEER, Creo Parametric, Inventor, and CATIA. Trained in Instructional Design, Mark uses his skills to develop instructor-led and web-based training products. Before joining ASCENT, Mark worked as a Technical Trainer with a focus on CATIA, Creo, and PLM systems. Mark holds a Bachelors degree in Computer Graphics Technology from Purdue University, West Lafayette, Indiana.

Mark has been the Lead Contributor for *3D Tolerancing and Annotation* since 2021.

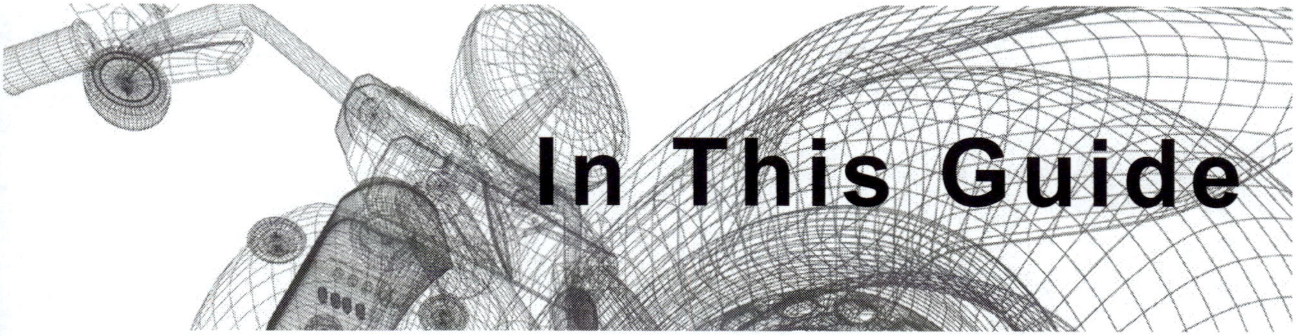

In This Guide

The following highlights the key features of this guide.

Feature	Description
Practice Files	The Practice Files page includes a link to the practice files and instructions on how to download and install them. The practice files are required to complete the practices in this guide.
Chapters	A chapter consists of the following: Learning Objectives, Instructional Content, and Practices. • **Learning Objectives** define the skills you can acquire by learning the content provided in the chapter. • **Instructional Content**, which begins right after Learning Objectives, refers to the descriptive and procedural information related to various topics. Each main topic introduces a product feature, discusses various aspects of that feature, and provides step-by-step procedures on how to use that feature. Where relevant, examples, figures, helpful hints, and notes are provided. • **Practice** for a topic follows the instructional content. Practices enable you to use the software to perform a hands-on review of a topic. It is required that you download the practice files (using the link found on the Practice Files page) prior to starting the first practice.
Appendices	Appendices provide additional information to the main course content. It could be in the form of instructional content, practices, tables, projects, or skills assessment.

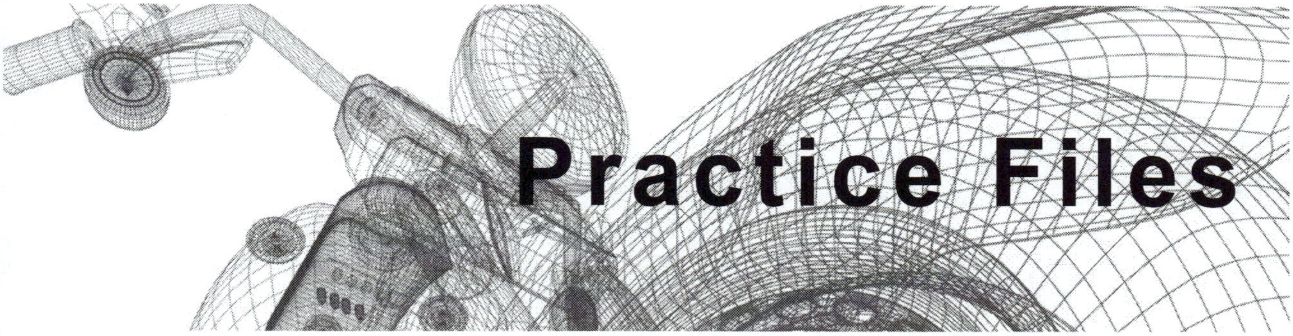

Practice Files

To download the practice files for this guide, use the following steps:

1. Type the URL ***exactly as shown below*** into the address bar of your Internet browser to access the Course File Download page.

   Note: If you are using the ebook, you do not have to type the URL. Instead, you can access the page simply by clicking the URL below.

   https://www.ascented.com/getfile/id/aymonieriPF

2. On the Course File Download page, click the **DOWNLOAD NOW** button, as shown below, to download the .ZIP file that contains the practice files.

3. Once the download is complete, unzip the file and extract its contents.

   The recommended practice files folder location is:
   C:\3DEXPERIENCE 3D T&A Practice Files

   Note: It is recommended that you do not change the location of the practice files folder. Doing so may cause errors when completing the practices.

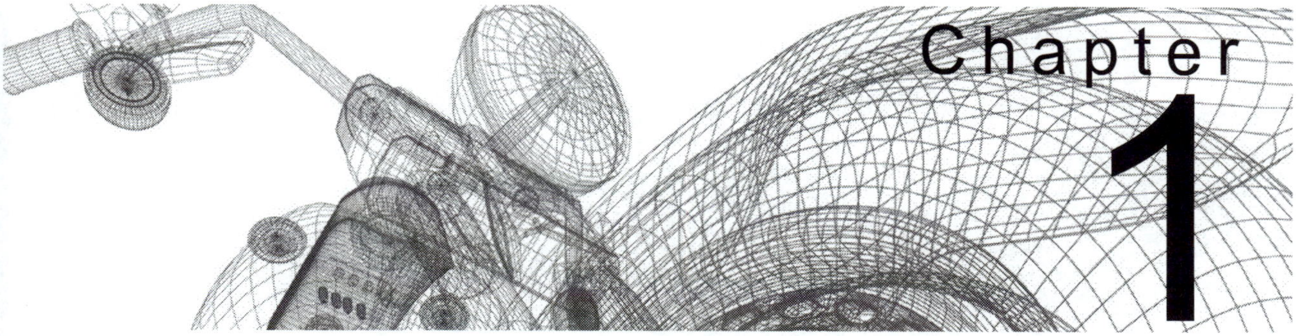

Introduction to 3D T&A

The goal of this guide is to teach you how to create tolerances and annotations to detail a model using the CATIA 3D Tolerancing & Annotation (3D T&A) app. You should already have a foundation-level understanding of the rules, standards, and types of geometrical tolerances, dimensions, and annotations.

Learning Objectives in This Chapter

- Understand the usage of tolerancing and annotations.
- Understand the use of the 3D T&A app.
- Recognize the 3D T&A interface and tools.
- Understand the annotation process.
- Create drawings from an annotated model.
- Learn how to access annotations and set annotation references.

1.1 Tolerancing and Annotations

Tolerances and annotations provide the details required to manufacture and fabricate a model designed in CATIA. Tolerances and annotations guide a Manufacturing group in the following ways:

- Details the acceptable standards.
- Provides the window for geometric variances and imperfections in parts and assemblies.
- Facilitates the production process and manufacturing standards.

Traditionally, these annotations are placed in the 2D drawing. Using the 3D Tolerancing & Annotation app, all annotations are stored directly in the 3D model. This eliminates the need to develop a drawing, and supports a paperless design and manufacturing environment. An example of an annotated part model is shown in Figure 1–1.

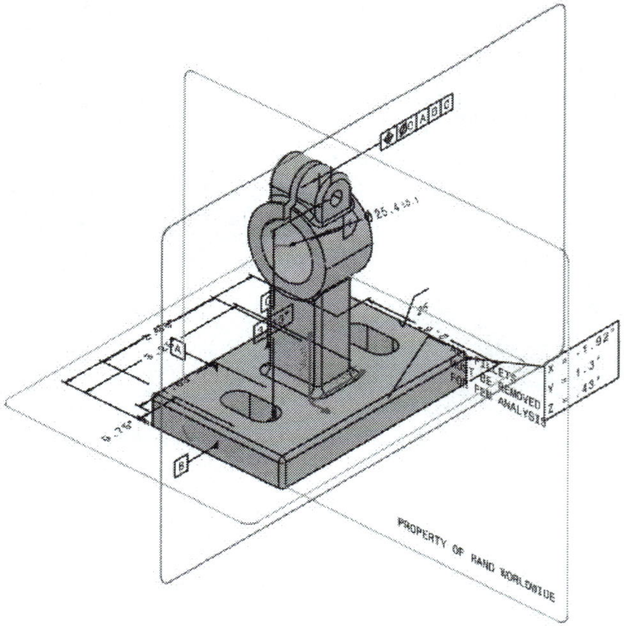

Figure 1–1

Placing the tolerances and annotations directly into the 3D design enables the manufacturing process to be considered throughout the design cycle, specifically in the initial stages. This helps avoid conflicts between design and manufacturing as early in the product life cycle as possible.

Annotations can be created in the following CATIA model types:

Model Type	File Type	Place Inside	App
Part	3D Part	3D Shape	3D Tolerancing & Annotation
Assembly	Physical Product	3D Shape	3D Tolerancing & Annotation

Although all annotations can be added to parts or products, they are placed within the *3D Shape* node of the specification tree. For 3D parts, the 3D shapes are automatically created; however, for products, the 3D shapes will have to be manually created by right-clicking on the product and selecting **Insert>3D Shape**.

Tolerances and annotations can be created and controlled when active within the 3D Shape view. If the top level of the part or product is active instead, you may find yourself in an app called 3D Annotation Insight. This app will only allow you to customize your display and apply filters. The creation of new objects isn't possible within the 3D Annotation Insight app.

All annotations are organized in specific branches of an annotation set in the specification tree. An example is shown in Figure 1–2.

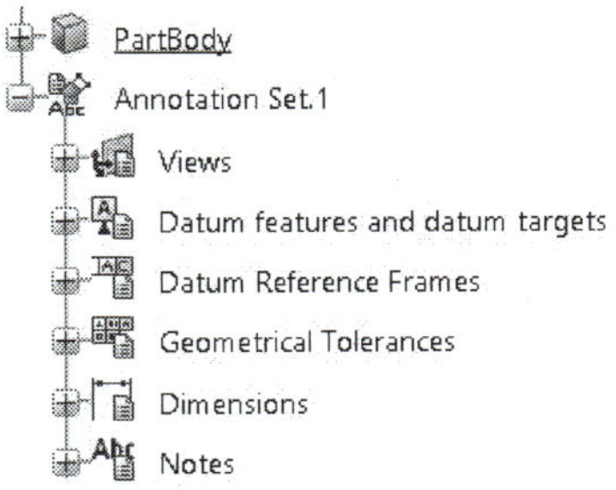

Figure 1–2

Annotation Standards

Similar to the drawing standards that are used to create 2D drawings, standards apply to the creation of annotations in a 3D model. For example, some annotations are created to match the ANSI-ASME standard.

Since it is possible to break a rule of the applied standard, two annotation categories can be created:

- Semantic
- Non-Semantic

Semantic

This type of annotation always matches the rules, specifications, and designations assigned by the active standard. Semantic annotations are created using the Tolerance Advisor or Framed (Basic) Dimensions icons. The Semantic Tolerancing Advisor dialog box is shown in Figure 1–3.

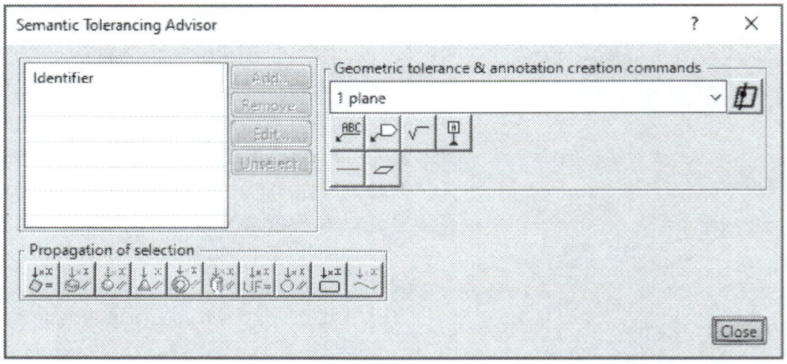

Figure 1–3

Non-Semantic

Non-semantic annotations might not necessarily match the active standard. Create this type of annotation when the active standard does not adequately represent the design intent of the model or the standards adopted by the designing company. Care should be taken when creating a non-semantic annotation to ensure that the end user of the annotation understands the designer's intent. Non-semantic annotations are created using the icons shown in Figure 1–4.

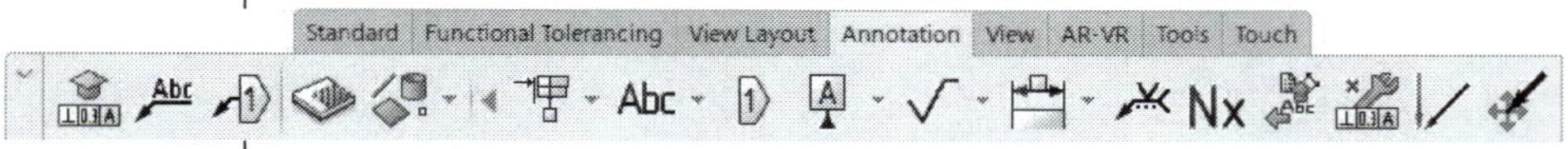

Figure 1–4

Icon	Name	Icon	Name
	Text		Flag Note
	Datum Element		Datum Target
	Geometrical Tolerance		Surface Texture
	Framed (Basic) Dimension		Dimensions
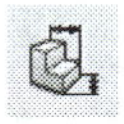	Generative Dimension		

1.2 Roles and Apps

The role used to create this material is the 3D Tolerancing & Annotation Designer role. While this role does grant access to many different apps within 3DEXPERIENCE, there are only two that will be focused on in this guide:

- 3D Tolerancing & Annotation
- 3D Annotation Insight

3D Tolerancing & Annotation

The majority of this learning material focuses on the creation of annotations and tolerances for part models in the 3D Tolerancing & Annotation app. However, this app is used for both parts and products within 3DEXPERIENCE. The 3D Tolerancing & Annotation app allows for the creation of views, tolerances, annotations, and filters to control the display of the model.

To access this app, first you will want to activate a 3D shape by double-clicking on it in the tree, then select the outer ring of the compass and select 

from under **My Apps**.

3D Annotation Insight

The 3D Annotation Insight app can only be used when active at the product level, either when dealing with an assembly and the product has been double-clicked on or if the 3D part has been activated instead of a 3D shape for a part model. The 3D Annotation Insight app is for display purposes only. The options available to you within the app only allow you to temporally customize and review the display of the model without creating any new objects.

To access this app, first you will want to activate a physical product or 3D part by double-clicking on it in the tree, then select the outer ring of the compass and select 

from under **My Apps**.

1.3 3D T&A Interface

The 3D Tolerancing & Annotation app interface is shown in Figure 1–5.

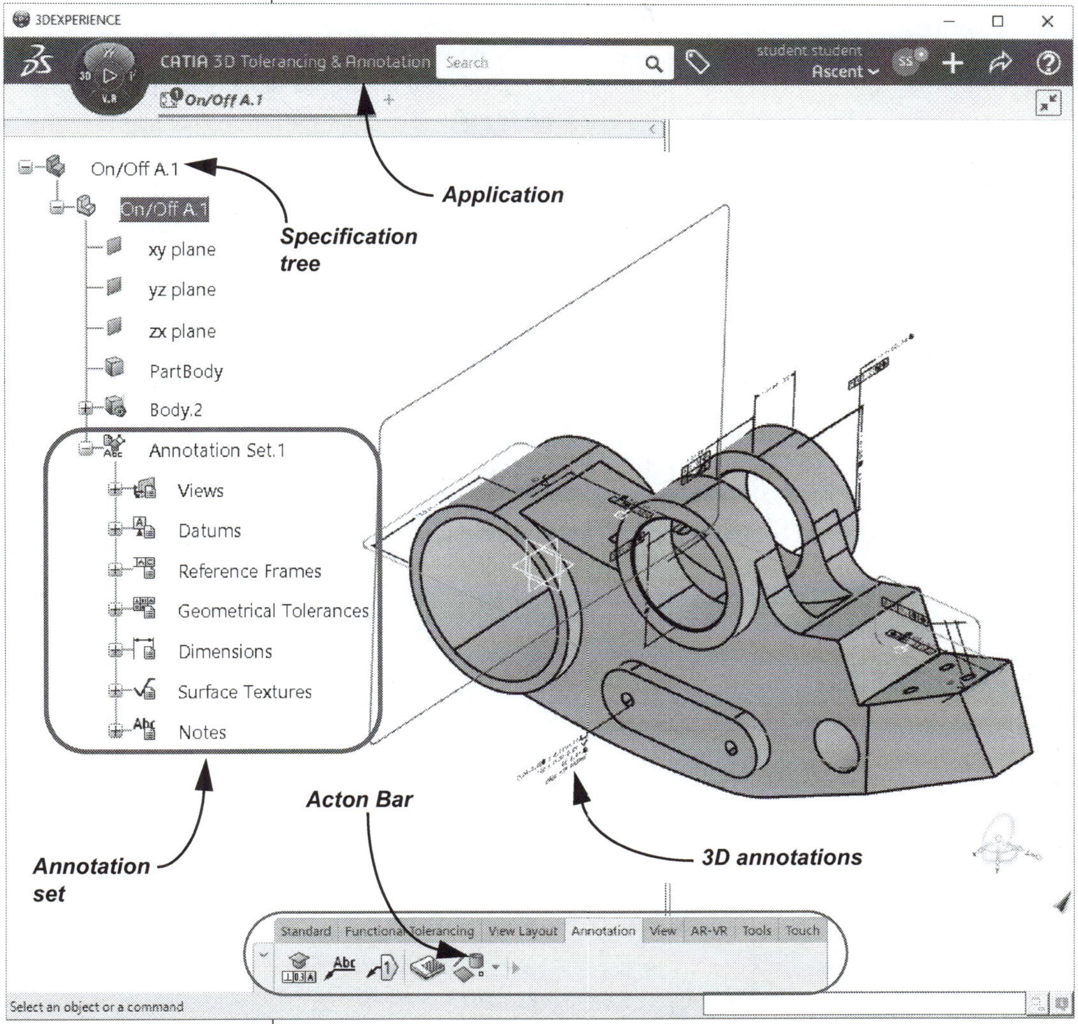

Figure 1–5

Hide/Show in 3D

Since 3D annotations add visual complexity to the model, they can be hidden as a group to simplify the display. If you receive a model that has no annotations displayed, you must toggle on the annotation set. To toggle the annotations on, right-click on the annotation set and select **Show in 3D**. This is useful when viewing an annotated model in an assembly.

When an annotation set has been hidden, the name of the annotation set still displays in the specification tree, as shown in Figure 1–6. The branch can still be expanded but no annotations display on the model.

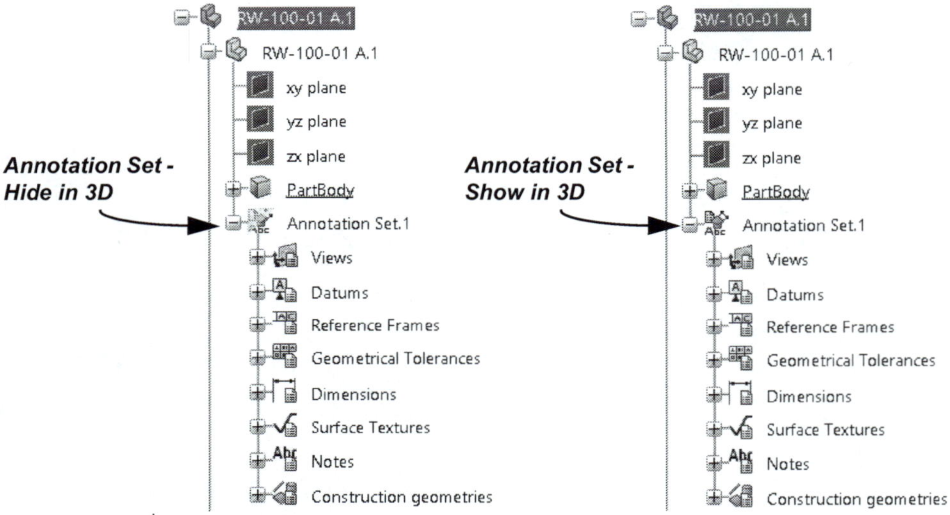

Figure 1–6

1.4 3D T&A Tools

This section provides an overview of the different tools available in the 3D Tolerancing & Annotation app. The Action Bar consists of eight sections, but this material will focus on the following four 3D T&A specific sections within the Action Bar:

- View Layout
- Annotation
- View
- Tools

View Layout

The View Layout section of the Action Bar contains the various view creation tools, as described in the following table. These views are used to hold all annotations for the part, and can be extracted with their annotations to a 2D representation.

Option	Icon	Description
Principal Views		Creates the principal views (Front, Left, Right, and so on).
View from Reference		Creates a view from the selected plane/planar surface.
Axonometric View		Creates a view from a 3D viewpoint.
Offset Section View/Section Cut		Creates an offset section view from the selected sketch.
Aligned Section View/Section Cut		Creates an aligned section view from the selected sketch.
View Layout		Creates 2D layout views from the selected annotation set, captures, and views.
Favorite Context		Defines the favorite context associated to the layout/annotation set.
Expanded View Layout		
Capture		Creates a capture in the 3D T&A app.

Annotation

The Annotation section of the Action Bar contains all of the tools required to fully annotate and tolerance the part. The Annotation tools are as follows:

Option	Icon	Description
Tolerance Advisor		Creates semantic annotations based on the selected geometry.
Text with Leader		Creates text with a leader to geometry in the annotation plane.
Flag Note with Leader		Creates a flag note with a leader to geometry in the annotation plane.
Restricted Area		Creates a restricted area from the selected geometry.
Geometry for 3D Annotations Flyout		
Constructed Geometry Creation		Creates construction geometry based on selected element(s).
Constructed Geometry Management		Shows details of constructed geometry references.
Thread Representation Creation		Creates thread representation construction geometry.
Expanded Action Bar		
Automatic Grouping		Automatically groups selected annotations together.
Annotations Positioning		Modifies the position of annotations in a view to ensure readability.
Text Flyout		
Text		Creates text in the annotation plane.
Text Parallel To Screen	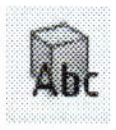	Creates text referencing geometry or an annotation plane that is always parallel to the screen.
Flag Note		Creates a flag note in the annotation plane.

Datum Feature Flyout		
Datum Feature		Creates a datum feature from selected geometry.
Datum Target		Creates a datum target from selected geometry.
Geometrical Tolerance		Creates a geometrical tolerance for the selected geometry.
Surface Texture Flyout		
Surface Texture		Specifies the surface roughness.
Edge of Undefined Shape		Creates annotations for undercuts and passing on internal and external edges.
Dimensions Flyout		
Framed (Basic) Dimensions		Creates a basic dimension for the selected geometry.
Dimensions		Creates dimensions for the selected geometry.
Cumulated Dimensions		Creates cumulated dimensions for the selected geometry.
Stacked Dimensions		Creates stacked dimensions for the selected geometry.
Coordinate Dimensions		Creates coordinate dimensions for the selected geometry.
Curvilinear Dimensions		Creates curvilinear dimensions for the selected geometry.
Generative Dimension		Creates selected model feature dimensions automatically.

View

The View section of the Action Bar has many generic commands that are found in most apps in 3DEXPERIENCE, but the following are the 3D T&A specific tools found within the View section. While these tools may be found in other apps, they all have an important use when working with 3D T&A.

Option	Icon	Description
Views...		Creates semantic annotations based on the selected geometry.
Annotation Blanking		Displays annotations with a blank background
3D Master Query		When this is active, selecting an element also highlights all associated geometry and annotations.
Display 3D Grid	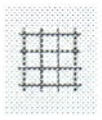	Toggles on/off the display of a grid on the active view.
Cutting Plane		Cuts the part by the selected annotation plane.
Elements' Analysis		Displays the various elements with particular status in different customizable colors.
Mirror Annotations		Mirrors the direction of the text in the annotation plane.

Tools

The Tools section, just like the View section, has many generic commands that are found in most apps in 3DEXPERIENCE. The following are the tools that are important for creating in the 3D T&A app.

Option	Icon	Description
3D Annotation Filter		Enables annotations to be filtered and displayed.
Object Properties		Toggles on/off the Object Properties window.
Action Pad		Toggles on/off the Action Pad window.

Additional Tools

These tools are not found on the Action Bar by default. However, they can be useful when needed. To be able to use these commands, they will need to be added to either the Action Bar or the Action Pad. Selecting **Me>Preferences>Customize...** is the easiest way add them to either location.

Option	Icon	Description
Non Semantic 3D Annotations Report		Generates a report based on annotations.
Report Customization		Customizes report generation options.
Manual Grouping	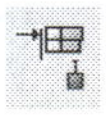	Manually groups selected annotations together.

1.5 Annotation Process

General Steps

Use the following general steps to add annotations and tolerances to a model:

1. Define the tolerancing standard.
2. Define the annotation planes.
3. Create dimensions and tolerances.
4. Create datum reference frames.
5. Create geometrical tolerances.
6. Create basic dimensions.
7. Create additional annotations.
8. (Optional) Extract 2D drawing views.

Step 1 - Define the tolerancing standard.

The tolerancing standard defines the properties to which the annotations must conform. To define the standard, select **Me>Preferences>App Preferences>3D Modeling> Mechanical Systems>3D Tolerancing and Annotation** and select the *Tolerancing* arrow. Select an option in the *Standard* drop-down list, as shown in Figure 1–7.

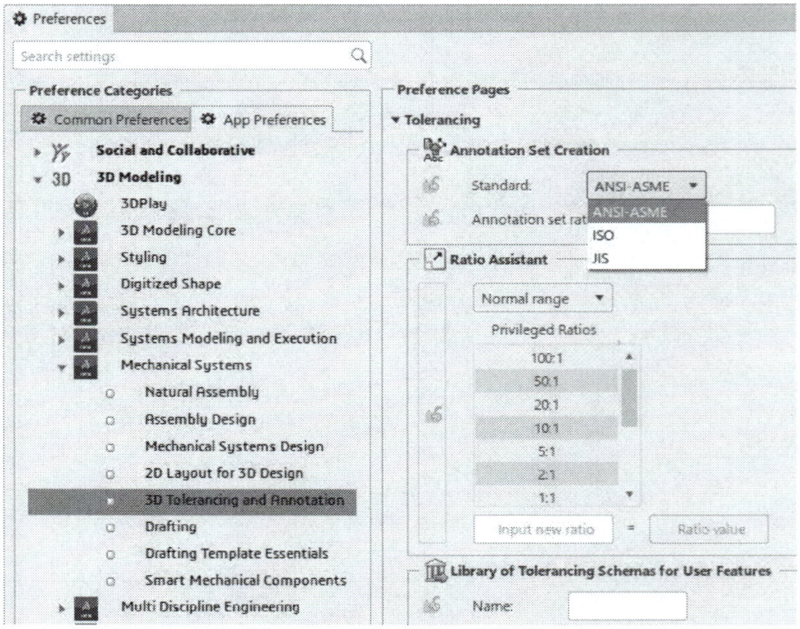

Figure 1–7

New models are created using the default standard. To change the standard for existing annotation sets, right-click on the Annotation Set.1 branch of the specification tree and select **Properties**. Use the drop-down list in the *Standards* tab of the Properties dialog box to change the standard for a model, as shown in Figure 1–8.

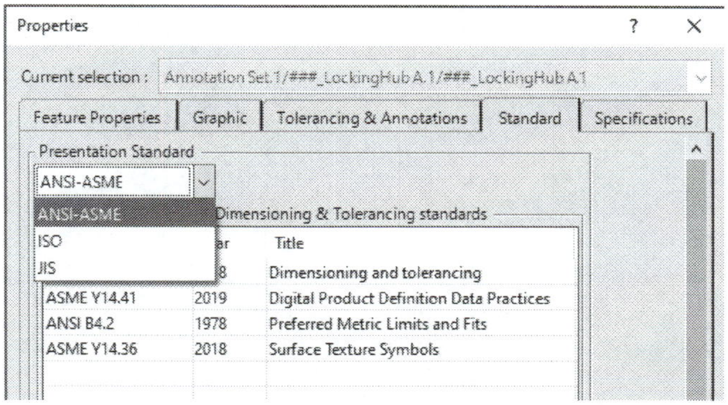

Figure 1–8

Step 2 - Define the annotation planes.

Before creating any annotations, define an annotation or view plane by referencing any planar face or reference plane in the model. The view plane provides an orientation reference for the annotation. When creating new annotations, they are associated with the active view plane. This enables annotations to be selected based on the view plane that was active during their creation.

The top face of the part shown in Figure 1–9 has been defined as an annotation plane.

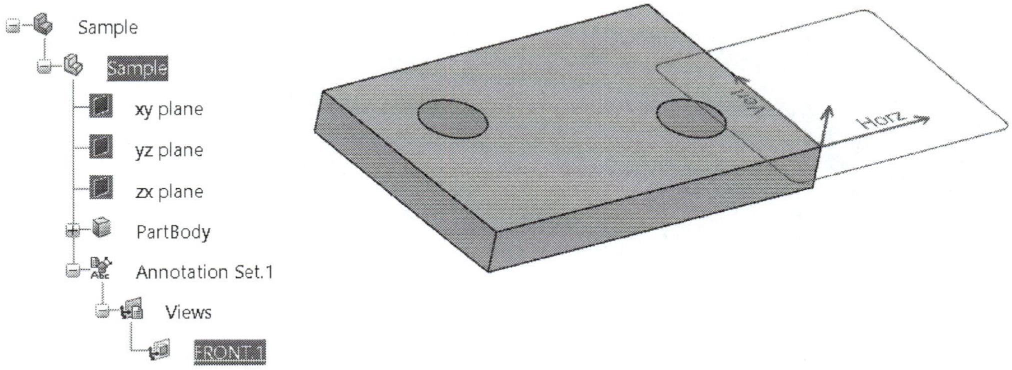

Figure 1–9

Active View

The active view plane is identified by a red border on the model. In the specification tree, the active view displays with a blue highlight and it is underlined, as shown in Figure 1–10. If no view planes exist, one is created that accommodates the annotation being defined.

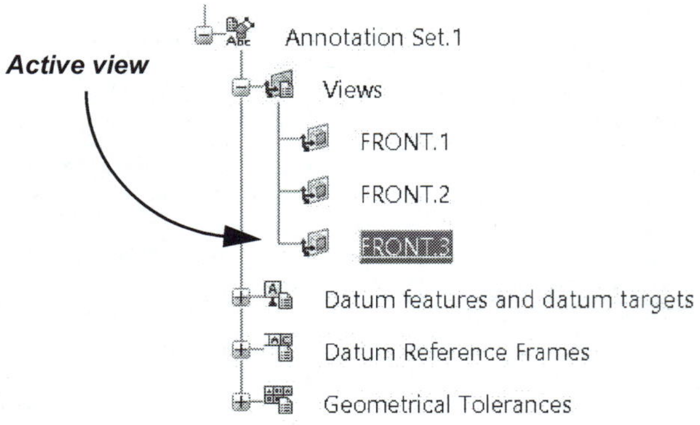

Figure 1–10

To activate a view plane, double-click on the view in the specification tree. You can also activate the view by double-clicking the view frame on the model.

Step 3 - Create dimensions and tolerances.

Dimensions and tolerances should be added as early as possible to support the datum reference frames and geometrical tolerances that are added to the model.

Dimensions can be toleranced using one of the following methods:

- General Tolerance (e.g., 90)
- Numerical Values (e.g., 90 ± 0.1)
- Tabulated Values (e.g., 90 H7)
- Single Limit (e.g., 90 MIN)

Some dimensions and tolerances have been added to the part, as shown in Figure 1–11.

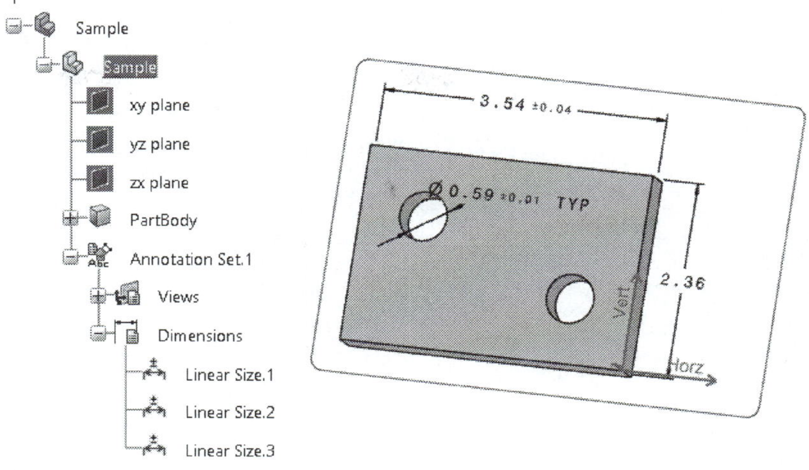

Figure 1–11

Step 4 - Create datum reference frames.

The next step is to define the semantic datums for the model. They can be defined on planar faces or reference planes in the model. If a non-planar surface is selected, datum target points must be defined to establish the datum.

In CATIA, datum reference frames are also called datum systems. The terms are used interchangeably.

Datum reference frames (DRF) provide the basis for all geometrical tolerancing in the model. The DRF's are developed from a selection of semantic datums. Once created, DRF's are added to the specification tree and the Semantic Tolerancing Advisor dialog box.

Three semantic datums (A, B, and C) and a datum reference frame (A|B|C) have been defined for the part model, as shown in Figure 1–12.

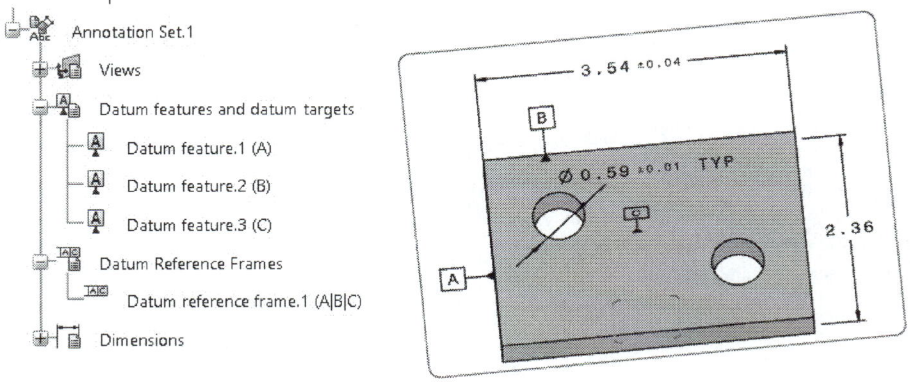

Figure 1–12

Step 5 - Create geometrical tolerances.

Since the geometrical tolerance must be constructed from one of the existing datum reference frames, they can only be added once the DRF's have been defined. A variety of geometrical tolerance types and conditions can be created in both semantic and non-semantic formats. A position tolerance has been added to the diameter dimension, as shown in Figure 1–13.

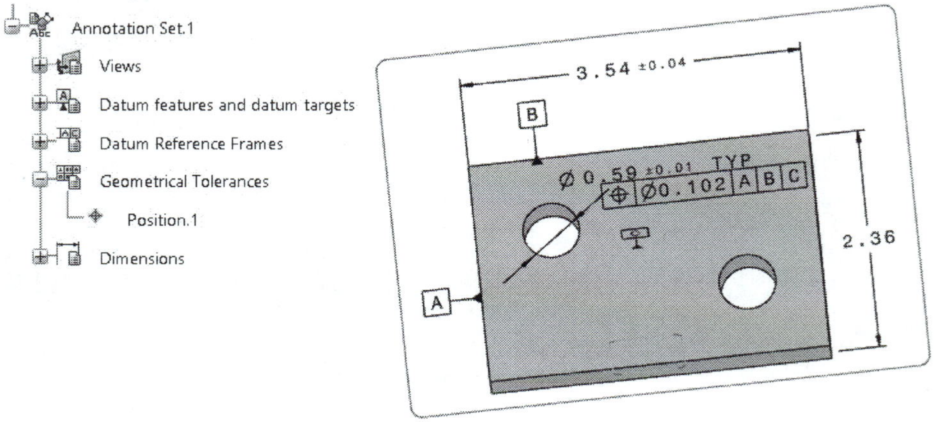

Figure 1–13

Step 6 - Create basic dimensions.

Basic dimensions are indicated by a frame or box around the dimension value. Since a basic dimension specifies a theoretically exact value, it must be associated with a datum reference frame to be created. A basic dimension has been added to the model, as shown in Figure 1–14.

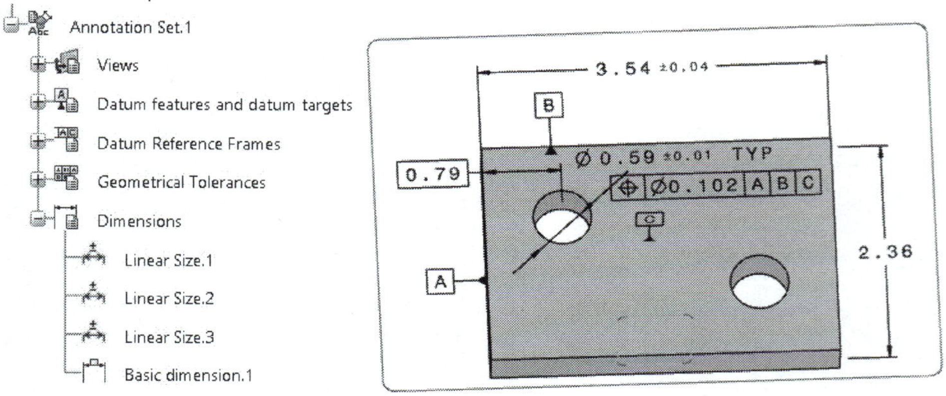

Figure 1–14

Step 7 - Create additional annotations.

The last step of the process is to complete the annotation of the model. The following list indicates some of the different types of additional annotations that can be defined:

- Text, including notes with leaders and title block information
- Flag notes
- Surface texture symbols

A completely annotated model is shown in Figure 1–15.

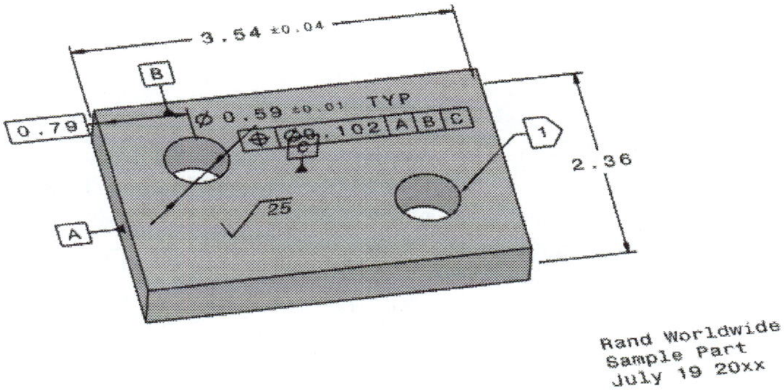

Figure 1–15

Step 8 - (Optional) Extract 2D drawing views.

Once the model has been fully annotated, you can extract drawing views directly from the annotation views.

1.6 Drawing Creation

Using the 3D T&A app simplifies the creation of drawing views. In the same way that drawing views can be extracted directly from the model, annotated views can also be taken directly from the model into the 2D drawing. This ability ensures that all engineering information is stored and extracted directly from the 3D model. It also enables the design and manufacturing process to minimize its reliance on the drawing for output.

General Steps

Use the following general steps to create a drawing using an annotated model.

1. Create a new drawing.
2. Extract a view from the 3D model.
3. Align the drawing views.

Step 1 - Create a new drawing.

With the annotated model open, create a new drawing. The tolerance standard and drawing standard must be the same to display an annotated view from a model.

Step 2 - Extract a view from the 3D model.

Before creating any drawing views, tile the widgets so that selections between the model and drawing can be facilitated. If the part and drawing widgets are open within the same tab, right-click on the tab and select **Tile Horizontally**. If the drawing and part widgets are in different tabs, you can toggle between widgets by selecting the tabs they are in.

In the expanded View Layout section of the Action Bar within the Drafting app, click  (View from 3D). Expand the specification tree for the annotated model and select an annotation plane in the Views branch. The system previews the annotated view in the drawing window. Position and orient the view using the drawing compass and then select anywhere in the drawing background to generate the view.

A drawing with multiple annotated views is shown in Figure 1–16.

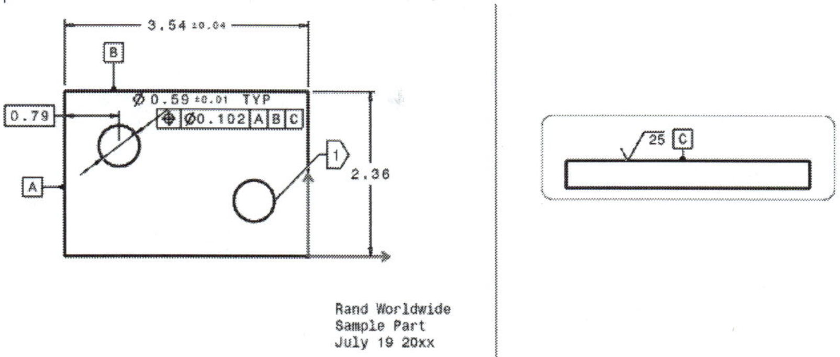

Figure 1–16

Step 3 - Align the drawing views.

By default, drawing views added from the model are not aligned correctly.

How To: Align the Views

1. Right-click on the border of the drawing view that moves into an aligned position and select **View Positioning>Align Views Using Elements**.
2. Select an element from each view to be aligned. For example, two edges are selected from the drawing views, as shown in Figure 1–17.

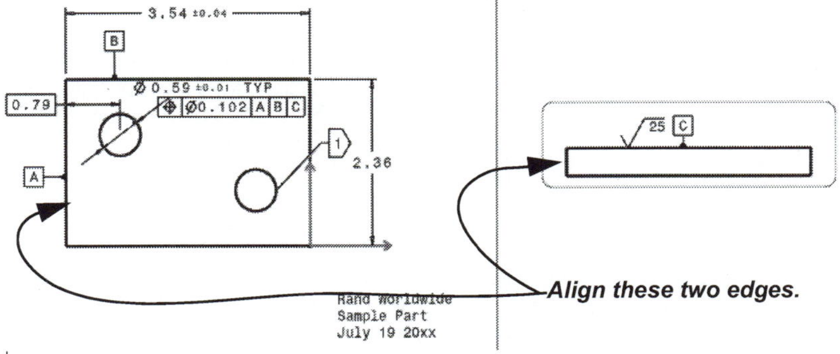

Figure 1–17

The aligned views are shown in Figure 1–18.

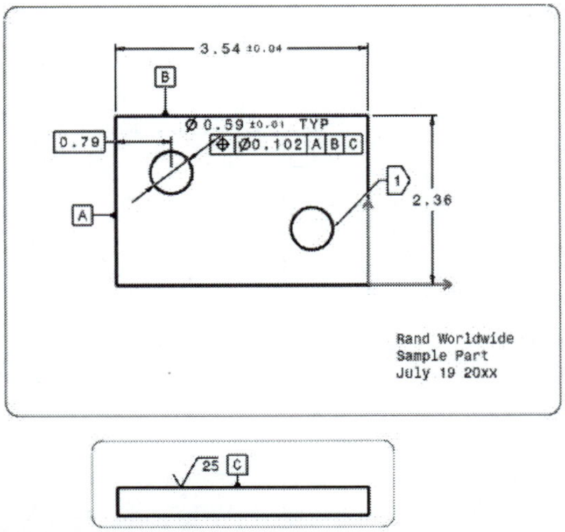

Figure 1–18

1.7 Accessing Annotations

An annotation set is created to store all elements created in the 3D Tolerancing & Annotation app and is viewable outside this application. Therefore, only the designers that are applying annotations require a role for 3D T&A. Anyone that is reviewing annotations and tolerances can do so using the 3D Annotation Insight app or can access them through another app that enables them to view part and product models.

If you are using the 3D Annotation Insight app to review part-level annotations, you have to activate the part at the top of the tree instead of at the 3D shape level that would need to be activated for 3D Tolerancing & Annotation. An example of an annotated model that has been activated at the part level in the 3D Annotation Insight app is shown in Figure 1–19.

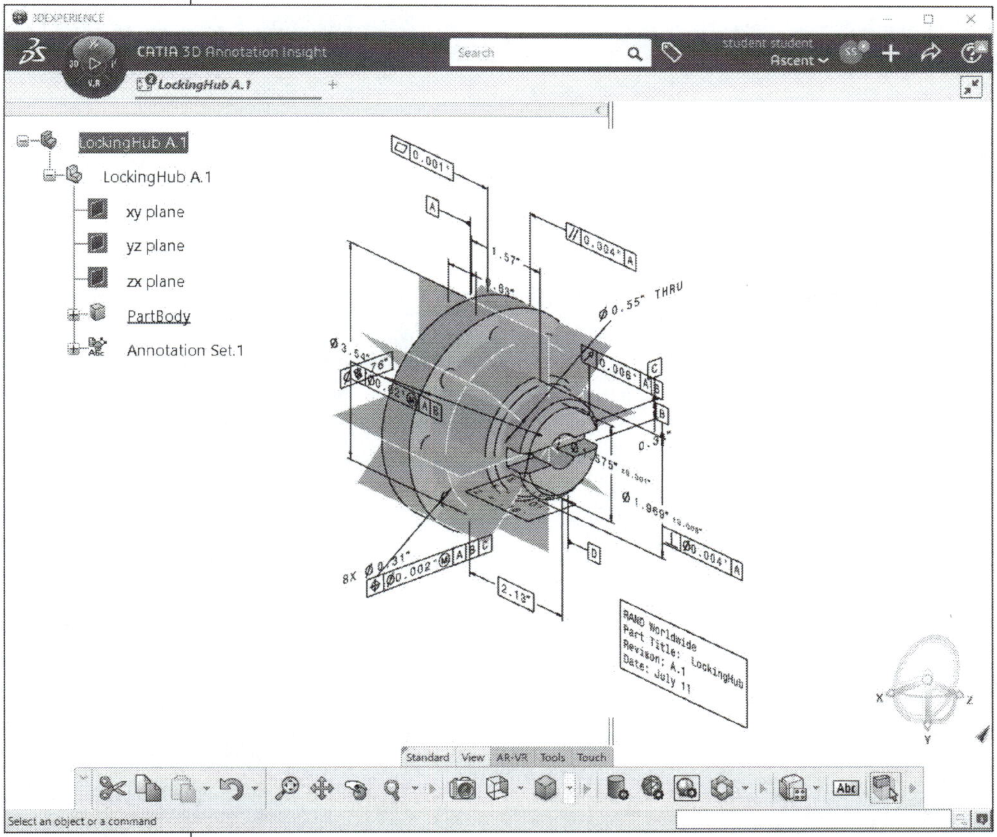

Figure 1–19

Remember that you might have to toggle on the annotation set before it can be viewed in the model. This is done by right-clicking on the annotation set and selecting **Show in 3D**.

1.8 Annotation References

You must select references when creating annotations. For example, the hole feature is selected to create the dimension and geometrical tolerance annotation shown in Figure 1–20. A parent-child relationship now exists between the hole and the annotation so that the annotation would fail if the hole were deleted.

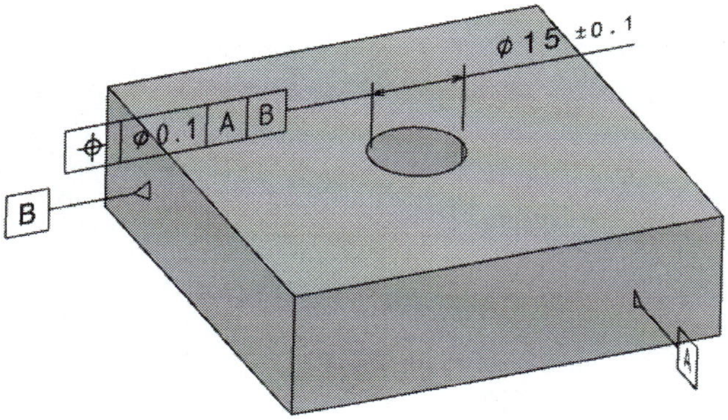

Figure 1–20

3D Master Query

The 3D Master Query tool () is used to identify the connection between a selected annotation and the rest of the model by highlighting elements on the model and in the specification tree when enabled. For example, the system highlights the hole feature if the toleranced dimension is selected, as shown in Figure 1–21.

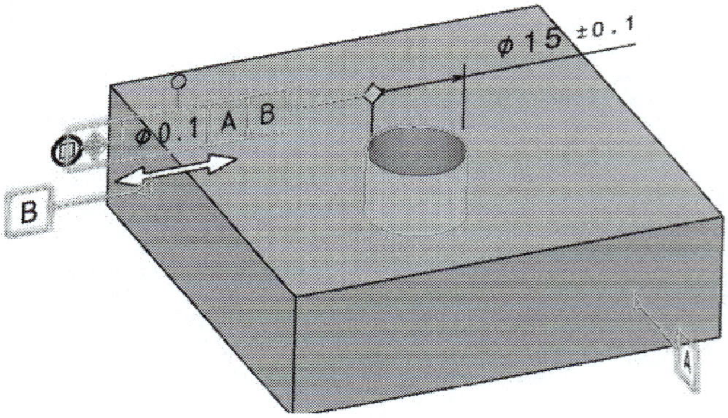

Figure 1–21

The 3D Master Query also considers the relationships between annotations. For example, if the geometrical tolerance is selected, the system highlights the hole feature and the Datum A and B annotations that are referenced by the geometrical tolerance.

By default, the **3D Master Query** tool is active. The icon is toggled on and off by selecting it in the View section of the Action Bar, as shown in Figure 1–22.

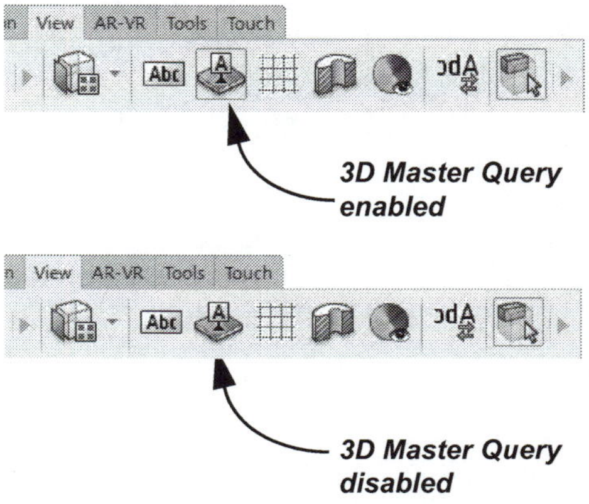

Figure 1–22

When active, the 3D Master Query tool will also section the model when a view is selected.

Practice 1a

3D T&A Overview

Practice Objectives

- Review an annotated model.
- Activate a view.
- Create a note.
- Create annotated drawing views from a 3D model.

In this practice, you will review a model that contains a variety of tolerances and annotations. The intent of this practice is to become familiar with the 3D T&A app and the different types of annotations that can be created.

After reviewing the model, you create a new drawing file and extract annotated views from the 3D geometry. The intent is to reinforce the concept that all engineering information must be stored and extracted directly from the 3D model. This enables the design and manufacturing process to minimize its reliance on the drawing for output.

The model and completed drawing displays, as shown in Figure 1–23.

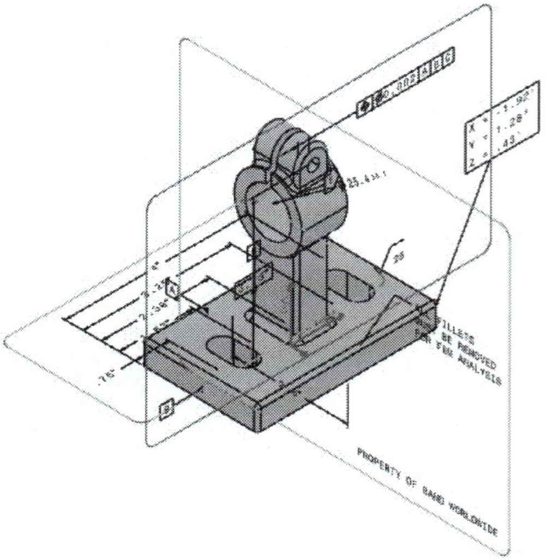

Figure 1–23

Task 1 - Import and open a part file.

1. Select (Add)>**Import**.
2. In the *Import* window, click (Browse) and navigate to your practice files folder.
3. Select the **FlangLock.3dxml** file, then click **Open** to place the file in the *Filename* field.

While this step isn't spelled out in all of the exercises, putting your initials in front of your imported files can help differentiate them from others that get saved.

4. Enter **###_** in the *Duplication String* field, where ### represents your personal initials. This will put your initials in front of the part title and help differentiate your files from others who might be doing the same exercises if you save them and open them later.
5. Click **OK** to complete the import process.
6. Click **OK** for the Operation report.
7. Right-click on **###_FlangeLock A.1** in the specification tree and select **Open**.

Task 2 - Switch to the 3D Tolerancing & Annotation app and adjust Preferences.

1. Verify that you are in the 3D Tolerancing & Annotation application. If not, select the outer ring of the compass and then select **3D Tolerancing & Annotation** from the **My Apps** list, as shown in Figure 1–24.

Figure 1–24

2. Select **Me>Preferences>Common Preferences> Parameters, Measures, and Units>Units** and select the *Units* arrow.

3. Select **Inch (in)** from the Length drop-down list, as shown in Figure 1–25.

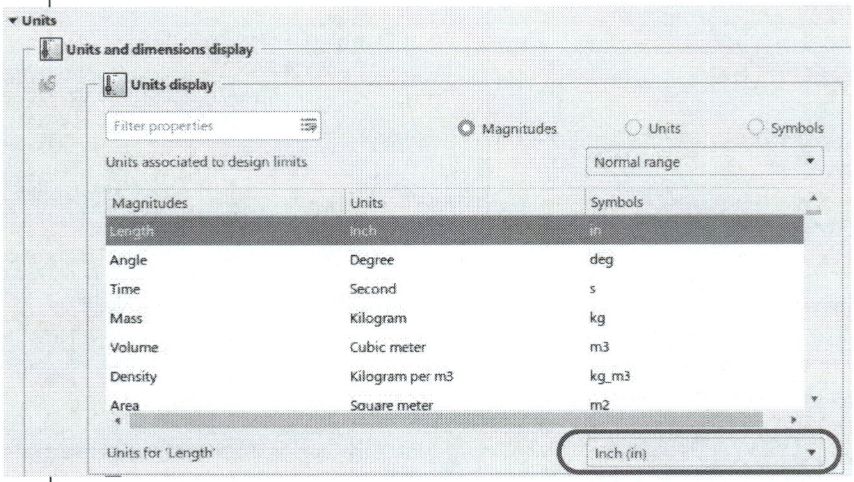

Figure 1–25

4. Click **OK**.

5. By default, the **3D Master Query** icon is enabled. This icon highlights geometry and reference frames that are associated to the selected annotation. If enabled, the icon is outlined with a blue square. For now, disable this option by clicking  (3D Master Query) in the View section of the Action Bar.

Task 3 - Review the annotations.

The presence of 3D T&A annotations in the model can be detected by the Annotation Set branch in the specification tree. You can toggle the display of annotations on and off to simplify the display of the model. Currently, the display of annotations is toggled off.

1. Right-click on **Annotation Set.1** in the specification tree and select **Hide in 3D**.

2. Right-click again on Annotation Set.1 in the specification tree and select **Show in 3D**. Annotations display on the model, as shown in Figure 1–26.

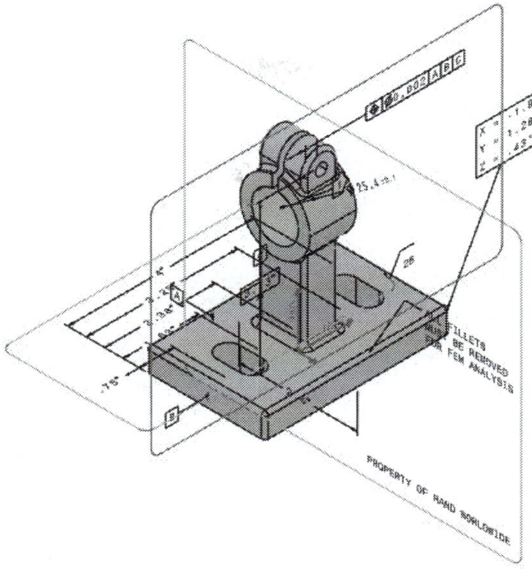

Figure 1–26

3. Expand the **Annotations** branch. A variety of annotations have been created in the model. Each annotation is organized in the tree by type, as shown in Figure 1–27.

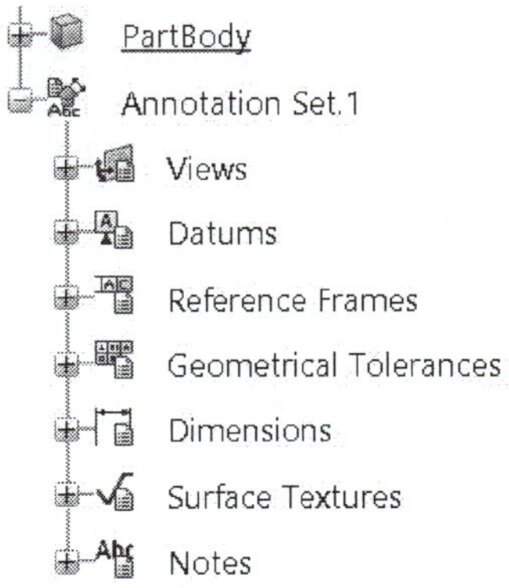

Figure 1–27

4. Expand the different branches of the specification tree and select a variety of annotations to become familiar with the different types. As tolerances are selected in the tree, they highlight on the model.

5. Click  (3D Master Query) so that it is enabled.

The other annotations are hidden in Figure 1–28 to simplify the display of the model.

6. Select the **Position.1** tolerance, as shown in Figure 1–28. It also highlights the geometry associated to the tolerance (Datum Reference Frame A|B|C and Hole.2).

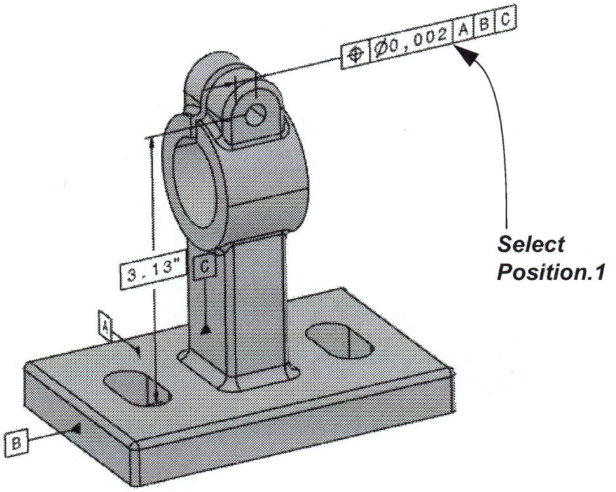

Figure 1–28

Task 4 - Modify the model.

The dimensional annotations are associative to the geometry on which they are based. In this task, you modify the Multipad base feature and then update the model to view changes to the associated annotations.

1. In the specification tree, expand **PartBody** and then **Multipad.1**. Double-click on **Sketch.1**. The sketch for the multipad feature displays.
2. Double-click on the **2.559** dimension shown in Figure 1–29.

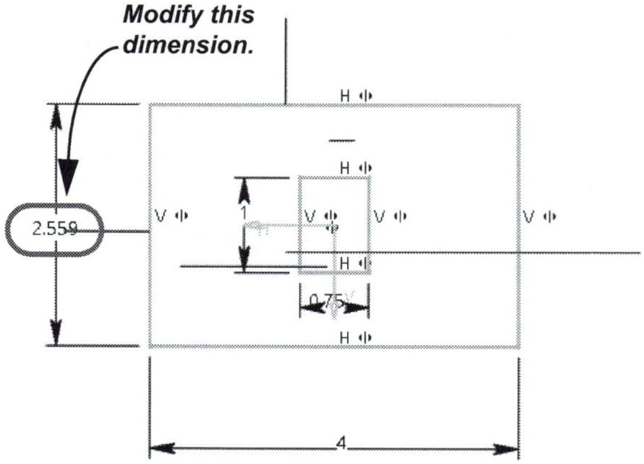

Figure 1–29

3. Enter a new value of **2.6** and click **OK**.

4. Click (Exit App) to exit Sketcher. The system updates all geometry and annotations based on the design change, as shown in Figure 1–30.

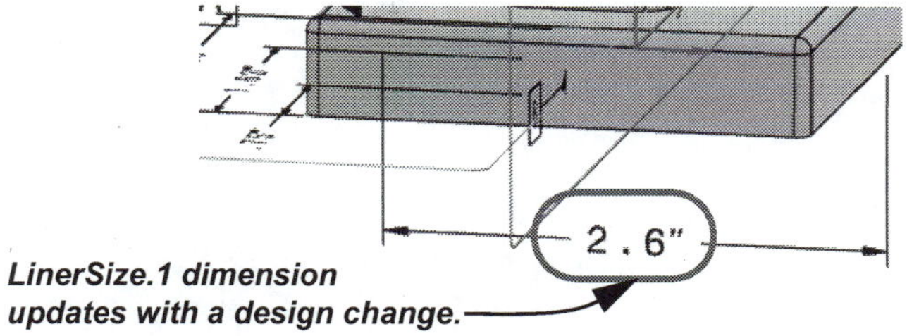

Figure 1–30

Task 5 - Activate a view and add a note.

The frame of the currently selected view highlights in cyan on the model and in the specification tree. Any annotations created are automatically associated with the activated view, which displays as red in the model and dark blue in the specification tree.

In this task, you add a text annotation to the model to demonstrate the properties of the active view.

1. Expand the **Annotation Set.1>Views** branch of the specification tree. The active view, **Front View.2**, is indicated by a red plane in the specification tree and on the model.

2. Double-click on **Front View.1** in the specification tree to activate the view.

3. Click Abc (Text) from the Annotation section of the Action Bar and select a location close to the one shown in Figure 1–31. The Text Editor dialog box opens.

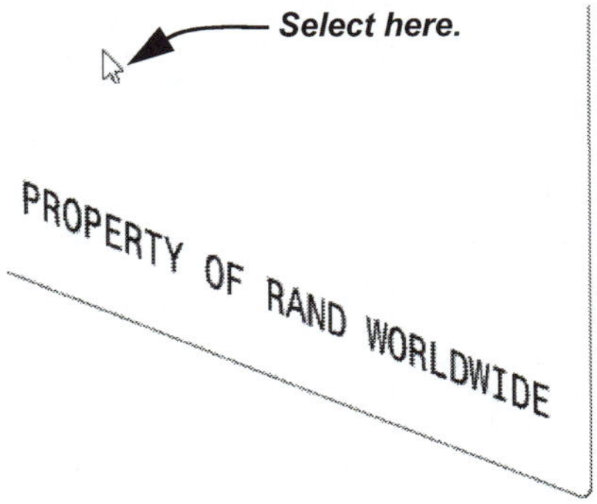

Figure 1–31

4. Enter the text **Material: Aluminum** and click **OK**. The annotation is added as **Text.3** to the Notes branch of the specification tree.

5. To orient the model using the view plane, click (Normal View) and then select **Front View.1** on the model or in the specification tree.

6. Position the text annotation as shown in Figure 1–32.

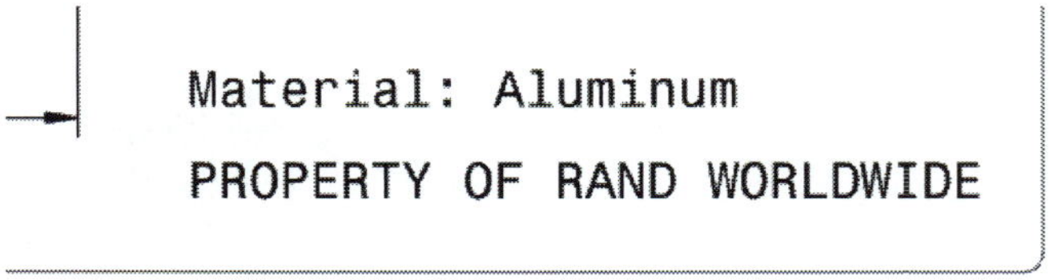

Figure 1–32

Task 6 - Create a drawing.

1. Select **(Add)>Drawing**. The New Drawing dialog box opens, as shown in Figure 1–33.

2. In the *Drawing Information* tab, create the drawing using the following parameters:

   - *Standard:* **ASME-ASME**
   - *Sheet Style:* **C ANSI**
   - *Automatic Layout:* **Empty sheet**

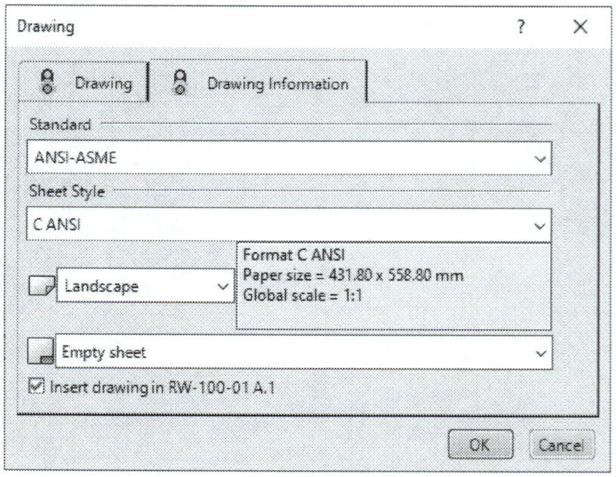

Figure 1–33

3. Click **OK** to create the new drawing.

4. In the newly created drawing widget, in the expanded View Layout section of the Action Bar, click (View from 3D).
5. Switch to the **RW-100-01** part widget and select **Front View.1** in the specification tree. The system displays this view and all annotations that are associated with it, as shown in Figure 1–34.

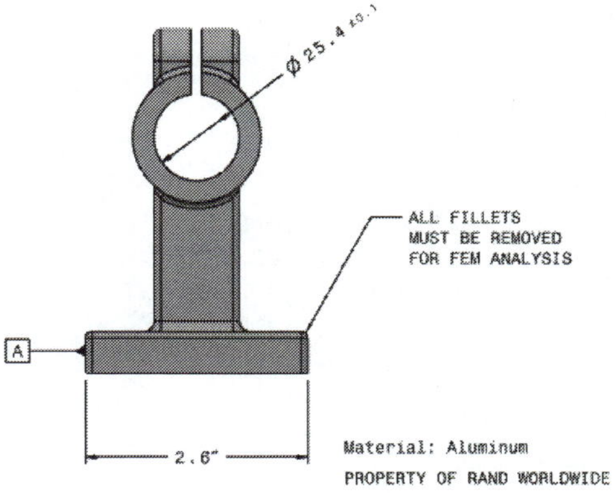

Figure 1–34

6. Click anywhere in the background of the drawing window to complete the view creation.
7. Create two more views using (View from 3D), selecting **Front View.2** and **Front View.3**. Position the drawing views as shown in Figure 1–35.

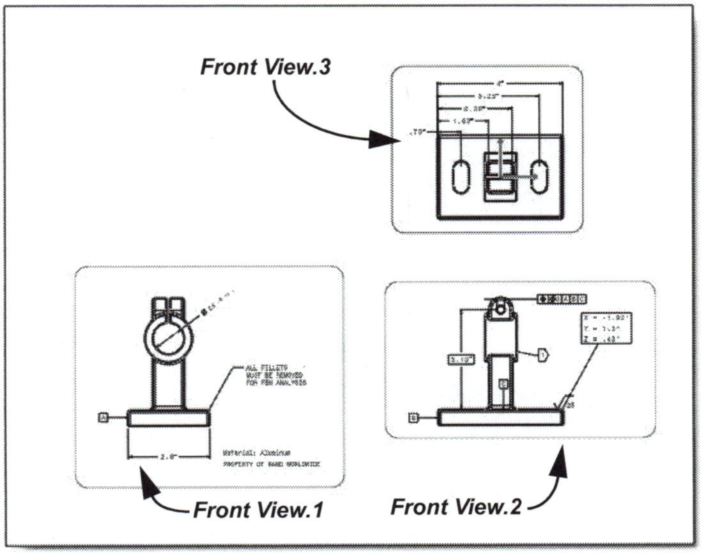

Figure 1–35

Task 7 - Align the drawing views.

1. Right-click on the border of **Front View.3** and select **View Positioning>Align Views Using Elements**.

2. Select the entities from **Front View.2** and **Front View.3**, as shown in Figure 1–36.

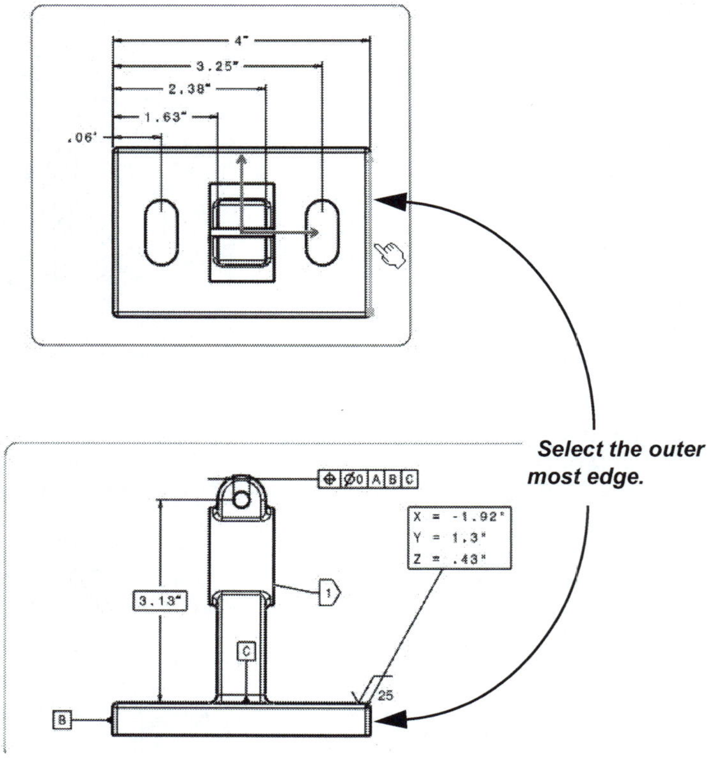

Figure 1–36

3. Repeat this operation to align **Front View.1** and **Front View.2**. The drawing displays, as shown in Figure 1–37.

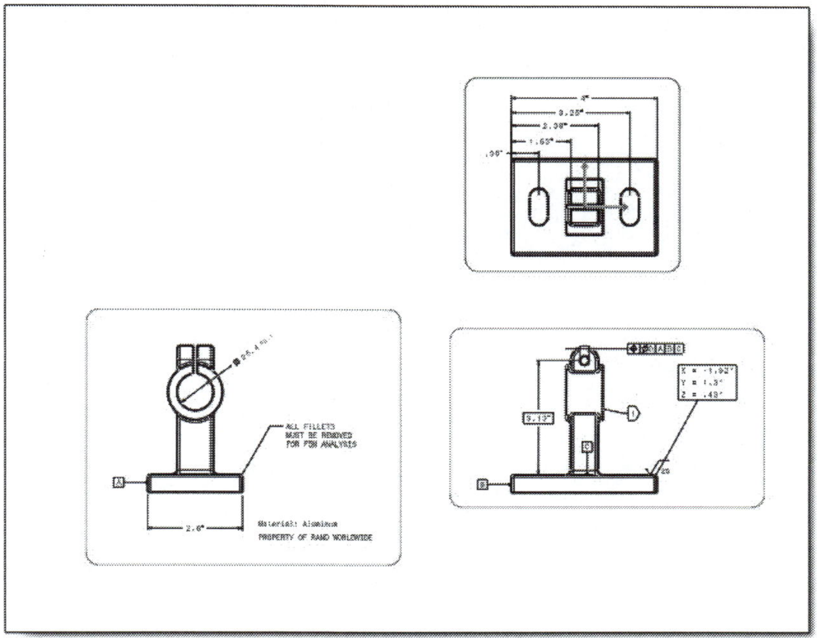

Figure 1–37

Task 8 - Transfer an annotation to another view.

1. Activate the **FlangeLock A.1** part window and maximize the window.

2. Right-click on the **2.6in** dimension and select **Transfer To View/Annotation Plane**, as shown in Figure 1–38.

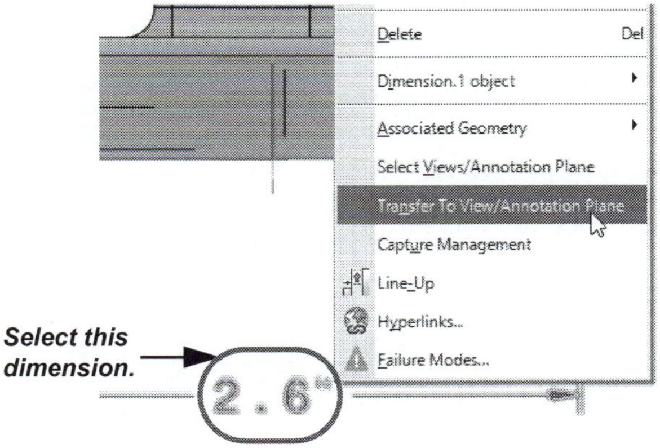

Figure 1–38

3. Select **Front View.3** in the specification tree. The system transfers the 2.6in dimension to this view plane.
4. Drag the dimension to an appropriate location.
5. Switch over to the Drawing widget.
6. Update the drawing to reflect the modification made to the 2.6in dimension. The Front View.3 drawing view displays, as shown in Figure 1–39.

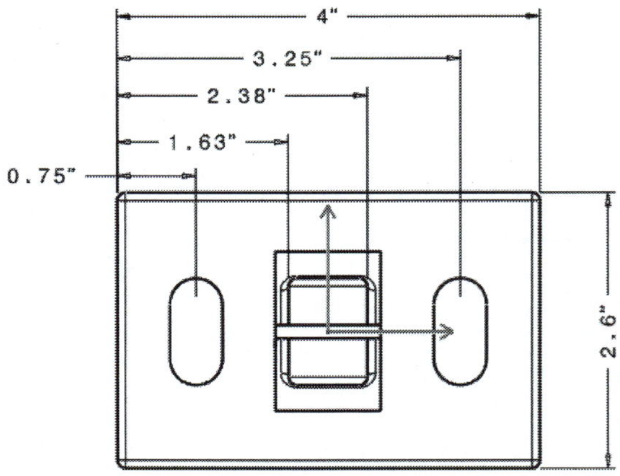

Figure 1–39

7. Save the model and drawing and close all windows.

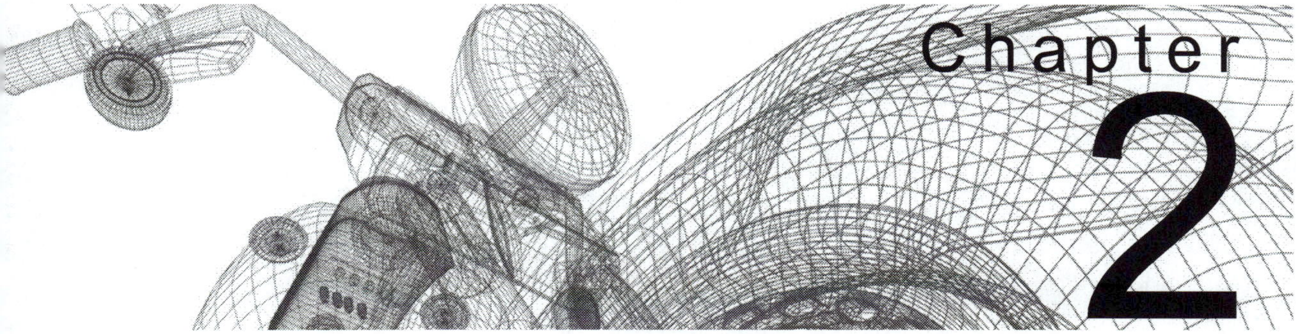

Preparing the Model

This chapter introduces how to create annotation planes and construction geometry. These features serve as the foundation of the annotations of a model.

Learning Objectives in This Chapter

- Create views, including planar and sketched views.
- Learn how to use a cutting plane.
- Understand the impact of view associativity.
- Understand the use of construction geometry.
- Create principal views.
- Create axonometric views.

2.1 Views

Views are used to locate and control the orientation of 3D annotations that are created on the model. Each annotation is associated with the view that was active during its creation. If a view has not been created, one is automatically added when the first annotation is created.

You can use views to orient the model. To do this, in the View section of the Action Bar, click  (Normal View) and then select the view in the model or specification tree.

The View Layout section of the Action Bar and the different types of views that can be created are shown in Figure 2–1.

Figure 2–1

Icon	Planar Views	Icon	Sketched Views
	Principal Views		Offset Section View/ Section Cut
	View From Reference (Projected View, Section View, Section Cut, Principal Views)		Aligned Section View/ Section Cut
	Axonometric View		

This can be divided into two types of views: planar and sketched. Planar views are created from a planar reference, while the sketched views are created from a sketch.

2.2 Planar Views

General Steps

Use the following general steps to create a planar view:

1. Select the view reference and planar view type.
2. Modify view parameters.

Step 1 - Select the view reference and planar view type.

Click  (View From Reference) to create a planar view. In the View Creation dialog box, select the Support-Reference geometric element and enter a view name, if required, in the *Name* field. In the Type drop-down list, select **Projection View**, **Section View**, or **Section Cut**, as shown in Figure 2–2.

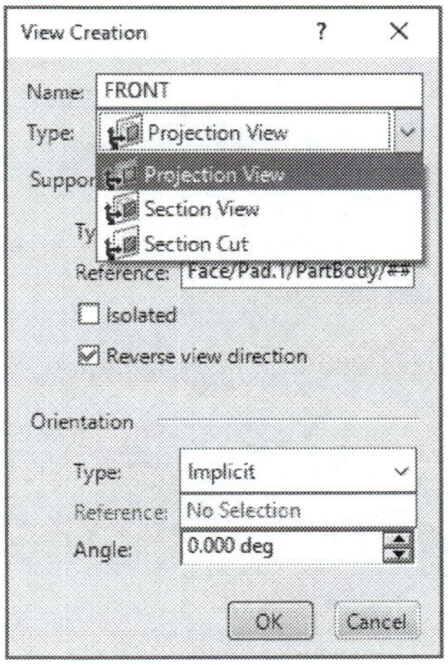

Figure 2–2

The type can also be preselected by selecting the icon of the desired type from the Tools Palette toolbar (shown in Figure 2–3) before selecting the Support-Reference geometric element. This toolbar will appear before the View Creation dialog box appears. The type can always be adjusted from the View Creation dialog box.

Figure 2–3

Projected View

This view type creates an annotation plane by selecting a planar face, surface, or reference plane on the model. When used to add a drawing view, the projected view orients the model so that the annotation plane is parallel to the screen. A projected view is identified by a blue datum plane when not active. An example is shown in Figure 2–4.

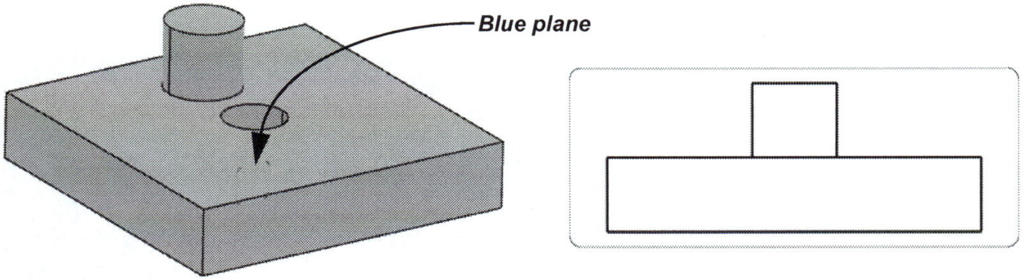

Figure 2–4

Section View

A section view annotation plane defines both a viewing orientation and a cutting plane. When the view is extracted to the Drafting app, a section view is automatically generated. A section view is identified by a green datum plane when not active. An example is shown in Figure 2–5.

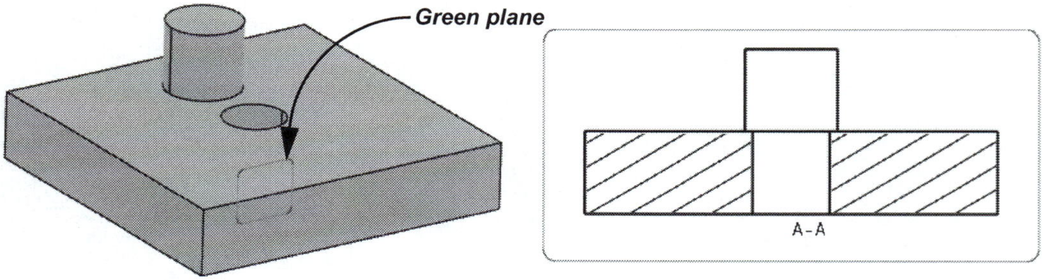

Figure 2–5

Section Cut

A section cut view annotation plane defines both a viewing orientation and a cutting plane. When the view is extracted to the Drafting app, a section cut view is automatically generated. The section cut only displays the geometry that lies on the cutting plane. All background geometry is not displayed. A section cut is identified by a yellow datum plane when not active. An example is shown in Figure 2–6.

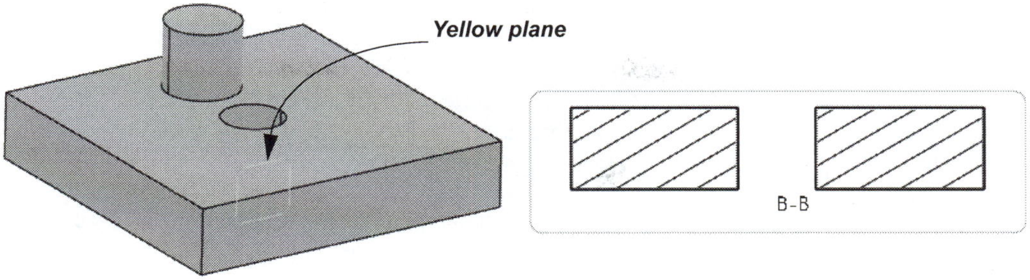

Figure 2–6

Step 2 - Modify view parameters.

Optionally, modify the view parameters, such as **Orientation** and **Reverse view direction**. Note that the reference element can also be replaced at this point, by clicking in the *Reference* field and selecting a new reference. Click **OK** to complete the view creation. The system adds the view to the model and specification tree and activates it. The active view is indicated by a red border.

Reverse View Direction

When a view is being created, a reference axis is placed on the view to indicate the orientation of the view, as shown in Figure 2–7. If required, to invert the normal axis, select **Reverse view direction** in the View Creation dialog box. The axis that is normal to the view plane initially displays red when no annotations have been associated with the view.

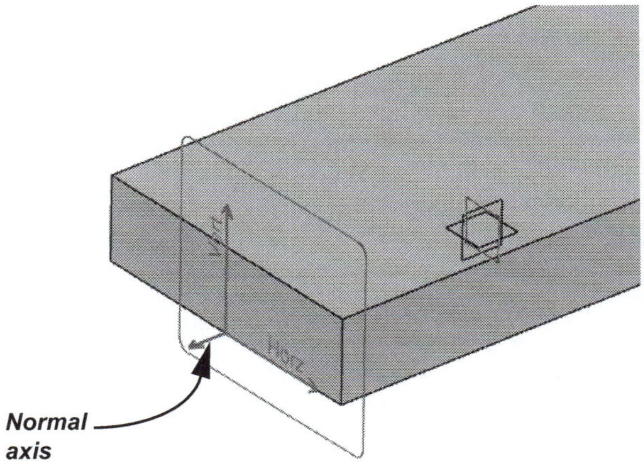

Figure 2–7

- Note: If the axis is not displayed, select **Me>Preferences> App Preferences>3D Modeling>Mechanical Systems>3D Tolerancing and Annotation** and select the **View/Annotation Plane** arrow. In the *View/Annotation Plane Display* section, enable **Display axis system of current view only**.

  Display axis system of the last selected view did not work as of the writing of this learning guide.

This normal axis determines the orientation of annotations that are placed on the view. An example is shown in Figure 2–8, where two parallel views have been created with normal axes in opposite directions. The annotation for Datum B has been inverted due to the orientation of the normal axis for FRONT.2.

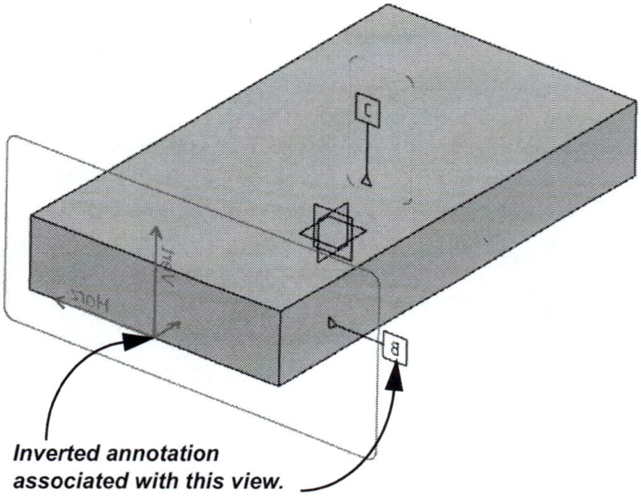

Figure 2–8

The view direction can only be reversed before annotations have been created on the view. If you want to reverse the view direction after annotations have been created, you can temporarily transfer the annotations off the view, reverse the view direction, and then transfer the annotations back. This enables you to reverse the view direction without deleting and recreating the annotations.

Displaying a Section

By default, the geometry of the section view (either planar or sketched) does not display on the 3D model. To display it, select **Me>Preferences>App Preferences>3D Modeling> Mechanical Systems>3D Tolerancing and Annotation** and select the *View/Annotation Plane* arrow.

Next, enable the **Visualization of the profile in the current view** option in the *View/Annotation Plane Display* area, as shown in Figure 2–9.

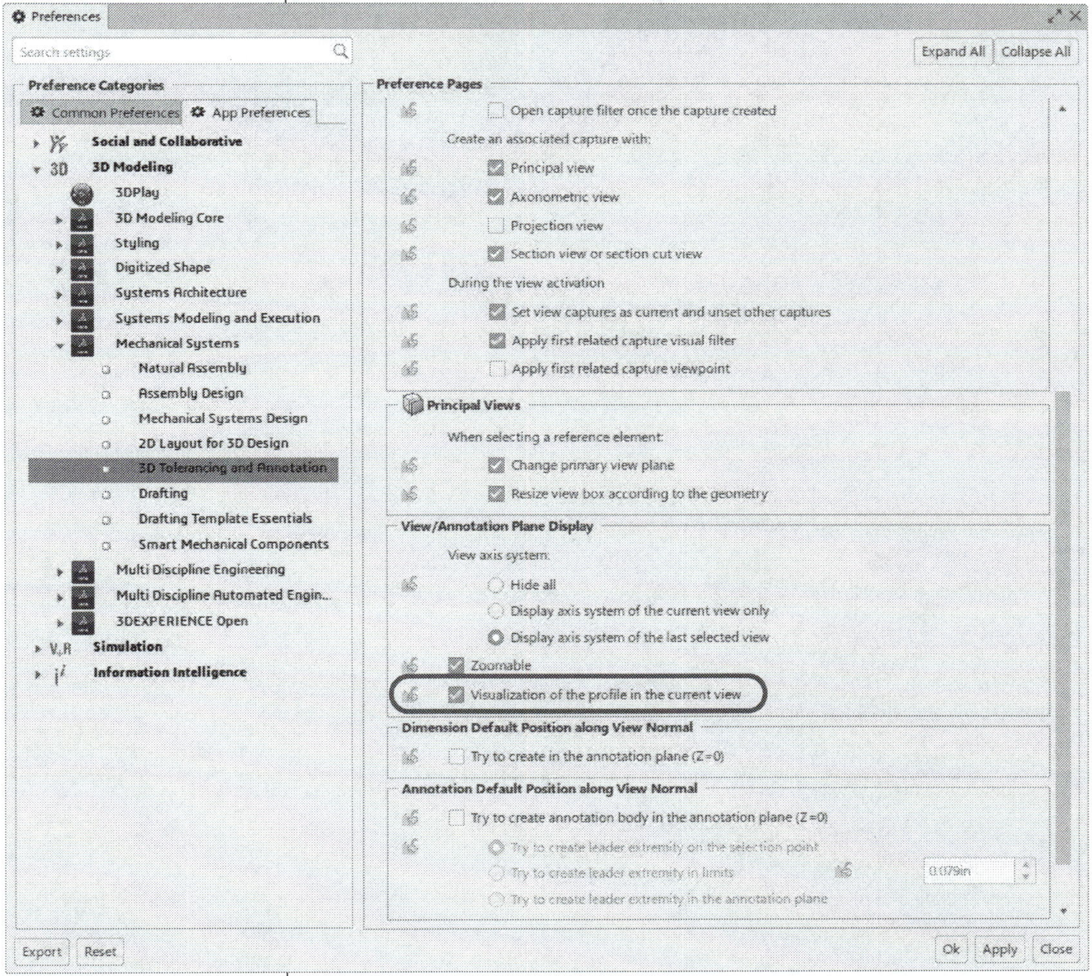

Figure 2–9

The model now displays the boundary generated by the section whenever the view is active, as shown in Figure 2–10.

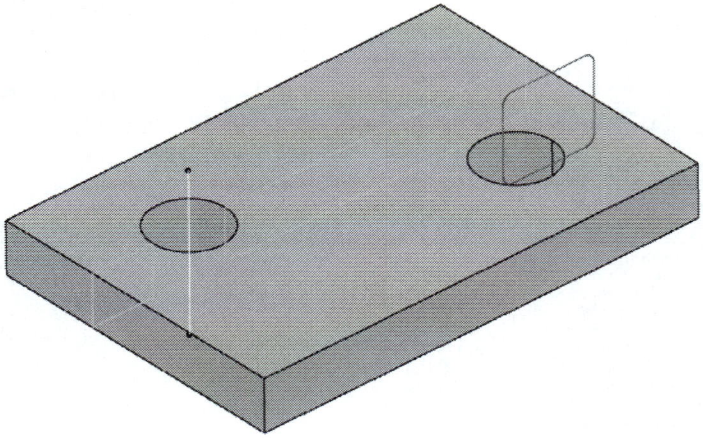

Figure 2–10

2.3 Sketched Views

This section provides the steps required to create Offset Section View/Section Cut and Aligned Section View/Section Cut views. These types of views are specifically targeted at preparing views for 2D extraction.

How To: Define a Sketched View

1. Define the type of section view to create by clicking one of the following two icons:

   -  (Offset Section View/Section Cut): The Offset View Creation dialog box opens, as shown in Figure 2–11.

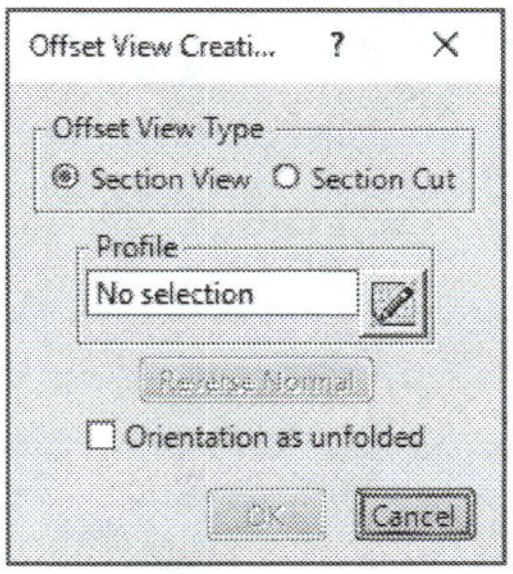

Figure 2–11

   -  (Aligned Section View/Section Cut): The Aligned View Creation dialog box opens, as shown in Figure 2–12.

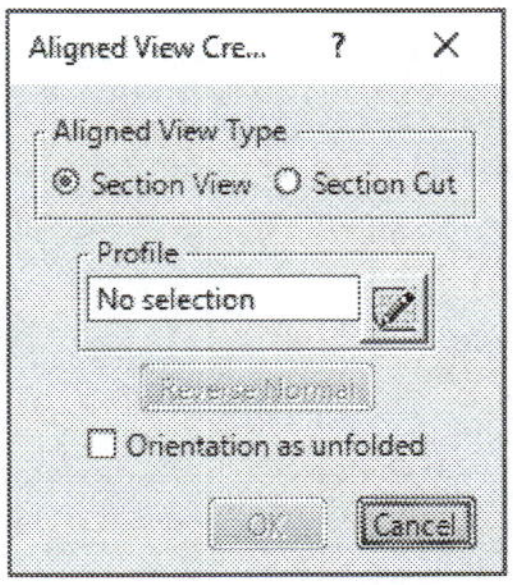

Figure 2–12

2. Select the type of view to be created by selecting the **Section View** or **Section Cut** option. The **Section View** option only impacts the drawing where a section view displays all geometry behind the cutting plane, while a **Section Cut** only displays the geometry on the cutting plane. An example is shown in Figure 2–13.

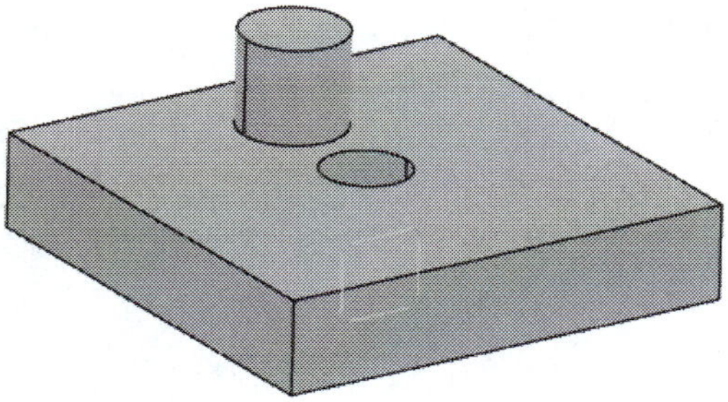

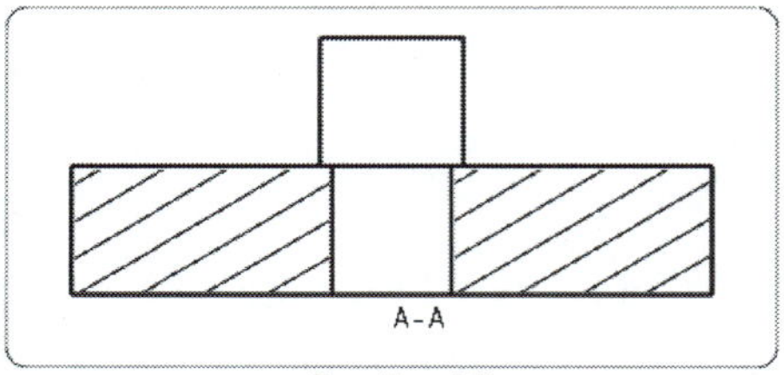

Section View

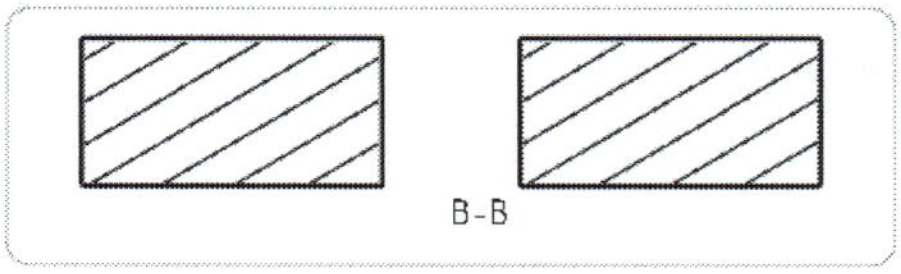

Section Cut

Figure 2–13

3. Click  (Sketch) and select a planar face, surface, or reference plane to sketch a profile for the extraction view. You can also select a predefined sketch feature. For an offset view, all of the lines in the sketch must be perpendicular or parallel to one another to be valid. An example sketch for an offset view is shown in Figure 2–14.

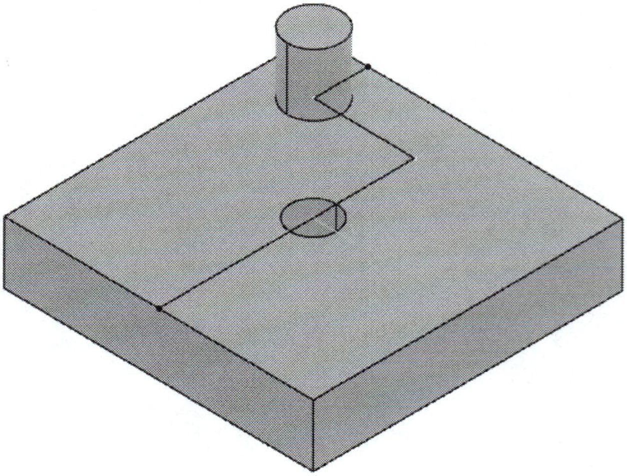

Figure 2–14

*You can reverse the normal for a sketched view at any time up until an annotation has been created. Activate the view, right-click, and select **Reverse Normal**.*

4. If required, use **Reverse Normal** to change the direction of the view normal. The arrow points opposite to the viewing direction.
5. Click **OK** to complete the view creation. The system adds the view to the model and specification tree, as shown in Figure 2–15. The **Offset Section ViewA-A** cannot be activated and is only available for drawing view creation purposes. Beneath the offset section view are several section views. Each section view behaves like a standard section view that can be activated to place annotations.

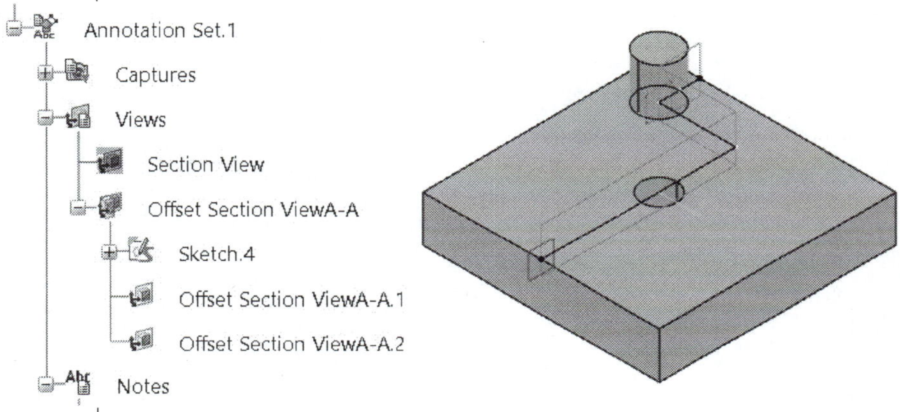

Figure 2–15

2.4 Cutting Plane

A cutting plane enables you to clip the geometry of the part using an existing view/annotation plane. A cutting plane is for visualization purposes only, as the view plane or part geometry are not permanently altered and no feature is created or added to the specification tree. An example is shown in Figure 2–16.

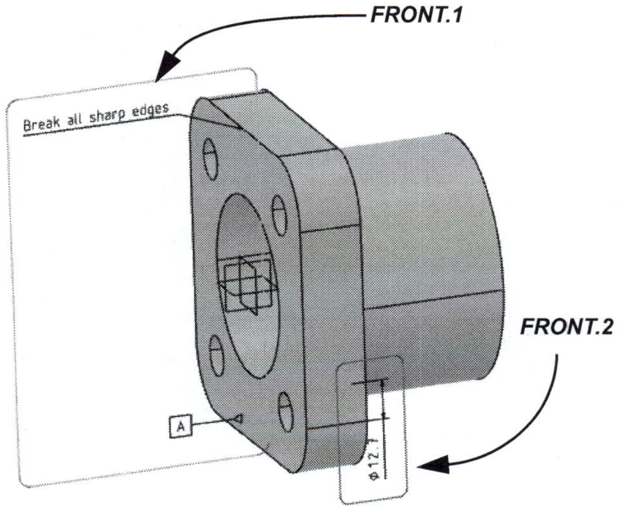

Figure 2–16

How To: View a Cutting Plane

1. In the View section of the Action Bar, click  (Cutting Plane), as shown in Figure 2–17.

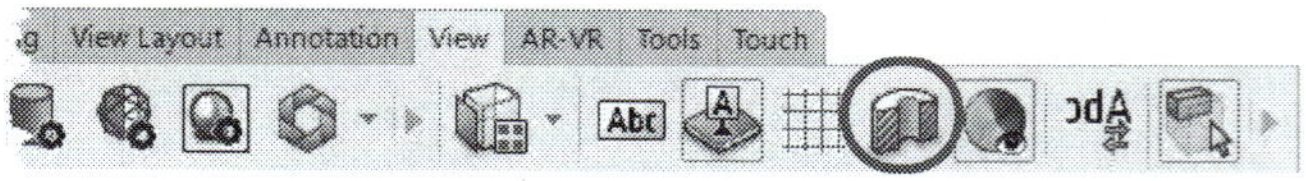

Figure 2–17

2. The application clips all of the geometry of the part at the active view/annotation plane.

Figure 2–18 shows the cutting plane using the **FRONT.1** annotation plane.

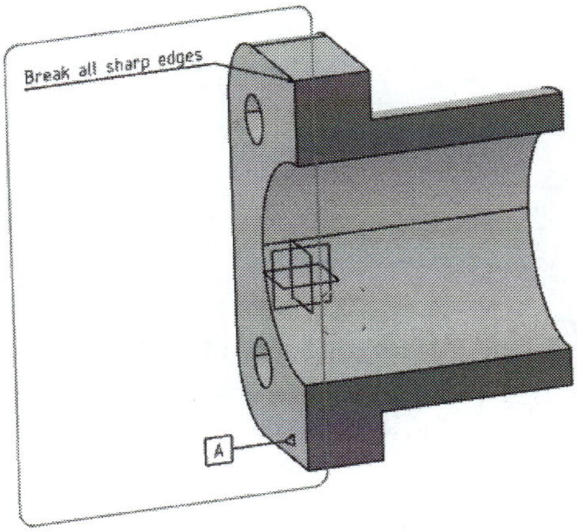

Figure 2–18

Figure 2–19 shows the cutting plane using the **FRONT.2** annotation plane.

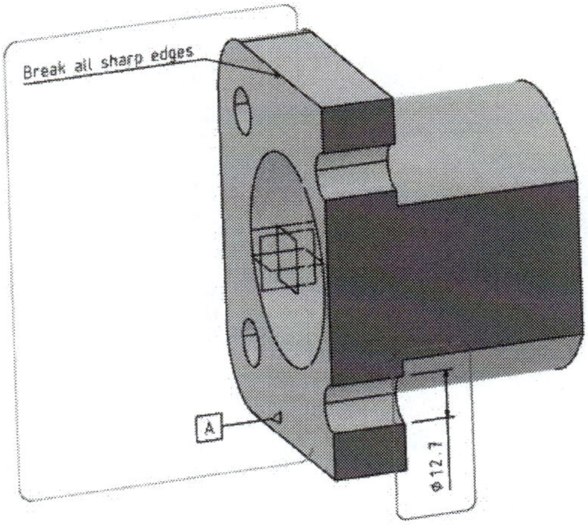

Figure 2–19

The cutting plane display is not saved with the model; however, they can be saved with the capture functionality.

3D Preview

When a view is selected, it is automatically displayed with the cutting plane regardless of whether or not  is active. If the view selected is a section view, the profile of the section displays as cyan-colored lines. You can disable this functionality by clearing  (3D Master Query).

Display Settings

The cutting plane can be customized to display a custom color or pattern based on material. This is very useful in assemblies to help distinguish the various components. Cross-hatching properties defined in the part also display in the drawing.

To display custom coloring or patterns in the cutting plane, select **Me>Preferences>App Preferences>3D Modeling> Mechanical Systems>3D Tolerancing and Annotation**. Select the *Display* arrow. In the *Sectioning Properties* section, the background Color and Pattern options can be customized.

2.5 View Associativity

When a view is created, a link is generated to the selected geometry reference(s). For example, if an offset reference plane is selected to define a front view, the view is dependent on the position of the plane. If the plane is moved, the view updates. This is driven by a CATIA option that controls the associativity of an annotation plane to its referenced geometry.

To access this option, select **Me>Preferences>App Preferences>3D Modeling>Mechanical Systems>3D Tolerancing and Annotation**, then select the *View/Annotation Plane* arrow to access the **Associate views with the geometry** option, as shown in Figure 2–20.

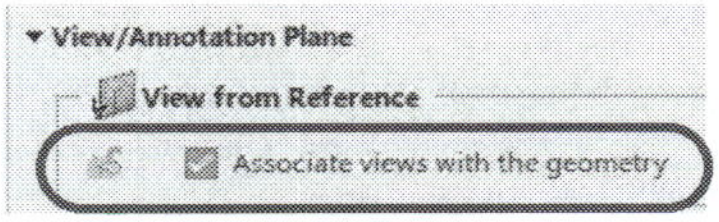

Figure 2–20

By default, this option is enabled. If it is disabled, the views do not update when modifications are made.

You can also disable or enable this option for specific annotation views. Right-click on the view and select **Change View Support**, as shown in Figure 2–21.

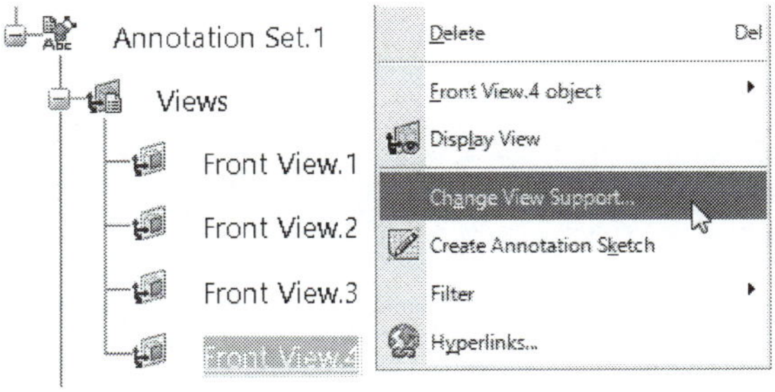

Figure 2–21

The Change View Support dialog box opens, as shown in Figure 2–22.

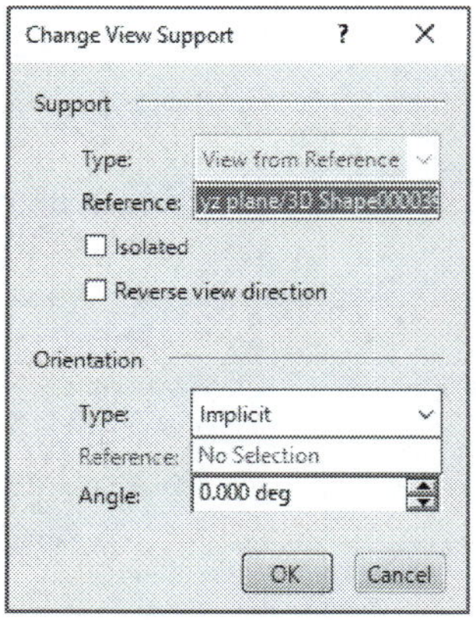

Figure 2–22

This dialog box is useful in the following situations:

- You require associativity, but views were created with **Associate views with the geometry** (in the Options dialog box) disabled. Toggle off the **Isolated** option and select reference element(s) for any views that you want to update with model changes.
- You require a view to reference a different geometric entity. In this case, you can click in the *Reference* field and select a new planar reference.

2.6 Principal Views

General Steps

Use the following general steps to create a principal view:

1. Start the creation of the principal view.
2. Select a plane to define plane orientation.
3. Select additional views to be created.

Step 1 - Start the creation of the principal view.

Click  (Principal Views) to create a principal view. The Principal Views dialog box opens, as shown in Figure 2–23.

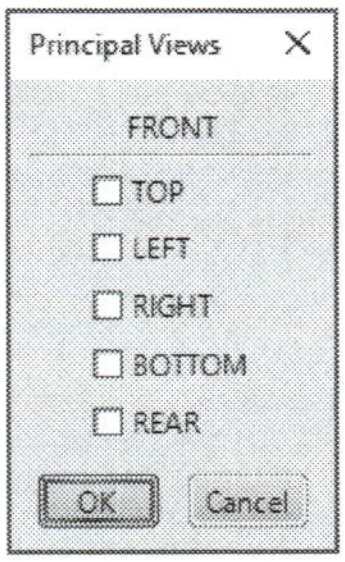

Figure 2–23

The primary view is **FRONT**. To change the primary view, click the control arrows, as shown in Figure 2–24.

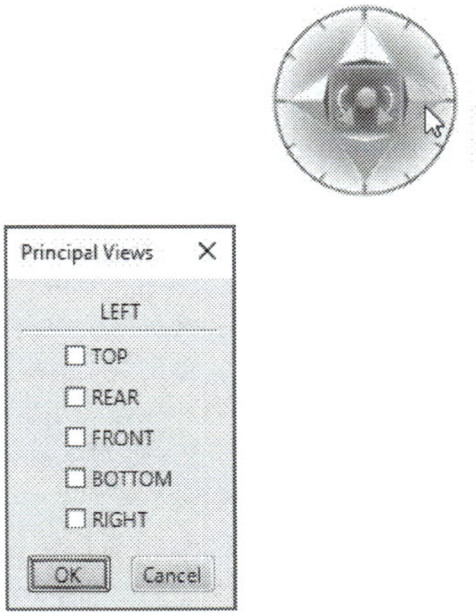

Figure 2–24

Depending on which arrow you clicked, the following combinations are applied:

- Right arrow: FRONT > LEFT > REAR > RIGHT > FRONT.
- Left arrow: FRONT > RIGHT > REAR > LEFT > FRONT.
- Up arrow: FRONT > BOTTOM > REAR > TOP > FRONT.
- Down arrow: FRONT > TOP > REAR > BOTTOM > FRONT.

The view bounding box displays as shown in Figure 2–25.

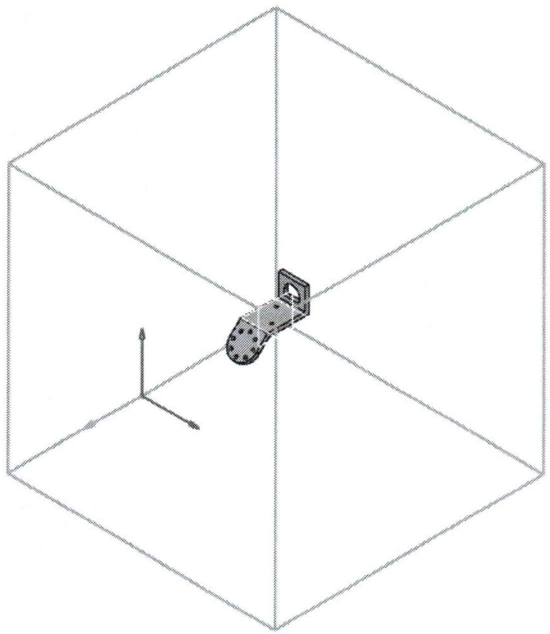

Figure 2–25

Step 2 - Select a plane to define plane orientation.

Select a plane to define the Front view plane orientation. The view box is resized according to the model size, as shown in Figure 2–26.

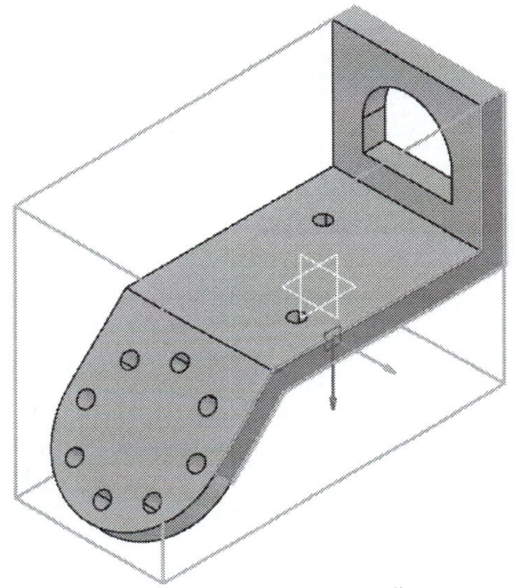

Figure 2–26

You can orient the view bounding box using the control and can modify the view bounding box angle using the green knob, as shown in Figure 2–27.

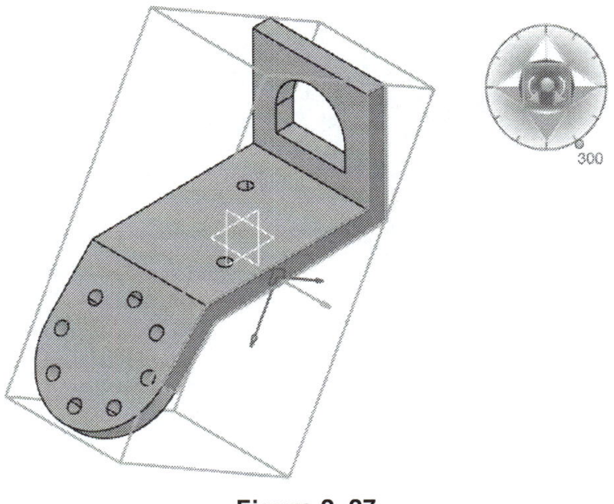

Figure 2–27

Step 3 - Select additional views to be created.

Select additional views to be created in the Principal View dialog box and click **OK**. Additional views display in the specification tree.

Created view/annotation planes are created as Projection View/Annotation and their reference planes are the faces of the bounding box.

Captures are automatically created and associated with the related views, and the names match, by default. However, if view names are edited, they will not automatically reflect in the capture names.

It is possible to have multiple views with the same name. If you want to ensure that all views have a unique name, click **Me>Preferences>Common Preferences>Object Properties>3D Shape>Display** and ensure that either **Under the same tree node** or **In the main object** are selected in the *Checking Operation when Renaming* area. A check is performed to ensure that two views do not bear the same name in a given annotation set.

2.7 Axonometric Views

An axonometric view enables you to manage 3D annotations in the same manner as for a projection view/annotation plane, but uses the screen view orientation.

General Steps

Use the following general steps to create an axonometric view:

1. Start the creation of a view from reference.
2. Select **Axonometric View** from the Tools Palette.
3. Select a 3D point or vertex, or indicate a point on a surface or a curve.
4. Complete the view.

Step 1 - Start the creation of a view from reference.

Click  (View From Reference) in the View Layout section of the Action Bar. The Tools Palette toolbar opens, as shown in Figure 2–28.

Figure 2–28

Step 2 - Select Axonometric View from the Tools Palette.

Select  (Axonometric View) from the Tools Palette. Blue borders display at the four corners of the screen enabling you to define the view point.

You can set a 3D viewpoint and/or select a point to define the axonometric view.

Step 3 - Select a 3D point or vertex, or indicate a point on a surface or a curve.

Select a 3D point or vertex, or indicate a point on a surface or a curve, in the 3D window to define the origin of the view. The View Creation dialog box displays, as shown in Figure 2–29.

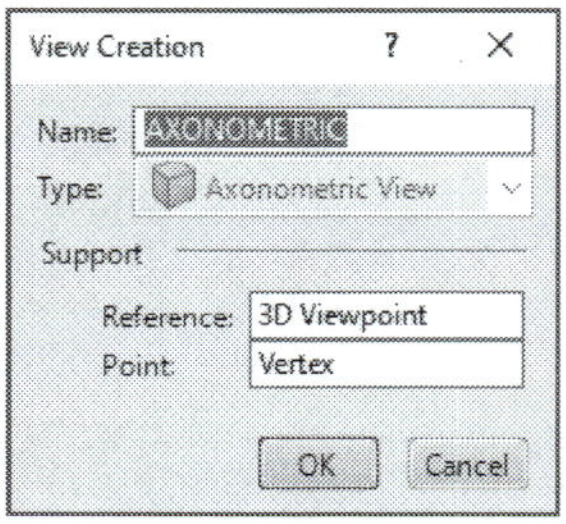

Figure 2–29

Step 4 - Complete the view.

Click **OK** in the View Creation dialog box or click anywhere on the screen. The axonometric view is created, as shown in Figure 2–30. Axonometric views are identified as Axonometric View in the specification tree.

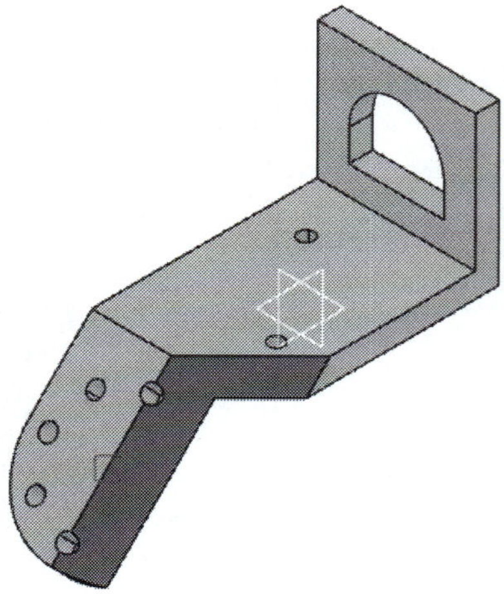

Figure 2–30

Alternatively,  (Axonometric View) can be selected and created directly from the View Layout section of the Action Bar. This creates the same Axonometric view, but no view creation window is shown. All that is required is the selection of a 3D point or vertex, or to indicate a point on a surface or a curve in the 3D window to define the origin of the view. The Axonometric view is then created.

2.8 Construction Geometry

Construction geometry enables you to generate references to geometry that is not present in the design model. This provides a consistent and complete referencing scheme for annotations in the model.

General Steps

Use the following general steps to create a construction geometry:

1. Select the geometrical element(s).
2. Start the creation of the construction geometry.
3. Complete the creation of the construction geometry.

Step 1 - Select the geometrical element(s).

The construction geometry is created solely by referencing existing geometry. The type of construction geometry created depends on the reference(s) used. For example, you must preselect a hole to create an axis for it.

Step 2 - Start the creation of the construction geometry.

In the Annotation section of the Action Bar, click

 (Constructed Geometry Creation). The Constructed Geometry Creation dialog box opens. Select the appropriate geometry to create from the available options, listed as follows:

Geometry	Image	Inputs and Outputs
Plane	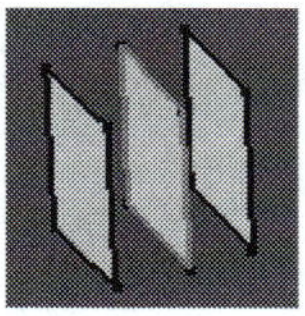	Select two surfaces to create a plane that is equidistant between them, or that bisects the angle created between them.

Plane	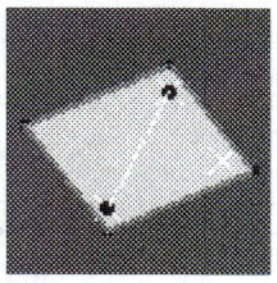	To create a plane on which all entities lie select one of the following: • two coplanar edges, • an edge and a point, • three points, • two cylinders, • a cylinder and an edge, or • a cylinder and a point.
Plane	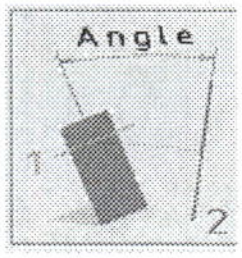	Select a surface and non-intersecting edge, or a surface and a cylinder to create a plane through the axis at an angle to the surface.
Plane	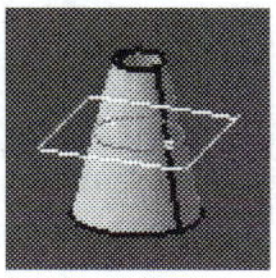	Select a cone to create a plane at either a specific cross-section diameter, offset from one plane, or equidistant between two planes. Selecting **Circle** creates a circle of the cone's cross-section.
Point	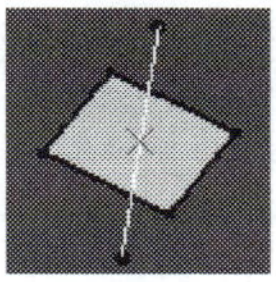	Select a surface and an edge, axis, or cylinder to create a point where the two intersect.
Point	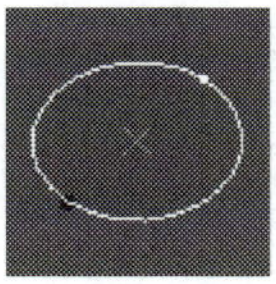	Select a circle to create a point at its center.
Point		Select a cone to create a point at its apex.
Axis		Select two intersecting surfaces to create an axis along their intersection.
Axis	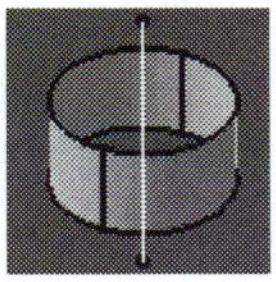	Select a cylinder or circular pattern to create an axis through its center.

Axis	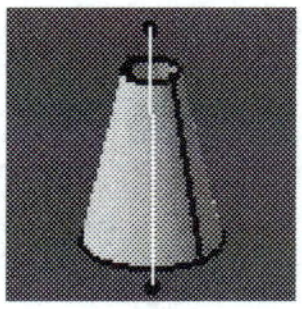	Select a cone to create an axis through its center.
Cylinder	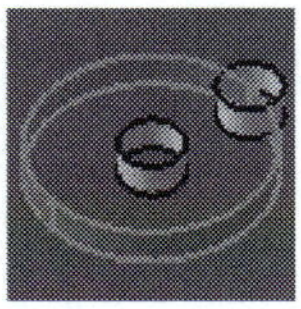	Select a cylinder and another cylinder, axis, or point to create a cylinder with its center as the first entity and a radius passing through the second entity.
Cylinder	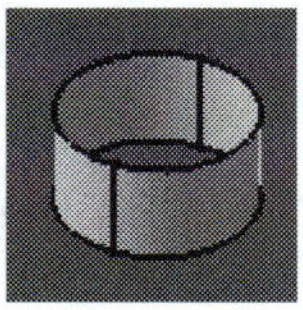	Select a circular pattern to create a cylinder through the entities.

Step 3 - Complete the creation of the construction geometry.

Click **OK** to complete the feature. The model and specification tree update to display the construction geometry, as shown in Figure 2–31.

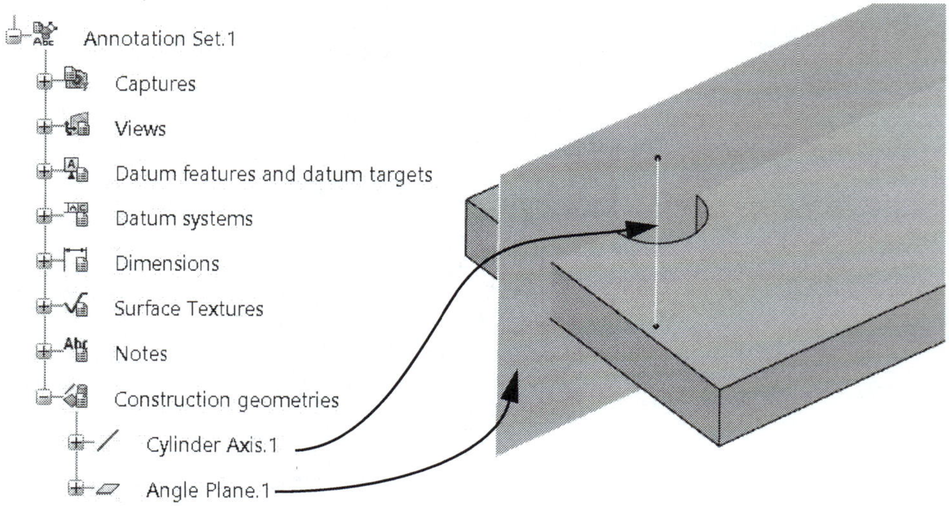

Figure 2–31

Practice 2a

Preparing the Model

Practice Objectives

- Define an annotation plane.
- Define a section plane.
- Create construction geometry.
- Reverse the view direction of an annotation plane.

In this practice, you will create section planes and construction geometry to prepare a model for annotation creation in the 3D T&A app. The completed model is shown in Figure 2–32.

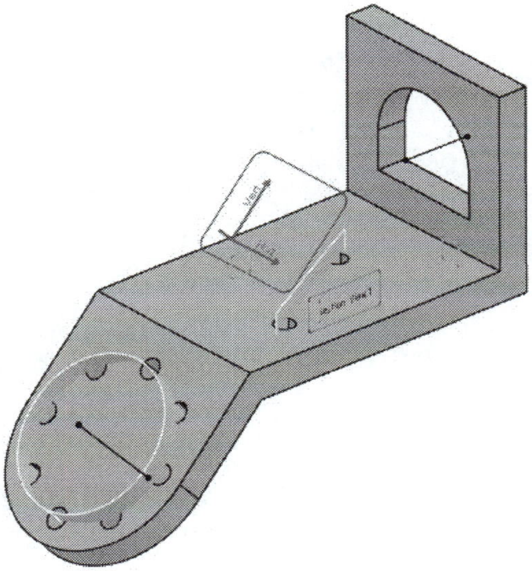

Figure 2–32

Once you finish preparing the model for annotations, you create a drawing for the model and add drawing views to show the properties of annotation planes and construction geometry.

Task 1 - Import and open a part file.

1. Import and open **Sample.3dxml**. The model displays as shown in Figure 2–33.

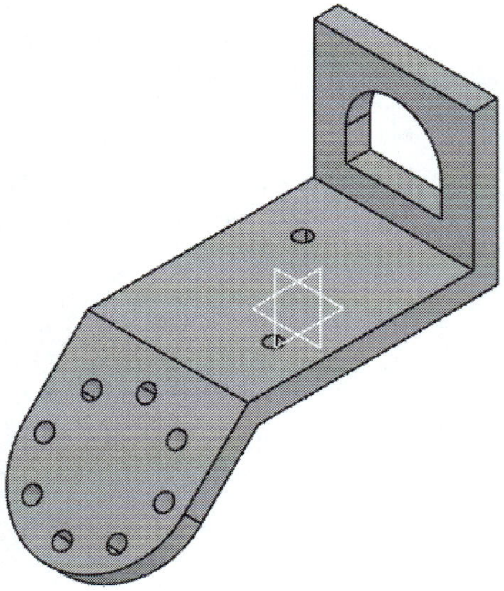

Figure 2–33

2. Select **Me>Preferences>App Preferences>3D Modeling> Mechanical Systems>3D Tolerancing and Annotation** and select the *Tolerancing* arrow.

3. In the *Annotation Set Creation* area, in the Standard drop-down list, select **ANSI-ASME**, as shown in Figure 2–34.

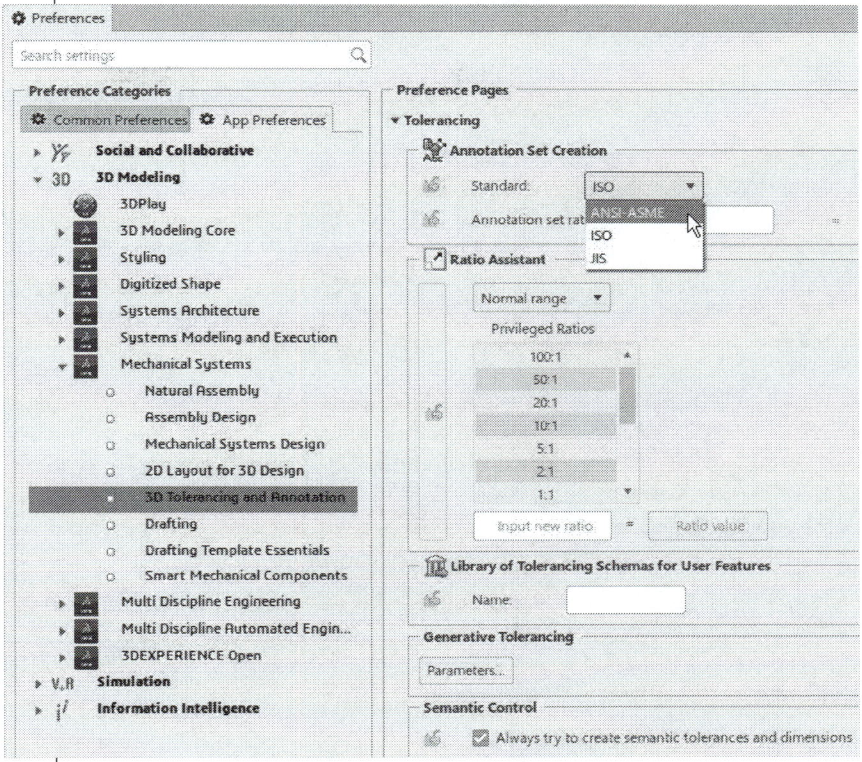

Figure 2–34

You may need to scroll down in the list to find the View/Annotation Plane Display area.

4. Select the *View/Annotation Plane* arrow.
5. In the *View/Annotation Plane Display* area, enable the **Display axis system for last selected view** option.
6. Select **Me>Preferences>Common Preferences> Parameters, Measures, and Units>Units** and select the *Units* arrow.

7. In the Length drop-down list, select **Millimeter (mm)**, as shown in Figure 2–35.

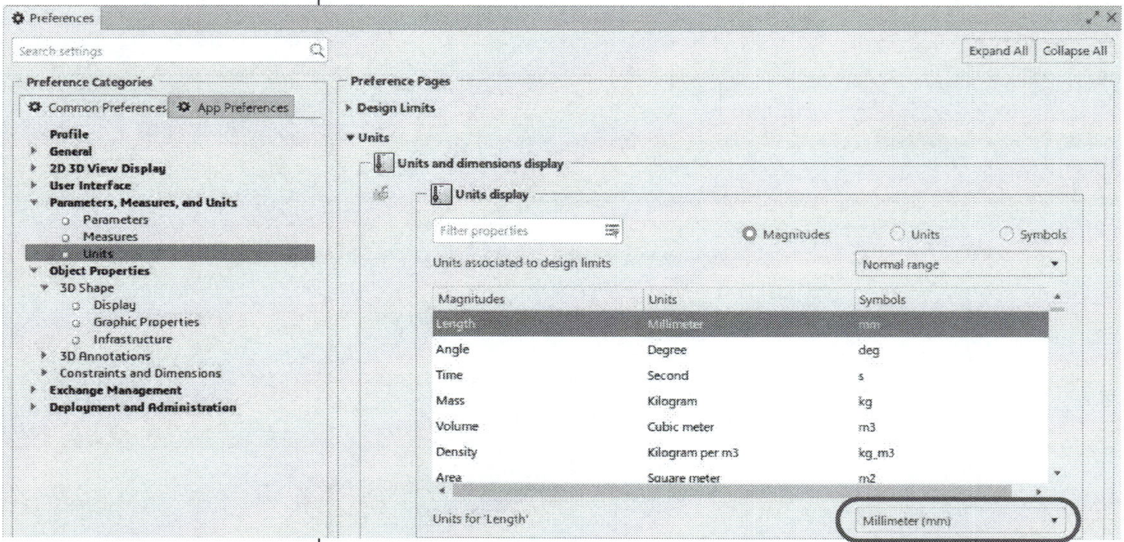

Figure 2–35

8. Click **OK**.

Task 2 - Define a projection view.

1. Select the View Layout section of the Action Bar, as shown in Figure 2–36.

Figure 2–36

2. Click  (View From Reference).

3. Select the face of the model, as shown in Figure 2–37. Once selected, the View Creation dialog box opens. The face selected is listed in the *Reference* field.

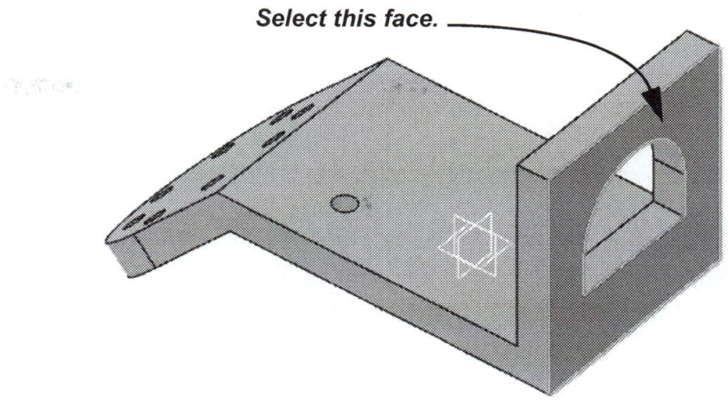

Figure 2–37

4. Accept all defaults and click **OK**. The system adds a view frame to the model and a **FRONT.1** entry is added to the Views branch of the specification tree, as shown in Figure 2–38.

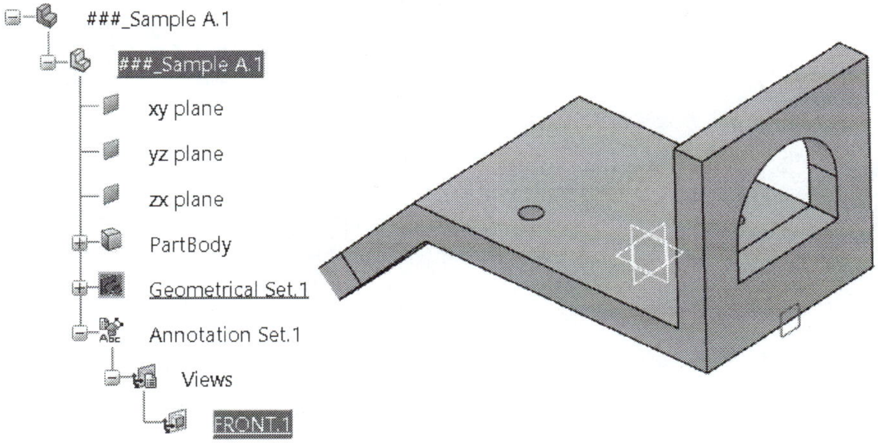

Figure 2–38

Task 3 - Define a section view.

In this task, you create a section view. A section view does not display a section profile on the 3D model by default. You can enable its display using the Options dialog box. A cross-section view is automatically created when this view is used to create a drawing view. You will display this view in a drawing at the end of the practice.

1. Click  (View From Reference).
2. Select the ZX plane.

3. In the Type drop-down list, select **Section View**.

4. Enter **Section View.1** in the *Name* field, accept all other defaults, and click **OK**. The system displays the section view frame on the model and adds it to the Views branch of the specification tree, as shown in Figure 2–39.

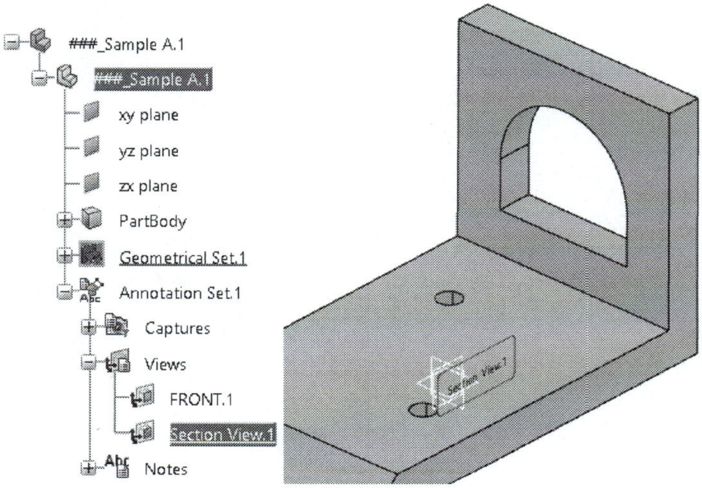

Figure 2–39

5. In the View section of the Action Bar, click  (Cutting plane). The model displays as shown in Figure 2–40.

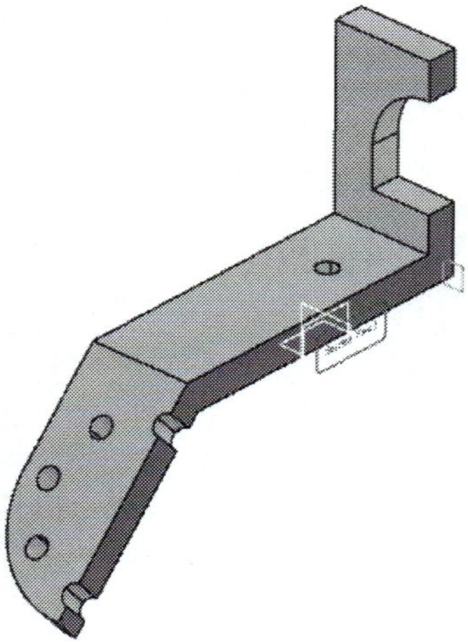

Figure 2–40

Design Considerations

Although the cutting plane can be used to cut the part in any view, the tool is especially useful when trying to visualize how a section cut will display on the 3D model.

6. Click  (Cutting plane) again to clear it.
7. Expand the Views branch of the specification tree and select **Section View.1**. Selecting a view applies a cutting plane. The section profile also highlights in cyan because this is a section view.
8. Click on the screen to clear the section view.
9. Select **Me>Preferences>App Preferences>3D Modeling>Mechanical Systems>3D Tolerancing and Annotation** and select the *View/Annotation Plane* arrow.
10. In the *View/Annotation Plane Display* area, enable the **Visualization of the profile in the current view** option, as shown in Figure 2–41.

You may need to scroll down in the list to find the visualization option.

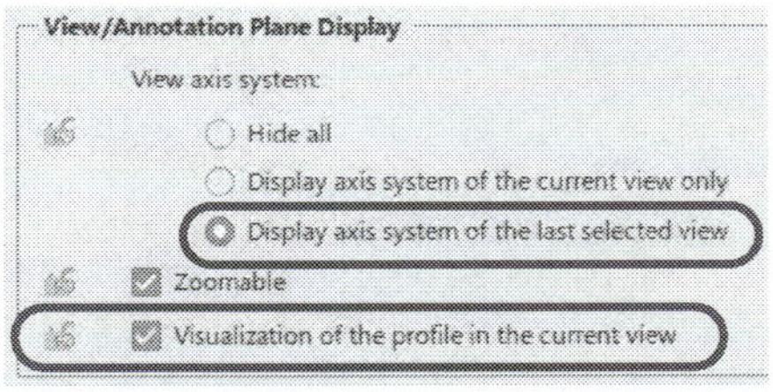

Figure 2–41

11. Click **OK**. The model updates to display the section profile, as shown in Figure 2–42.

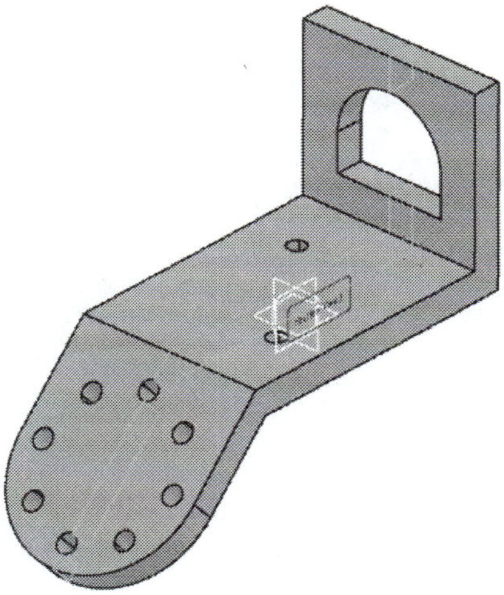

Figure 2–42

12. Clear the **Visualization of the profile in the current view** option.

13. Hide the three default reference planes to simplify the display of the model.

Task 4 - Create a construction plane.

In this task, you create a construction plane that passes through the axes of the two holes on the top face of the part. This plane is then used to develop an annotation plane.

1. In the Annotation section of the Action Bar, click  (Constructed Geometry Creation), as shown in Figure 2–43.

Figure 2–43

2. Select the cylindrical surface of the hole shown in Figure 2–44. Ensure that you select the hole from the model and not from the specification tree. Based on the selection, the Constructed Geometry dialog box opens with the option to create an axis.

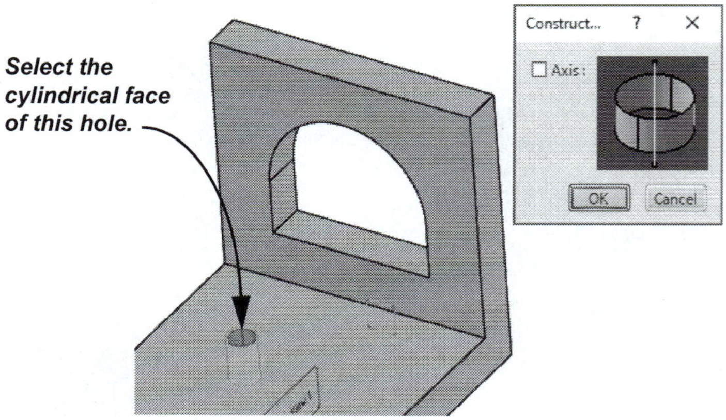

Figure 2–44

3. Select the second hole, as shown in Figure 2–45. This time, the Constructed Geometry dialog box prompts you to create a Plane or Reference cylinder.

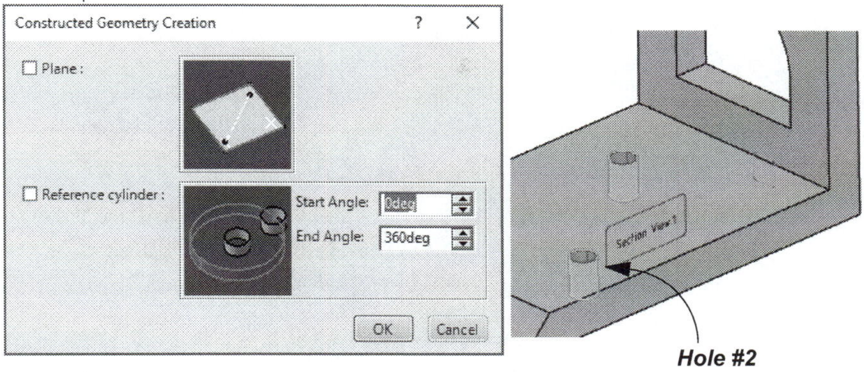

Figure 2–45

4. Select **Plane** and click **OK**. The system adds a Passing Plane to the model and specification tree, as shown in Figure 2–46.

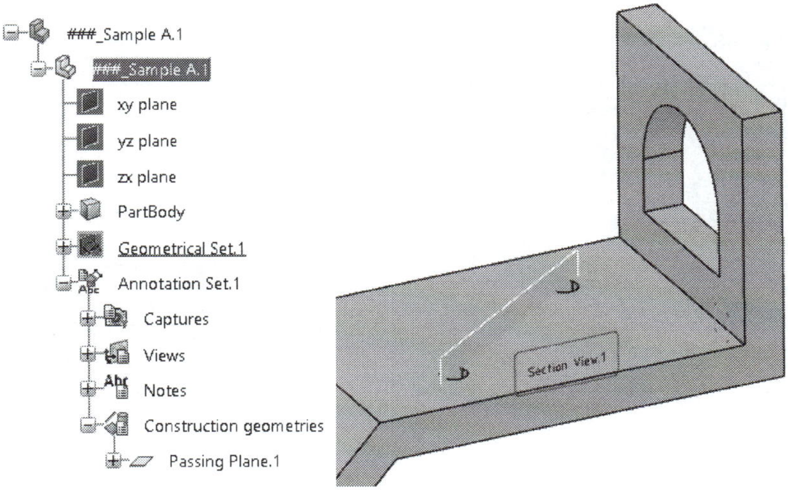

Figure 2–46

Design Considerations

This plane is associative with the geometry selected during its construction. If the position of the holes changes, the plane updates with the new locations.

Task 5 - Create two annotation planes.

1. Select **Me>Preferences>App Preferences>3D Modeling>Mechanical Systems>3D Tolerancing and Annotation** and select the *View/Annotation Plane* arrow.

2. In the *View/Annotation Plane Display* area, enable the **Displayed for current view only** option and click **OK**.

3. Click  (View From Reference) from the View Layout section of the Action Bar and select **Passing Plane.1** in the model or specification tree.

4. Select **Projection View** in the Type drop-down list, if required. **FRONT.2** is added to the Views branch of the specification tree

5. Ensure that the axis system matches Figure 2–47.

    - The **Displayed for current view only** option displays the axis as shown in Figure 2–47. In most images in this guide, the axes are toggled off to keep the images uncluttered.

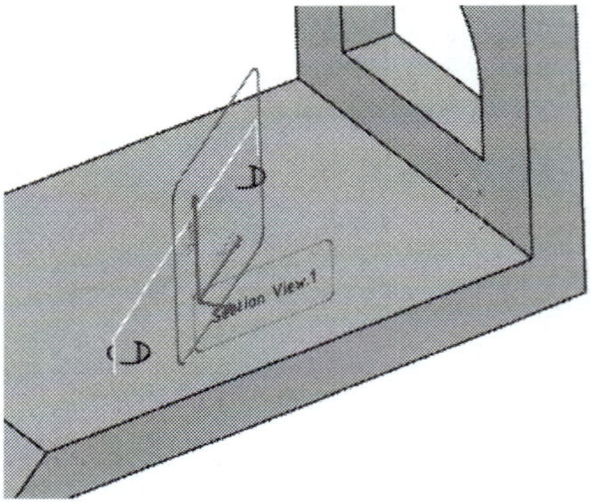

Figure 2–47

6. Click **OK**.

7. Create a final front view annotation plane using the face shown in Figure 2–48.

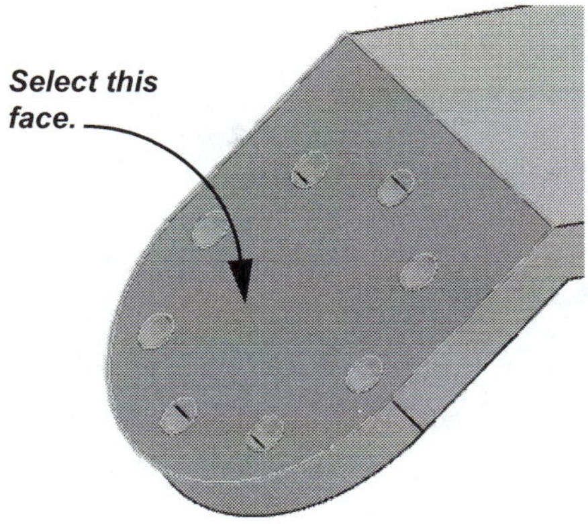

Figure 2–48

The model displays as shown in Figure 2–49.

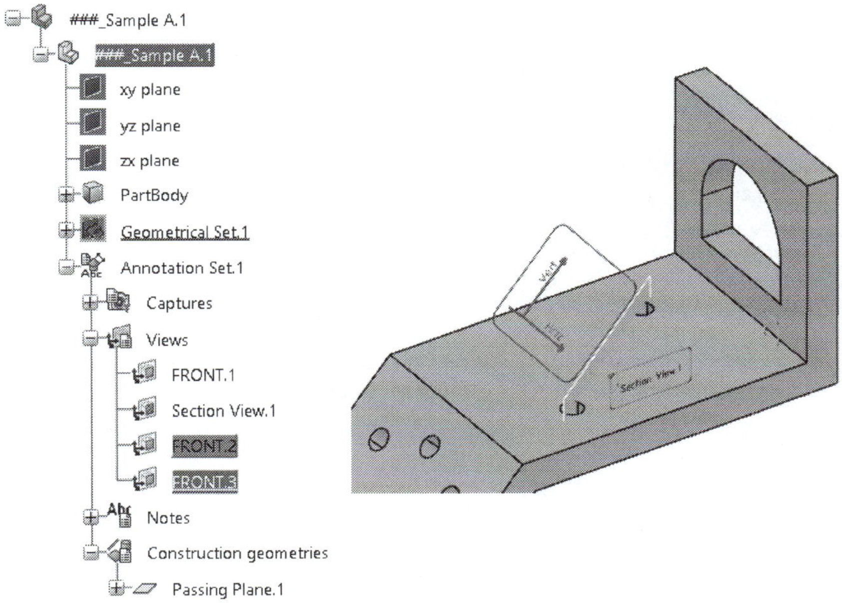

Figure 2–49

8. Select **Me>Preferences>App Preferences>3D Modeling> Mechanical Systems>3D Tolerancing and Annotation** and select the *View/Annotation Plane* arrow.

9. In the *View/Annotation Plane Display* area, enable **Displayed for last selected view** and click **OK**.

Task 6 - Create a reference cylinder and axis.

1. Click  (Construction Geometry Creation).
2. Expand the PartBody branch in the specification tree and select **CircPattern.1**. The Constructed Geometry dialog box opens, enabling you to create a cylinder.

*The **Axis** option in the Constructed Geometry dialog box is not displayed until **Cylinder** is selected.*

3. Select **Cylinder**. The system places a cylindrical surface on the model that passes through each instance of the patterned hole. In addition, the system now enables you to create a constructed axis that passes through the center of the patterned holes, as shown in Figure 2–50.

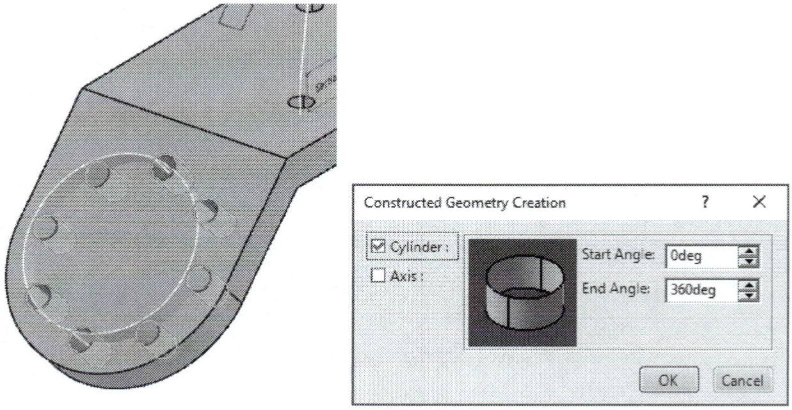

Figure 2–50

4. Select **Axis** and complete the operation. Click **OK**. The model displays as shown in Figure 2–51.

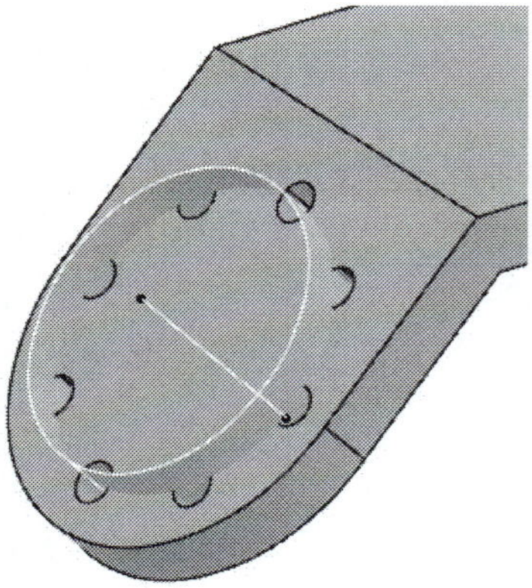

Figure 2–51

Task 7 - Create a constructed axis.

1. Create an additional constructed geometry axis by selecting the face shown in Figure 2–52. Ensure that you select the **Axis** option in the dialog box.

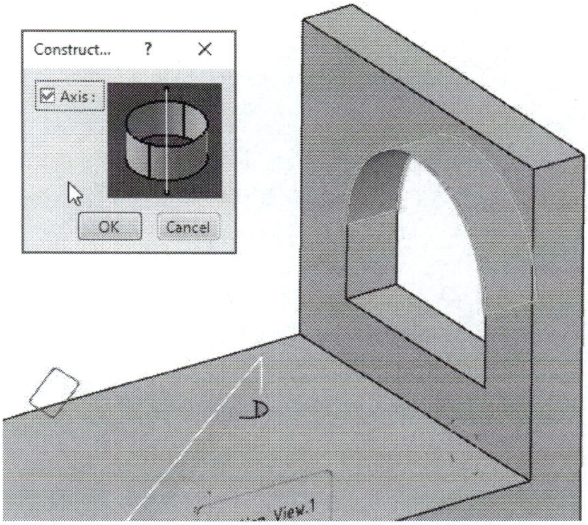

Figure 2–52

2. Save the part. The model displays as shown in Figure 2–53.

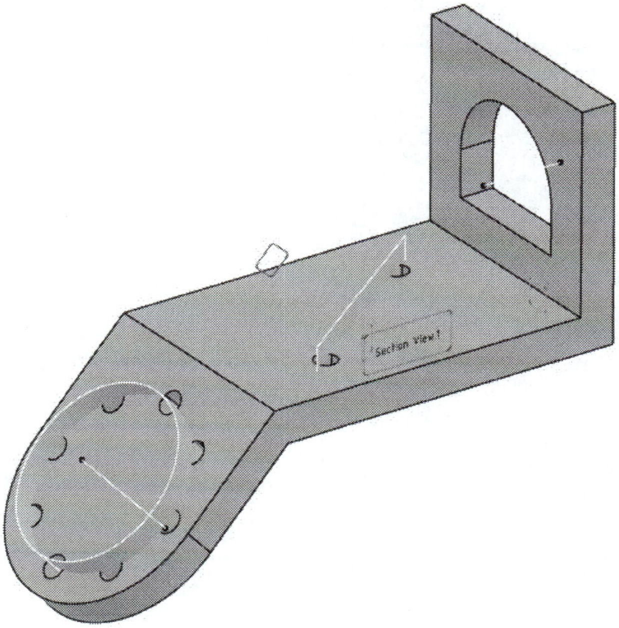

Figure 2–53

Task 8 - (Optional) Drawing view creation.

In this optional task, you develop drawing views using the views created in the part model. Modifications to the annotation set are updated in the drawing views to demonstrate the associativity between 3D T&A features, the model, and drawing views.

1. Create an empty ANSI-ASME standard, E-ANSI size drawing.

2. Click  (View from 3D) and create a view using **Section View.1**. The drawing view displays, as shown in Figure 2–54.

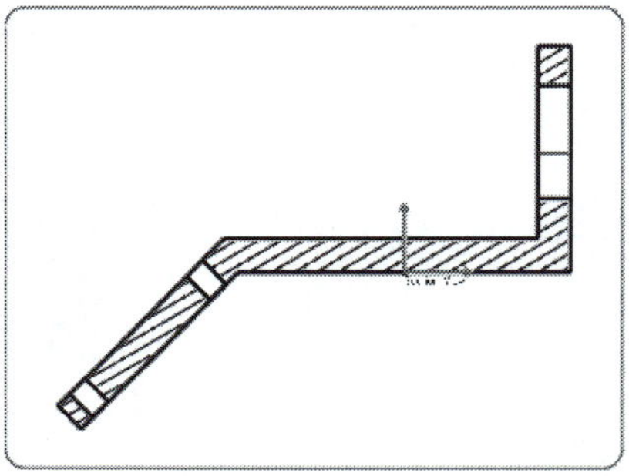

Figure 2–54

Design Considerations

As previously indicated, a section view created in the 3D T&A app automatically generates a section view in the Drafting app. The properties of this view can be modified identically to the methods used to modify a section view generated in Drawing mode.

3. Create a second view that references **FRONT.2** from Sample.3dxml. The drawing view displays as shown in Figure 2–55.

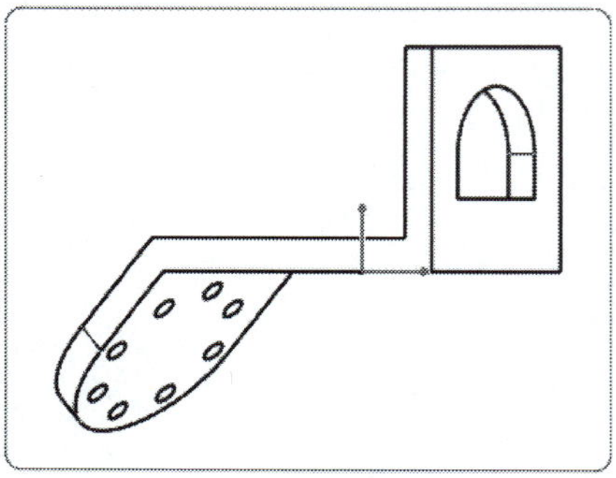

Figure 2–55

 *(Normal View) may need to be selected to flip the sketch into the orientation shown in Figure 2–56.*

Task 9 - Modify the part.

1. Activate the Sample part widget.
2. Double-click on **Sketch.5** and modify the dimensional values, as shown in Figure 2–56. This sketch is used to position **Hole.4** that was referenced during the construction of **Passing Plane.1** and **Front View.2**.

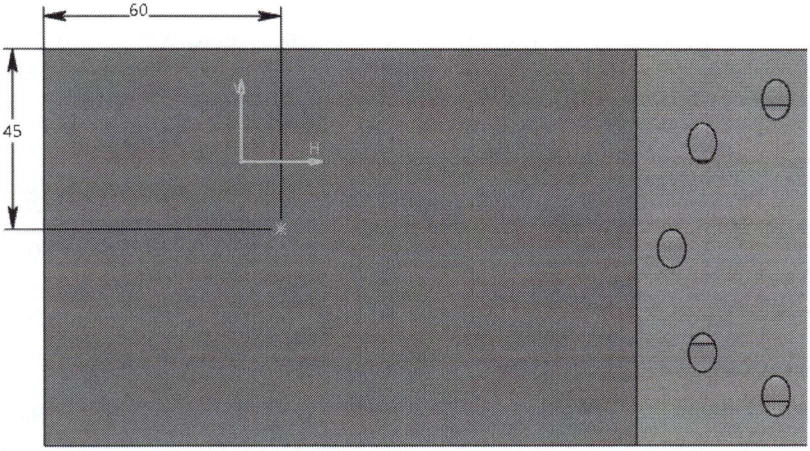

Figure 2–56

3. Click  (Exit app) to exit Sketcher.
4. Click  (Update All), if required, to update the model. The model displays, as shown in Figure 2–57.

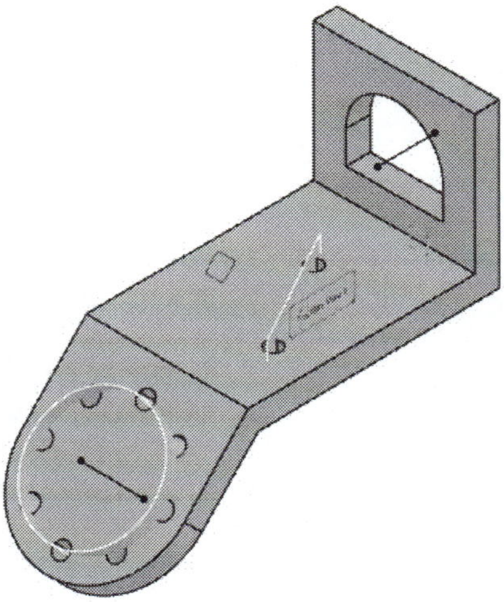

Figure 2–57

Design Considerations

The constructed geometry remains associative to the hole features in the model. In addition, the annotation plane created from the passing plane also updates with the new hole position.

5. Return to the drawing window and update. **Front View.2** changes position based on the modified hole.

Task 10 - Invert the normal for Front View.2.

In this task, you invert the normal for **Front View.2**. When creating an annotation view, you should check the normal direction, indicated by the red arrow, and modify it immediately if it is incorrect. Once an annotation has been added to a view, the normal cannot be modified.

1. Activate the Sample part widget.
2. Activate **Front View.2** by double-clicking on it in the specification tree.
3. Right-click on **Front View.2** and select **Change View Support**.
4. Select **Reverse view direction** and click **OK**.
5. Return to the drawing widget.

Design Considerations

The view does not change in the drawing. Since the drawing view was oriented before placement, changes to the normal for the front view are not reflected in the drawing. The normal only determines the default orientation of a drawing view. This is demonstrated by placing a second drawing view for **Front View.2**.

6. Create a third drawing view and reference **Front View.2**. The drawing view displays as shown in Figure 2–58.

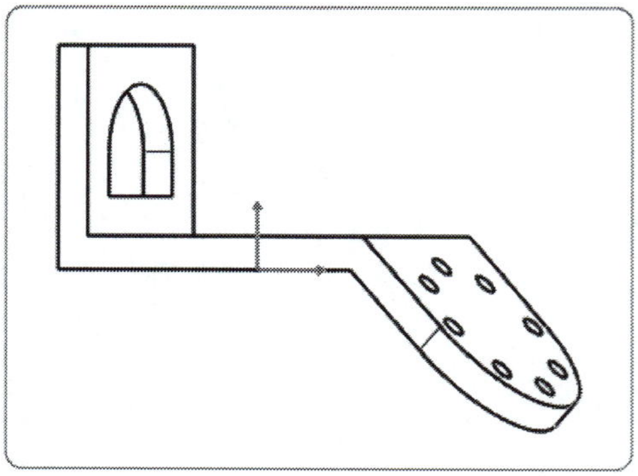

Figure 2–58

Design Considerations

Drawing views can be created as soon as annotation and section views are added to the model. As annotations and other 3D T&A features are added, they can be updated in the drawing.

This drawing was created for demonstration purposes only and does not need to be maintained.

7. Close the drawing without saving.

8. Save the model and close the widget.

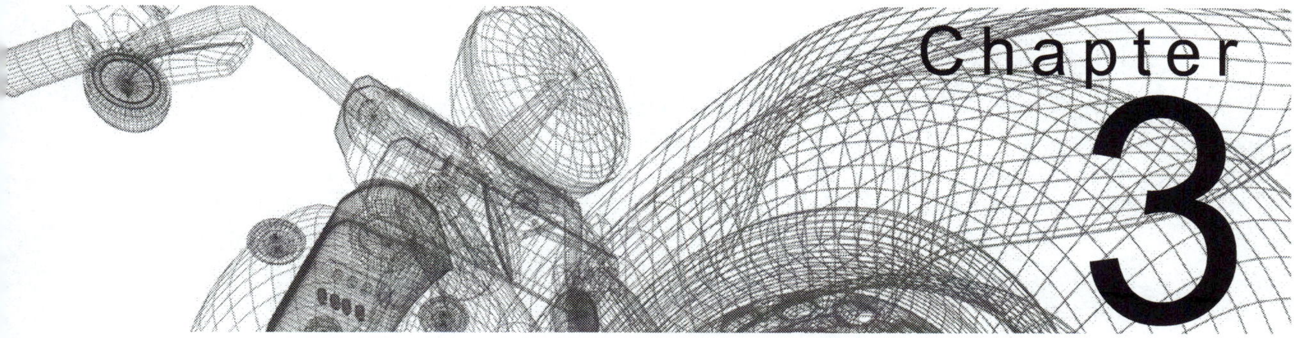

Semantic Annotations

This chapter introduces the Semantic Tolerance Advisor. This tool is used to build almost all annotations required for a model, while maintaining the rules defined by the active standard. In addition, this chapter describes the process used to create basic dimensions.

Learning Objectives in This Chapter

- Understand datum reference frames.
- Learn how to use the Tolerance Advisor tool.
- Create basic dimensions.

3.1 Datum Reference Frames

In CATIA, datum reference frames are also called datum systems. The terms are used interchangeably.

Datum reference frames (DRF) provide the basis for all geometrical tolerancing in the model. The DRF defines an origin from which the location or geometric characteristics of all of the geometry of a part or assembly model are established. For example, datums A and B have been defined for the simple part shown in Figure 3–1. The left and bottom sides of the part will be used as an origin to locate the position of the hole using the 0.1mm boundary defined by the geometrical tolerance.

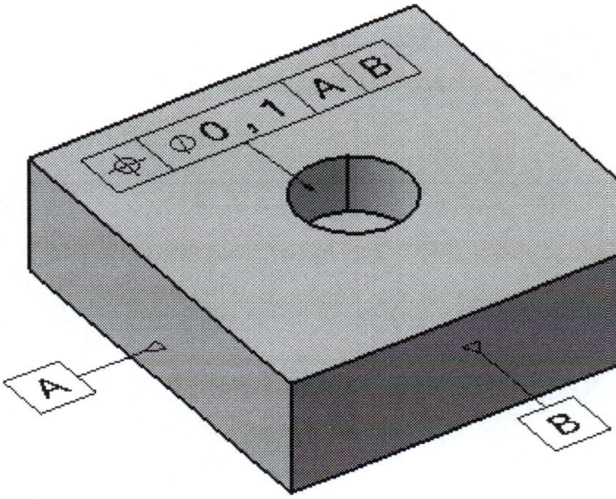

Figure 3–1

General Steps

Use the following general steps to create a datum reference frame for geometrical tolerancing:

1. Activate an annotation plane.
2. Create the semantic datums.
3. Create the required datum reference frame.

Step 1 - Activate an annotation plane.

Double-click on the required annotation plane in the specification tree or directly from the model to activate it. The orientation of the selected annotation plane is used to define the orientation of the text.

Step 2 - Create the semantic datums.

Once you have selected the annotation plane, you must define the semantic datums required to locate your part for geometrical dimensioning and tolerancing. Datums can be created by selecting one of the following types of geometry:

- Point or vertex
- Line, axis, or edge
- Face, surface, or reference plane

The selection of geometry for a datum depends on the geometric shape of the part and the types of tolerances required. You can create as many datums as required to locate the part and all of its geometry in 3D space.

How To: Create a Semantic Datum

1. Select the datum geometry. A face is selected, as shown in Figure 3–2.

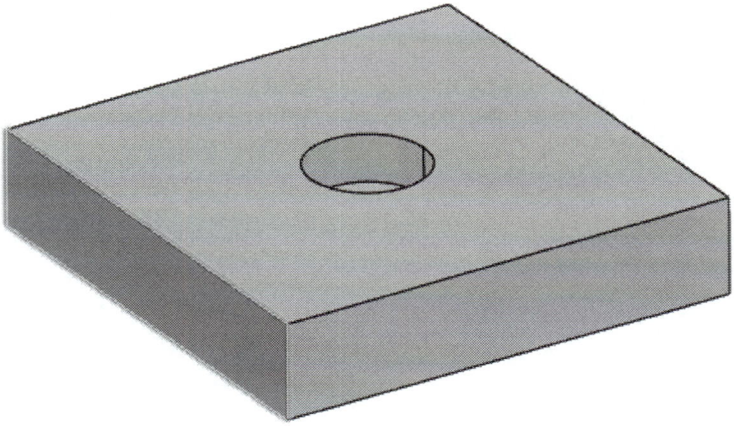

Figure 3–2

2. In the Annotation section of the Action Bar, click (Tolerancing Advisor). The Semantic Tolerancing Advisor dialog box opens, as shown in Figure 3–3.

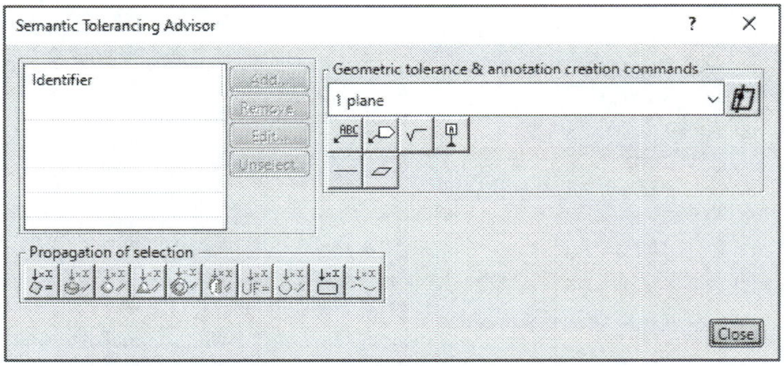

Figure 3–3

3. Click (Datum Feature). The Datum feature dialog box opens, as shown in Figure 3–4.

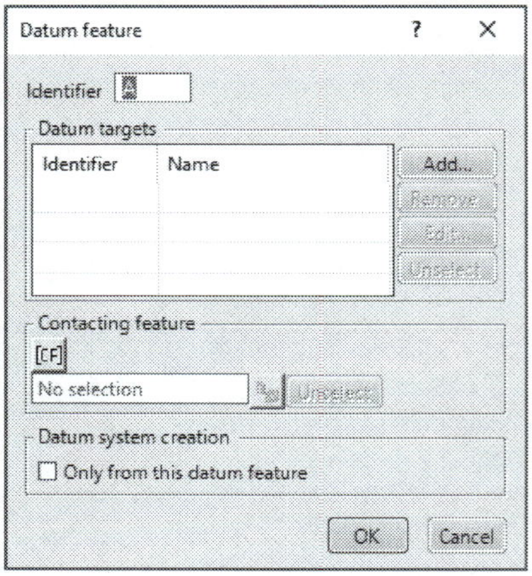

Figure 3–4

4. Enter a name in the *Identifier* field. If the selected geometry is non-planar, you can define the datum targets. These are discussed at the end of this section.

5. Click **OK** once you have defined the datum. The system places a datum flag onto the selected geometry, as shown in Figure 3–5.

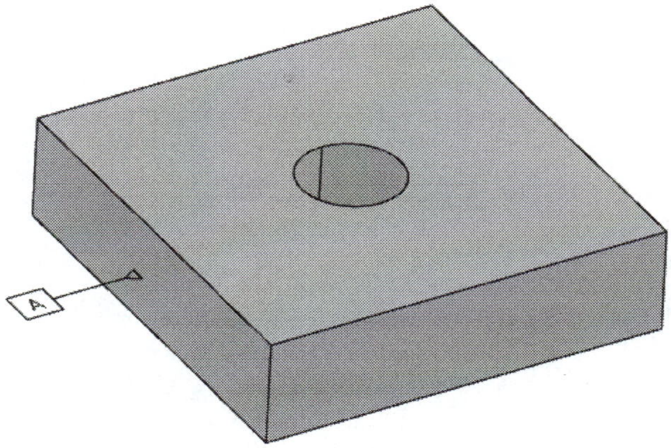

Figure 3–5

6. At this point, the Semantic Tolerancing Advisor dialog box remains open. Selecting additional geometry enables you to define more semantic datums to locate the model in 3D space, as shown in Figure 3–6. Click **Close** once you have completed creating datums.

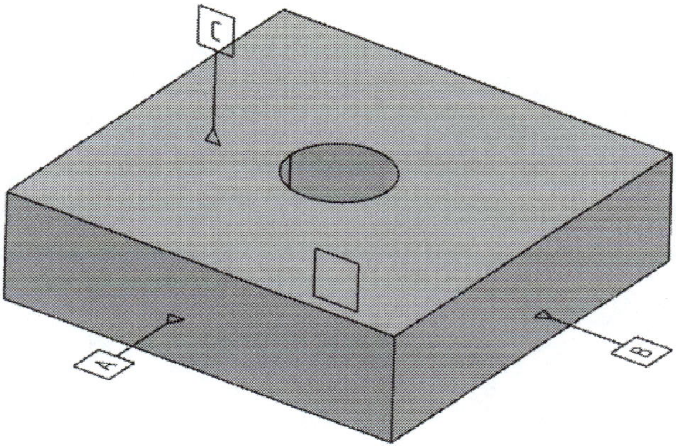

Figure 3–6

Datum Targets

When defining a non-planar or non-linear element as a datum, the system requires you to select datum targets to correctly locate the geometry. For example, the surface shown in Figure 3–7 would require up to three datum targets to correctly define the semantic datum.

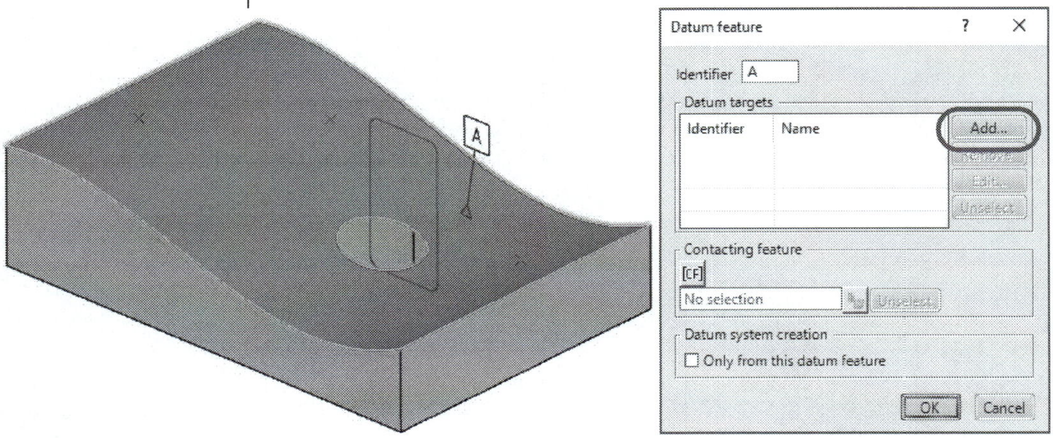

Figure 3–7

Click **Add**. The Datum Target dialog box opens as shown in Figure 3–8.

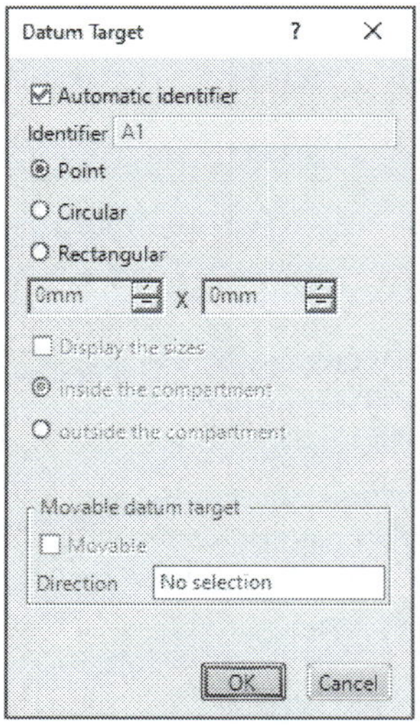

Figure 3–8

This dialog box enables you to create multiple datum target annotations at once by selecting any number of points. Ideally, reference points would be predefined to locate the datum targets; however, you can select anywhere on the datum surface to define a target.

The **Automatic naming** option enables you to meet naming standards (A1, A2, etc.). To manually name the target, clear this option and enter a new name in the *Identifier* field.

Select **Circular** or **Rectangular** to define the size of the target area. You can select the **Display the size(s)** check box. This option enables you to view the sizes:

- Inside the compartment
- Outside the compartment

The **Display the size(s)** check box is unavailable when the selected datum target feature is a point and the **Point only** option is selected, or neither a rectangular nor a circular face.

Click **OK** once the targets are defined. The model displays as shown in Figure 3–9.

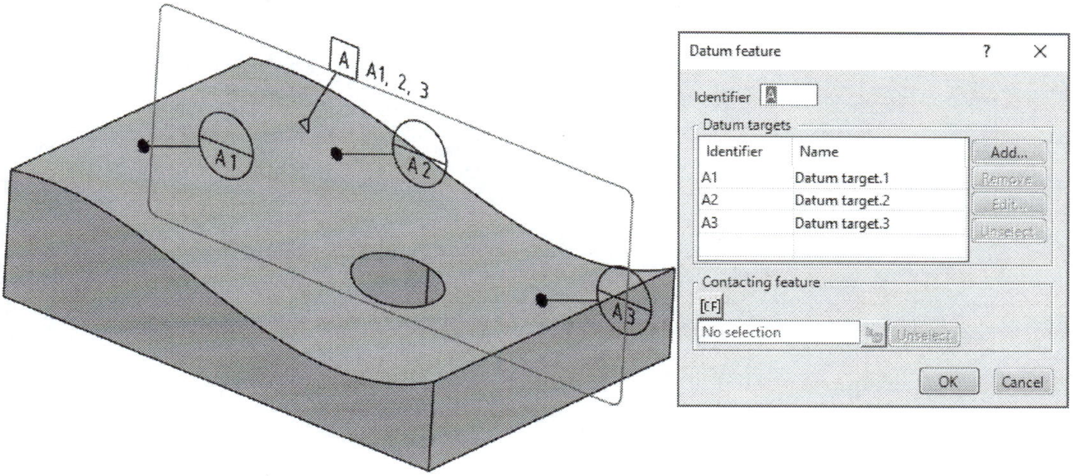

Figure 3–9

Click in the *Datum Direction* field and select a plane that represents the orientation of the datum surface (i.e., the plane's normal direction must be on the external material side).

Step 3 - Create the required datum reference frame.

Although semantic datums have been defined, they cannot yet be used to define a geometrical tolerance. To do this, you must define a datum reference frame for each unique set of datums used in a geometrical tolerance.

How To: Create a Datum Reference Frame

1. Verify that nothing is preselected and then click  (Tolerancing Advisor). The Semantic Tolerancing Advisor dialog box opens as shown in Figure 3–10.

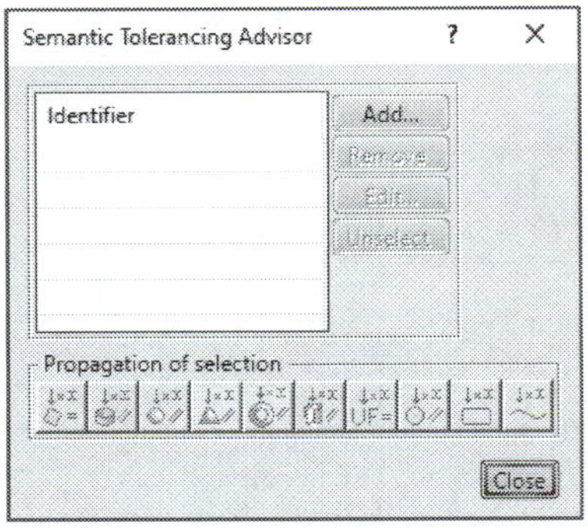

Figure 3–10

2. Click **Add**. The Datum system dialog box opens, as shown in Figure 3–11.

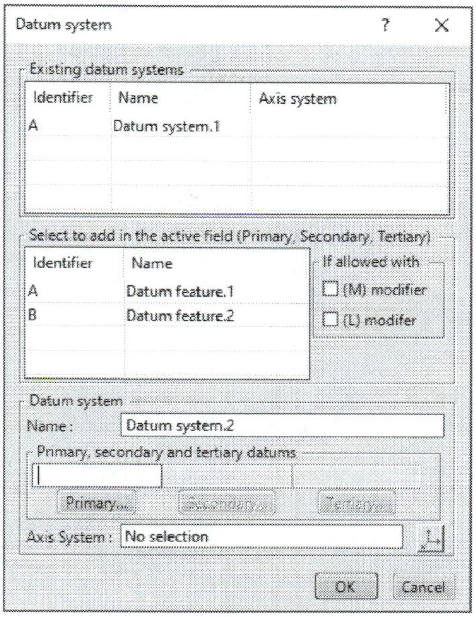

Figure 3–11

3. Select a datum in the list of datum features to add it to the datum frame boxes below. Any combination of datums can be arranged by selecting in the appropriate datum frame boxes field. For example, an A|B datum has been created in Figure 3–12.

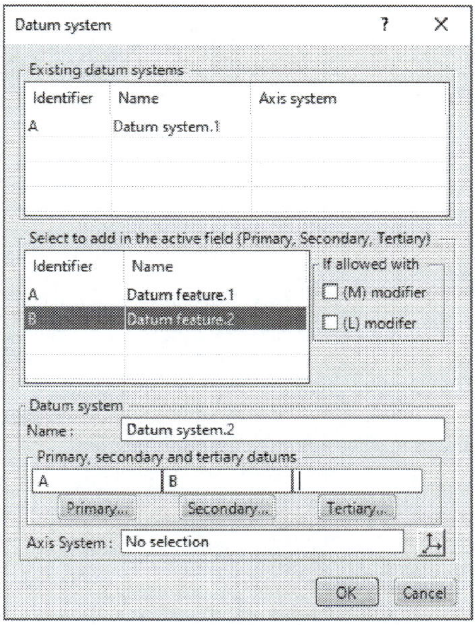

Figure 3–12

4. Click **OK** to complete the operation. The Semantic Tolerancing Advisor and specification tree display, as shown in Figure 3–13.

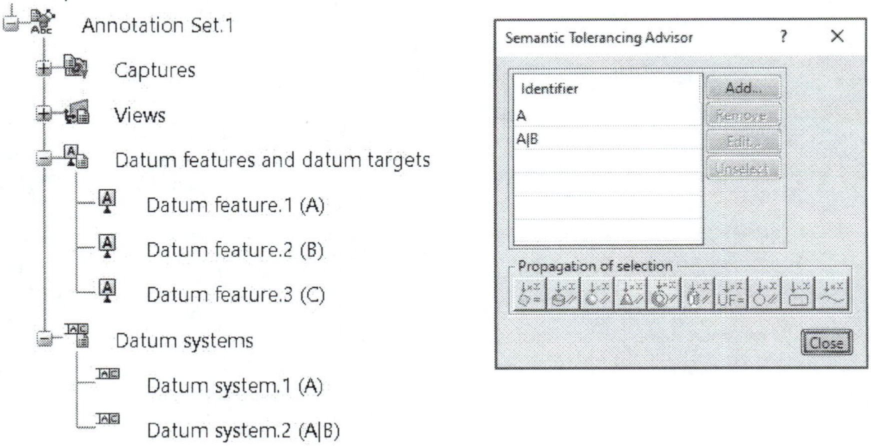

Figure 3–13

If required, select the options highlighted in Figure 3–14 to automatically create a datum reference frame from the semantic datums just created.

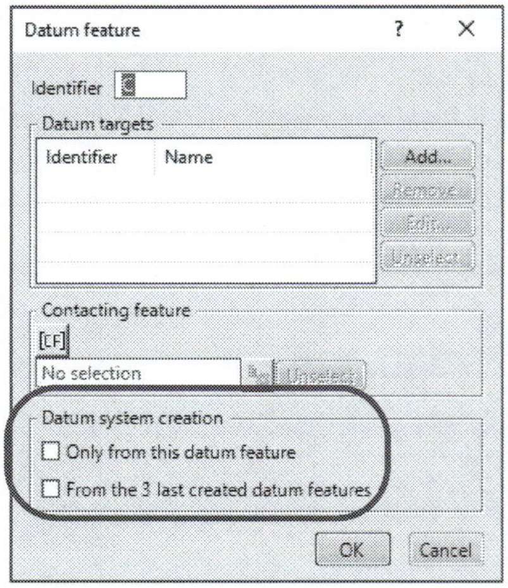

Figure 3–14

3.2 Tolerance Advisor

The Semantic Tolerancing Advisor dialog box is not only used to create semantic datums and datum reference frames. The Tolerance Advisor enables you to develop almost all of the semantic tolerances required for your model. The following list includes some of the types of annotations that can be created:

- Text with Leader
- Flag Note
- Roughness
- Semantic Datum
- Geometrical Tolerances
- Dimensions

The Tolerance Advisor only enables you to create an annotation that corresponds to the tolerancing standard based on the selections made. Therefore, as datum reference frames, geometry, or annotations are selected, the options in the Semantic Tolerancing Advisor dialog box change to show only the appropriate annotations.

General Steps

Use the following general steps to create a geometric tolerance:

1. Start the creation of the geometric tolerance.
2. Select the references.
3. Specify and define the annotation.

Step 1 - Start the creation of the geometric tolerance.

In the Annotation section of the Action Bar, click

 (Tolerancing Advisor). The Semantic Tolerancing Advisor dialog box opens, as shown in Figure 3–15. Without any preselected elements, the dialog box displays all of the currently defined datum reference frames.

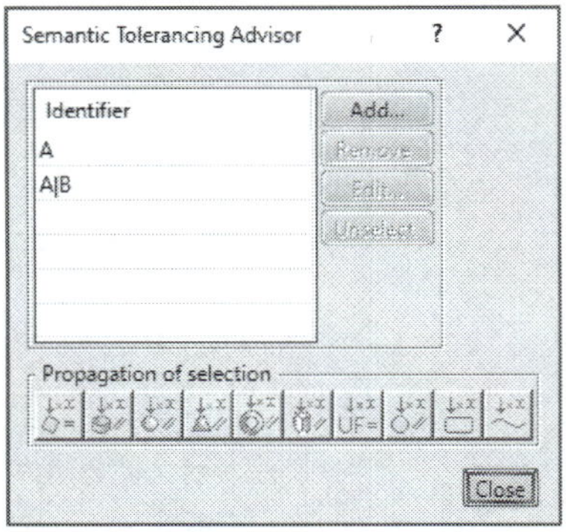

Figure 3–15

Step 2 - Select the references.

If you are defining a geometrical tolerance, select the datum reference frame in the list. Next, select the geometric entity that is referenced by the annotation. Press and hold <Ctrl> to select multiple entities. The Semantic Tolerancing Advisor dialog box updates with the available annotations. For example, the A|B datum reference frame and a cylindrical face are selected in the dialog box shown in Figure 3–16.

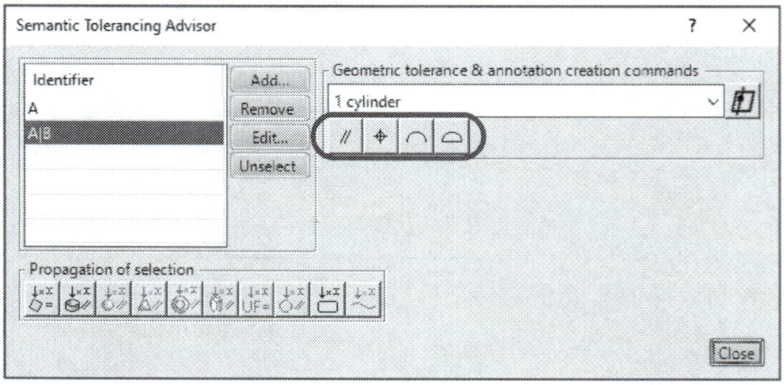

Figure 3–16

If multiple geometric elements are selected, the **Geometric tolerance & annotations creation commands** drop-down list provides additional options, as shown in Figure 3–17.

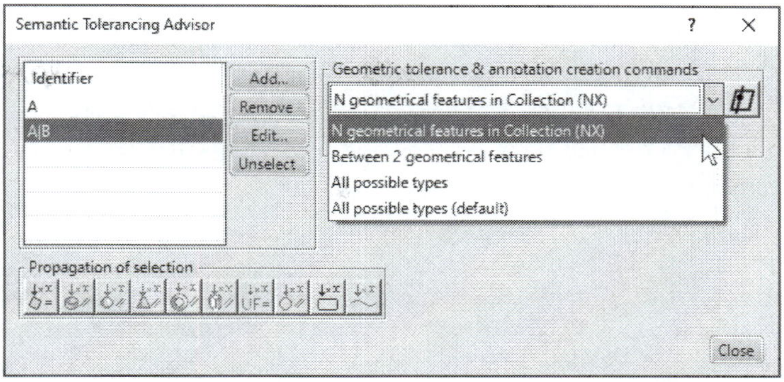

Figure 3–17

Selecting Multiple Items

The propagation selection tools at the bottom of the Semantic Tolerancing Advisor dialog box lets you automatically propagate geometry selection. The tools can be used to select all the faces of the same sphere, plane, cylinder, cone, or torus surface. The three propagation options are as follows.

Options	Description
	The **All same canonicity faces** option selects all the faces of a part that are on the same plane.
	The **All same diameter parallel cylinders** option selects all the faces of a part that have the same cylindrical shape and diameter, and are parallel to the cylindrical face that was selected.
	The **All same diameter parallel sphere** option selects all the faces of a part that have the same spherical shape and diameter as the selected face.
	The **All same apex angle cones** option selects all the faces of a part that have the same cone shape with the same apex angle.
	The **All same user defined features** option selects all the user features or technological results of user features of the same type in the part.
	The **All same diameter, same pitch, parallel CG thread cylinders** option selects all the constructed geometry thread cylinders of a part that have the same diameter and pitch, and have an axis parallel to the Constructed Geometry Thread Cylinder that was selected.

	The **All same diameter parallel circular edge** option selects all parallel circular edges with same diameter.
	The **All elongated, rectangular, or rectangular round pin/hole** option selects all faces of elongated, rectangular, or rectangular round pins or holes to which the selected face or edge belongs.
	The **All the in between edges with tangent continuity** option selects all border edges in a tangent continuity of the selected edge including it.

Step 3 - Specify and define the annotation.

Click an icon from the list of annotations that are available based on the selected datum reference frame and geometry. Depending on the type of annotation selected, a Definition dialog box opens, enabling you to completely define the annotation. For example, the Geometrical Tolerance dialog box opens, as shown in Figure 3–18, if a position geometrical tolerance is created.

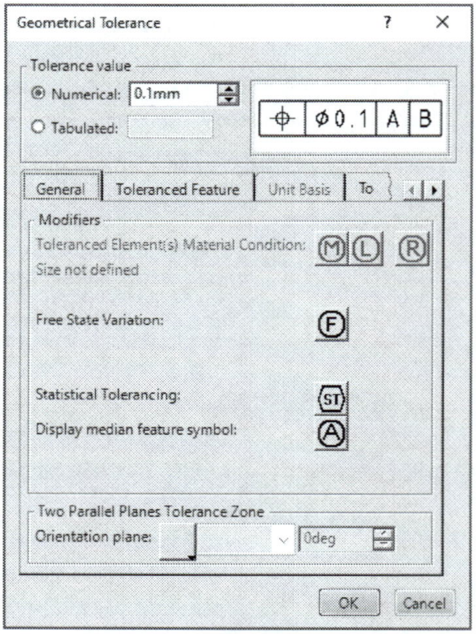

Figure 3–18

A variety of tolerance parameters can be defined in this example, including:

- Tolerance Feature
- Unit Basis
- Tolerance Zone
- Notes

As parameters are defined, the tolerance updates on the model and in the dialog box.

Click **OK** to complete the definition of the annotation. The model displays as shown in Figure 3–19.

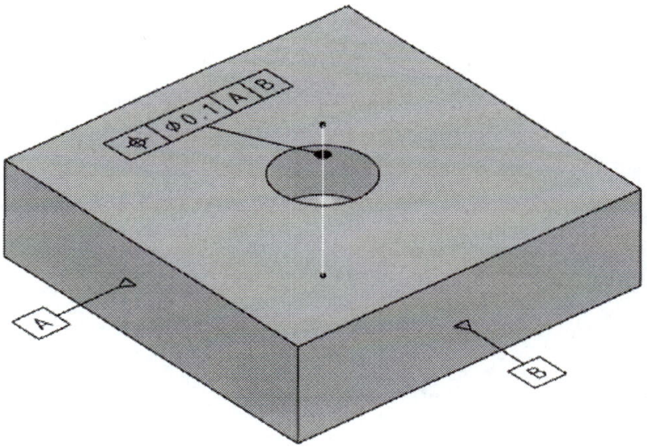

Figure 3–19

Once the annotation has been defined, the Semantic Tolerancing Advisor dialog box remains open for further annotation creation. Click **Close** once you have completed all possible annotations.

3.3 Basic Dimensions

Basic or framed dimensions provide a theoretically exact value that is used to define the size of a feature. Basic dimensions are identified by a rectangle that encloses the value, as shown in Figure 3–20.

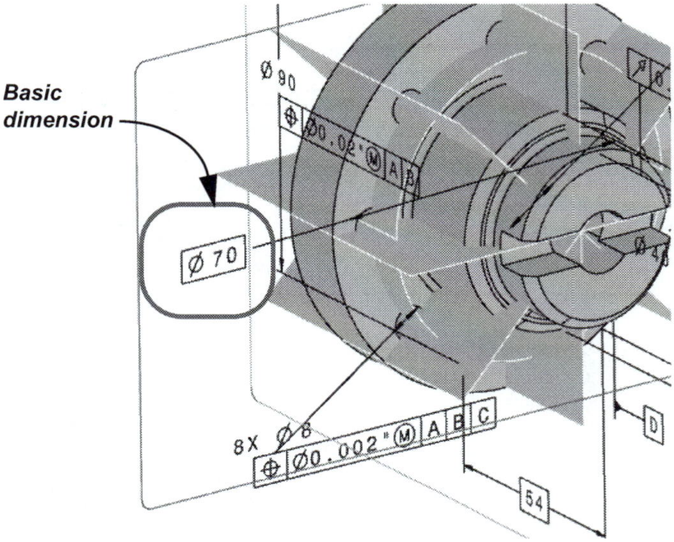

Figure 3–20

General Steps

Use the following general steps to create a basic dimension:

1. Start the creation of a basic dimension.
2. Select a context for the dimension.
3. Start the creation of the dimension.
4. End the creation of the dimension.

Step 1 - Start the creation of a basic dimension.

In the Annotation section of the Action Bar, click  (Framed (Basic) Dimensions). The system prompts you to define a context for the dimension.

Step 2 - Select a context for the dimension.

Since the basic dimension defines a theoretically exact dimension, you must relate the dimension to a specific context. The basic dimension can be related to a datum reference frame, a restricted area, a datum target, or Profile of a Line, Profile of a Surface, Angularity, or Position geometrical tolerances.

Select the appropriate context in the specification tree. The Framed (Basic) Dimensions Management dialog box opens, as shown in Figure 3–21.

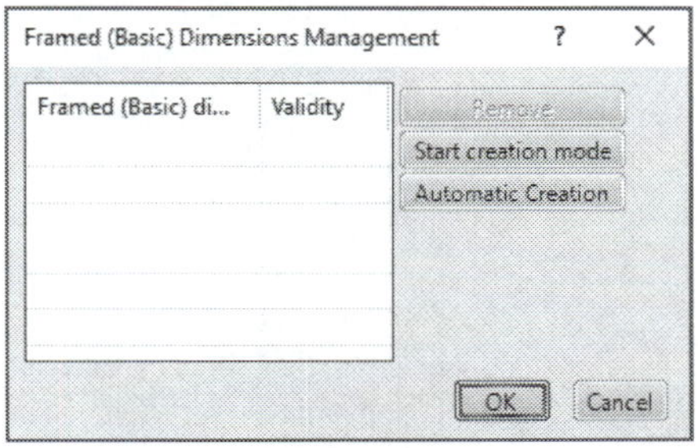

Figure 3–21

Step 3 - Start the creation of the dimension.

Click **Start creation mode** to start the creation of the dimension.

Next, select the geometry to dimension. The system previews the dimension that has been defined, as shown in Figure 3–22.

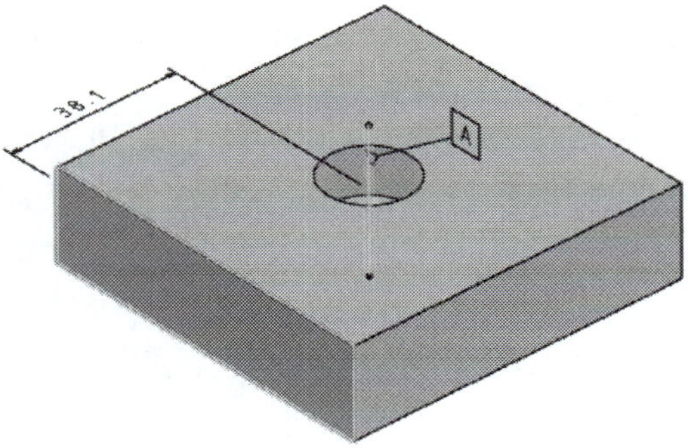

Figure 3–22

Step 4 - End the creation of the dimension.

Select anywhere on the background of CATIA to accept this dimension. The system places a rectangular frame around the dimension and adds it to the dialog box, as shown in Figure 3–23.

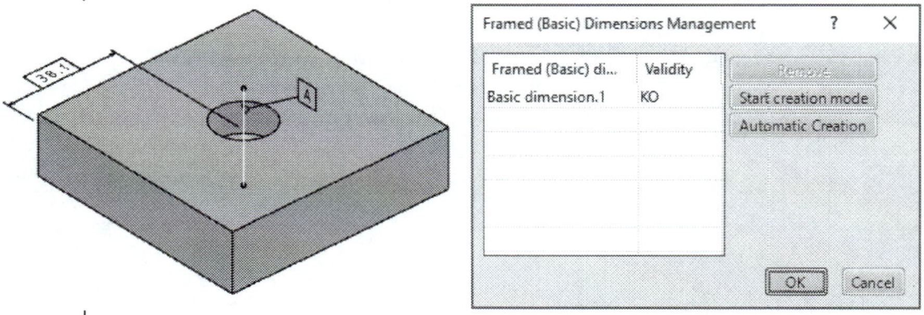

Figure 3–23

At this point, you can continue adding basic dimensions to the model. If you are finished creating basic dimensions, click **End creation mode** and then **OK** to complete the operation.

Automatic Creation

Basic dimensions can be automatically created for patterned features.

How To: Create a Basic Dimension Automatically

1. Click 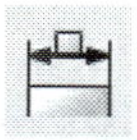 (Framed (Basic) Dimensions).
2. Select the context for the dimension. For example, select the position tolerance that was created for the pattern of holes, as shown in Figure 3–24.

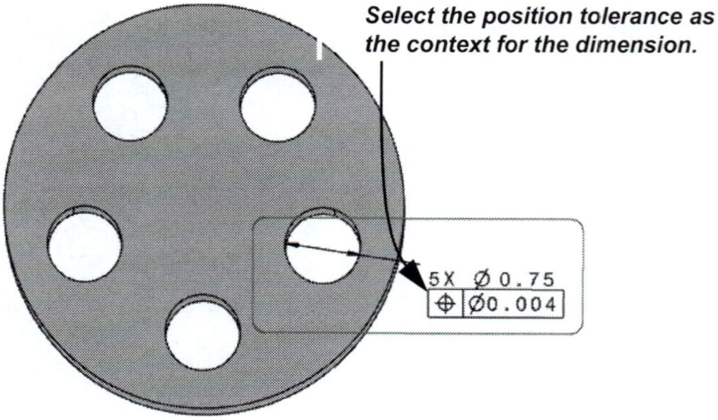

Figure 3–24

The Framed (Basic) Dimensions Management dialog box opens, as shown in Figure 3–25.

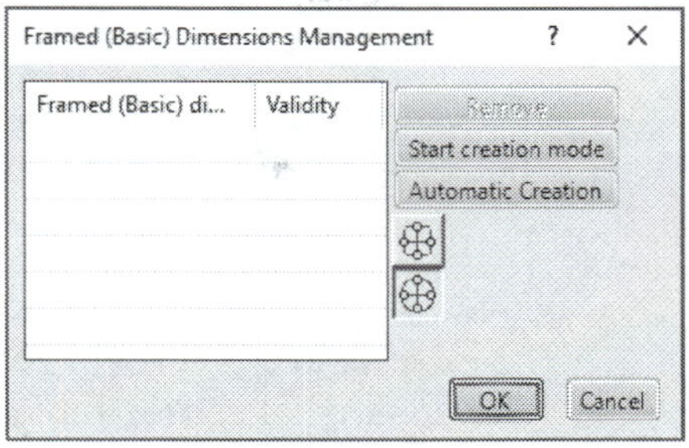

Figure 3–25

3. For circular patterns, two modes are available to define the position of the patterned features. The following describes the two available modes.

Mode	Description
	The position of the patterned features will be defined using rectangular coordinates
	The position of the patterned features will be defined using cylindrical coordinates.

4. Click **Automatic Creation**.
5. The dimensions are automatically generated for the selected feature. Any required construction elements are also created, as shown in Figure 3–26.

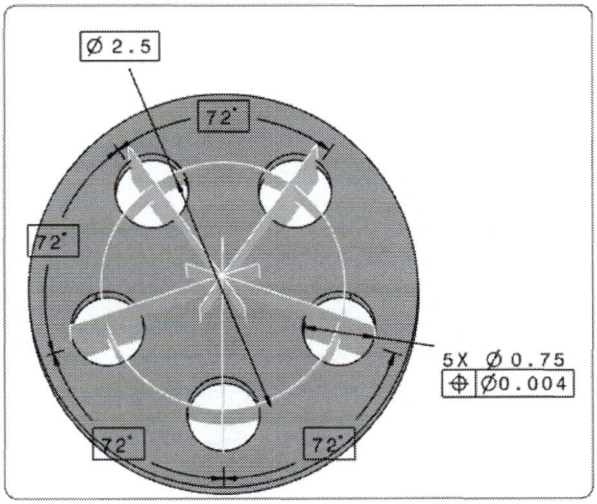

Figure 3–26

6. Click **OK**.

Practice 3a Dimensions and Tolerances

Practice Objectives

- Define the tolerancing standard.
- Create annotation planes.
- Create dimensions with general tolerances and with symmetrical tolerances.

In this practice, you will add annotations to the LockingHub model shown in Figure 3–27.

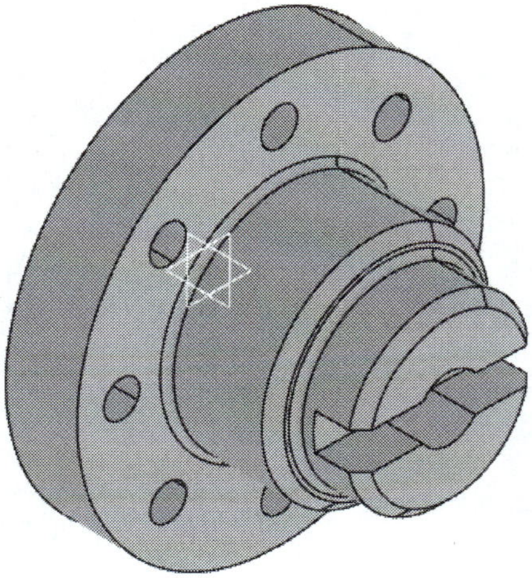

Figure 3–27

Adding dimensions and tolerances to the model should be the first step in any annotation activities, since it enables you to specify material conditions for the geometric tolerances. The completed model displays as shown in Figure 3–28.

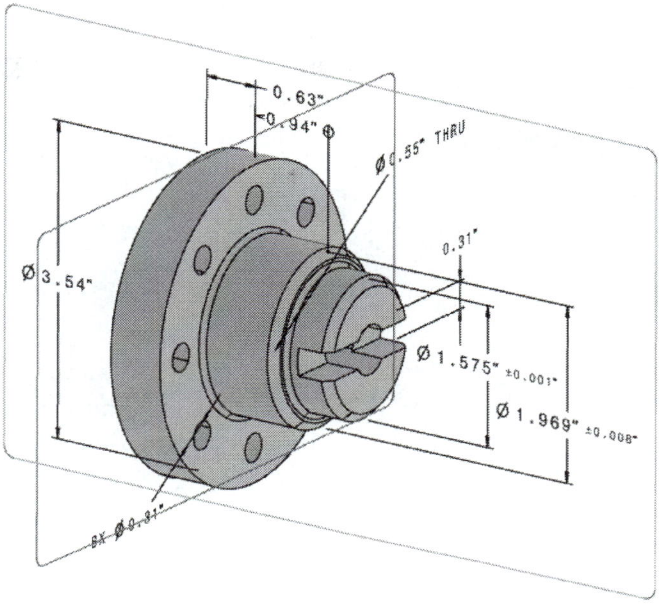

Figure 3–28

Task 1 - Import and open a part file.

1. Import and open **LockingHub.3dxml**. The model displays as shown in Figure 3–29.

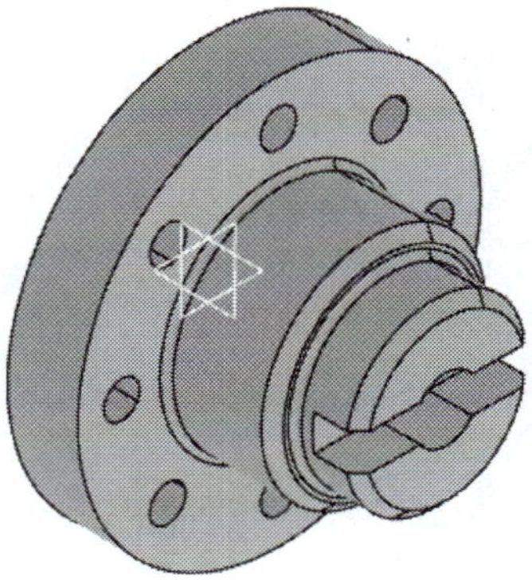

Figure 3–29

2. Ensure you are in the 3D Tolerancing & Annotation app. If not, select on the outer ring of the compass and then pick **3D Tolerancing & Annotation** from under **My Apps**, as shown in Figure 3–30.

Figure 3–30

Task 2 - Set the tolerancing standard.

Design Considerations

Before you begin the creation of any tolerances and annotations using the 3D T&A app, ensure that the correct tolerancing standard has been defined in the Options dialog box. As annotations are created, they use the standard that has been defined. Although this standard can be changed in the *Standard* tab of the Properties dialog box for the Annotation Set.1 feature, it is best to ensure the correct standard before creating any annotation.

1. Select **Me>Preferences>App Preferences>3D Modeling> Mechanical Systems>3D Tolerancing and Annotation** and select the *Tolerancing* arrow.

2. In the Standard drop-down list, select **ANSI-ASME**, as shown in Figure 3–31.

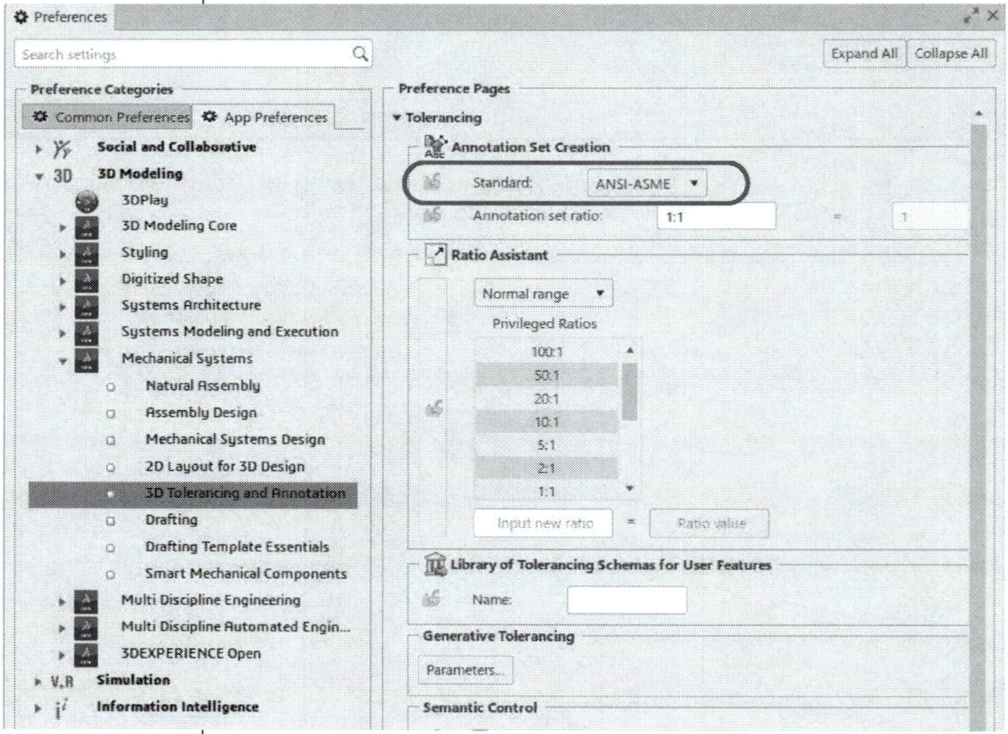

Figure 3–31

3. Select **Me>Preferences>Common Preferences> Parameters, Measures, and Units>Units** and select the *Units* arrow.

4. Select **Inch (in)** in the Length drop-down list, as shown in Figure 3–32.

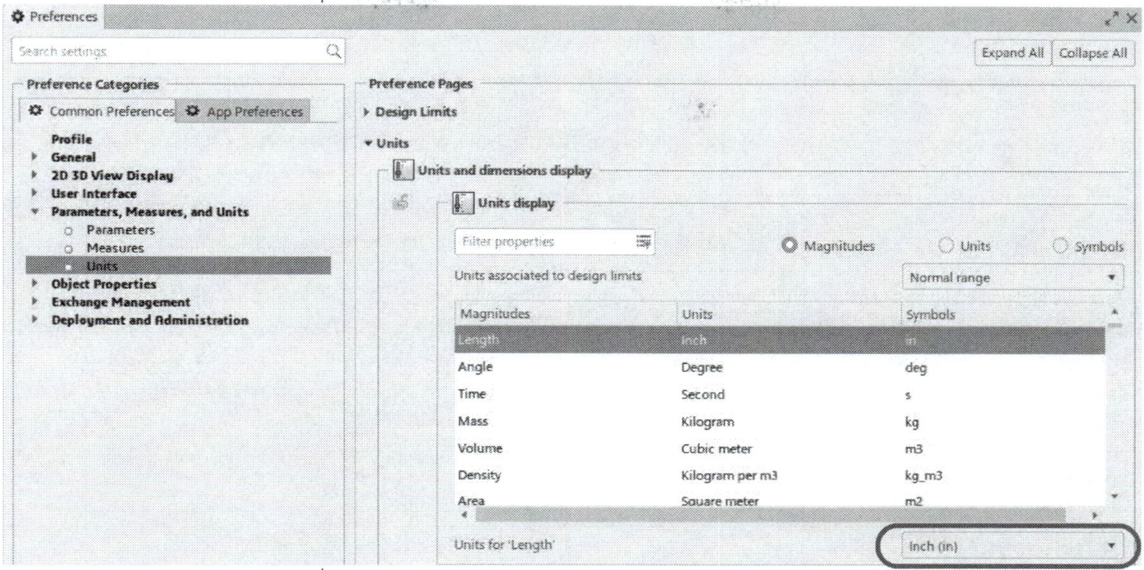

Figure 3–32

5. Click **OK**.

Task 3 - Create annotation planes.

1. Create a Projection View annotation plane on the XY plane with the name **FrontView**.

2. Create a second Projection View annotation plane on YZ plane with the name **SideView**.

3. Ensure that SideView is the active view. The specification tree displays as shown in Figure 3–33.

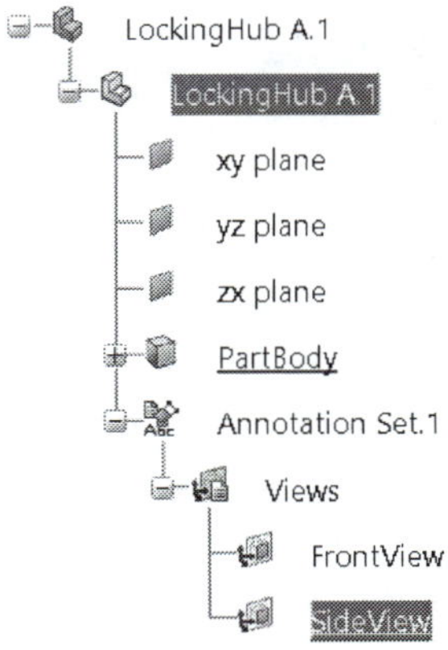

Figure 3–33

4. Hide the three default reference planes to simplify the display of the model.

Task 4 - Create a general tolerance dimension using the Tolerance Advisor.

In the following tasks, you will add a series of dimensions and tolerances to the model. You will use the Tolerance Advisor to ensure that the dimensions conform to the ASME standard defined at the beginning of this practice.

*Note that the View axis is hidden in the following images for clarity. It can be controlled in the **Me>Preferences>App Preferences>3D Modeling>Mechanical Systems>3D Tolerancing and Annotation**> View/Annotation Plane arrow.*

1. In the Annotation section of the Acton Bar, click  (Tolerancing Advisor). The Semantic Tolerancing Advisor dialog box opens, as shown in Figure 3–34.

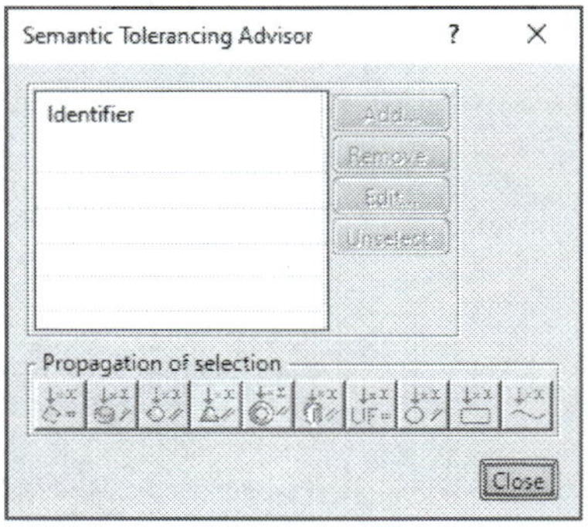

Figure 3–34

2. Select the cylindrical face highlighted in Figure 3–35. The Semantic Tolerancing Advisor dialog box updates with annotation options for the selected face.

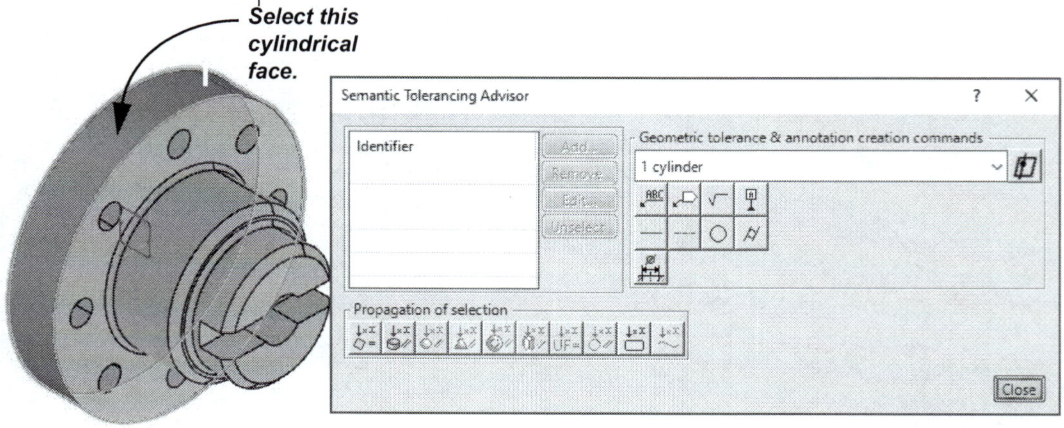

Figure 3–35

3. Click  (Diameter) in the dialog box. The system places a 0.3' diameter dimension in a default location on the model. Additionally, the Limit of Size Definition dialog box opens, enabling you to configure a tolerance for the diameter dimension.

4. Select **General Tolerance** and accept the default standard, as shown in Figure 3–36. Note that if your system is configured so that the Tolerance can be edited, then you should leave it unchanged.

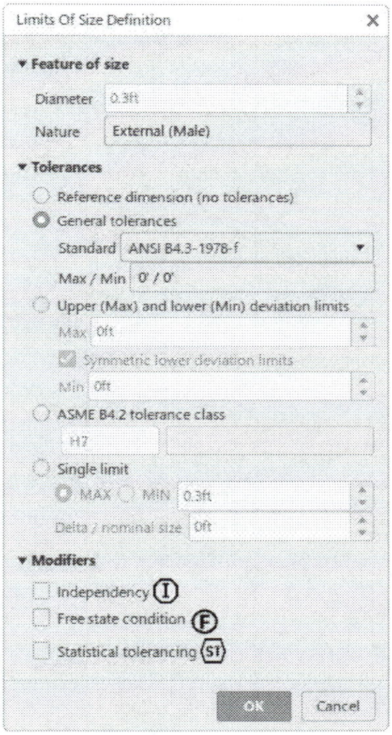

Figure 3–36

5. Click **OK** to return to the Semantic Tolerancing Advisor dialog box.

6. Click **Close** to finish the operation.

7. Select the 0.3' diameter dimension and drag it to an appropriate location on the model. The model displays, as shown in Figure 3–37.

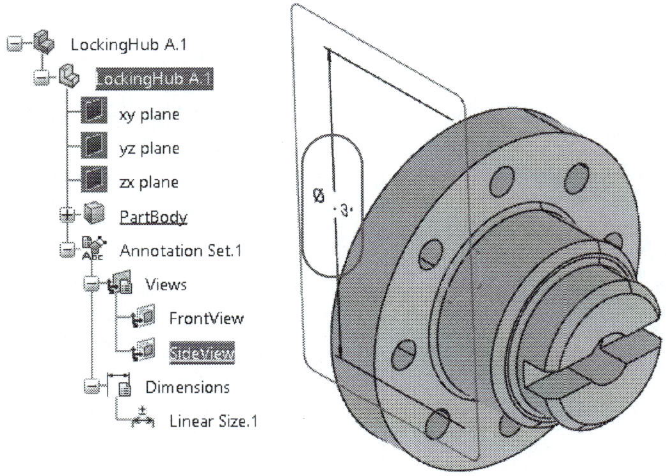

Figure 3–37

Task 5 - Create a symmetric tolerance dimension.

1. Preselect the cylindrical face shown in Figure 3–38 and then click (Tolerancing Advisor).

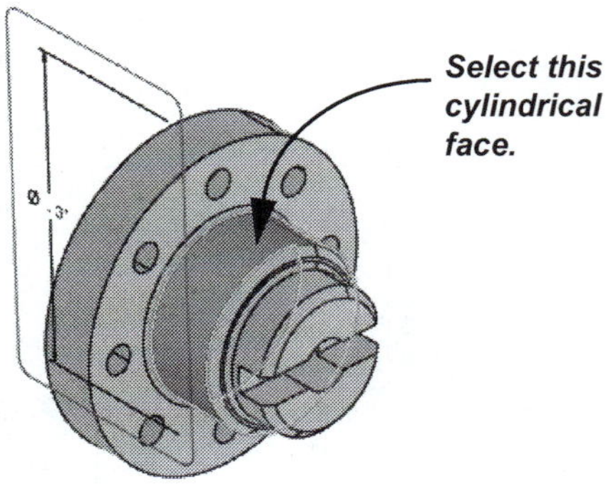

Figure 3–38

2. Click (Diameter) to create a second diameter dimension.
3. Make the following selections in the Limit of Size Definition dialog box, as shown in Figure 3–39:
    - Select **Upper (Max) and lower (Min) deviation limits**.
    - In the *Max* field, enter **0.008in**.
    - Select **Symmetric lower deviation limits**.

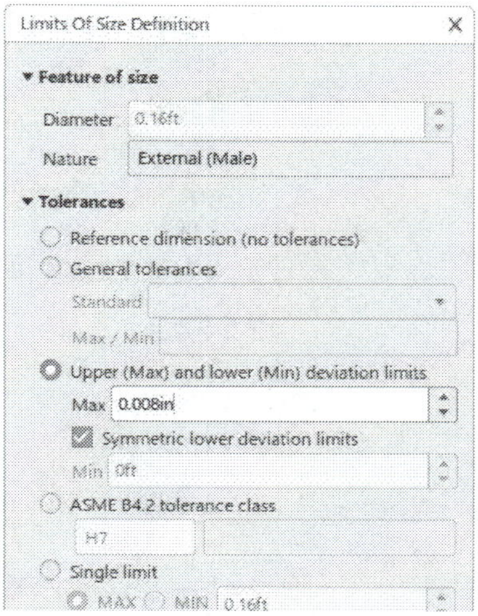

Figure 3–39

4. Click **OK**, then move the dimension to an appropriate location, as shown in Figure 3–40.

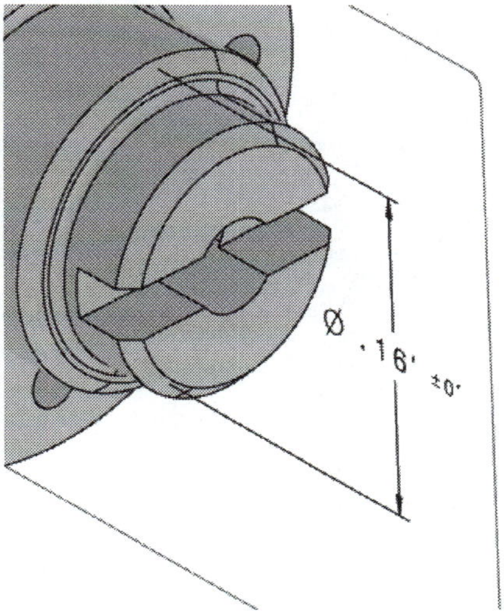

Figure 3–40

5. Click **Close** to close the Semantic Tolerancing Advisor dialog box.

Design Considerations

Note that the tolerance value is 0. This is because the value format is, by default, in Feet. The tolerance is too small. In a later task, you will change all the values to inches at the same time.

Task 6 - Create a dimension for a pattern.

In this task, you create a diameter dimension for the pattern of eight holes. You place this dimension on the FrontView annotation plane.

1. Activate FrontView.
2. Select the surface of the hole shown in Figure 3–41.

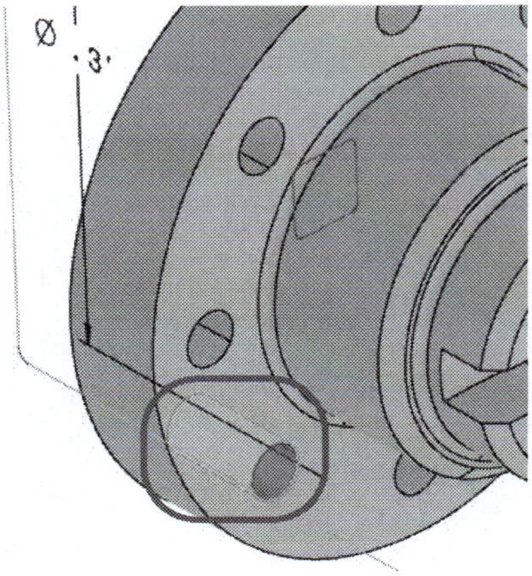

Figure 3–41

3. Click  (Tolerancing Advisor).
4. In the *Propagation Selection* area of the Semantic Tolerancing Advisor dialog box, click  (All same diameter parallel cylinders).
5. Note that all eight holes in the pattern highlight and the Semantic Tolerancing Advisor has **N cylindrical slots/tabs in Collection (NX)** selected in the *Geometric tolerance & annotation creation commands* drop-down list, as shown in Figure 3–42.

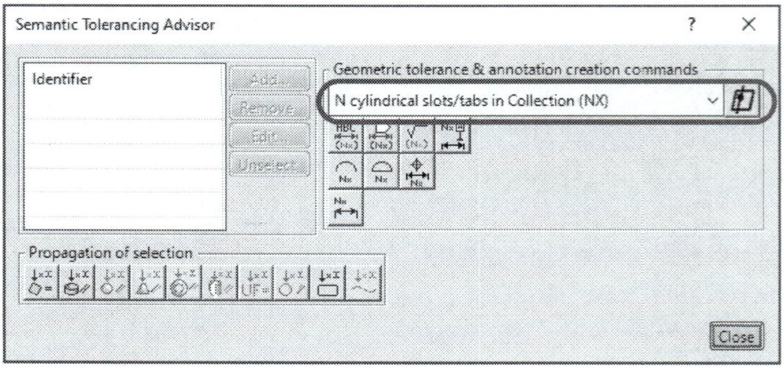

Figure 3–42

6. Select **N cylinders in collection (NX)** in the *Geometric tolerance & annotation creation commands* list, as shown in Figure 3–43.

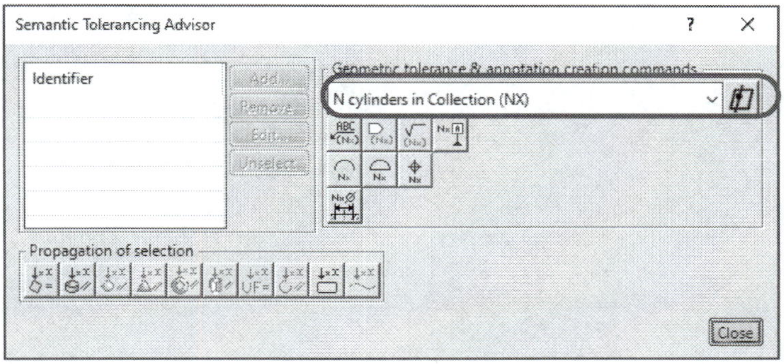

Figure 3–43

7. Click  (Pattern Diameter) and apply a **General Tolerance**. Leave *Tolerance* set to the default values.

8. Complete the operation and position the dimension appropriately, as shown in Figure 3–44.

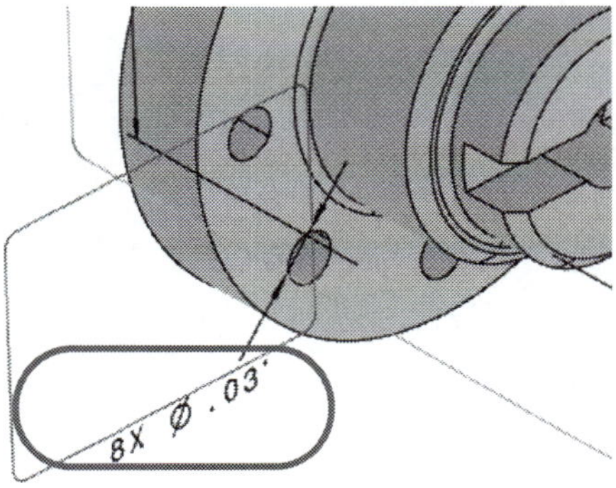

Figure 3–44

Task 7 - Create text with a leader that references a dimension.

In this task, you will need to create a dimension for the center hole. The dimension should be followed with some text that describes the feature as a “thru” hole. You need to modify the properties of the dimension to add additional text.

1. In the specification tree, right-click on **FrontView** and select **Display View** to orient the model.

2. Preselect **Hole.2** in the specification tree and activate the Tolerance Advisor.

3. Create a diameter dimension with a general tolerance. Leave tolerance set to default values.

4. Complete the operation and move it to an appropriate position, as shown in Figure 3–45.

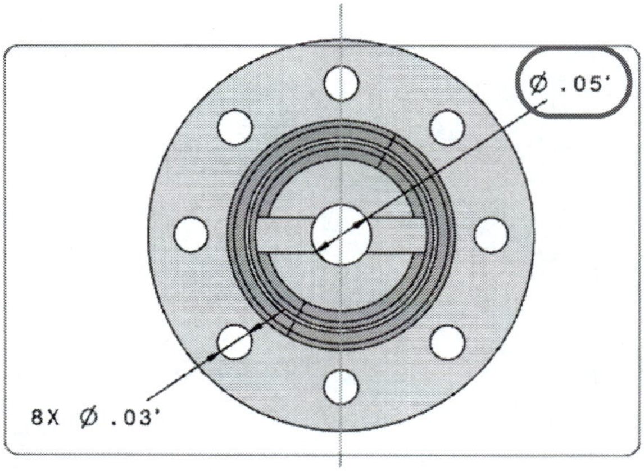

Figure 3–45

5. Right-click on the dimension and select **Properties**. Leave *Tolerance* set to default values.

6. Select the *Dimension Texts* tab and enter **THRU** in the *Associated Texts* field, as shown in Figure 3–46.

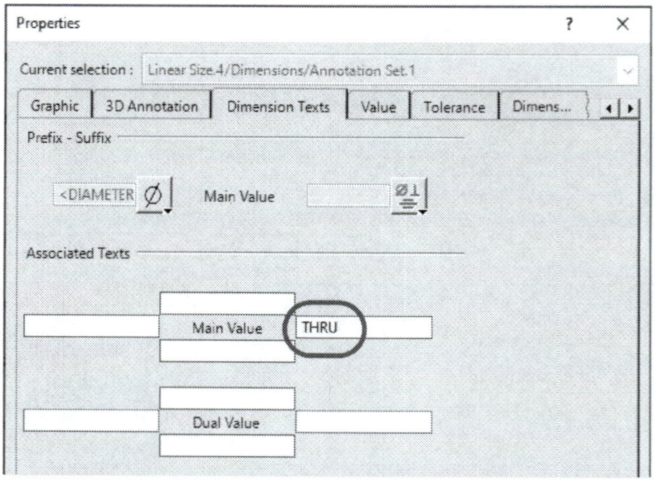

Figure 3–46

7. Click **OK**. The model displays as shown in Figure 3–47.

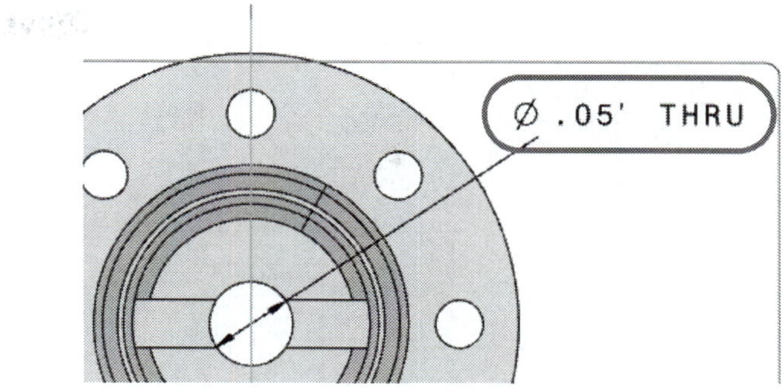

Figure 3–47

Task 8 - Create a distance dimension.

1. Activate SideView.
2. Hold <Ctrl> and select the two parallel faces shown in Figure 3–48.

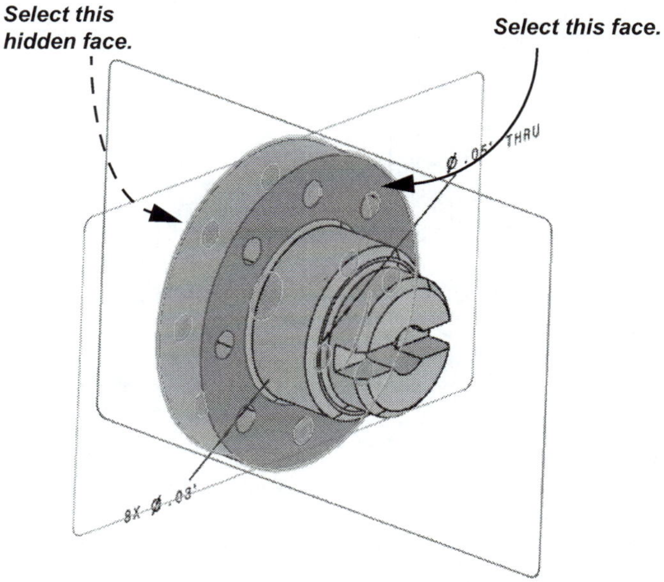

Figure 3–48

3. Activate the Tolerance Advisor. The default Geometric feature type is **1 slot/tab**, as shown in Figure 3–49.

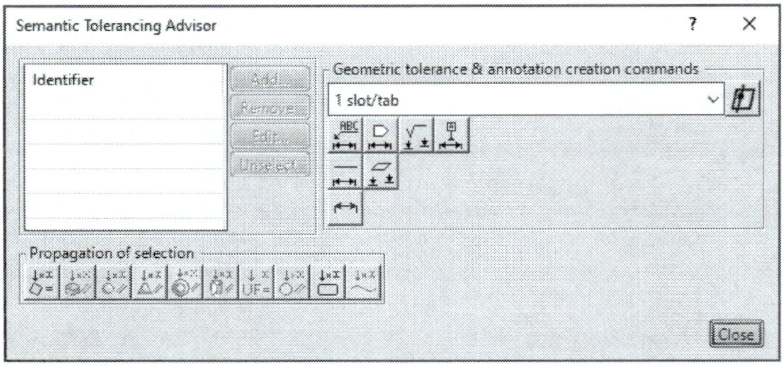

Figure 3–49

4. Click (Distance Creation) to add a distance dimension to the model. Create the dimension using a general tolerance.

5. Complete the operation and move the dimension to an appropriate position, as shown in Figure 3–50.

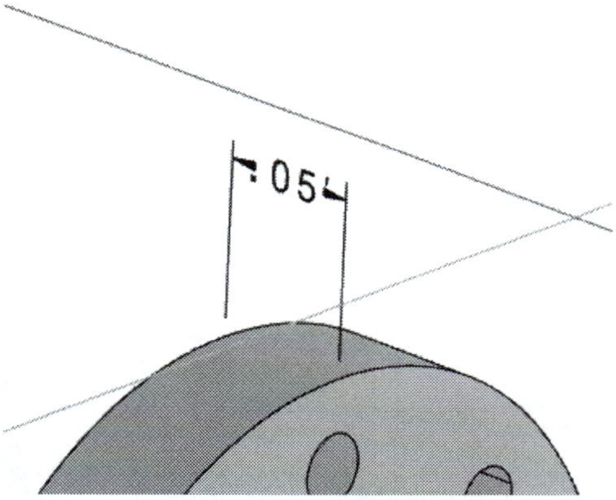

Figure 3–50

6. Remove the current FrontView filter applied to the model by clicking the ✕ in the upper right corner, as shown in Figure 3–51. This will display all of the dimensions again.

Figure 3–51

Task 9 - Create additional annotations.

1. With the SideView activated and using the Semantic Tolerancing Advisor dialog box, create the additional annotations shown in Figure 3–52.

   - Create the 0.13' diameter dimension with a +/- 0.001" tolerance.
   - Create the 0.13' dimension shown.

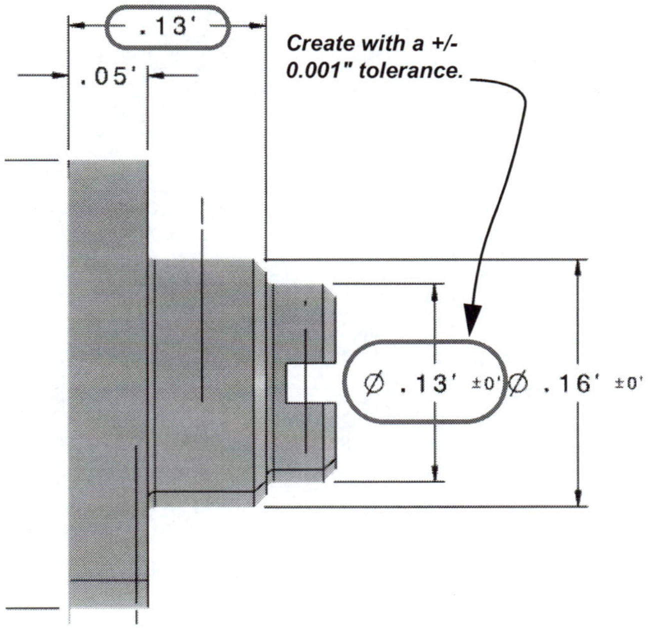

Figure 3–52

2. Activate FrontView and create the additional annotation shown in Figure 3–53.

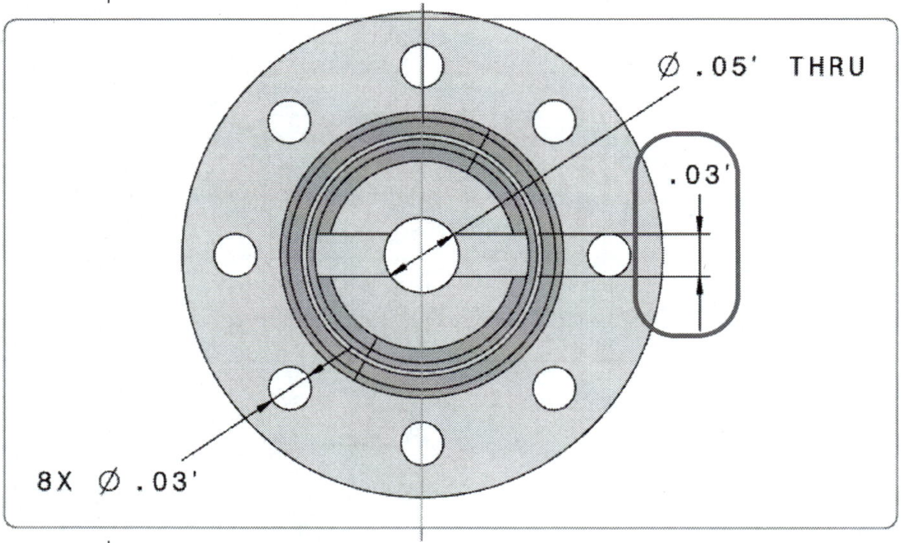

Figure 3–53

Task 10 - Change the dimension units.

The tolerances in this model do not display because they are too small for the default units (feet). In this task, you change the units of the dimensions to inches.

1. From the specification tree, select the first dimension under the Dimensions branch.
2. Press and hold <Shift> and select the last dimension. All the dimensions highlight.
3. In the Object Properties window, select **DISTINCH**, as shown in Figure 3–54.

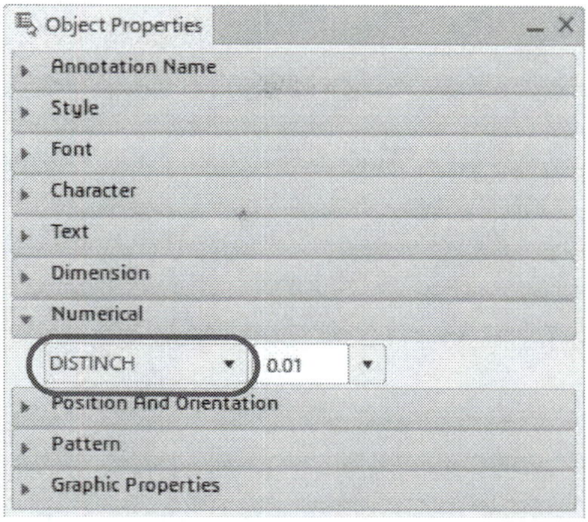

Figure 3–54

The model units update, as shown in Figure 3–55.

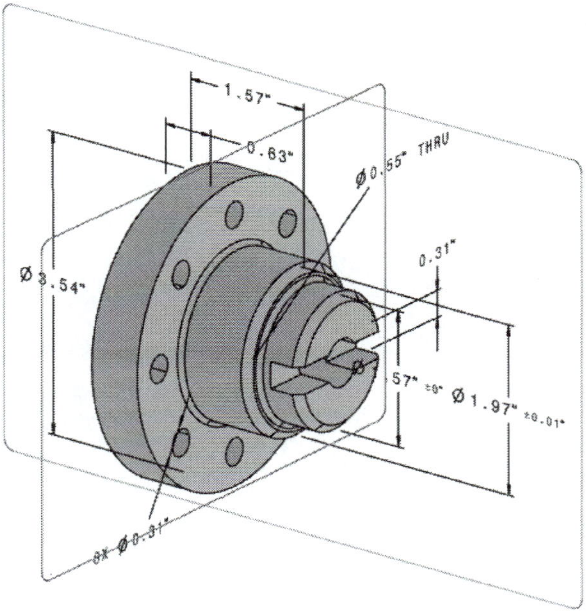

Figure 3–55

4. Note that the tolerances still do not display. To correct this, precision must be increased.

5. Using <Ctrl>, multi-select the 1.57" and the 1.97" dimensions.

6. In the Object Properties window, set the precision to **0.001**. The model units update, as shown in Figure 3–56. Update the position of those two dimensions as needed. Holding <Shift> while dragging them will release the snap function.

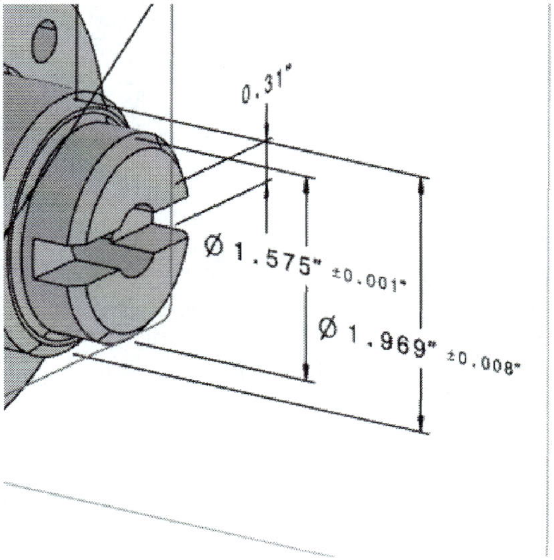

Figure 3–56

7. Save the model.

Practice 3b Geometric Tolerances

Practice Objectives

- Create a semantic datum.
- Create a datum reference frame.
- Create a geometric tolerance.
- Create a framed (basic) dimension.

In this practice, you will create datum reference frames (DRF), geometric tolerances, and basic (or framed) dimensions. The completed model is shown in Figure 3–57.

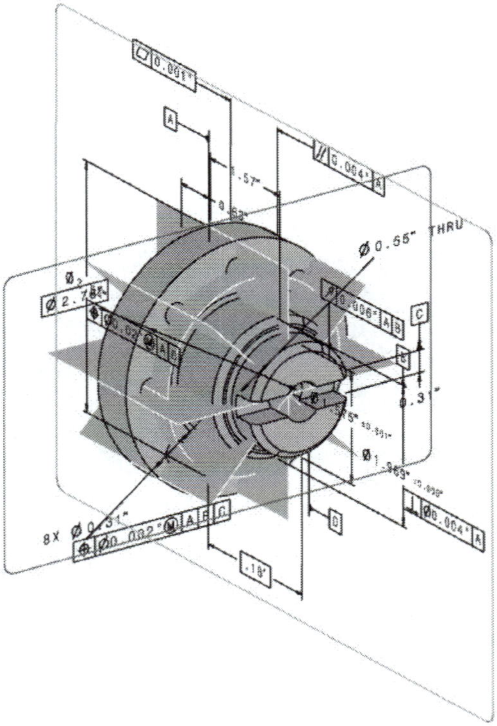

Figure 3–57

Task 1 - Import and open a part file.

1. Import and open **LockingHub_Ex3a.3dxml**. The model displays as shown in Figure 3–58.

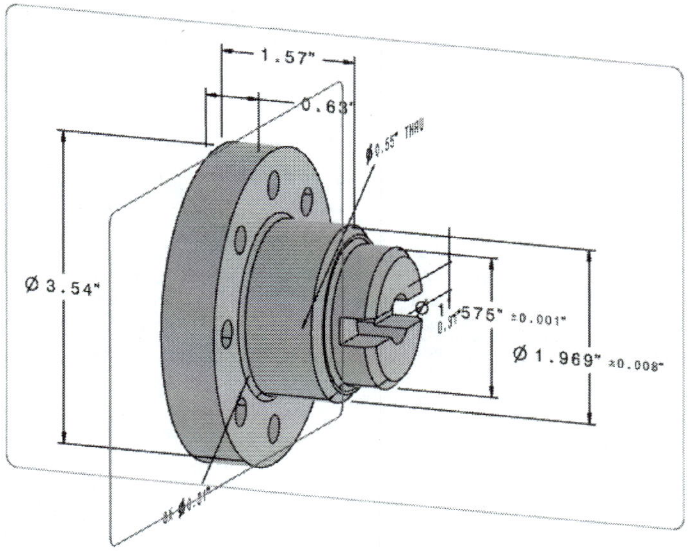

Figure 3–58

Task 2 - Create a semantic datum and datum reference frame.

In this task, you will define the first semantic datum for the model. In addition, you will automatically create a datum reference frame using semantic datum A. This datum reference frame will be referenced during the creation of geometric tolerances for the model.

1. Activate SideView.

2. Preselect the face shown in Figure 3–59.

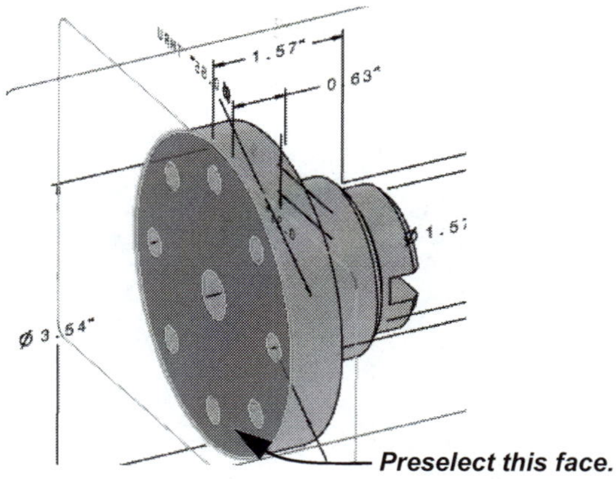

Figure 3–59

3. Click (Tolerancing Advisor) and then (Datum Feature). The Datum feature dialog box opens as shown in Figure 3–60.

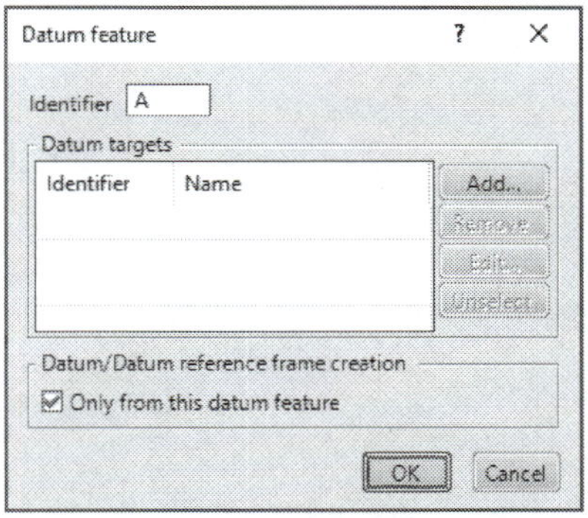

Figure 3–60

4. Ensure that the following selections are made:

- *Datum Label:* **A**
- Select **Only from this datum feature**.

5. Complete the operation. The model displays as shown in Figure 3–61.

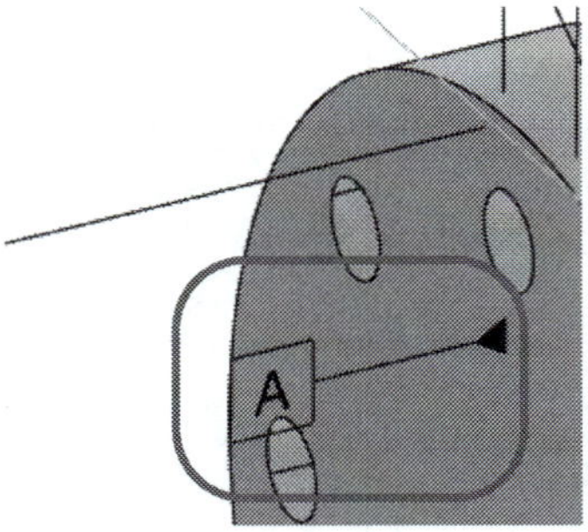

Figure 3–61

Datum feature.1 and **Datum reference frame.1** have been added to the specification tree, as shown in Figure 3–62.

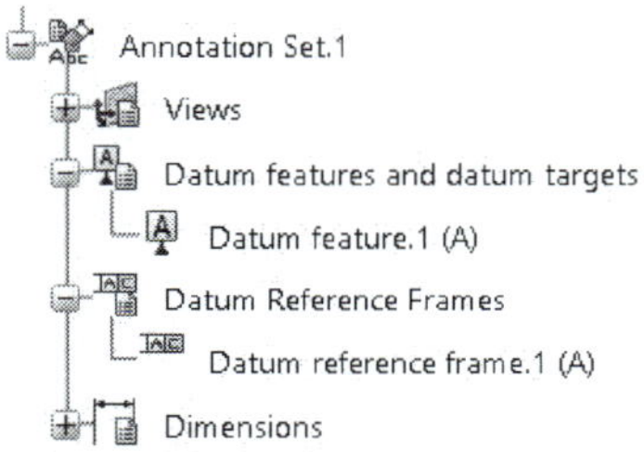

Figure 3–62

Task 3 - Position the semantic datum.

1. Select **Datum A**. The system places a yellow diamond on the datum, enabling you to modify the attachment point.

2. Experiment with positioning the datum and attachment point.

3. Right-click on the yellow diamond and select **Extremity Link>Perpendicular**, as shown in Figure 3–63.

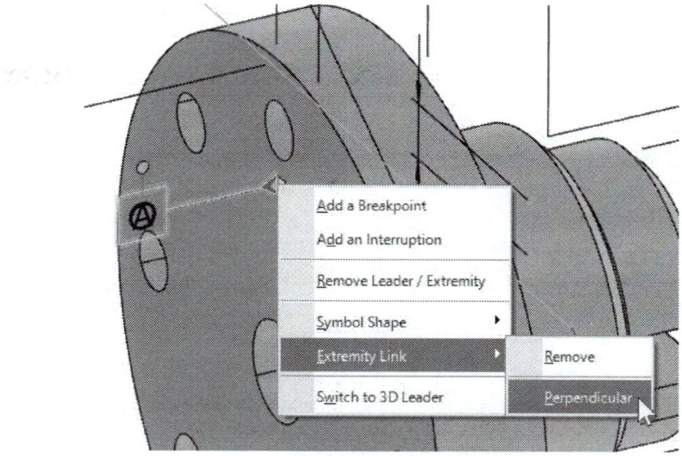

Figure 3–63

4. Drag the datum to the position shown in Figure 3–64.

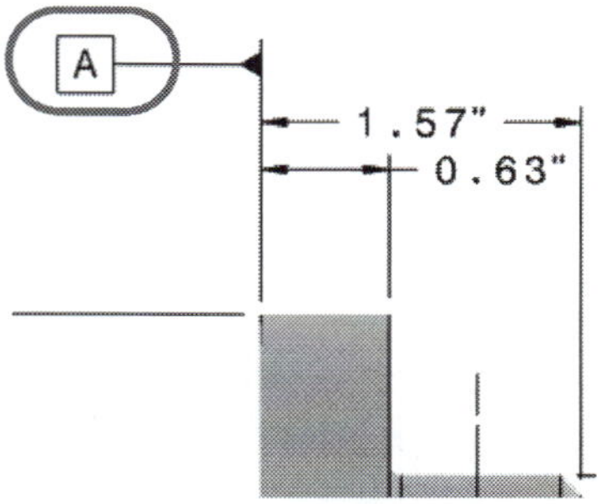

Figure 3–64

Task 4 - Create additional semantic datums.

In this task, you create three more semantic datums to annotate the model. Datum B will reference the 1.969" diameter cylindrical surface. Therefore, you can select the **1.969"** diameter dimension to define this datum.

1. Select the **1.969"** diameter dimension and then click  (Tolerancing Advisor).

2. Click  (Datum Feature) to create a semantic datum. Define the following properties in the Datum feature dialog box:

   - *Datum Label:* **B**
   - Clear the **Only from this datum feature** option.

3. Complete the operation. The model displays as shown in Figure 3–65. The datum displays attached to the 1.969" diameter dimension.

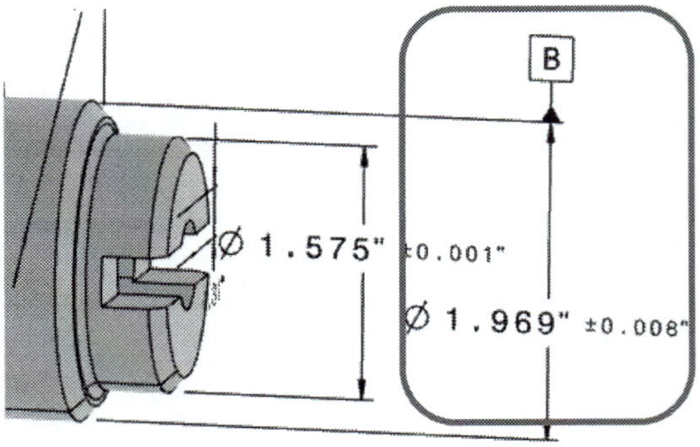

Figure 3–65

4. Activate FrontView.

5. Create a semantic datum that references the 0.31" toleranced dimension. Do not create any datum reference frames during this operation. The model displays as shown in Figure 3–66.

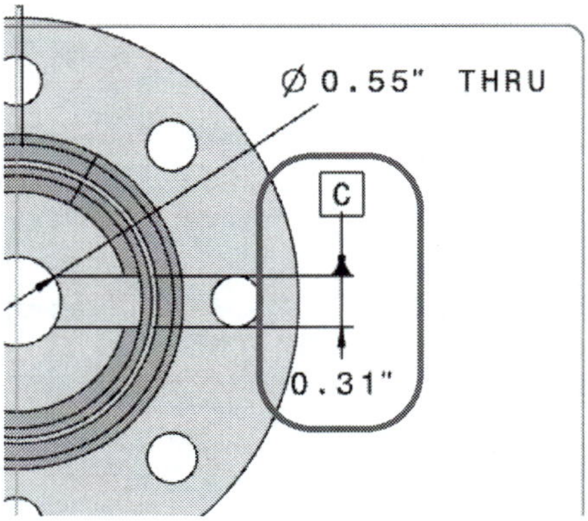

Figure 3–66

6. Activate SideView.

7. Create a final semantic datum named **D** that references the planar face shown in Figure 3–67. Do not create any datum reference frames during this operation.

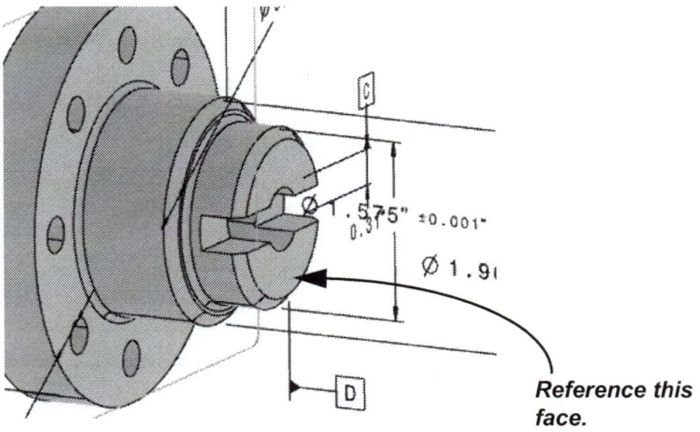

Figure 3–67

Task 5 - Manually create a datum reference frame.

In this task, you will manually define the datum reference frame A|B.

1. With nothing preselected, click (Tolerancing Advisor). The Semantic Tolerancing Advisor dialog box opens, as shown in Figure 3–68.

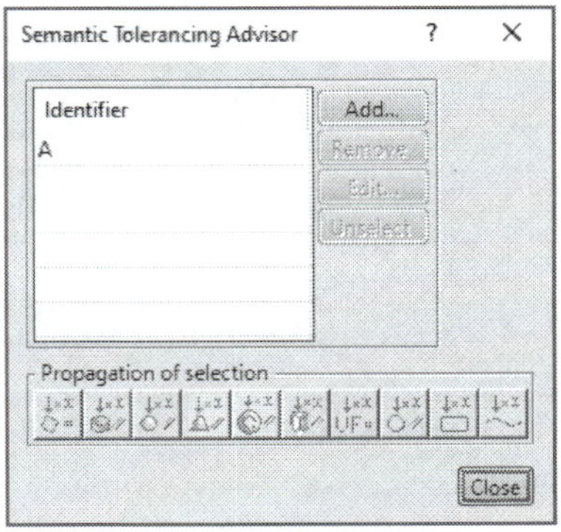

Figure 3–68

2. Click **Add**. The Datum reference frames dialog box opens, as shown in Figure 3–69.

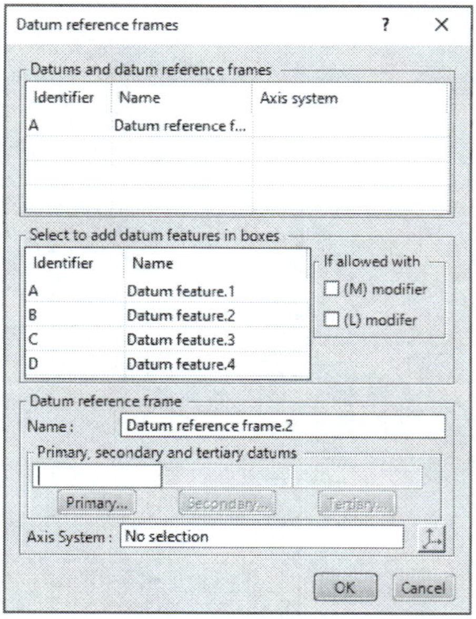

Figure 3–69

3. In the *Select to add datum features in boxes* area, select **A** and then **B**. The *Datum reference frame* area updates, as shown in Figure 3–70.

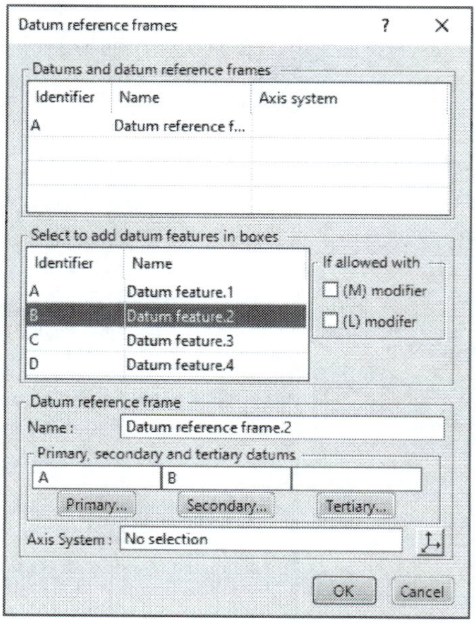

Figure 3–70

4. Click **OK** and then **Close**. The specification tree displays as shown in Figure 3–71.

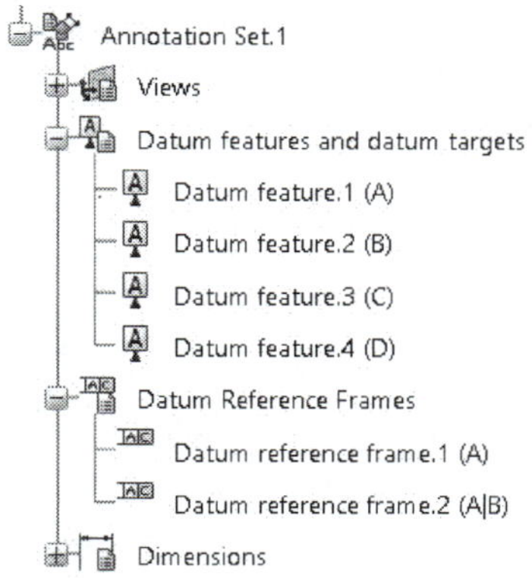

Figure 3–71

5. Save the model.

Task 6 - Change the geometrical tolerance precision.

The model requires geometrical tolerances with a precision of 0.001. By default, CATIA will create them with a tolerance of 0.01. In this task, you increase the global geometric tolerance precision.

1. Select **Me>Preferences>App Preferences>3D Modeling>Mechanical Systems>3D Tolerancing & Annotation** and select the *Tolerances* arrow.

2. Set the *Description* to **DISTINCH** and *Precision* to **0.001**, as shown in Figure 3–72.

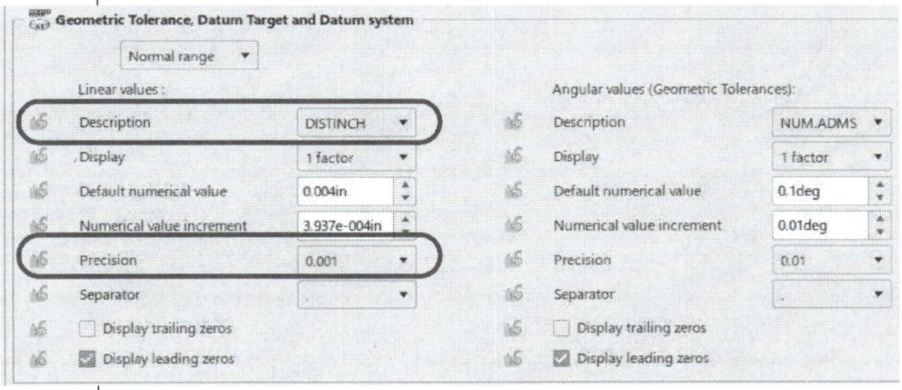

Figure 3–72

3. Click **OK**.

Task 7 - Create a flatness tolerance.

1. Select the model face referenced by datum A and then click  (Tolerancing Advisor). The Semantic Tolerancing Advisor dialog box opens, as shown in Figure 3–73. The Semantic Datum icon is highlighted, indicating that a datum has already been created on this face.

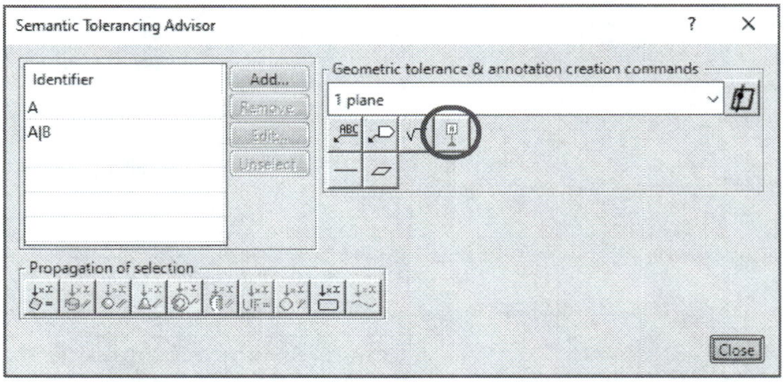

Figure 3–73

2. Click  (Flatness Specification). The Geometrical Specification dialog box opens, as shown in Figure 3–74.

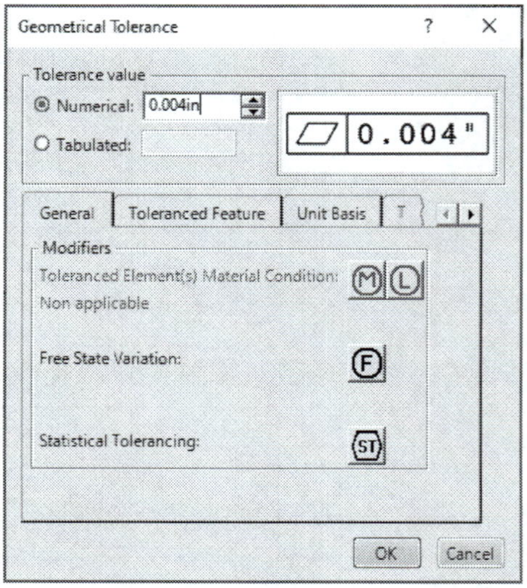

Figure 3–74

3. Enter a numerical tolerance value of **0.001** and complete the operation. **Flatness.1** is added to the **Geometrical Tolerances** branch of **Annotation Set.1**, as shown in Figure 3–75.

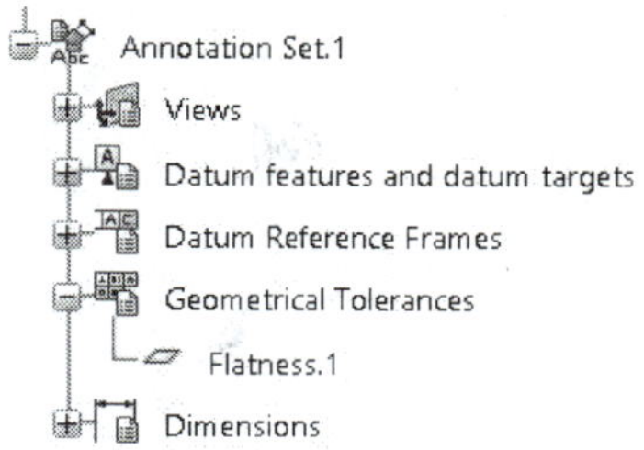

Figure 3–75

4. Right-click the yellow dot on the leader and select **Extremity Link>Perpendicular**, then position the tolerance as shown in Figure 3–76.

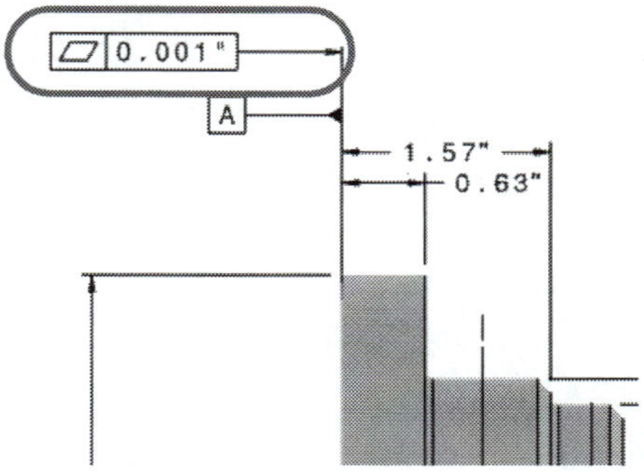

Figure 3–76

Task 8 - Create a positional tolerance.

1. Preselect the **3.54"** diameter dimension and then access the Tolerance Advisor.

2. Select **A|B** in the *Datums and datum reference frames* area. The Semantic Tolerancing Advisor dialog box updates, as shown in Figure 3–77.

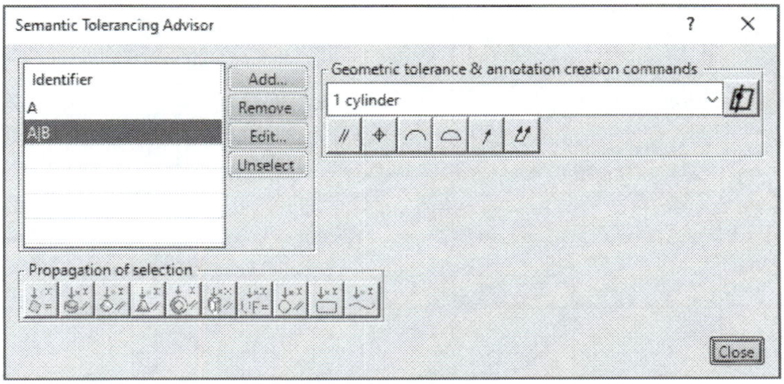

Figure 3–77

3. Click (Position-with-DRF Specification). The Geometrical Tolerance dialog box opens.

4. Enter a numerical tolerance of **0.02in** and click to define a maximum material condition for the toleranced elements. The dialog box displays as shown in Figure 3–78.

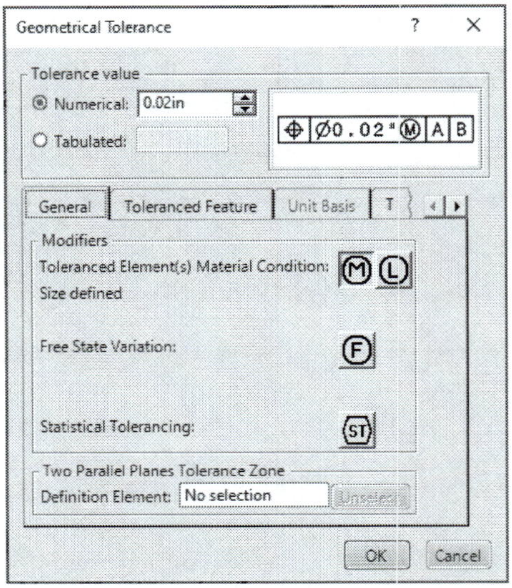

Figure 3–78

5. Complete the operation and appropriately position the tolerance. The model displays as shown in Figure 3–79.

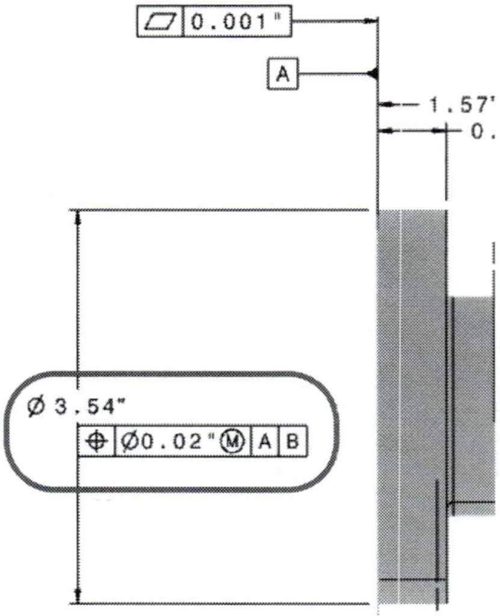

Figure 3–79

Task 9 - Create additional tolerances.

1. With SideView active, create the additional tolerances shown in Figure 3–80, using the information provided in the following table.

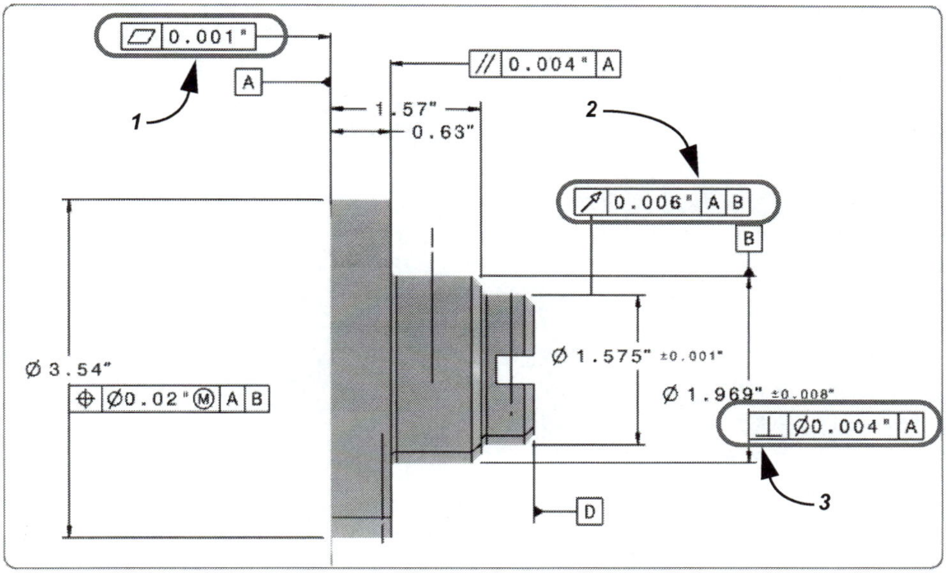

Figure 3–80

Item	Reference	DRF	Type	Tolerance
1	Back face of part	A	Parallelism	0.004"
2	Top horizontal leader of the 1.575" diameter dimension	A|B	Circular Runout	0.006"
3	1.969" diameter dimension	A	Perpendicularity	0.004"

2. Activate FrontView.

3. Access the Tolerance Advisor and click **Add**.

4. Define an A|B|C datum reference frame, as shown in Figure 3–81, and click **OK**.

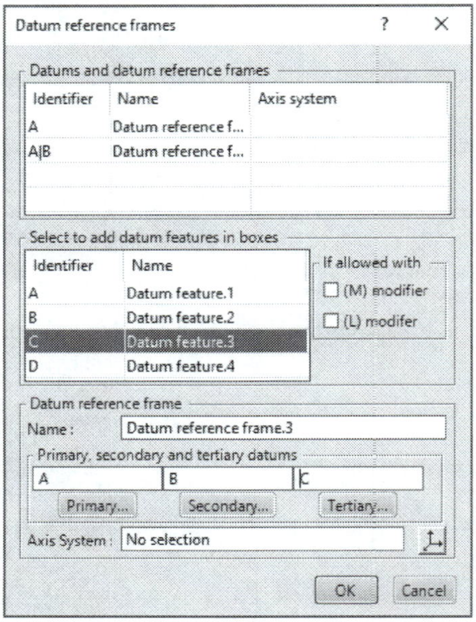

Figure 3–81

5. Select **A|B|C** in the Semantic Tolerancing Advisor dialog box.

6. Select the **8 x 0.31"** diameter dimension from the model.

7. Define the tolerance shown in Figure 3–82.

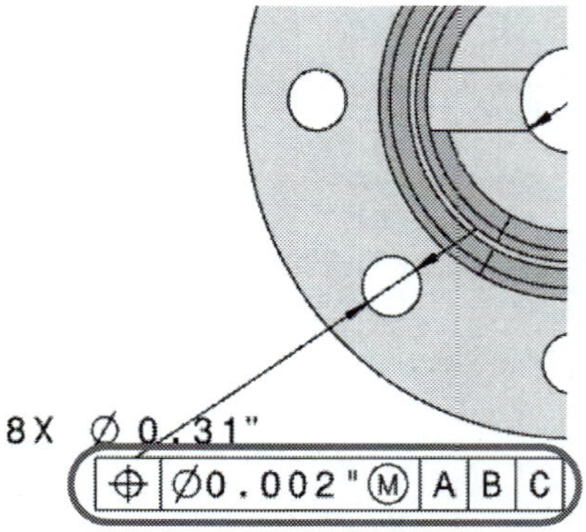

Figure 3–82

8. Complete the operation.

Task 10 - Create a datum reference frame.

In this task, you will manually create the datum reference frame A|D. This datum reference frame is used in the next task to create a basic dimension.

1. Access the Tolerance Advisor.
2. Add a new datum reference frame, select **A** and **D**, and complete the operation.
3. Click **OK** in the Semantic Tolerancing Advisor dialog box.

Task 11 - Create a basic dimension.

In the next two tasks, you will develop basic or framed dimensions. Two dimensions are created that accomplish the following:

- Locate the front face of the model with respect to the semantic datum A.
- Define the bolt circle diameter with respect to the position tolerance on the holes.

1. Activate SideView.
2. In the Annotation section of the Action Bar, click 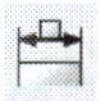 (Framed (Basic) Dimensions).
3. The system prompts you to select a context. Select **Datum reference frame.4 (A|D)** in the specification tree. The Framed (Basic) Dimensions Management dialog box opens, as shown in Figure 3–83.

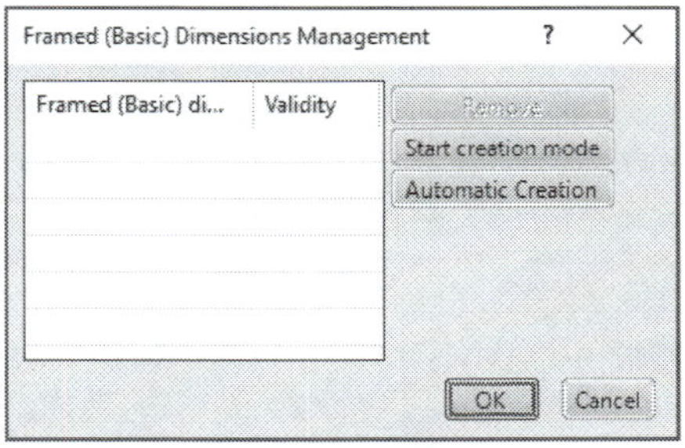

Figure 3–83

4. Click **Start creation mode**.

5. Select the two faces, as shown in Figure 3–84.

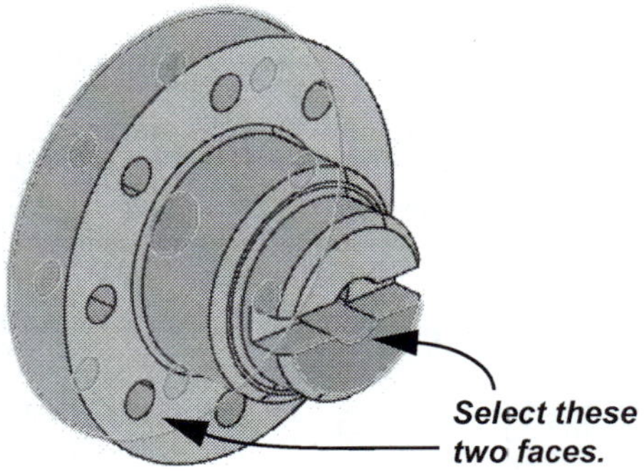

Figure 3–84

6. The system places a dimension on the model. if required, right-click on the dimension and select **Dimension Representation>Force Horizontal Dimension in view**, so that the dimension displays as shown in Figure 3–85.

The dimension might appear across the geometry. It can be moved once the operation is complete.

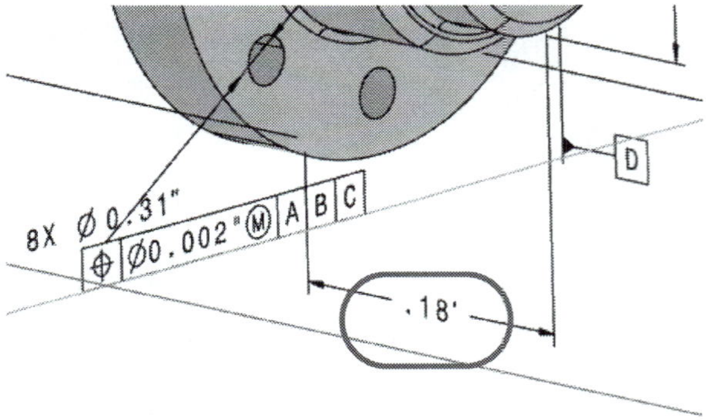

Figure 3–85

7. Select anywhere on the background to frame the dimension. The dimension displays as shown in Figure 3–86.

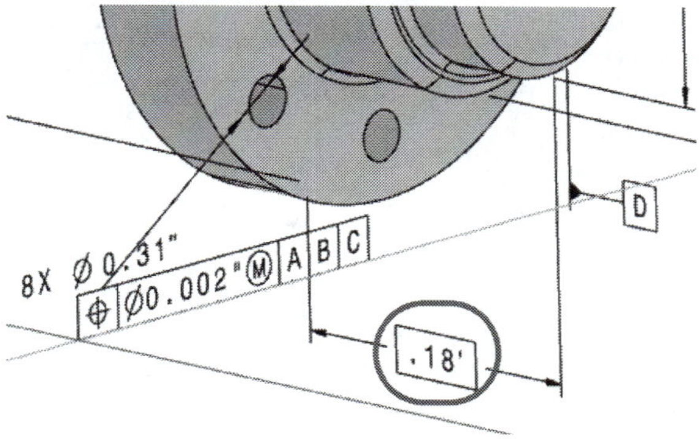

Figure 3–86

8. Click **End creation mode**. The Framed (Basic) Dimensions Management dialog box displays as shown in Figure 3–87.

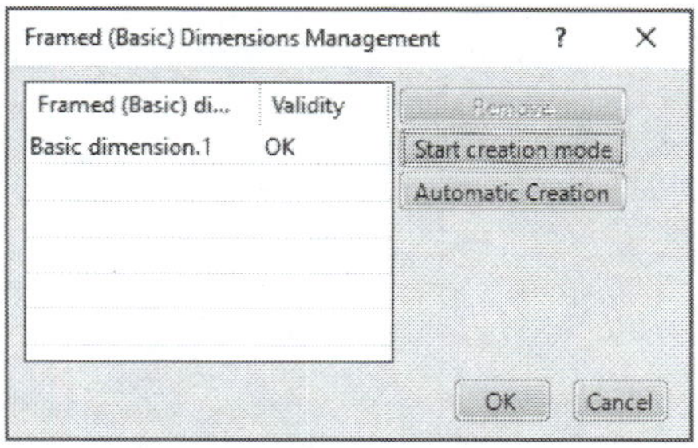

Figure 3–87

9. Click **OK** to complete the operation.

10. Use the Numerical Properties toolbar to set the format of the 12' dimension to **DISTINCH**.

Task 12 - Create a second framed dimension.

1. Activate the FrontView.

2. In the Annotation section of the Action Bar, click  (Framed Basic Dimensions).

3. Select the position tolerance for the pattern of eight holes to set the context.

4. In the Framed (Basic) Dimensions Management dialog box, click **Automatic Creation**.

Note that in addition to the dimensions, the system creates reference planes and a reference cylinder. Should you delete these dimensions later, the reference entities will not automatically be deleted.

All associated dimensions display as shown in Figure 3–88.

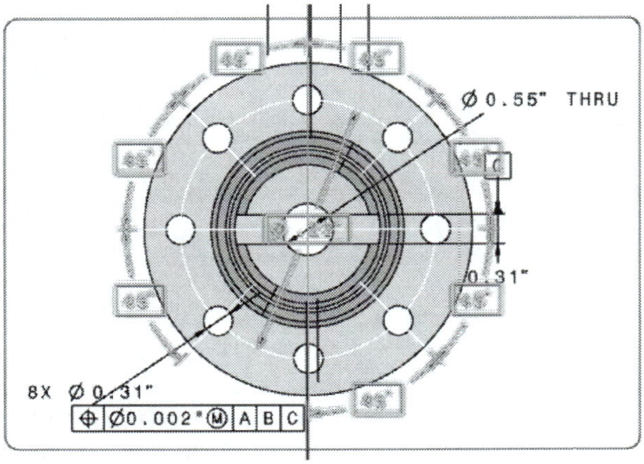

Figure 3–88

Use <Ctrl> to multi-select the dimensions in the dialog box.

5. Select the dimensions in the dialog box to highlight them on the model.
6. Highlight all of the 45deg dimensions in the dialog box and click **Remove** to remove them from the display.
7. Click **OK**.
8. Change the format of the .23' diameter dimension to **DISTINCH** and position it as shown in Figure 3–89.

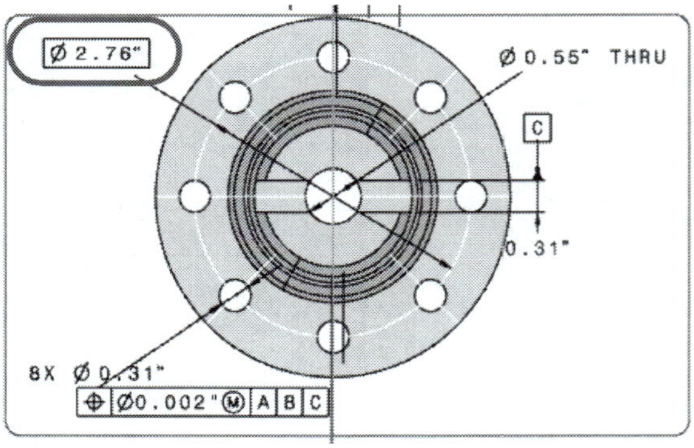

Figure 3–89

9. Save the model and close the window.

Practice 3c

Surface 3D T&A

Practice Objectives

- Create a semantic datum using datum targets.
- Create a semantic datum on surface geometry.
- Create a positional tolerance on surface geometry.

In this practice, you will add datums and tolerances to a surface part model. The placement of semantic datums and datum reference frames can be challenging due to the complex shapes that can be developed for a surfaced part. Therefore, this practice focuses on the development of these annotations. The completed model is shown in Figure 3–90.

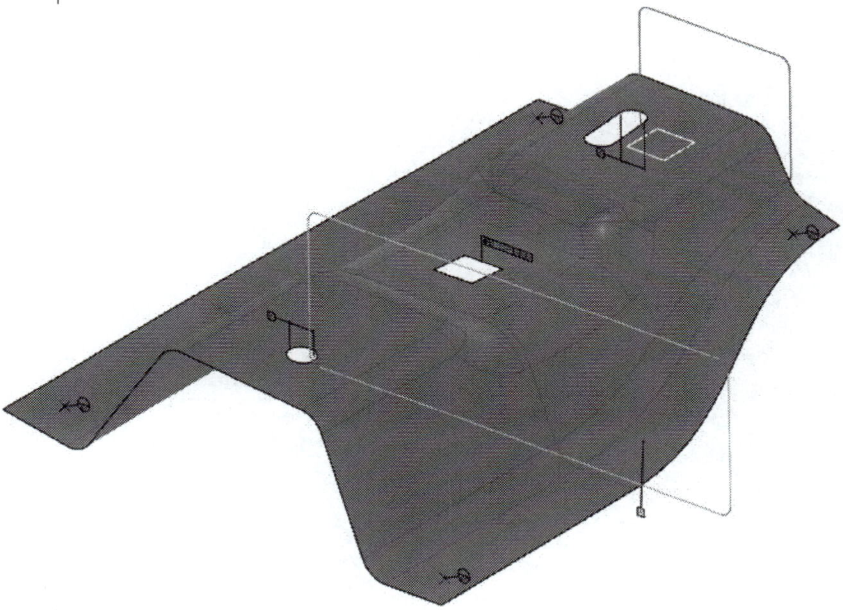

Figure 3–90

Task 1 - Import and open a part file.

1. Import and open **Skin.3dxml**. The model displays as shown in Figure 3–91.

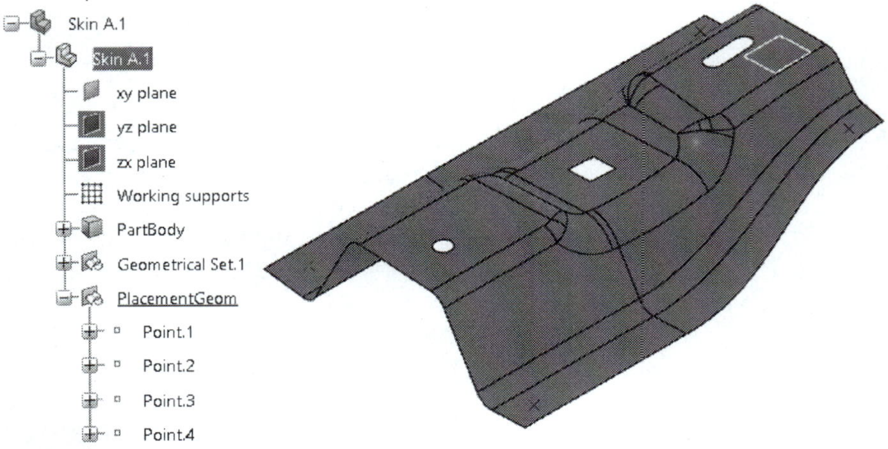

Figure 3–91

2. Expand the **PlacementGeom** geometrical set. It consists of four reference points that lie on the exterior surfaces of the part. These points are used to locate datum targets that define the datum A.

Task 2 - Create Datum A.

1. Hold <Ctrl> and select the four surfaces in the order shown in Figure 3–92.

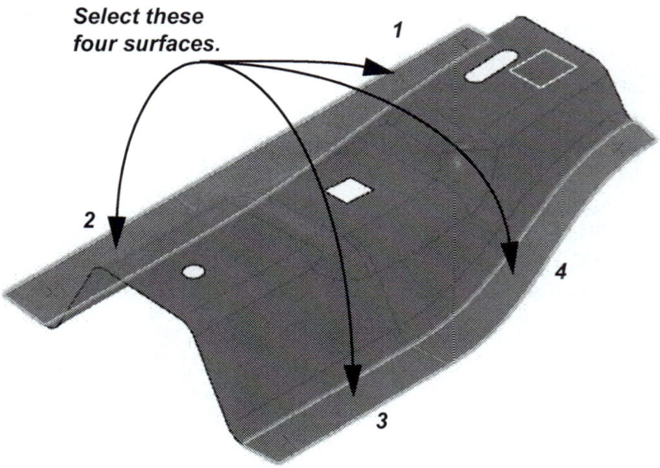

Figure 3–92

2. Click (Tolerancing Advisor). The Semantic Tolerancing Advisor dialog box opens.

3. In the *Geometric tolerance & annotation creation commands* drop-down list, select **All possible types**. The dialog box updates as shown in Figure 3–93.

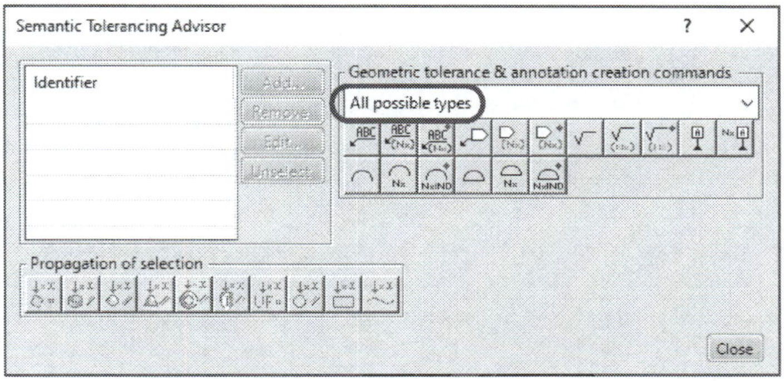

Figure 3–93

4. Click (Datum Feature). The Datum feature dialog box opens.

Design Considerations

To define a datum on these surfaces, you must define datum targets to position the part. You can add these targets on the fly using the icons in the Datum Targets field.

5. Click **Add**. The Datum Target dialog box opens, as shown in Figure 3–94. This dialog box enables you to create multiple datum target annotations at once.

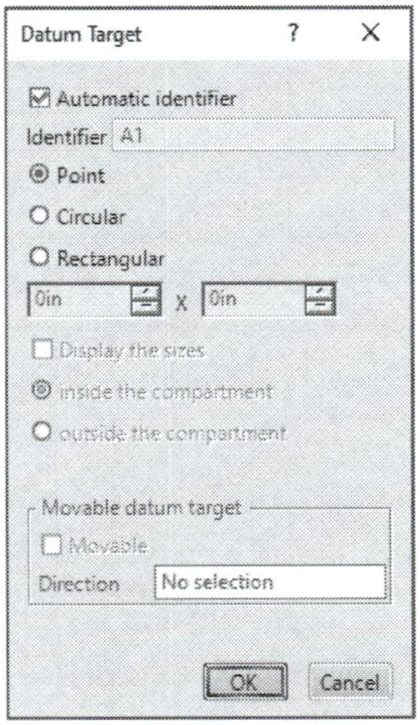

Figure 3–94

6. Select **Point.1** in the model. A datum target is added to the model, as shown in Figure 3–95.

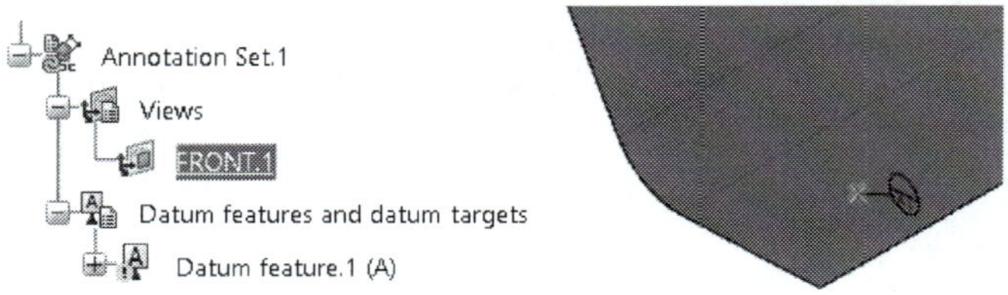

Figure 3–95

7. Continue to select **Point.2**, **Point.3**, and **Point.4**. The system creates a target for each point.

8. Click **OK** to close the Datum Target dialog box. The Datum feature dialog box displays, as shown in Figure 3–96.

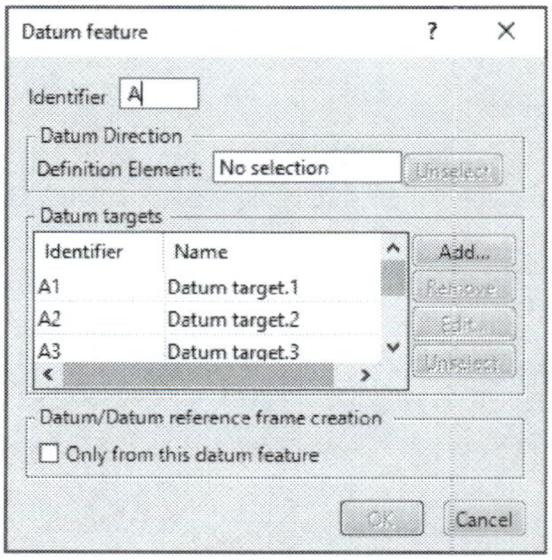

Figure 3–96

9. Click in the Definition Element field and select the XY plane in the specification tree.

10. Verify that the **Only from this datum feature** option is cleared, and complete the operation. The model displays as shown in Figure 3–97.

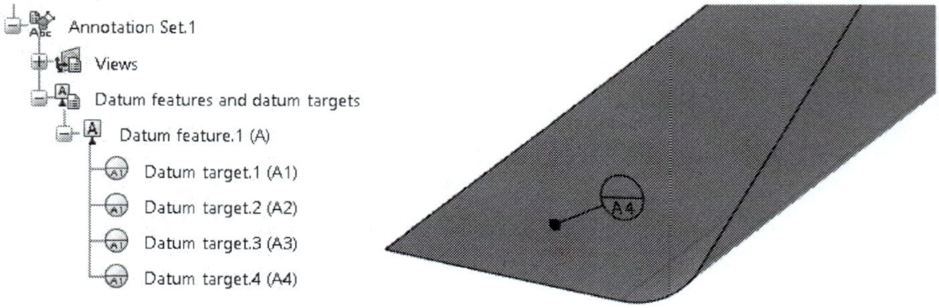

Figure 3–97

Design Considerations

Note the creation of **FRONT.1**. Since no annotation plane was created when the datum was defined, the system creates a view that accommodates the selected references.

Task 3 - Create Datum B and C.

1. Click 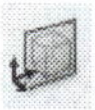 (View From Reference) and select the yz plane. Rename the view to **SideView** and click **OK**.
2. Select the edge of the hole, as shown in Figure 3–98.

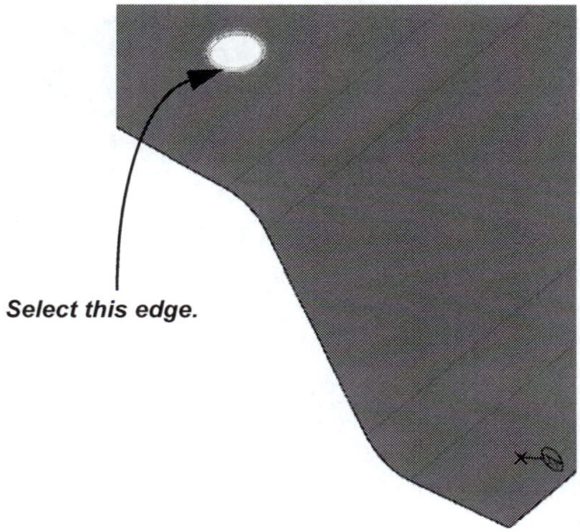

Figure 3–98

3. Activate the Tolerance Advisor and create a semantic datum. The model displays as shown in Figure 3–99.

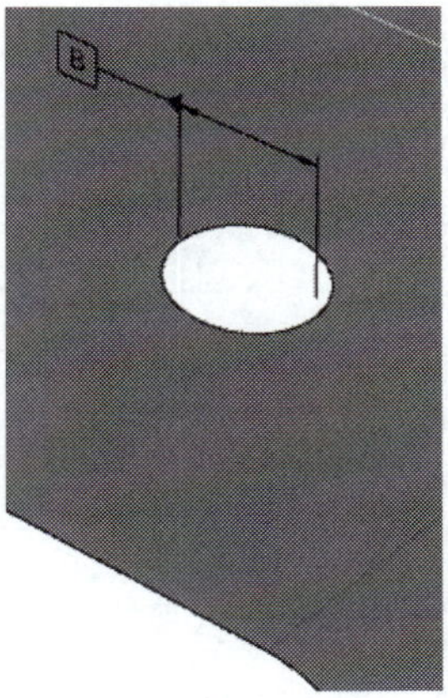

Figure 3–99

4. Preselect the edge shown in Figure 3–100 and access the Tolerance Advisor.

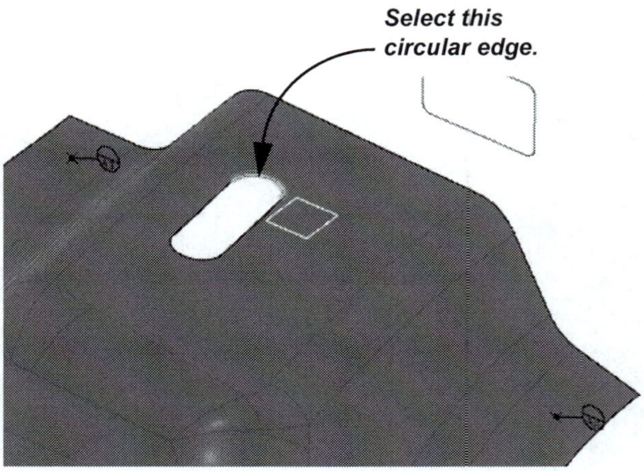

Figure 3–100

5. Create a semantic datum. Verify that the **From the 3 last created datum features** option is enabled, as shown in Figure 3–101, and complete the operation.

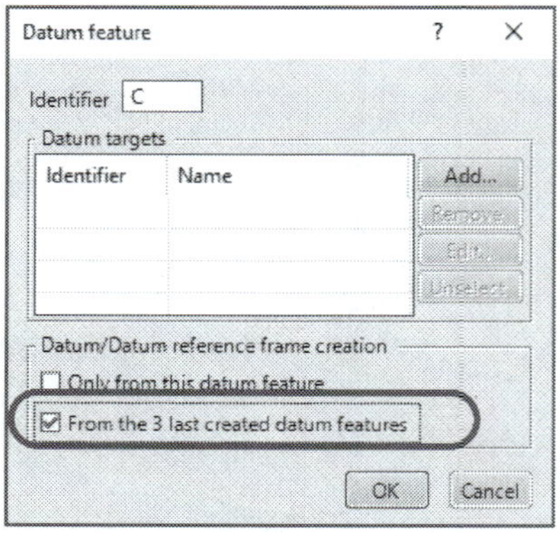

Figure 3–101

Task 4 - Create a position tolerance.

1. Preselect the four edges of the square cutout, as shown in Figure 3–102.

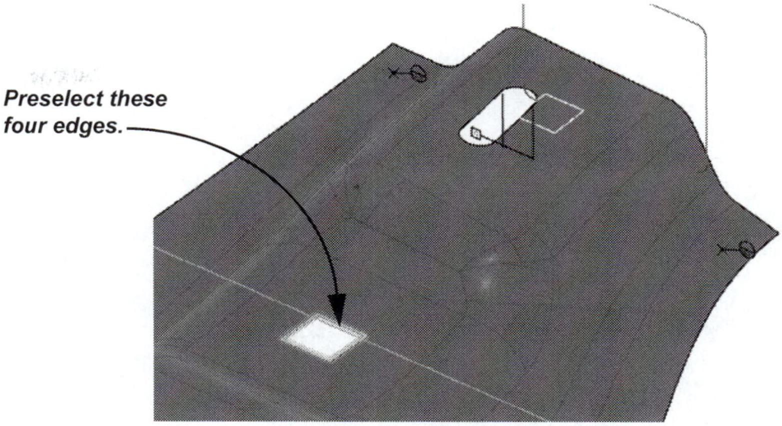

Figure 3–102

2. Access the Tolerance Advisor and make the following selections to create the position tolerance shown in Figure 3–103:

   - Select **A|B|C** from the *Identifier* area.
   - Click (Position-with-DRF Specification) to create a position tolerance.

Accept the default options in the Geometrical Tolerance dialog box and complete the operation. The model displays as shown in Figure 3–103.

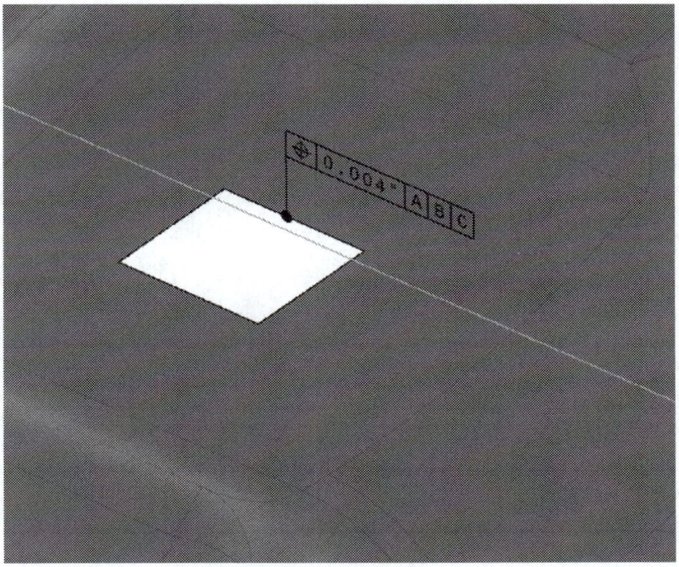

Figure 3–103

3. Save the model and close the window.

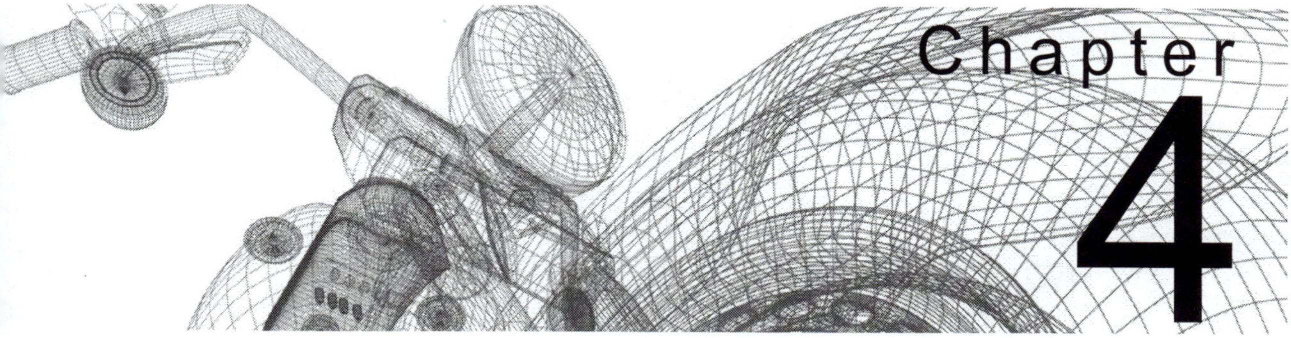

Non-Semantic Annotations

Non-semantic annotations enable user input that might not meet the defined tolerancing standards. These annotations should be used when the company standard does not match these standards, or the designer has a unique annotation that cannot be made using a semantic annotation. This chapter introduces non-semantic methods of creating annotations.

Learning Objectives in This Chapter

- Create text and flag notes.
- Create datum elements and datum targets.
- Create geometric tolerances.
- Learn how to place roughness symbols.
- Create dimensions.
- Understand the diagnostic reporting tool.

4.1 Text

Text can be added to 3D models to communicate additional information about the model. You can create three kinds of text annotations:

- Text with Leader
- Text
- Text Parallel to Screen

You have the option to add text with or without a leader. The text in either case is defined on an annotation plane; as a result, the orientation of the text is based on the orientation of the annotation plane you select. If an annotation plane is not parallel to the screen, then all the text created with or without a leader is not parallel to the screen, as shown in Figure 4–1.

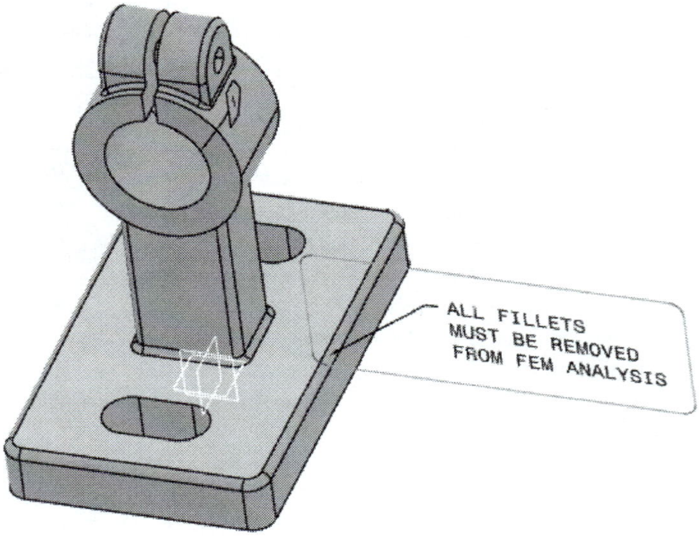

Figure 4–1

If you want some text to remain parallel to the screen, regardless of the orientation of the annotation plane, use  (Text Parallel To Screen).

General Steps

Use the following general steps to create any of the three types of 3D text:

1. Activate an annotation plane.
2. Select the required 3D text icon.
3. Select a reference element.
4. Enter text in the Text Editor.
5. Complete the feature.

Step 1 - Activate an annotation plane.

Double-click on the required annotation plane in the specification tree or directly from the model to activate it. The orientation of the selected annotation plane defines the orientation of the text.

Step 2 - Select the required 3D text icon.

In the Annotation section of the Action Bar, click one of the following tools:

- 

(Text with Leader)
- 

(Text)
- 

(Text Parallel To Screen)

Step 3 - Select a reference element.

Select a geometric or annotation element in the specification tree or model. The selected element is used as a reference for the Leader. If the Text tool is being used, you can also indicate a location on the annotation plane to place the text.

Step 4 - Enter text in the Text Editor.

To add multiple lines of text press <Shift> + <Enter>.

The Text Editor opens after a reference element is selected, as shown in Figure 4–2. Enter the required text.

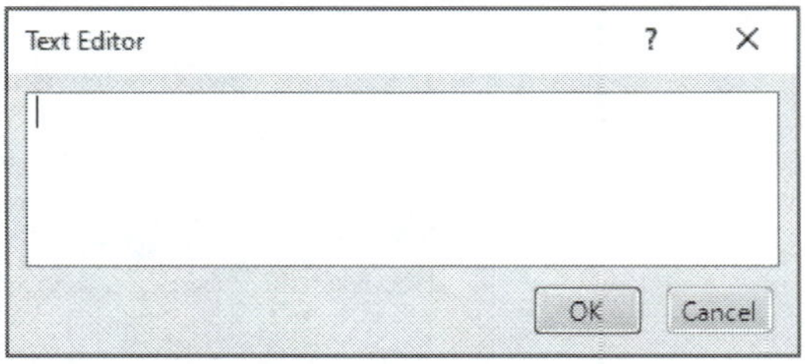

Figure 4–2

Step 5 - Complete the feature.

Click **OK** to complete the creation of the text. The text feature displays under the *Notes* node in the specification tree, as shown in Figure 4–3.

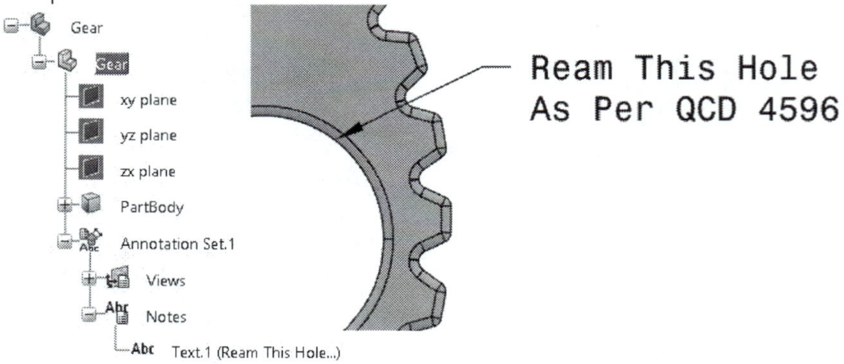

Figure 4–3

Editing Text

Formatting for all text is applied using the Object Properties window, as shown in Figure 4–4. If needed,  (Object Properties) can be turned on from the Tools section of the Action Bar.

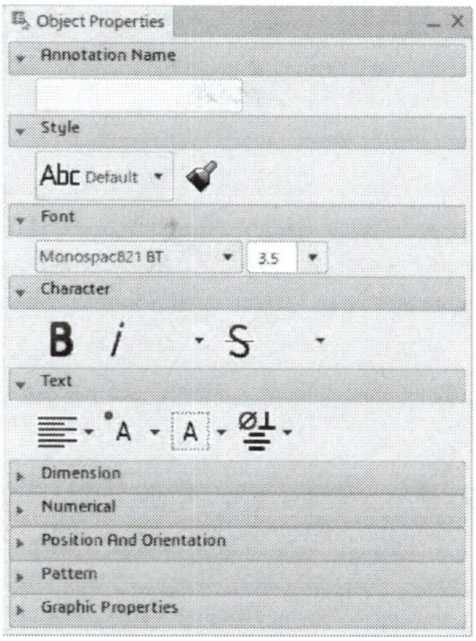

Figure 4–4

Handling Text Features

Select the text and move it using the handles shown in Figure 4–5.

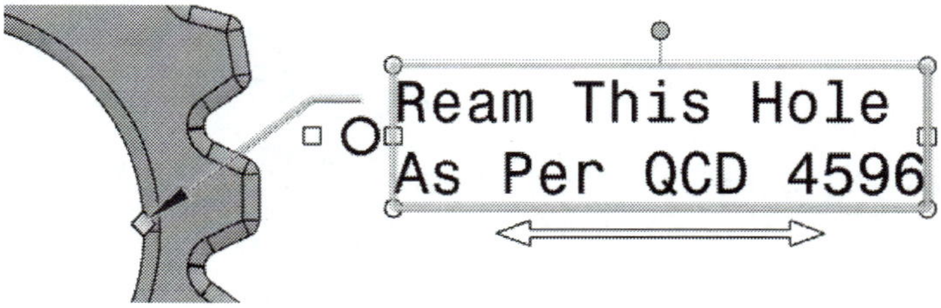

Figure 4–5

Select the yellow diamond and right-click to access the text leader handling options, as shown in Figure 4–6.

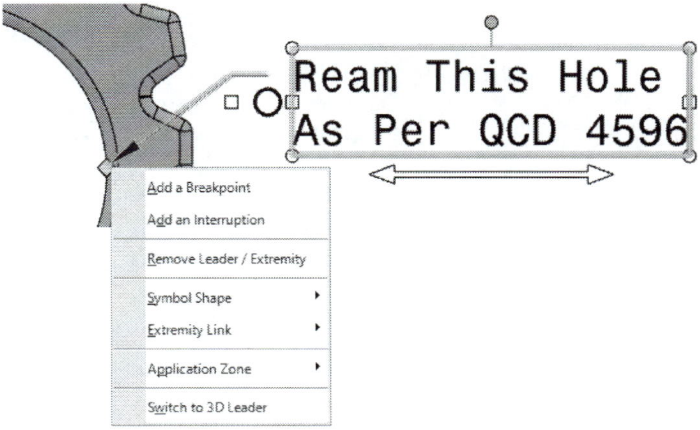

Figure 4–6

Attribute Link

You can associatively add model parameter values to a text note. Right-click outside the Text Editor dialog box and select **Insert Attribute Link**, as shown in Figure 4–7.

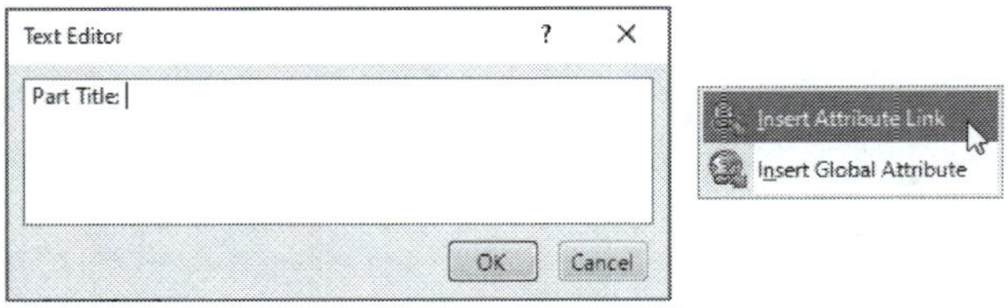

Figure 4–7

Select a feature or body in the specification tree to filter the parameters. The Attribute Link Panel dialog box opens, as shown in Figure 4–8, enabling you to select a parameter from the model.

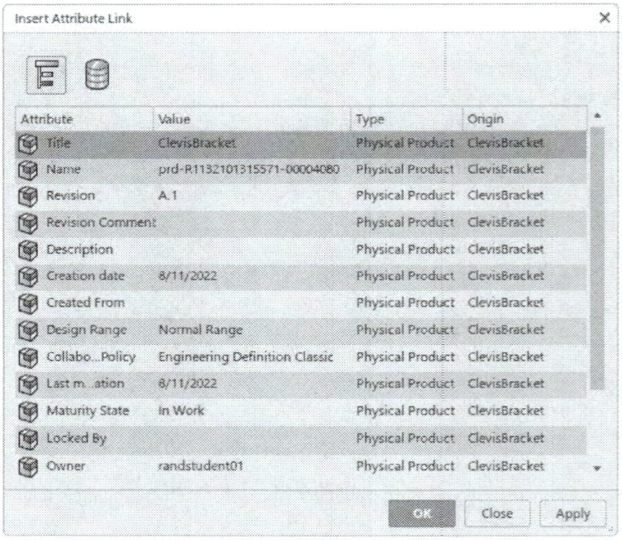

Figure 4–8

Once the parameter has been selected, its value is added to the Text Editor, as shown in Figure 4–9. This value is associative, so it updates with changes to the model.

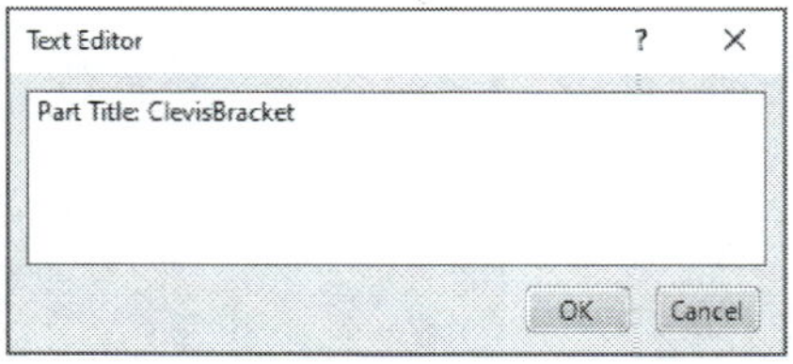

Figure 4–9

4.2 Flag Notes

Flag notes enable you to add a list of files or web links to the document. You can quickly open a related spreadsheet, presentation, or web site from the CATIA document from a flag note. An example displays, as shown in Figure 4–10.

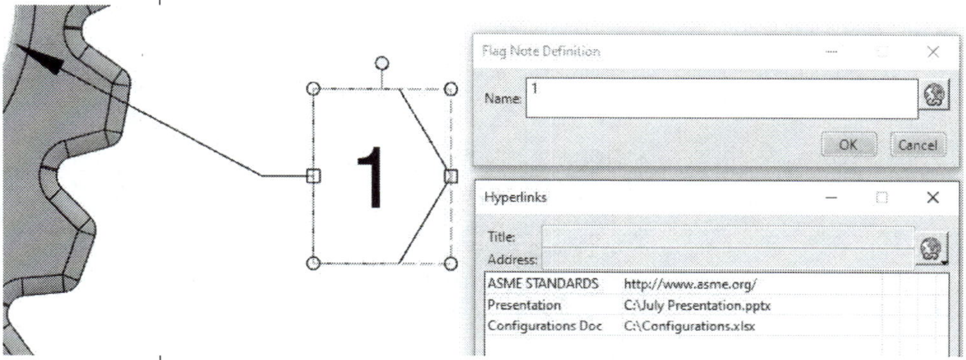

Figure 4–10

You have the option of adding flag notes with or without a leader. The flag note in either case is defined on an annotation plane similar to 3D text.

General Steps

Use the following general steps to create flag notes with or without a leader:

1. Activate an annotation plane.
2. Select the required flag note icon.
3. Select a reference element.
4. Add links in the Hyperlinks dialog box.
5. Complete the feature.

Step 1 - Activate an annotation plane.

Double-click on the required annotation plane in the specification tree or directly from the model to activate it. The orientation of the selected annotation plane defines the orientation of the flag note.

Step 2 - Select the required flag note icon.

In the Annotation section of the Action Bar, click one of the following tools:

-  (Flag Note with Leader)
-  (Flag Note)

Step 3 - Select a reference element.

Select a geometric or annotation element in the specification tree or directly from the model. The selected element is used as a reference for the leader.

Step 4 - Add links in the Hyperlinks dialog box.

The Flag Note Definition dialog box opens after a reference element is selected, as shown in Figure 4–11.

Figure 4–11

The *Name* field is populated with a number that is incremented each time a new flag note is created. You can modify this *Name* value as needed.

To link the flag note to a related document or website, select the  (Hyperlinks) icon to the right of the *Name* field. The Hyperlinks window opens, as shown in Figure 4–12.

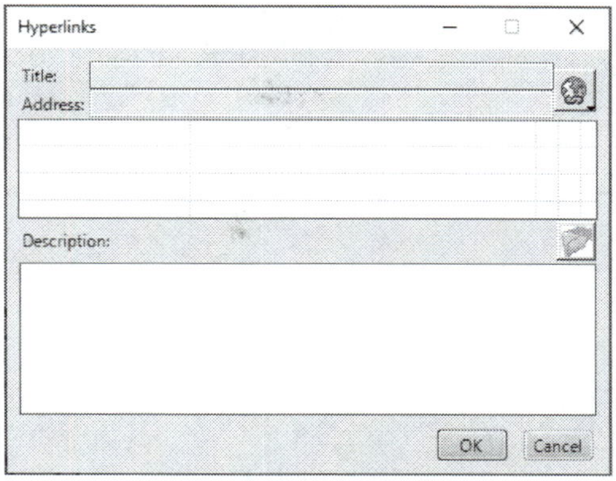

Figure 4–12

Select the  (Adds an URL) icon to create a blank URL in the list. The *Title* and *Address* fields become editable for that URL. The *Address* field can be used to point to URLs or to local file paths. Double-clicking on the listed item opens that file automatically in its default program. Selecting  (Adds an URL) again will add to the list, as shown in Figure 4–13.

The *Description* field allows for text to be included to better understand why the URLs are linked to the flag note.  can be selected to import text from a local .TXT file into the *Description* field.

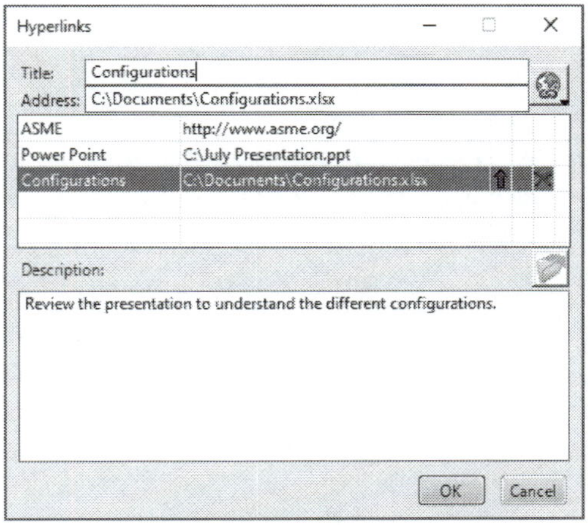

Figure 4–13

If the document you are looking to link to exists within the 3DEXPERIENCE database, it can also be linked to by expanding the arrow next to  (Adds an URL), as shown in Figure 4–14.

Figure 4–14

Each of these options will immediately open a *Select or search* window, as shown in Figure 4–15. Selecting one will add it to the Hyperlinks window.

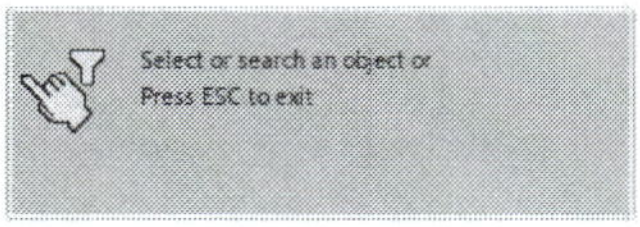

Figure 4–15

Step 5 - Complete the feature.

Click **OK** twice to complete the creation of the flag note. The flag note feature displays under the *Notes* node in the specification tree, as shown in Figure 4–16.

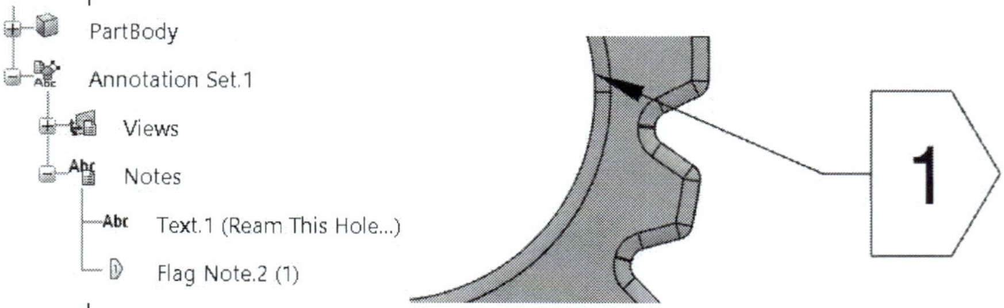

Figure 4–16

Free and Linked Annotations

Any text or flag note annotation that is created by selecting geometry from the model is termed a “linked” annotation. A linked annotation is related to the geometry used to place the annotation. It fails if the associated geometry no longer exists in the model. The symbol for a linked annotation displays in the specification tree, as shown in Figure 4–17.

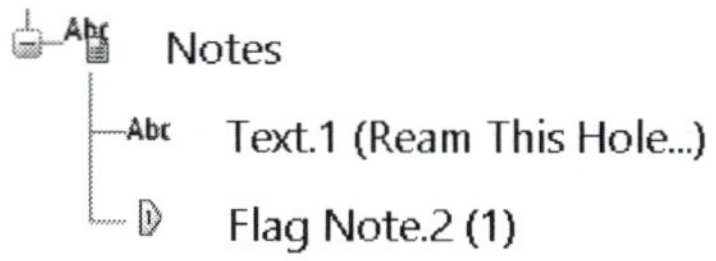

Figure 4–17

A free annotation is created by selecting anywhere in the annotation plane to place the annotation. A free annotation can be created using the following options:

-  (Text)
-  (Text Parallel to Screen)
-  (Flag Note)

The symbol for a free annotation displays in the specification tree, as shown in Figure 4–18.

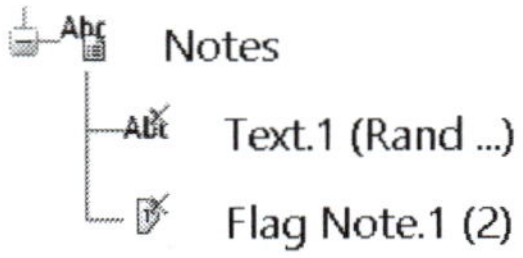

Figure 4–18

When transferring free annotations between annotation planes, the system always positions the annotation at the origin of the reference axes of the new view. The annotation might appear lost, because it is no longer positioned relative to the background location selected during creation. Find the annotation by activating the view the annotation was transferred to, and then centering the model on the reference axes.

4.3 Datum Features

Datum features can be added for geometrical tolerancing.

General Steps

Use the following general steps to create datum features:

1. Activate an annotation plane.
2. Start the creation of the datum feature.
3. Select a reference element.
4. Enter an identifier.
5. Complete the feature.

Step 1 - Activate an annotation plane.

Double-click on the required annotation plane in the specification tree or directly from the model to activate it. The orientation of the selected annotation plane defines the orientation of the datum feature.

Step 2 - Start the creation of the datum feature.

In the Annotation section of the Action Bar, click  (Datum Feature).

Step 3 - Select a reference element.

Select a geometric element or feature in the specification tree or directly from the model. The selected element is used as a reference for the location of the datum feature.

Step 4 - Enter an identifier.

The Datum Feature Creation dialog box opens after a reference element is selected, as shown in Figure 4–19. Enter an identifier.

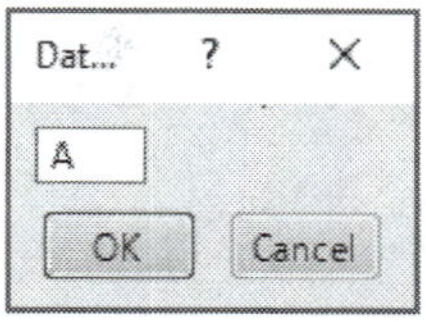

Figure 4–19

Step 5 - Complete the feature.

Click **OK** to complete the creation of the datum element. The datum element feature displays under the *Datum features and datum targets* node in the specification tree, as shown in Figure 4–20.

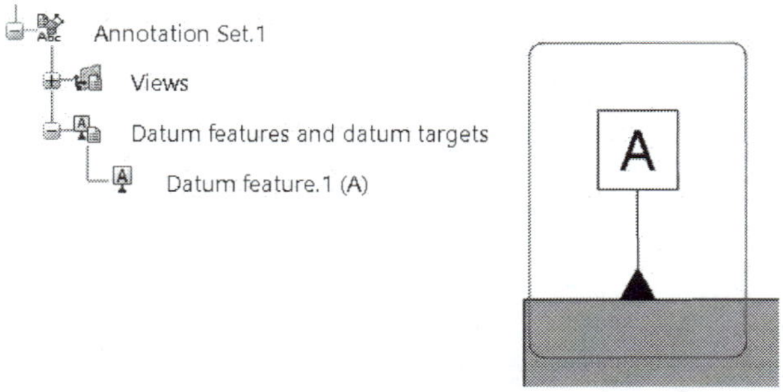

Figure 4–20

Non-Planar Datums

If a non-planar face or surface is selected to define the datum element, you can add datum targets to constrain the datum. To do this, create the datum and then double-click on it in the model or specification tree. The Datum feature dialog box displays, as shown in Figure 4–21. Click **Add** to create datum targets.

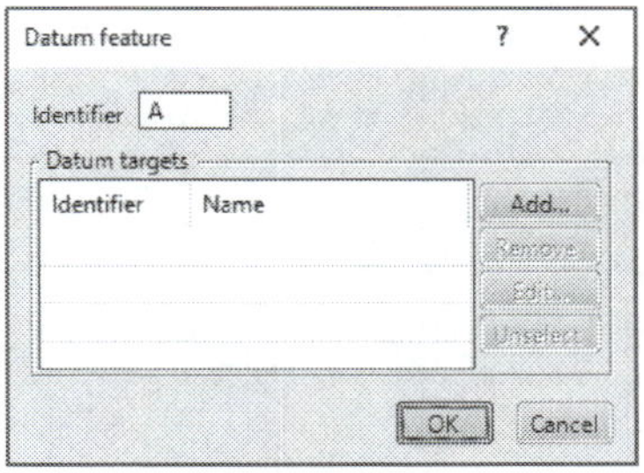

Figure 4–21

DRFs for Non-Semantic Annotation

Once you have defined a simple datum, use the Tolerance Advisor to assign it as a datum reference frame before using it in a geometrical tolerance. The process is identical to defining a semantic datum reference frame.

When non-semantically annotating a model, a datum reference frame is automatically defined when the datum is added to a non-semantic geometrical tolerance.

4.4 Datum Target

A datum target is typically defined using the Datum Feature dialog box. Defining a datum target makes it associative to the datum element. In some cases, this association is undesirable or not possible. In such cases, you can use the Datum Target tool.

General Steps

Use the following general steps to create datum targets:

1. Activate an annotation plane.
2. Start the creation of the datum target feature.
3. Select a reference element.
4. Enter the parameters.
5. Complete the feature.

Step 1 - Activate an annotation plane.

Double-click on the required annotation plane in the specification tree or directly from the model to activate it. The orientation of the selected annotation plane defines the orientation of the datum target.

Step 2 - Start the creation of the datum target feature.

In the Annotation section of the Action Bar, click  (Datum Target), as shown in Figure 4–22.

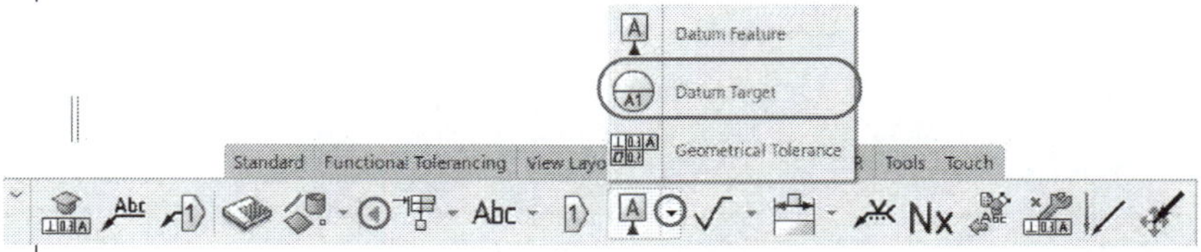

Figure 4–22

Step 3 - Select a reference element.

Select a geometric element or feature in the specification tree or directly from the model. The selected element is used as a reference for the location of the datum target.

Step 4 - Enter the parameters.

The Datum Target Creation dialog box displays after a reference element is selected, as shown in Figure 4–23.

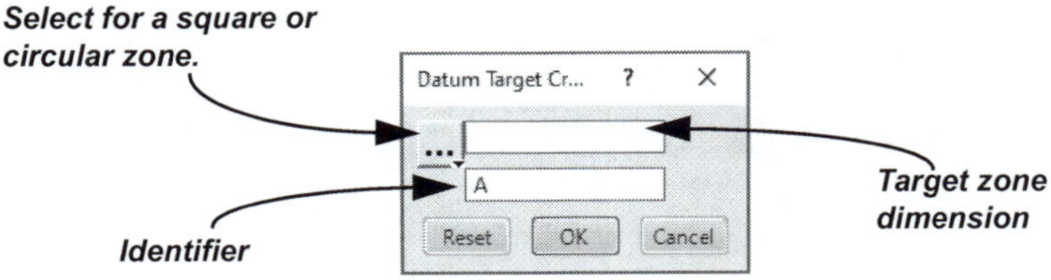

Figure 4–23

Enter the required parameters in the Datum Target Creation dialog box. An example is shown in Figure 4–24.

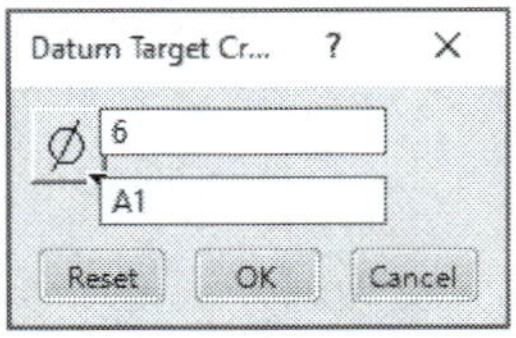

Figure 4–24

Step 5 - Complete the feature.

Click **OK** to complete the creation of the datum target. The datum target feature displays under the *Datums* node in the specification tree, as shown in Figure 4–25.

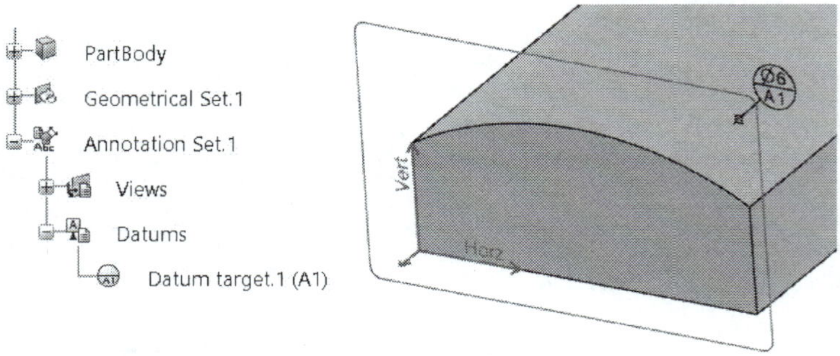

Figure 4–25

4.5 Geometric Tolerances

General Steps

Use the following general steps to create geometric tolerances:

1. Activate an annotation plane.
2. Start the creation of the Geometrical Tolerance feature.
3. Select a reference element.
4. Enter the parameters.
5. Complete the feature.

Step 1 - Activate an annotation plane.

Double-click on the required annotation plane in the specification tree or directly from the model to activate it. The orientation of the selected annotation plane defines the orientation of the geometrical tolerance.

Step 2 - Start the creation of the Geometrical Tolerance feature.

In the Annotation section of the Action Bar, click

(Geometrical Tolerance), as shown in Figure 4–26.

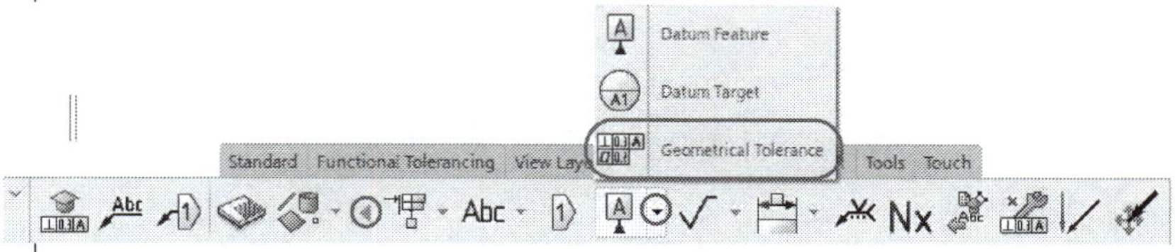

Figure 4–26

Step 3 - Select a reference element.

Select a geometric element or feature in the specification tree or directly from the model. The selected element is used as a reference for the location of the geometrical tolerance.

Step 4 - Enter the parameters.

The Geometrical Tolerance dialog box opens after a reference element is selected, as shown in Figure 4–27.

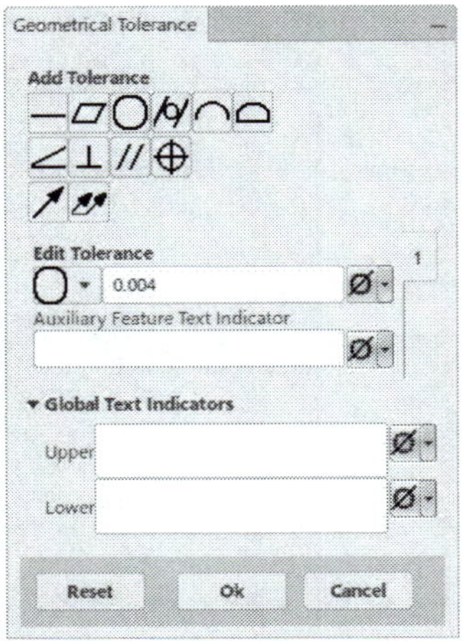

Figure 4–27

Enter the required parameters in the Geometrical Tolerance dialog box. An example is shown in Figure 4–28. The Geometrical Tolerance window will change based on the tolerance being applied.

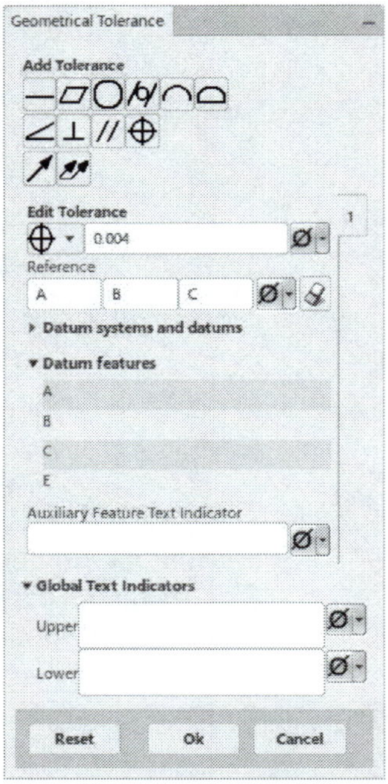

Figure 4–28

Step 5 - Complete the feature.

Click **OK** to complete the creation of the geometrical tolerance. An example of a geometrical tolerance is shown in Figure 4–29.

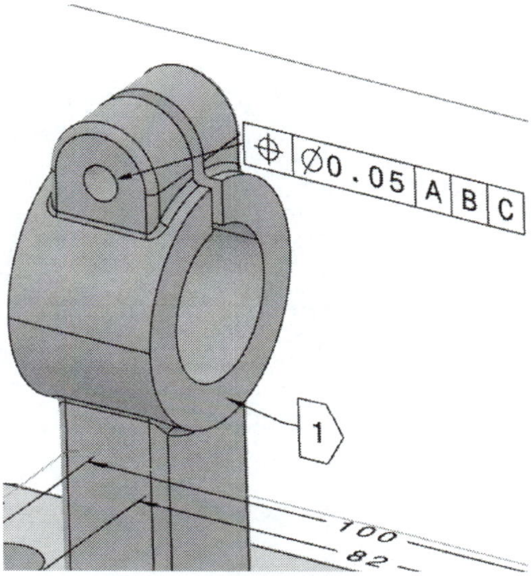

Figure 4–29

The geometrical tolerance feature displays under the *Geometrical Tolerances* node in the specification tree.

4.6 Surface Texture

General Steps

Use the following general steps to create roughness symbols:

1. Activate an annotation plane.
2. Start the creation of the surface texture.
3. Select a reference element.
4. Enter the parameters.
5. Complete the feature.

Step 1 - Activate an annotation plane.

Double-click on the required annotation plane in the specification tree or directly from the model to activate it. The orientation of the selected annotation plane defines the orientation of the roughness symbol.

Step 2 - Start the creation of the surface texture.

In the Annotation section of the Action Bar, click  (Surface Texture), as shown in Figure 4–30.

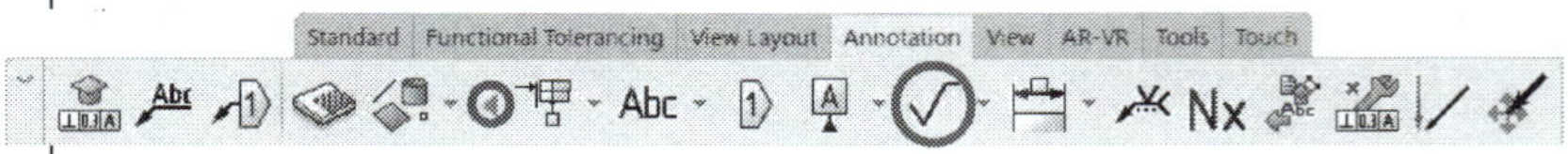

Figure 4–30

Step 3 - Select a reference element.

Select a geometric element or feature in the specification tree or directly from the model. The selected element is used as a reference for the location of the surface texture symbol.

Step 4 - Enter the parameters.

The Surface Texture dialog box displays after a reference element is selected, as shown in Figure 4–31.

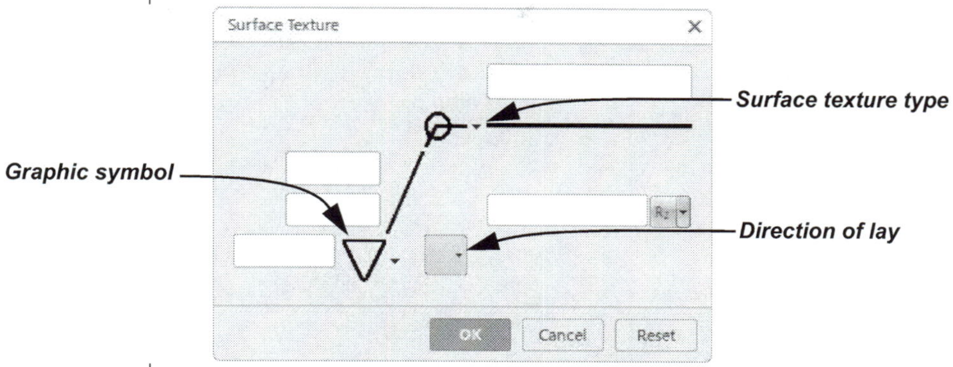

Figure 4–31

Enter the required parameters in the Surface Texture dialog box.

Step 5 - Complete the feature.

Click **OK** to complete the creation of the surface texture symbol. An example of a surface texture symbol is shown in Figure 4–32.

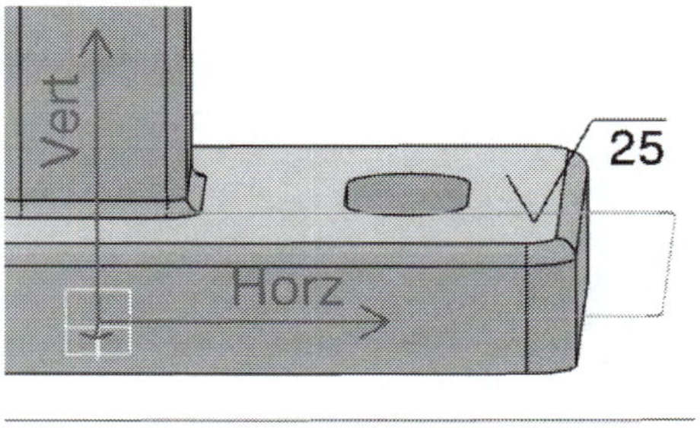

Figure 4–32

The surface texture symbol feature displays under the *Surface Textures* node in the specification tree.

4.7 Dimensions

General Steps

Use the following general steps to create dimensions:

1. Activate an annotation plane.
2. Start the creation of dimensions.
3. Select the references required to create the required dimension.
4. Place the dimension.
5. Modify the dimension properties, as required.

Step 1 - Activate an annotation plane.

Double-click on the required annotation plane in the specification tree or directly from the model to activate it. The orientation of the selected annotation plane defines the orientation of the dimension.

Step 2 - Start the creation of dimensions.

In the Annotation section of the Action Bar, click

 (Dimensions), as shown in Figure 4–33.

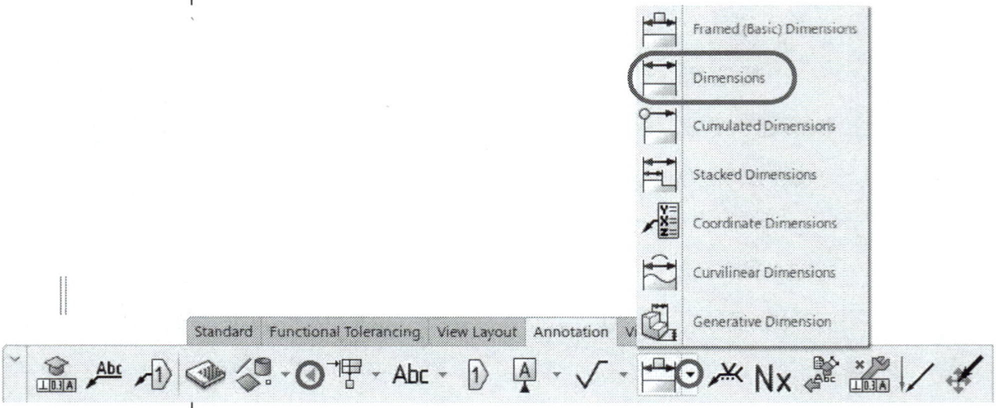

Figure 4–33

Step 3 - Select the references required to create the required dimension.

Select the references required to create the required dimension. The references selected determine the type of dimension created. For example, select two edges or surfaces that are at an angle to one another to create an angular dimension.

Step 4 - Place the dimension.

When all references have been selected, click anywhere on the CATIA background to place the dimension. An example is shown in Figure 4–34.

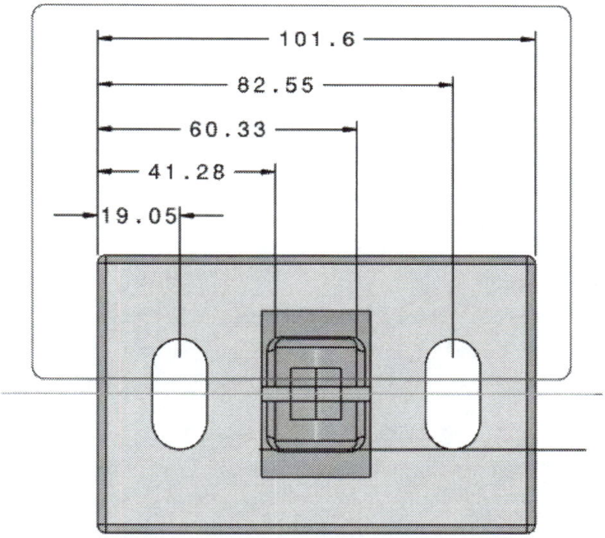

Figure 4–34

Step 5 - Modify the dimension properties, as required.

Modify the line type, tolerance standard, tolerance value, and tolerance precision using the Object Properties window, as shown in Figure 4–35. If needed,  (Object Properties) can be turned on from the Tools section of the Action Bar.

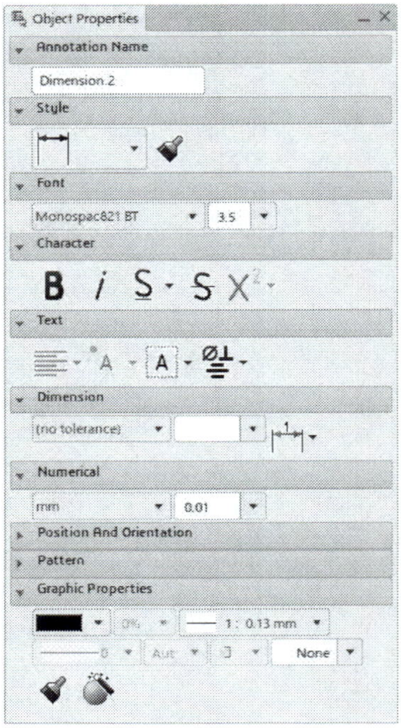

Figure 4–35

Cumulated Dimension

In the Dimensions flyout of the Annotation section of the Action Bar, click  (Cumulated Dimensions) to create a series of cumulated dimensions. The first reference selected is the baseline and further selections are dimensioned from the baseline, as shown in Figure 4–36.

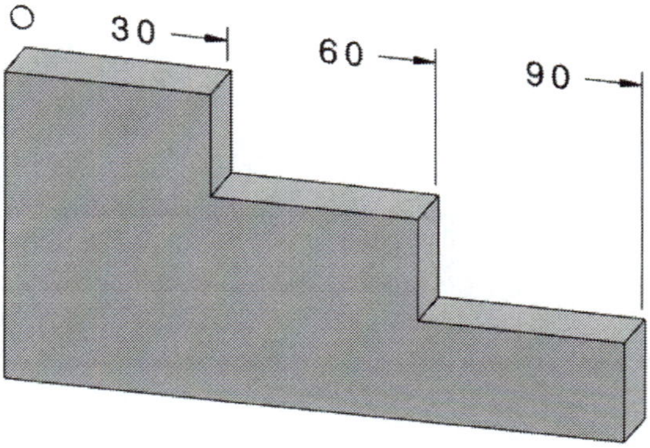

Figure 4–36

Stacked Dimension

In the Dimensions flyout in the Annotation section of the Action Bar, click 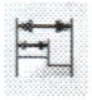 (Stacked Dimensions) to create stacked dimensions. An example of stacked dimensions is shown in Figure 4–37.

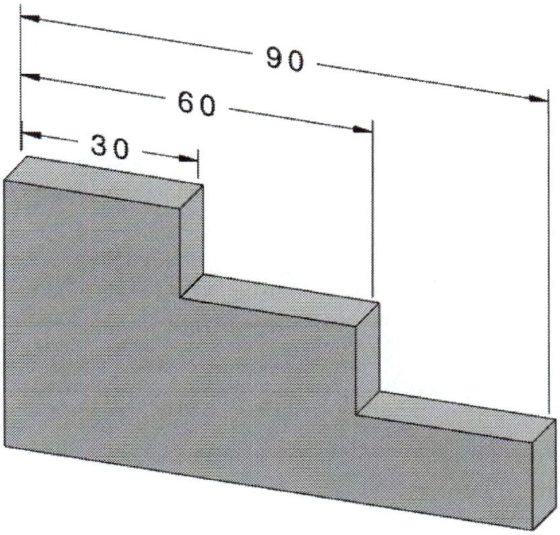

Figure 4–37

Coordinate Dimension

In the Dimensions flyout of the Annotation section of the Action Bar, click  (Coordinate Dimensions) to create a coordinate dimension. Select a vertex on the model to display its coordinates, as shown in Figure 4–38.

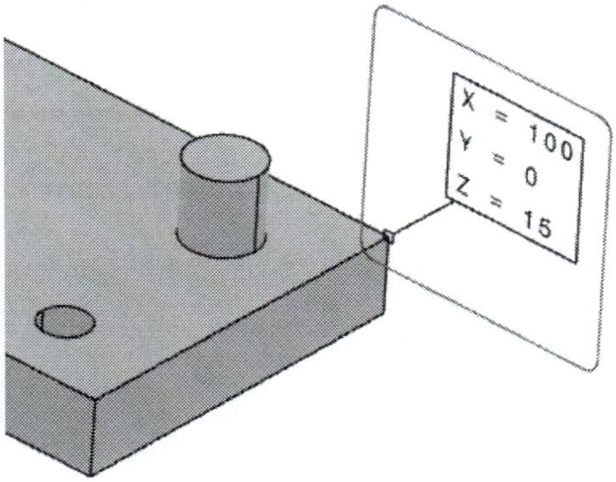

Figure 4–38

Curvilinear Dimension

In the Dimensions flyout of the Annotation section of the Action Bar, click  (Curvilinear Dimensions) to create a length dimension for a non-linear edge or curve. Select the edge to display the dimension, as shown in Figure 4–39.

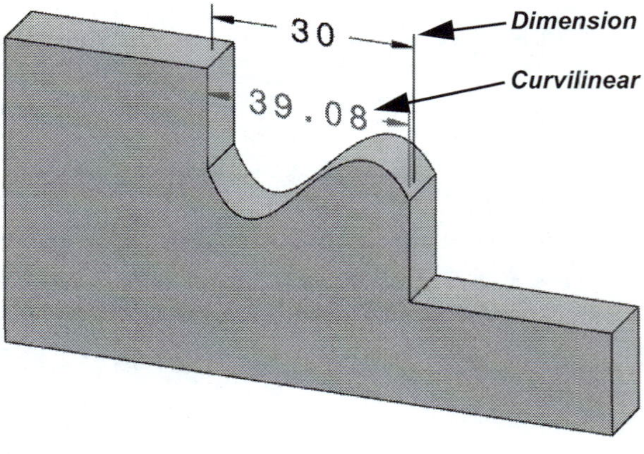

Figure 4–39

4.8 Generative Dimensions

General Steps

Use the following general steps to create generative dimensions:

1. Activate an annotation plane.
2. Start the creation of generative dimensions.
3. Select the features to dimension.
4. Select the dimensions to create.
5. Complete the feature(s).

Step 1 - Activate an annotation plane.

Double-click on the required annotation plane in the specification tree or directly from the model to activate it. The orientation of the selected annotation plane defines the orientation of the text.

Step 2 - Start the creation of generative dimensions.

In the Annotation section of the Action Bar, click  (Generative Dimension). The Generate 3D Tolerancing dimensions dialog box opens, as shown in Figure 4–40.

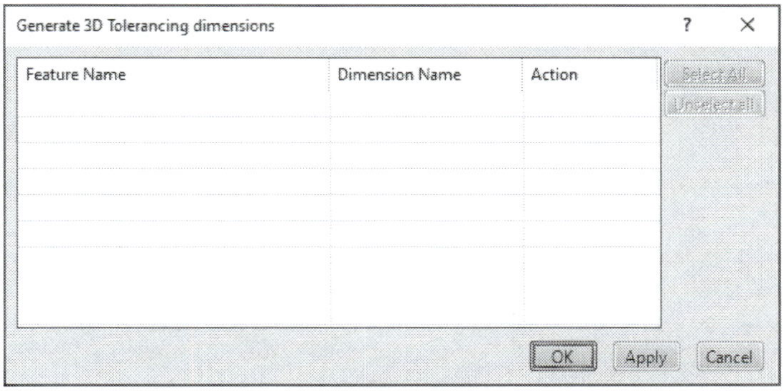

Figure 4–40

Step 3 - Select the features to dimension.

Select the feature(s) to dimension. The dimensions related to each selected feature automatically populate in the Generate 3D Tolerancing dimensions dialog box, as shown in Figure 4–41.

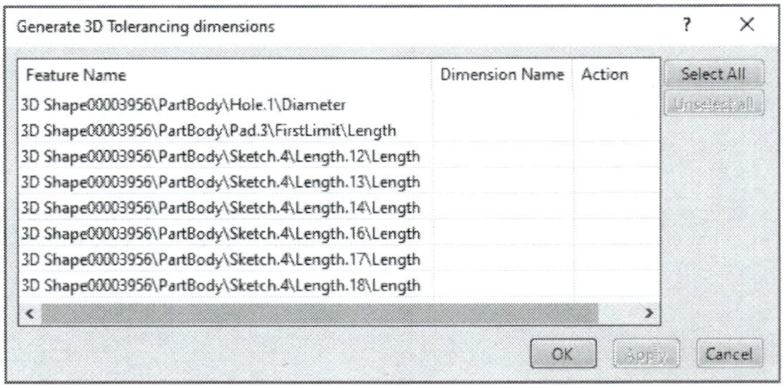

Figure 4–41

The dimensions also display on the model.

Step 4 - Select the dimensions to create.

Not all of the dimensions listed need to be created. Select the dimensions you want to create in the list. The **Create** action displays in the *Action* column for that dimension, as shown in Figure 4–42.

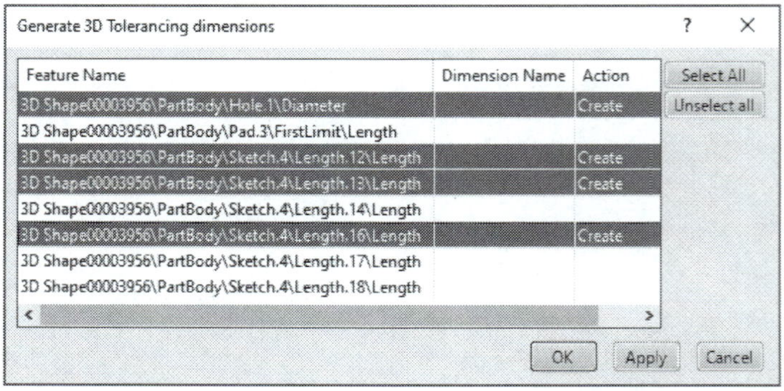

Figure 4–42

Selected dimensions are highlighted in the model. Clear a dimension by selecting it again and the **Create** action is removed from the *Action* field.

If the dimension already exists on the model, **Delete** is shown in the *Action* column.

Step 5 - Complete the feature(s).

Once all of the required dimensions have been set with the appropriate action, click **Apply** to preview the created dimensions on the model. Click **Cancel** to return to the model's previous state or **OK** to accept the new dimensions.

The dimensions are created under the *Dimensions* node in the specification tree.

Semantic Dimensions

If non-semantic annotations are correctly defined, they can conform to the rules of the tolerancing standard that has been defined; however, they are not required to do so.

For example, a tolerance sketched dimension displays with a semantic representation if it is annotated using the Generative Dimension tool. Alternatively, you can create a dimension using the Semantic Tolerancing Advisor dialog box and then modify it (using the Object Properties window) so that it does not conform to the applied standard.

The best method of ensuring that your annotations meet the tolerancing standard is to know the parameters of the standard and to check your annotations to ensure that they conform.

4.9 Reporting Diagnostics

Annotation failures are typically due to a lost reference. If an annotation does fail, you can view a diagnostic report and obtain information to help solve the failure.

The example in Figure 4–43 shows a part that has a text annotation attached to a hole feature. The annotation indicates that this hole feature is used as an indexing reference with a mating part.

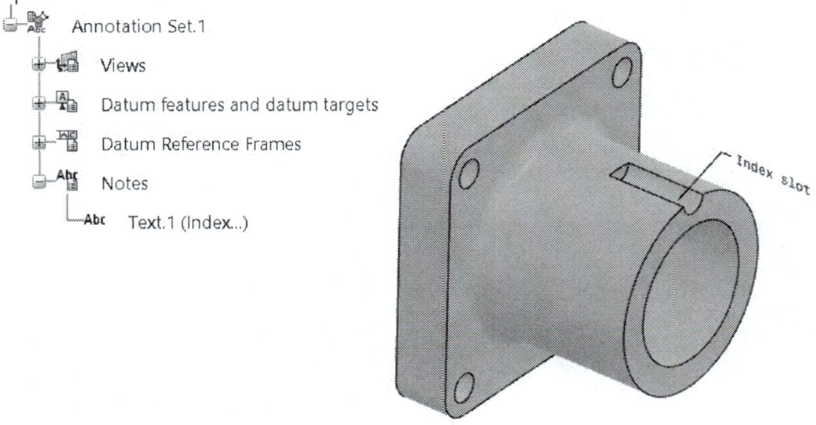

Figure 4–43

If the hole that the annotation references is deleted, the text listed in the specification tree changes by displaying a yellow exclamation mark, as shown in Figure 4–44.

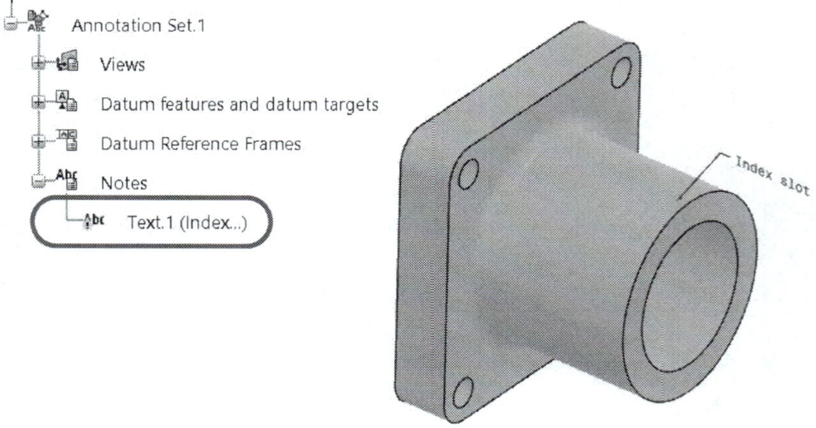

Figure 4–44

You can view the diagnostic report by right-clicking on the failed text in the specification tree and selecting **Diagnostic Report**, as shown in Figure 4–45.

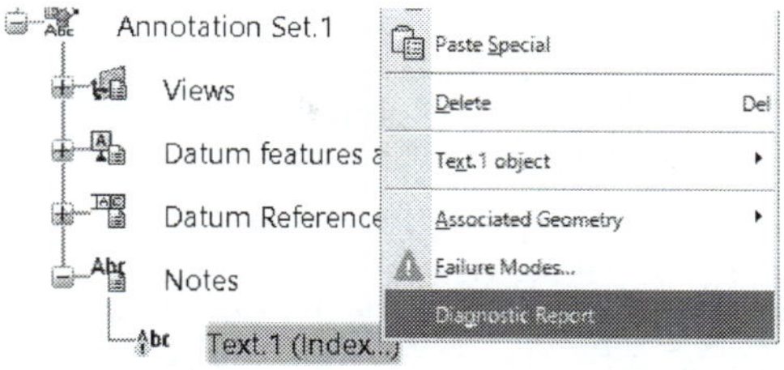

Figure 4–45

In this case, the 3D annotation diagnostics report description reports that a feature is an **Invalid component**, as shown in Figure 4–46.

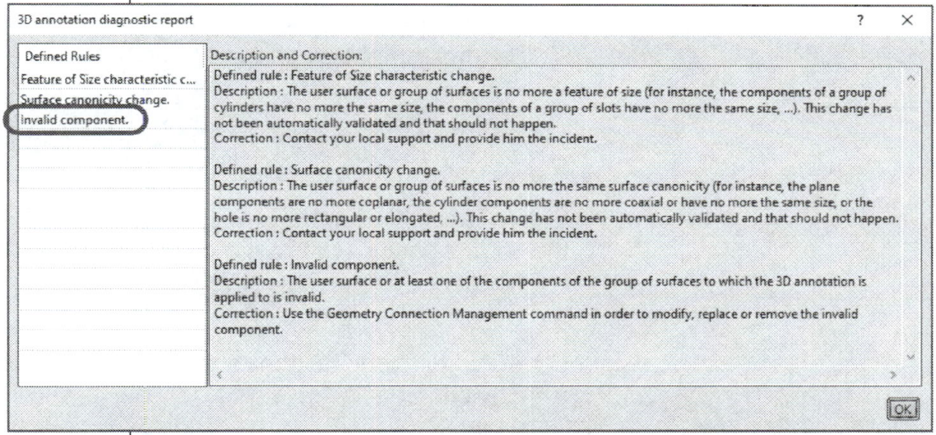

Figure 4–46

The 3D annotation diagnostic report is informational only. No actual changes can be made through this dialog box.

4.10 Reporting

The reporting tool in the 3D T&A app enables you to review the non-semantic tolerances that have been created in the model and to verify that they meet specific tolerancing rules. Since non-semantic tolerances do not need to obey any tolerancing standards, this is a good method of ensuring that mistakes have not been made during the annotation of the model.

*To add commands, go to **Me>Preferences> Customize**.*

The Reporting tools are not found on the Action Bar by default.

Both the (Report Customization) and (Non Semantic 3D Annotation Report) tools will need to be added to the Action Bar or Action Pad if you want to use them in the 3D T&A app.

Use the following general steps to perform a report:

1. Customize the report.
2. Run the report and analyze the results.

Step 1 - Customize the report.

Before running a report, you should customize it to ensure that the correct settings are specified. These settings are used for all reports performed in the active CATIA session.

Click (Report Customization). The Non-Semantic Annotations Settings dialog box opens, as shown in Figure 4–47.

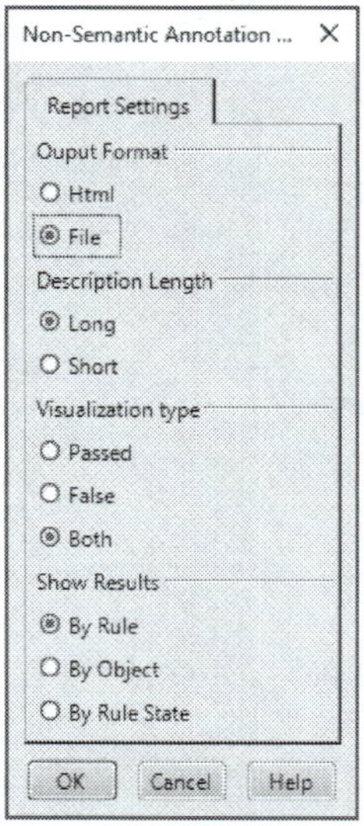

Figure 4–47

The following describes the options in the Non-Semantic Annotation dialog box.

Option		Description
Output Format		
	Html	The report is generated in an Html format and automatically opened in a web browser.
	File	The report is generated in a text format and automatically opened in a Report dialog box.
Description Length		
	Long	A descriptive help message is added for each check in the report.
	Short	Only the check name is reported.
Visualization type		
	Passed	Only checks that were successful are reported.
	False	Only checks that were unsuccessful are reported.
	Both	All checks are reported.
Show Results		These options are only available for a file report.
	By Rule	The report is organized by the type of check.
	By Object	The report is organized by annotation feature.
	By Rule State	The report is organized by unsuccessful annotation features, and then followed by successful annotation features.

Click **OK** once the report customization has been completed.

Step 2 - Run the report and analyze the results.

To run a report, click  (Non Semantic 3D Annotation Report). Report opens in either a web browser or Report window, as shown in Figure 4–48, depending on the settings made.

8/30/2022

Only Non-Semantic Annotations are reported.

List of Expert Checks :

Visualization Settings : All objects

Validity	Hierarchy	Check Name	Percent of Success	Assessment	Help	Correct Function
		datum label unicity	Not Pertinent		A datum label shall be unique in the tolerancing set	Edit the datum label and replace it with a non-already used label
		datum label capital letter	0%		A datum label shall only contain capital letter(s) (upper case)	Edit and Replace the datum-label small letter(s) with the corresponding capital letter(s)
		authorized or proposed datum label letter	Not Pertinent		A datum label should not contain the capital letters I, O or Q. according to ASME Y14.5M-1994 standard.	Edit and Replace the datum label
		datum label length	Not Pertinent		A datum label shall not be composed with more than two letters (ASME standard)	Edit and check the datum label length

Figure 4–48

Read the Validity column to analyze the report. There are three possible values, described as follows:

Validity	Description
	The check has completely succeeded.
	The check has failed. Look at the Percent of Success column to see what percentage of the possible annotation features have failed the check.
Blank	The check did not apply to the model being reported. The Percent of Success column reads "Not Pertinent".

Any check that has failed can be investigated by selecting on the check name. This opens a new browser window and displays the name of the failed annotation feature. For example, the report for the “datum label capital letter” link displays, as shown in Figure 4–49. This window indicates that Geometrical Tolerance.1 has failed the check and must be resolved.

8/30/2022

Validity	Hierarchy	Check Name	Percent of Success	Assessment	Help	Correct Function
		coherence of datums specified in the GDT and datum unicity	0%		- A datum specified in a reference frame//GDT shall be defined in the annotation set. - A datum shall not be specified several times in a the same reference frame//GDT	Edit the annotation to specify an existing datum and//or create the lacking datum

Validity	Object name	Weight	Comment
	Geometrical Tolerance.1(Geometrical Tolerance.1)		

Figure 4–49

Practice 4a

Creating Text Annotations

Practice Objectives

- Add a text annotation.
- Add a coordinate dimension.

In this practice, you will complete the annotation of the LockingHub part model. This includes the creation of annotations to convey the standard titleblock information on the 3D part model. The completed model is shown in Figure 4–50.

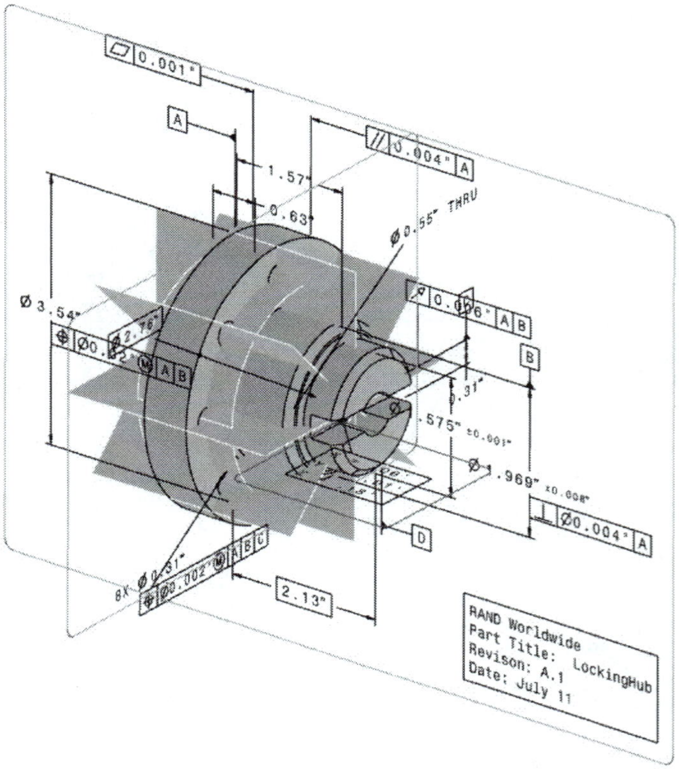

Figure 4–50

Task 1 - Import and open a part file.

1. Import and open **LockingHub_Ex3b.3dxml**. The model displays as shown in Figure 4–51.

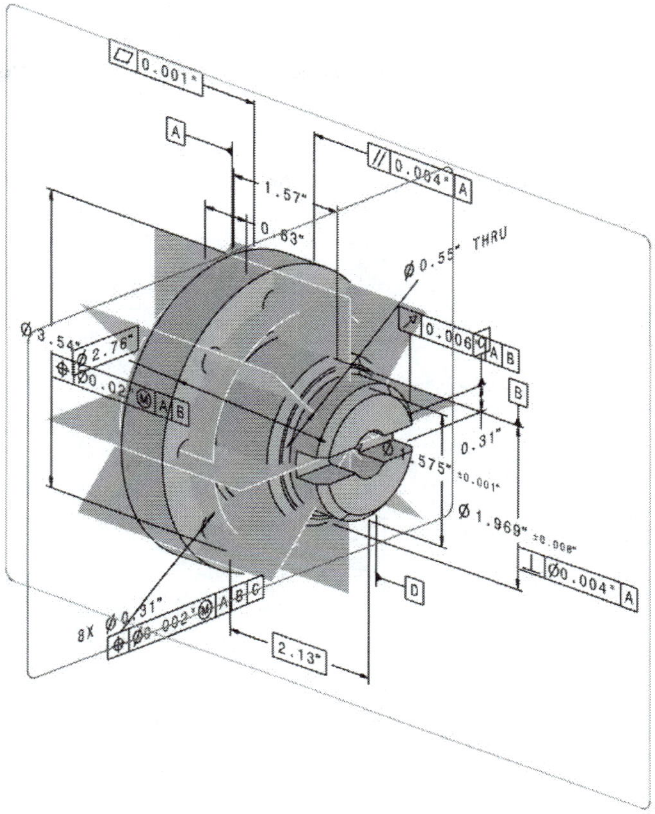

Figure 4–51

2. Activate SideView.

Task 2 - Add titleblock notes.

1. In the Annotation section of the Action Bar, click Abc (Text).
2. Select a location at the bottom right corner of SideView, as shown in Figure 4–52.

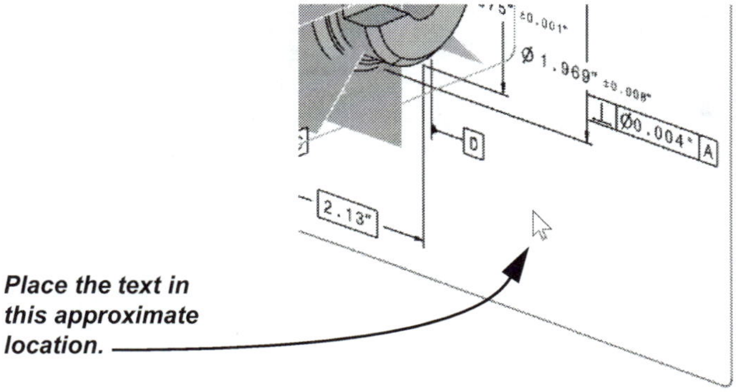

Figure 4–52

3. Enter the text shown in Figure 4–53 into the Text Editor dialog box. To add the second line of text, press <Shift>+<Enter>. Do not close the dialog box.

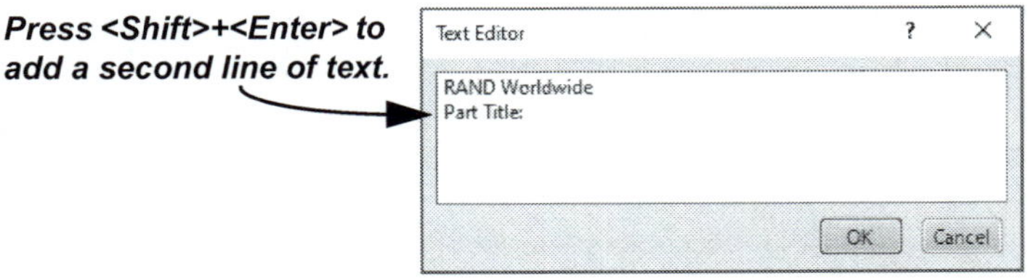

Figure 4–53

4. Right-click outside the Text Editor dialog box and select **Insert Attribute Link**, as shown in Figure 4–54.

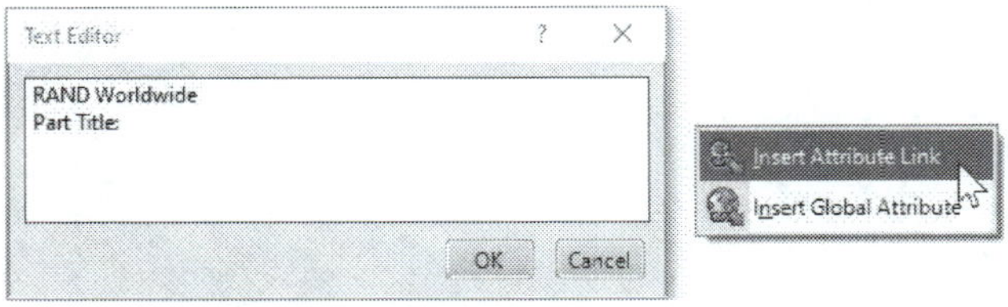

Figure 4–54

5. Select **LockingHub** in the specification tree. The Insert Attribute Link dialog box opens.

6. At the top of the list of parameters, select the **Title** parameter that has a value of **LockingHub**, as shown in Figure 4–55.

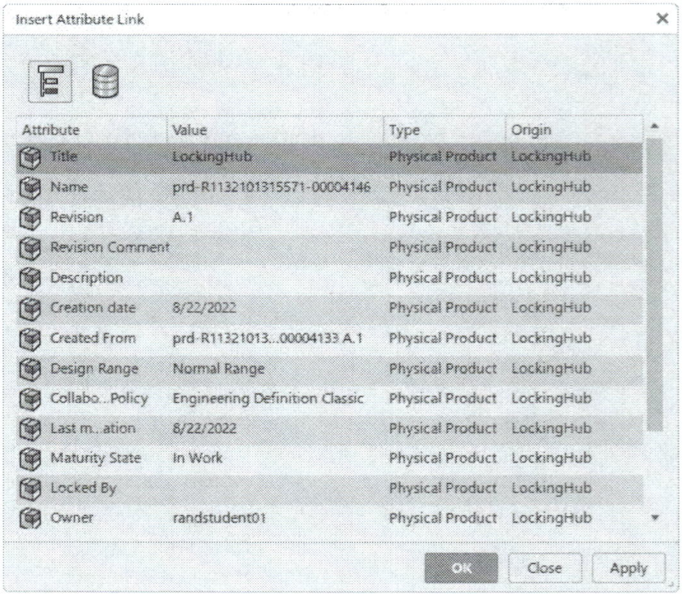

Figure 4–55

7. Click **OK**. The title is added to the Text Editor dialog box.

Design Considerations

By using the **Insert Attribute Link** option, you are creating associative text in the title block. If the **Title** parameter is changed, the text in this annotation updates with the modification.

8. Complete the Text Editor dialog box, as shown in Figure 4–56. **Note:** Do not use the **Attribute Link** option for the remaining two lines in the text.

Press <Shift>+<Enter> to add another line of text in the Text Editor.

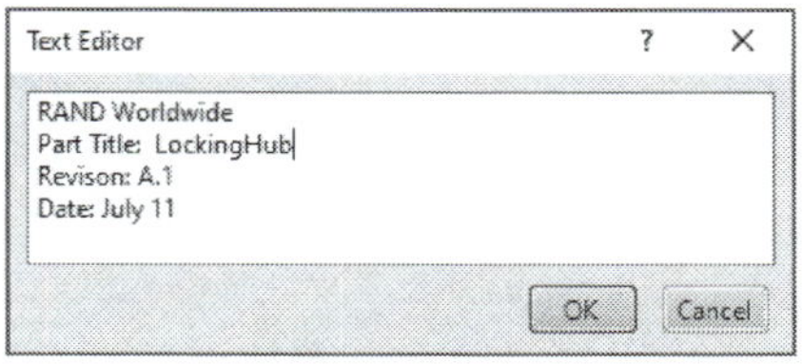

Figure 4–56

9. Click **OK**. The model displays as shown in Figure 4–57.

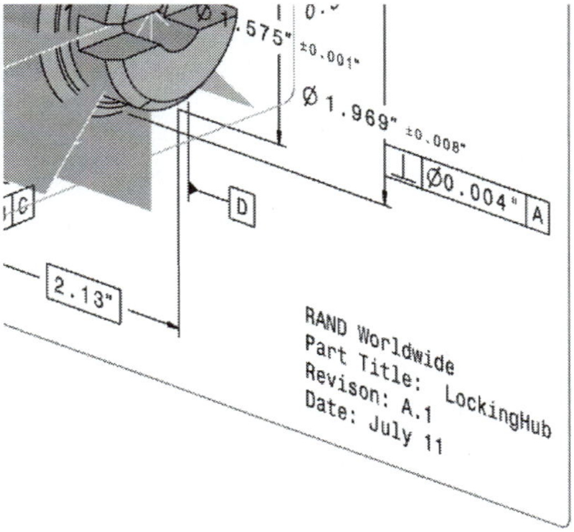

Figure 4–57

10. To add a frame to the title block information, verify that the text is highlighted. In the Text section of the Object Properties window, click (Rectangle), as shown in Figure 4–58.

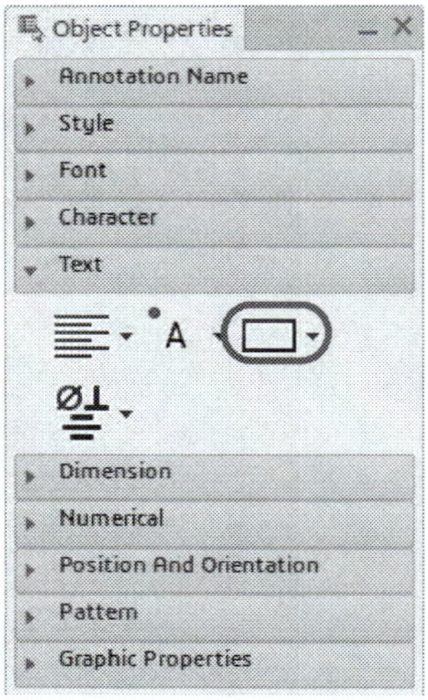

Figure 4–58

The title block displays as shown in Figure 4–59.

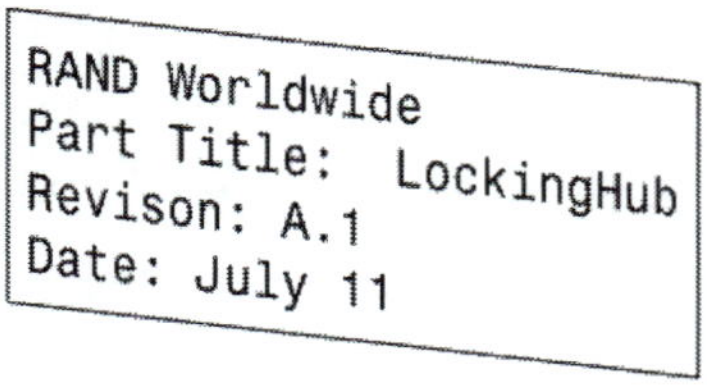

Figure 4–59

Task 3 - Create a coordinate dimension.

1. Create an additional projection view annotation plane named **TopView** using the ZX plane.
2. In the Dimensions flyout of the Annotation section of the Action Bar, click (Coordinate Dimensions).
3. Select the vertex shown in Figure 4–60.

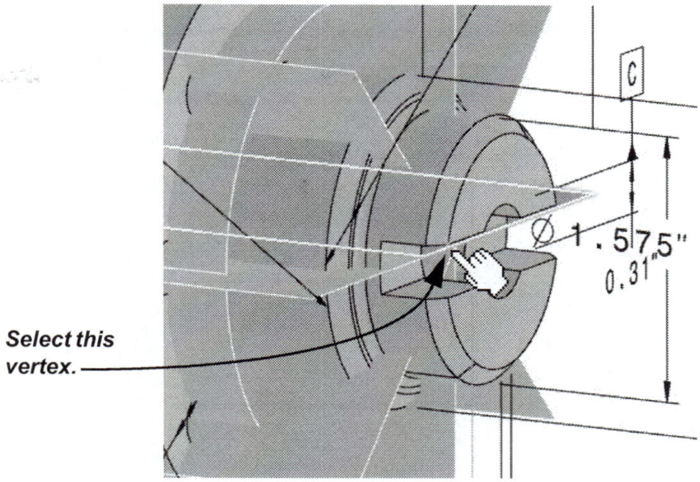

Figure 4–60

4. Position the annotation appropriately. The model displays as shown in Figure 4–61.

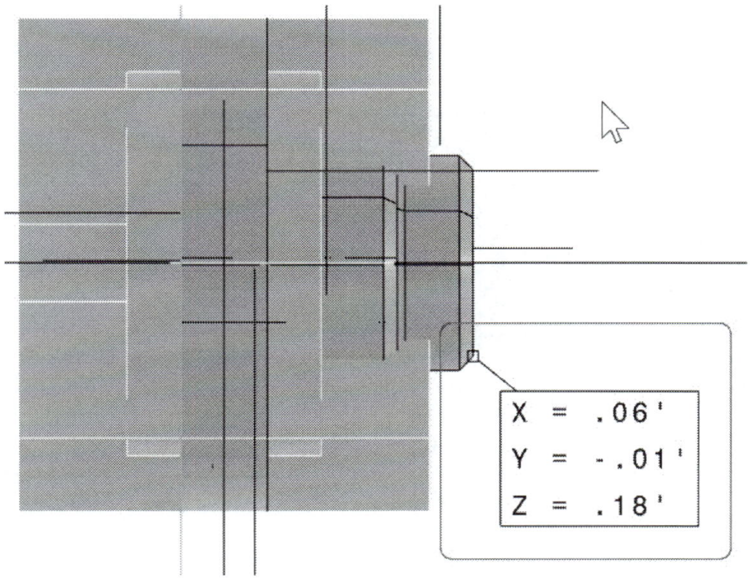

Figure 4–61

5. Hide the three annotation views.

6. Save the model and close the window.

Practice 4b Non-Semantic Annotations

Practice Objectives

- Add generative and stacked dimensions.
- Add a datum element and tolerance.

In this practice, you will practice creating non-semantic annotations. You will create the annotations using the non-semantic tools in the Annotations toolbar for demonstration purposes only. Ideally, these annotations would be developed using the Tolerance Advisor to ensure that they conform to the applied standard. The completed model displays, as shown in Figure 4–62.

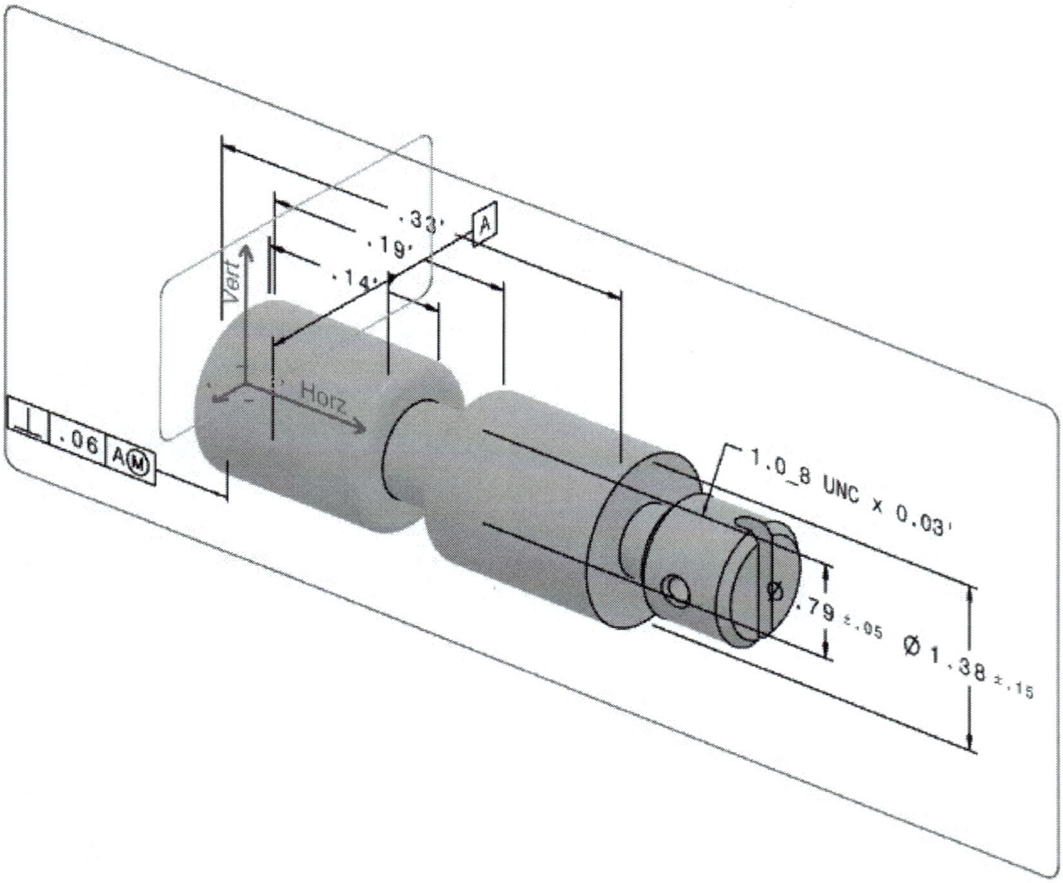

Figure 4–62

Task 1 - Import and open a part file.

1. Import and open **StandOff.3dxml**. The model displays as shown in Figure 4–63.

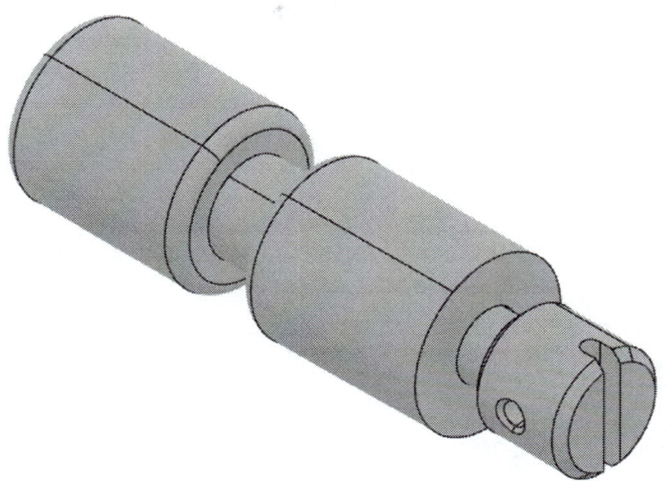

Figure 4–63

2. Right-click on **Annotation Set.1** and select **Show in 3D**.

3. Expand the **Annotation Set.1** branch of the specification tree and review the three views that have been established, as shown in Figure 4–64.

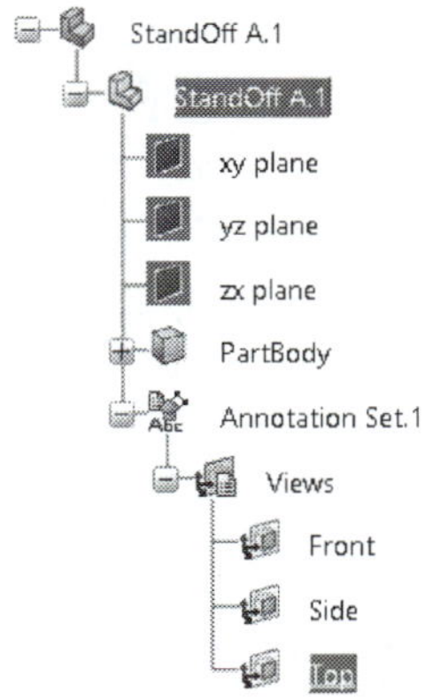

Figure 4–64

4. Activate the view named **Side**.

Task 2 - Add generative dimensions.

In this task, you will use the Generative Dimensions tool to display model dimensions. You will select a feature from the model and the dimensions for this feature can be selected for display as an annotated dimension.

1. In the Annotation section of the Action Bar, click  (Generative Dimension). The Generate 3D Tolerancing dimensions dialog box opens, as shown in Figure 4–65.

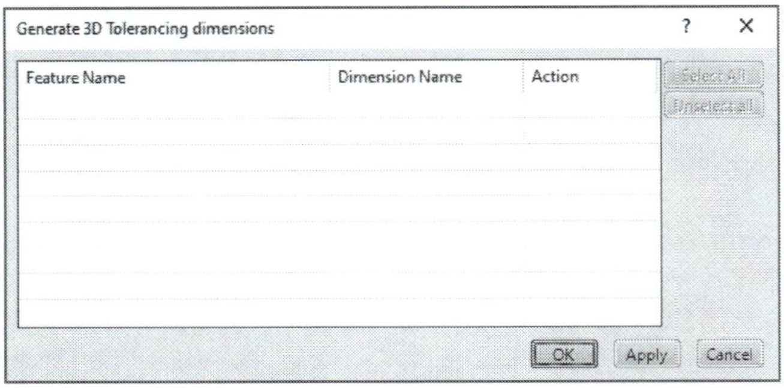

Figure 4–65

2. Expand PartBody and select **Shaft.1** in the specification tree. The dimensions for the shaft feature display on the model. These dimensions are also listed in the Generate 3D Tolerancing dimensions dialog box, as shown in Figure 4–66.

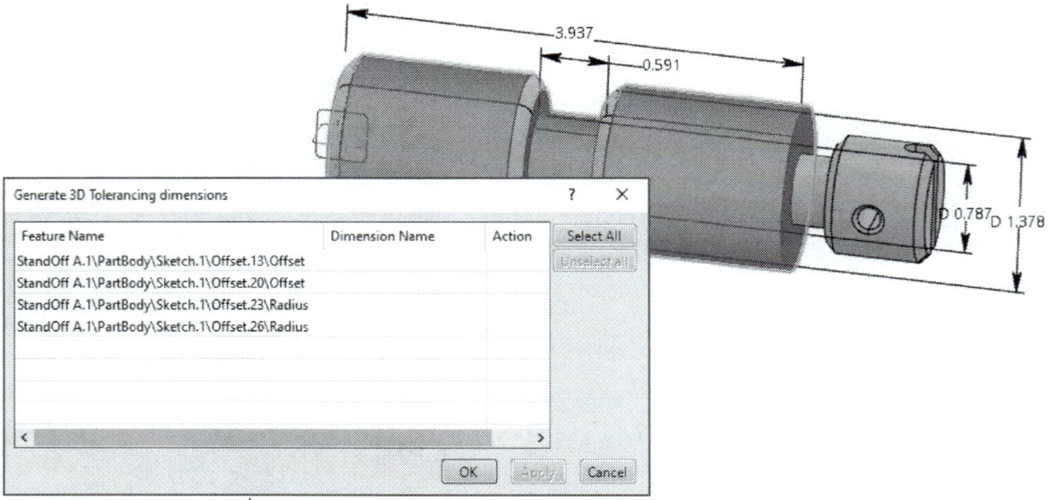

Figure 4–66

3. Select the **0.787in** and **1.378in** diameter dimensions from the model. These dimensions are highlighted in the dialog box and their *Action* value is set to **Create**, as shown in Figure 4–67.

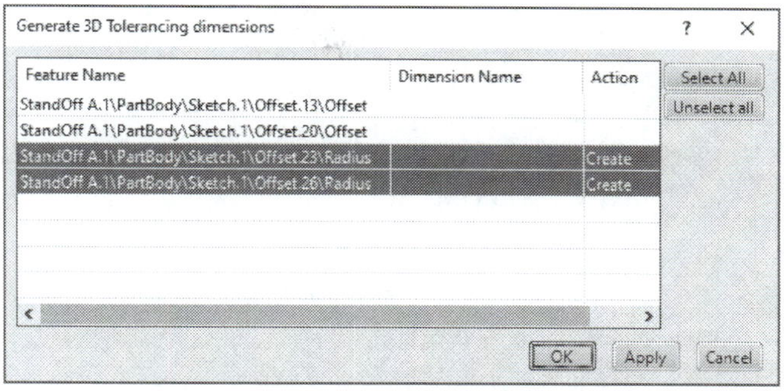

Figure 4–67

4. Click **OK** to complete the operation. The system automatically generates annotations for the selected dimensions, as shown in Figure 4–68. Adjustment of the dimensions maybe required.

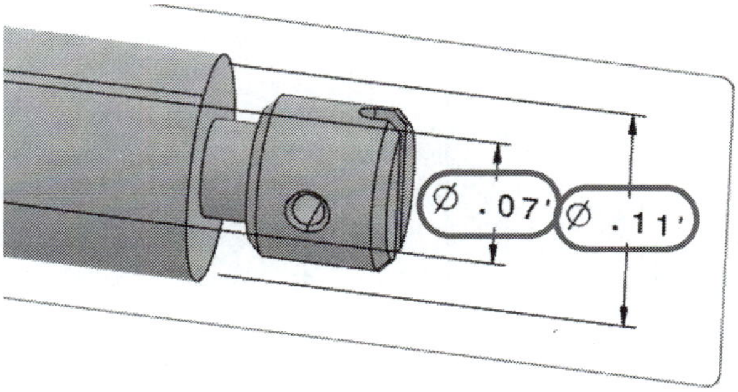

Figure 4–68

Task 3 - Add tolerances to the dimensions.

By default, the dimensions are created with a general tolerance. In this task, you will add specific tolerances to the generated dimensions created in the previous task.

1. Verify that the Object Properties window is displayed. To display the window, toggle on  (Object Properties) from the Tools section of the Action Bar.

2. Select the **.07ft** diameter dimension.

3. Make the following selections in the Object Properties window:

   - Select **NUM.DINC**.
   - Select **TOL_NUM2**.
   - Select **+- 0.05**.

   The toolbar and model display as shown in Figure 4–69.

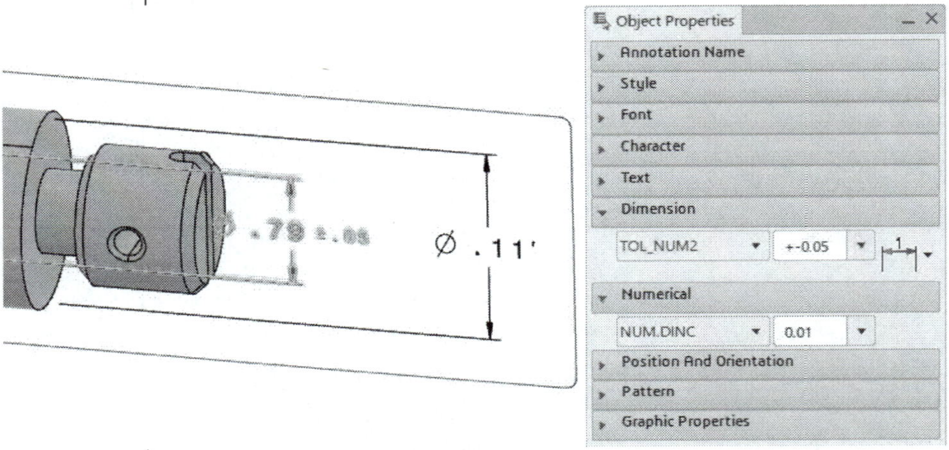

Figure 4–69

4. Repeat this process to add a +/- 0.15 tolerance to the 1.38in diameter dimension. The model displays as shown in Figure 4–70.

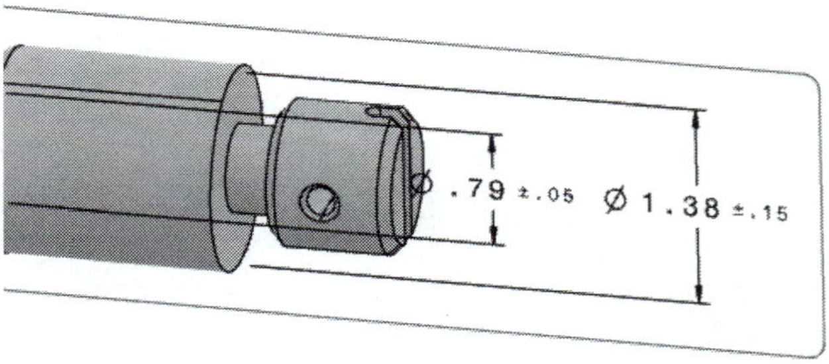

Figure 4–70

Task 4 - Create stacked dimensions.

1. In the Dimensions flyout of the Annotation section of the Action Bar, click 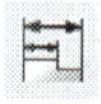 (Stacked Dimensions).
2. Select the two faces of the model, as shown in Figure 4–71. The system adds a distance dimension between these faces.

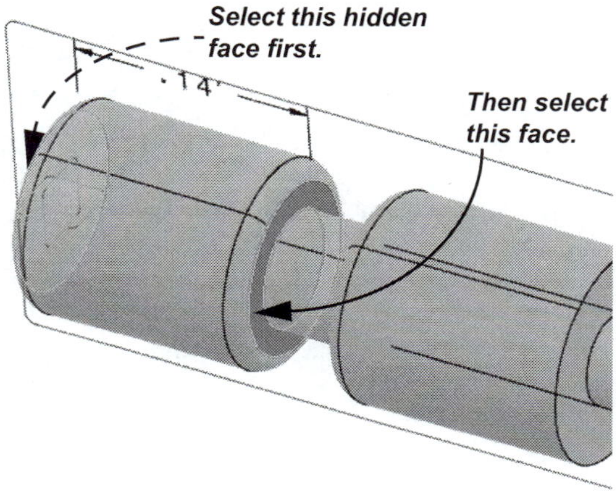

Figure 4–71

3. Select the face shown in Figure 4–72. The system adds a dimension between this reference and the first face selected.

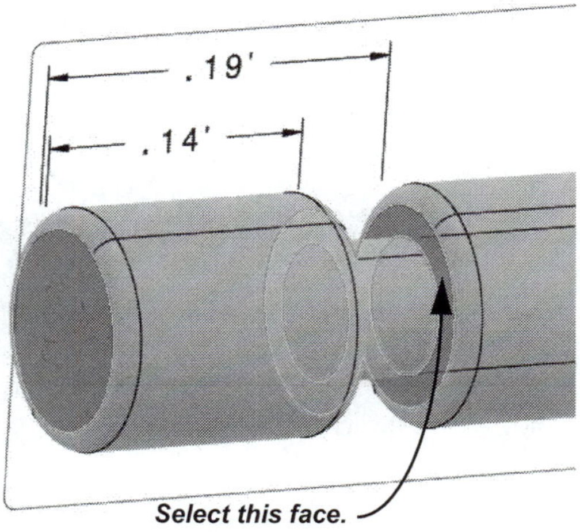

Figure 4–72

4. Select the face shown in Figure 4–73.

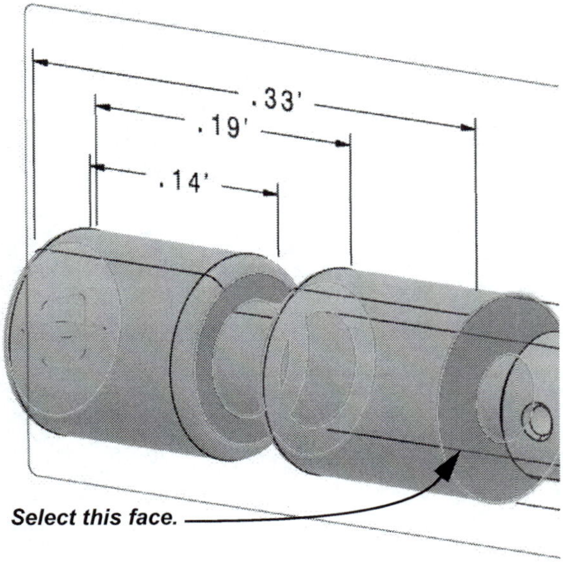

Figure 4–73

5. Select anywhere on the background to complete the dimension creation. The model displays as shown in Figure 4–74.

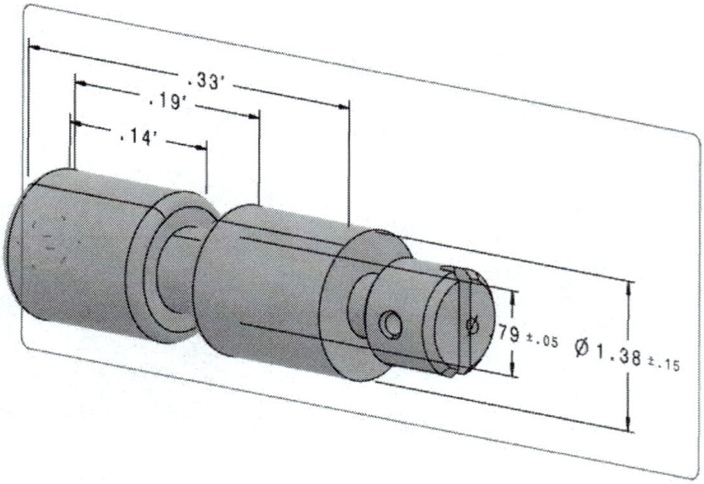

Figure 4–74

Task 5 - Add text with a leader.

1. In the Annotation section of the Action Bar, click (Text with Leader).
2. Select the cylindrical face highlighted in Figure 4–75. The Text Editor dialog box opens.

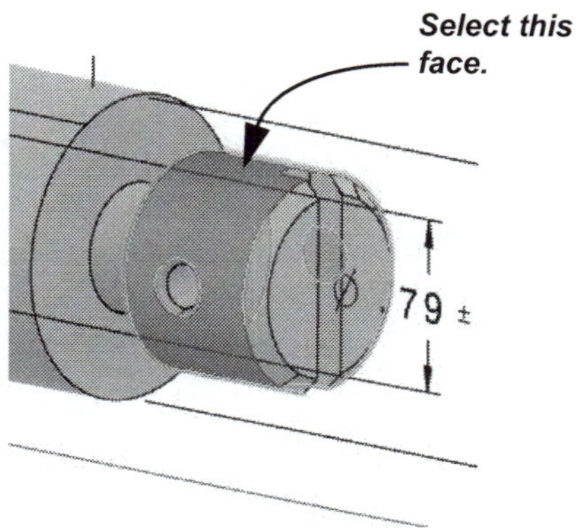

Figure 4–75

3. Enter **1.0_8 UNC x 0.03'** in the Text Editor dialog box and click **OK**. The model displays as shown in Figure 4–76.

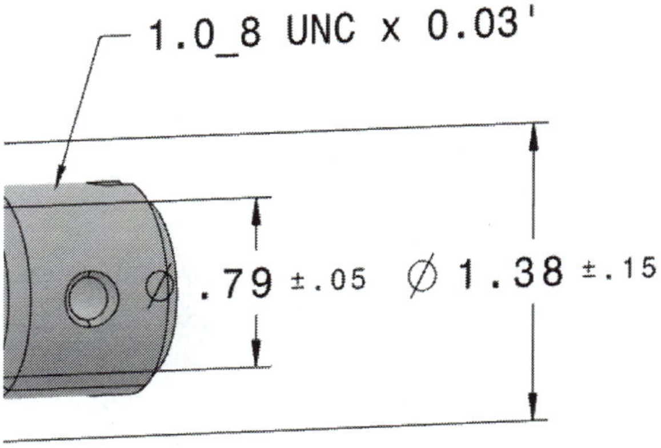

Figure 4–76

Task 6 - Create a datum and tolerance.

1. Activate the view named Front.

2. In the Annotation section of the Acton Bar, click  (Datum Element).

3. Select the cylindrical face highlighted in Figure 4–77. The Datum Feature Creation dialog box opens.

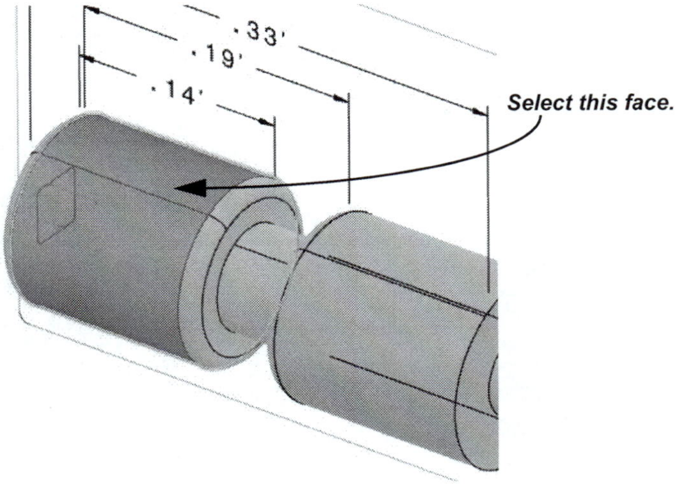

Figure 4–77

4. Accept the default name of **A** and click **OK**. The model displays as shown in Figure 4–78.

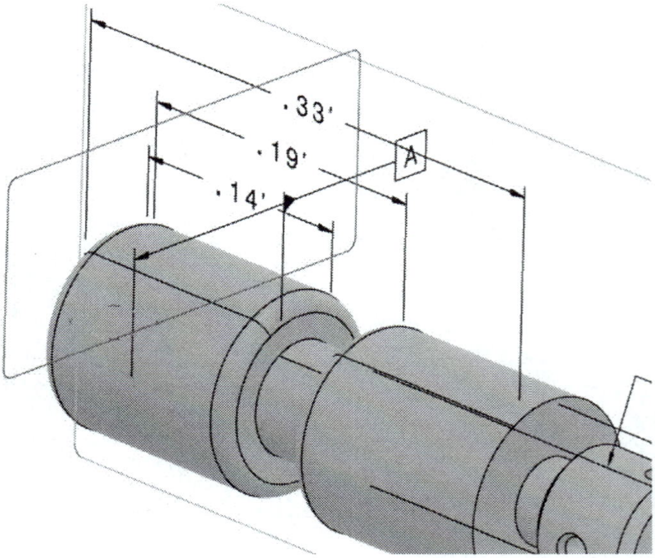

Figure 4–78

5. Activate the view named Side.

6. In the Annotation section of the Action Bar, click  (Geometrical Tolerance).

7. Select the face shown in Figure 4–79.

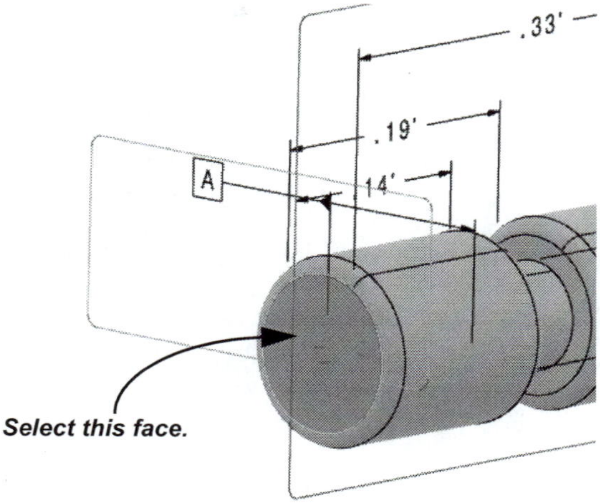

Figure 4–79

The Geometrical Tolerance dialog box opens, as shown in Figure 4–80.

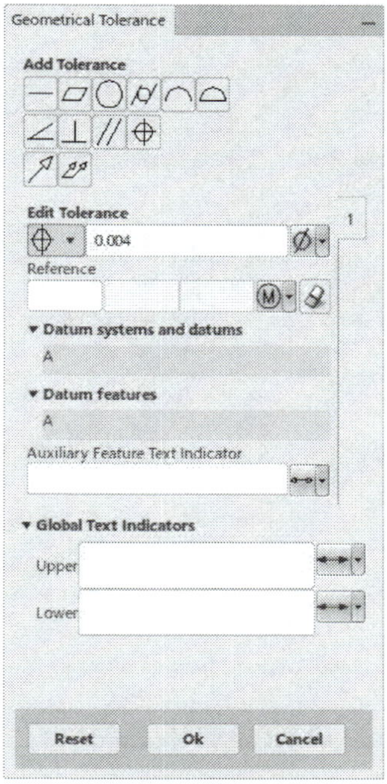

Figure 4–80

8. Make the following selections in the Geometrical Tolerance dialog box:

   - Select **Perpendicularity** in the Tolerance flyout.
   - Enter **0.06** in the *Tolerance* field.
   - Enter **A** in the first *Reference* field.
   - Click  in the Insert Symbol flyout with the cursor in the *Reference* field.

   The Geometrical Tolerance dialog box displays as shown in Figure 4–81.

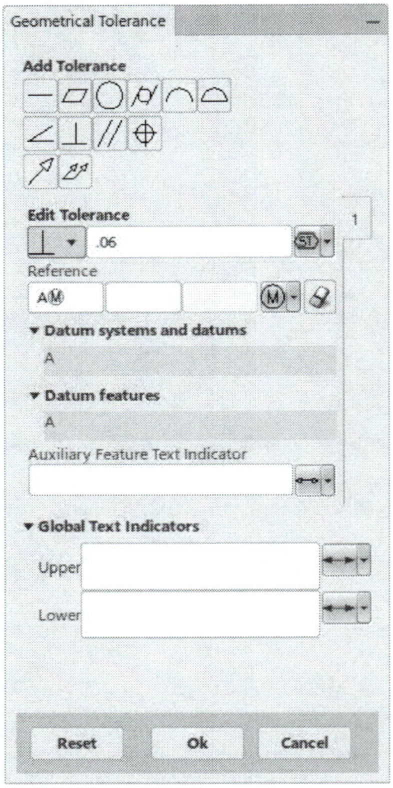

Figure 4–81

9. Click **OK**.

10. Right-click the yellow diamond at the end of the leader and click **Extremity Link>Perpendicular**.

    The model displays as shown in Figure 4–82.

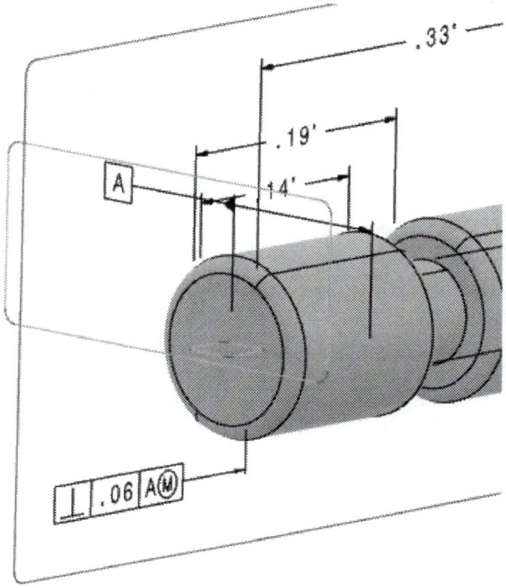

Figure 4–82

11. Save the model and close the window.

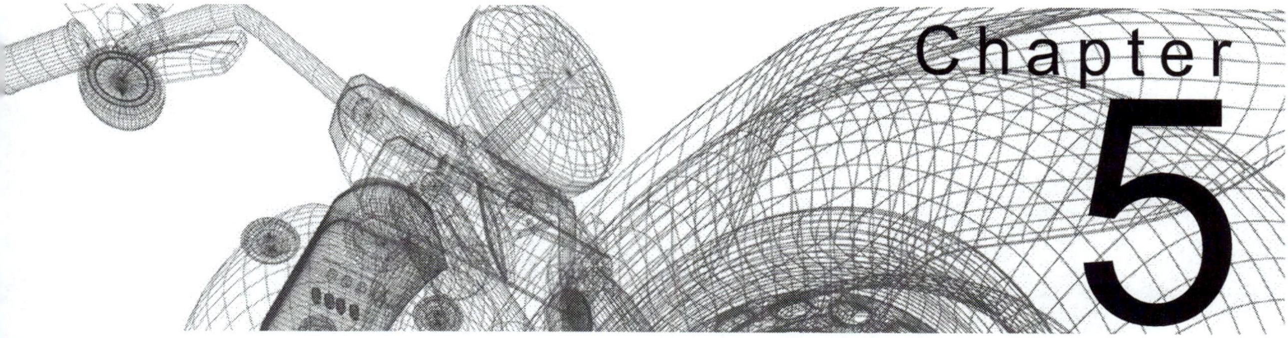

Annotation Management

This chapter introduces the tools and operations that enable you to manage your annotations.

Learning Objectives in This Chapter

- Create leader symbols.
- Learn how to mirror, transfer, and group annotations.
- Understand how to apply annotation filters.
- Learn how to use cameras and captures.
- Learn how to use geometry connection management.

5.1 Leader Symbols

Depending on the leader type and feature being referenced, a particular leader symbol might be required by your company standards, as shown in Figure 5–1.

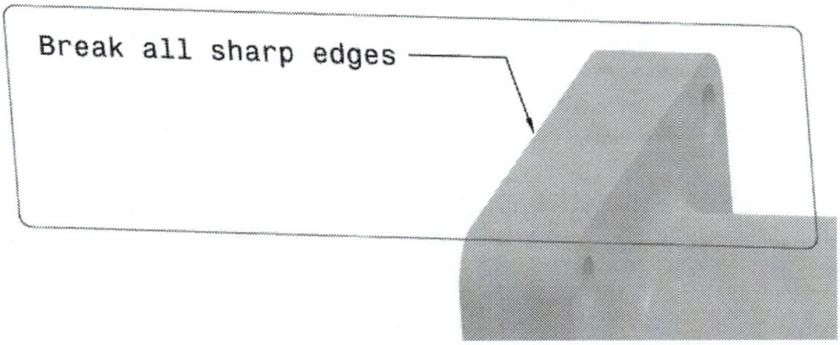

Figure 5–1

General Steps

Use the following general steps to change leader symbols:

1. Select the annotation.
2. Select the end manipulator.
3. Select the symbol.

Step 1 - Select the annotation.

Select the annotation for which you want to change the leader symbol. The handles for the test display and the end manipulator turn blue, as shown in Figure 5–2.

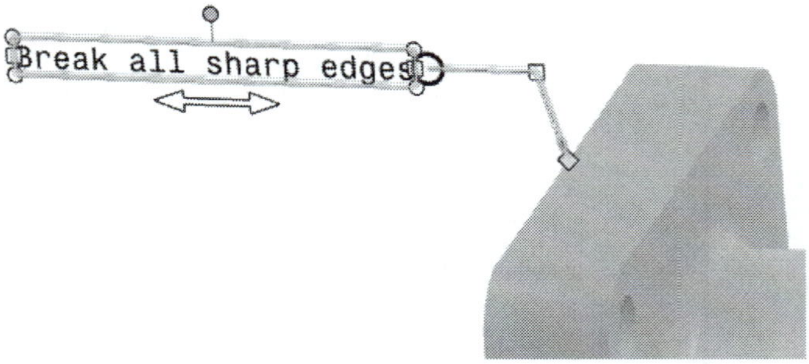

Figure 5–2

Step 2 - Select the end manipulator.

Right-click and select **Symbol Shape**, as shown in Figure 5–3.

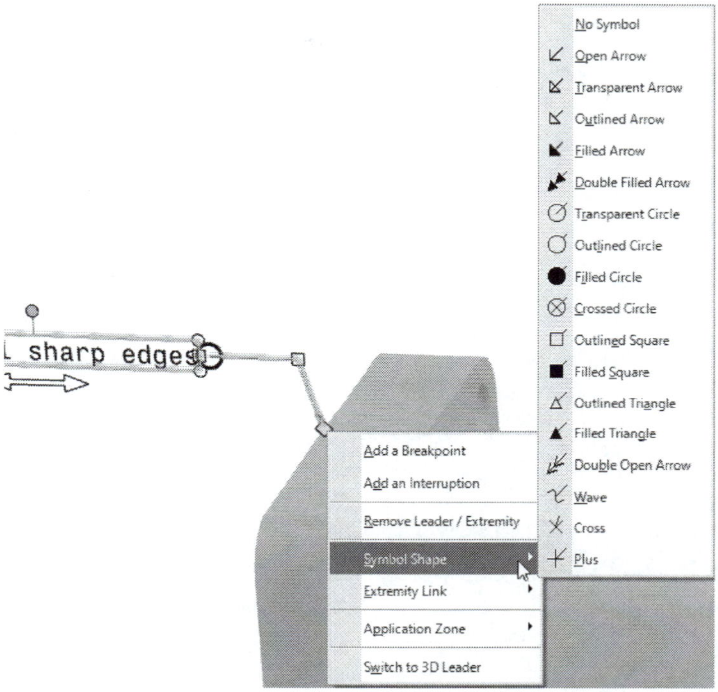

Figure 5–3

Step 3 - Select the symbol.

Select the required symbol shape to complete the change, as shown in Figure 5–4.

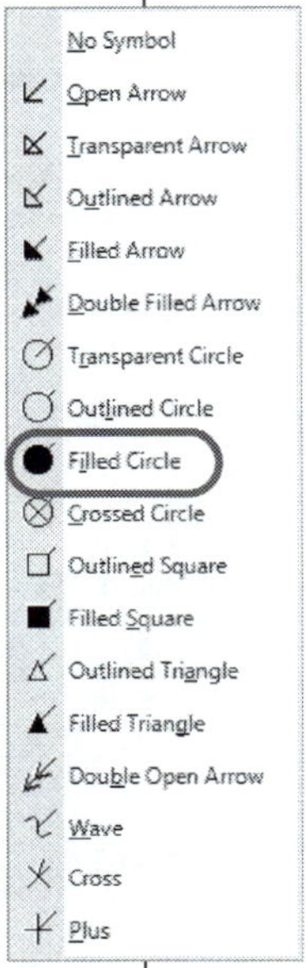

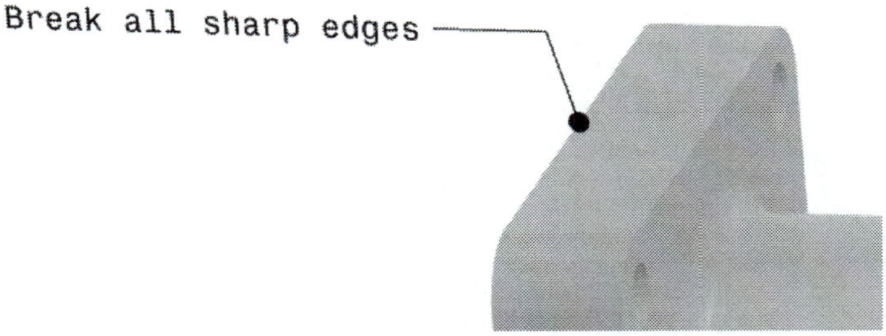

Figure 5–4

5.2 Mirror Annotations

As the model is oriented, the annotations remain fixed and the direction of the text might not display as required. For example, the model shown in Figure 5–5 has been oriented so that the annotated text reads backwards.

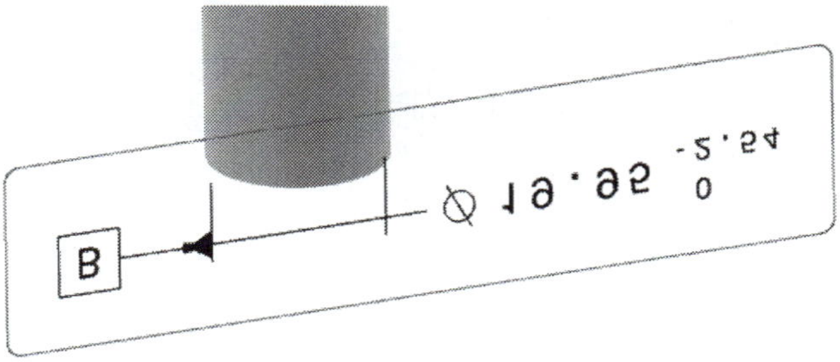

Figure 5–5

At any time, you can flip text using  (Mirror Annotations) in the View section of the Action Bar. All reversed annotations are mirrored, as shown in Figure 5–6.

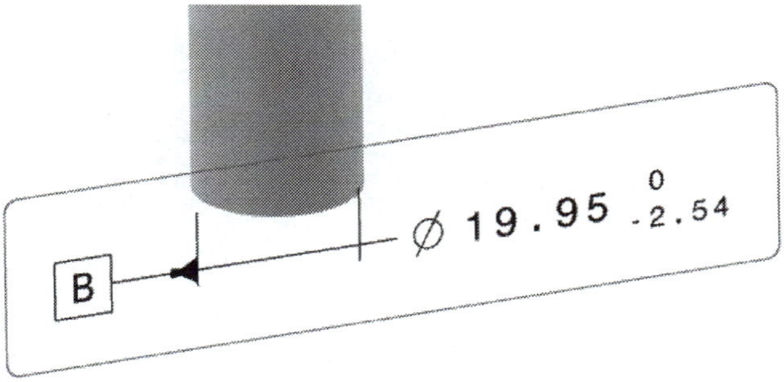

Figure 5–6

5.3 Transferring Annotations

Each annotation is placed in a particular view to better organize and display the information. This view can easily be changed to improve the organization of the model.

General Steps

Use the following general steps to transfer annotations:

1. Select the annotation to be transferred.
2. Transfer the annotation.
3. Select the destination view.

Step 1 - Select the annotation to be transferred.

Select the parent annotation. In this case, the geometric tolerance frame follows the selected semantic diameter dimension, as shown in Figure 5–7.

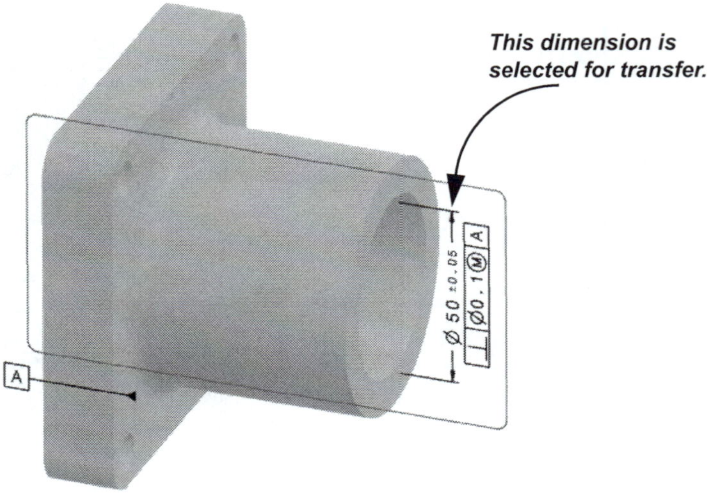

Figure 5–7

Step 2 - Transfer the annotation.

Right-click and select **Transfer to View/Annotation Plane**, as shown in Figure 5–8.

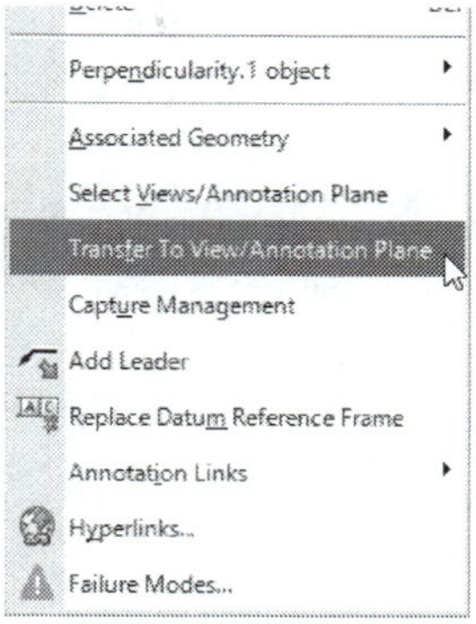

Figure 5–8

Step 3 - Select the destination view.

Select the destination view. The annotation is transferred, as shown in Figure 5–9.

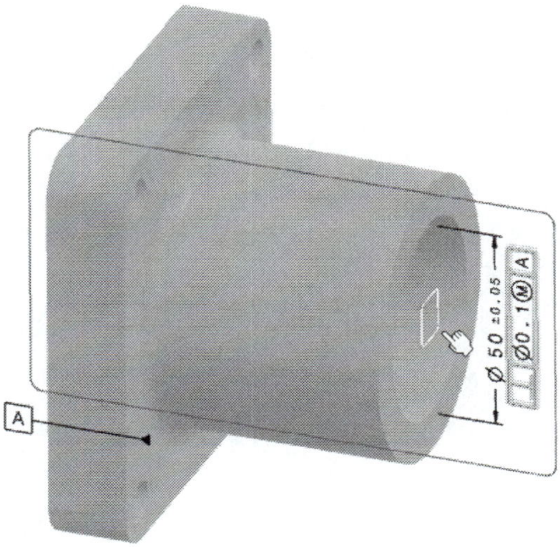

Figure 5–9

The annotation plane must exist before performing the transfer operation, as shown in Figure 5–10.

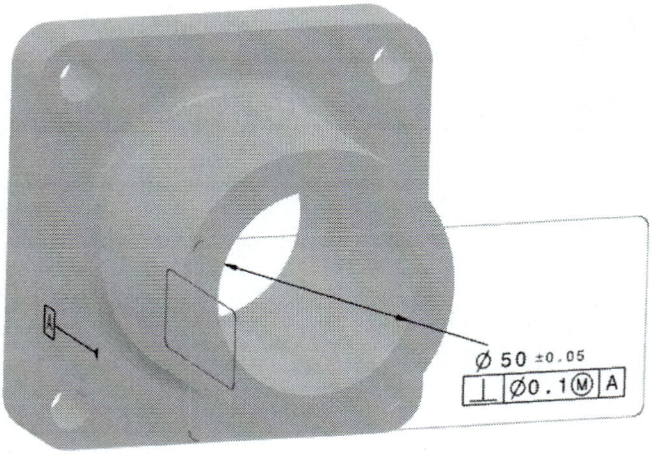

Figure 5–10

5.4 Grouping Annotations

One element of a model can have many different annotations. It might have a text note, a surface condition, and a geometrical tolerance. To simplify the display of information, these elements can be grouped together.

A new annotation can be grouped with an existing annotation by preselecting the existing annotation during the creation of the new annotation. This section focuses on the manual grouping of existing annotations.

General Steps

Use the following general steps to group annotations:

1. Start the grouping operation.
2. Select the annotations to group.
3. Specify the positioning options.
4. Group additional annotations, if required.
5. Complete the grouping.

Step 1 - Start the grouping operation.

The **Manual** grouping command isn't on the Action Bar by default. Use **Me>Preferences>Customize** to add  (Manual) to either the Action Bar or Action Pad, then select the  (Manual) icon from the custom location. CATIA prompts you to select annotations. In this example, the annotations shown in Figure 5–11 are grouped.

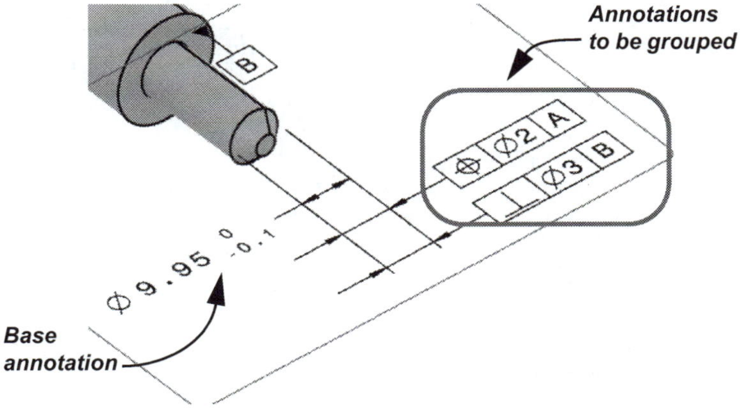

Figure 5–11

Step 2 - Select the annotations to group.

Multiple annotations can be grouped in one operation. The system always groups the selected annotation with the previously selected annotation. For example, if annotations are selected in the order shown in Figure 5–12, the following groups are formed:

- Group 1: Toleranced dimension and position geometrical tolerance
- Group 2: Position and perpendicular geometrical tolerances

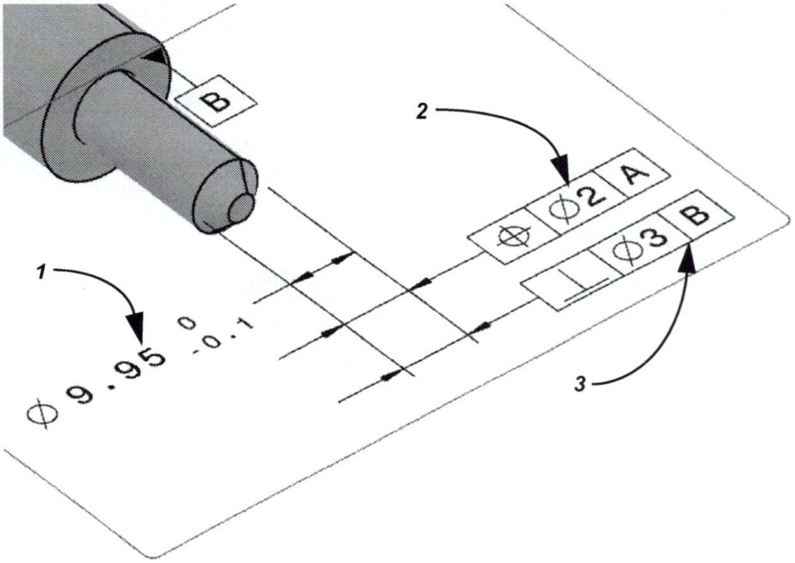

Figure 5–12

As a result, all three annotations move if the toleranced dimension is moved. Likewise, the perpendicular tolerance moves if the position tolerance is moved.

When you need to group more than one annotation, you must define the positioning options for each annotation before continuing to the next one. Start by selecting the base annotation, and then the first annotation to group. The system groups the annotations in a default position after you finish selecting them, and the Positioning dialog box opens, as shown in Figure 5–13.

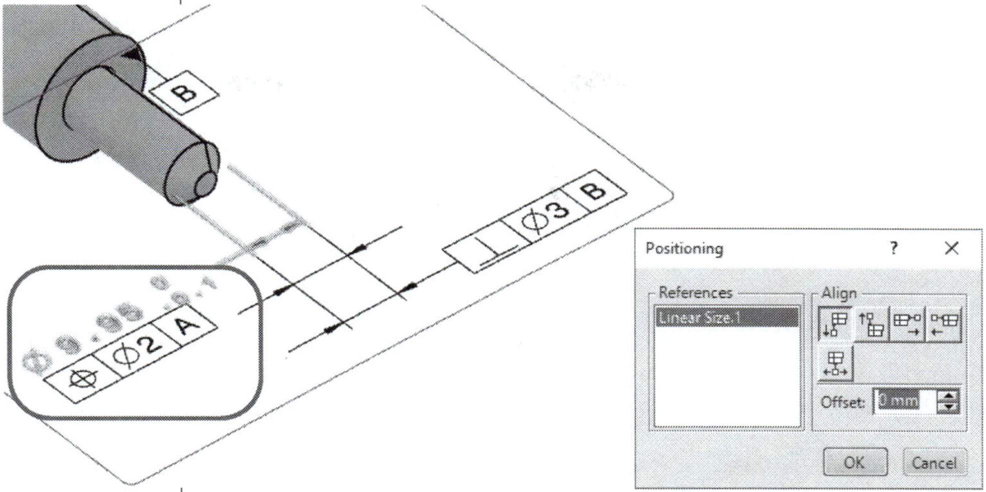

Figure 5–13

Step 3 - Specify the positioning options.

Use the Positioning dialog box to specify the alignment and offset parameters for the active annotation. The options are described as follows:

Option	Description
Align	
 **Align Bottom**	Position the annotation beneath the base annotation, as shown below. 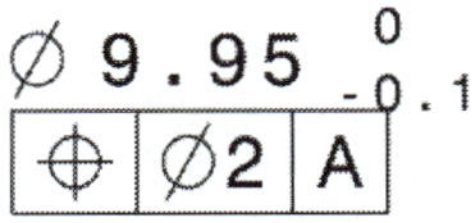
 **Align Top**	Position the annotation above the base annotation, as shown below. 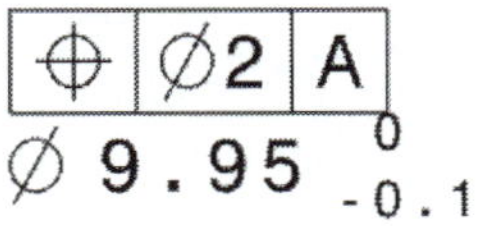

 **Align Right**	Position the annotation to the right of the base annotation, as shown below. 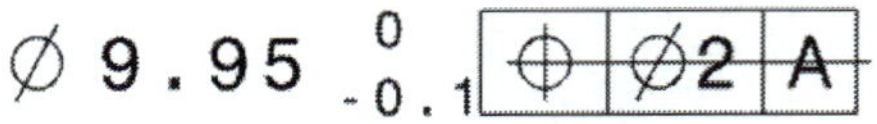
 **Align Left**	Position the annotation to the left of the base annotation, as shown below. 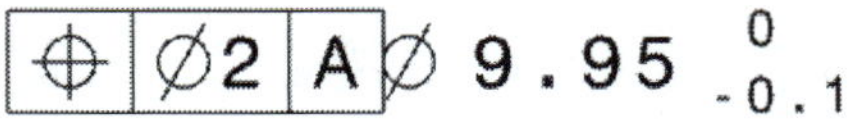
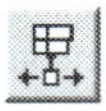 **Center Horizontally**	Position the left side of the annotation at the center of the base annotation. This option can be used in conjunction with the other four alignment options. A bottom-center alignment is shown below. 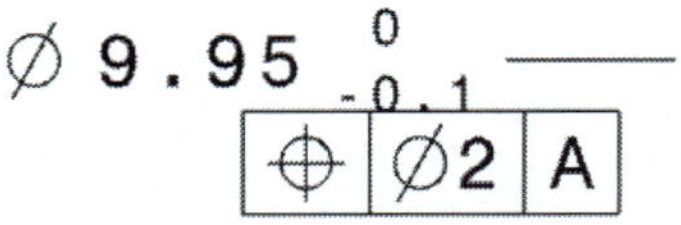
Offset	Move the annotation by the specified distance in the alignment direction. A bottom alignment that is offset by 4mm is shown below. Since a bottom alignment is used, the annotation is offset downwards. 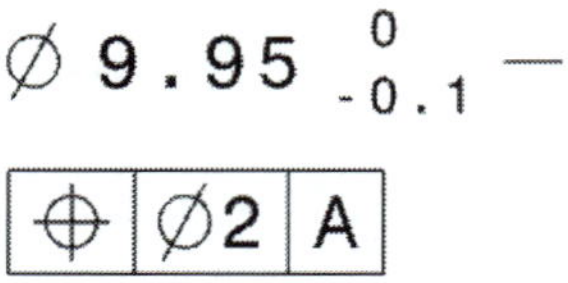

Once the positioning options have been specified, you can group additional annotations to the base annotation.

Step 4 - Group additional annotations, if required.

To group further annotations to the base annotation, select them in the model. The annotation is added to the References list and the **Alignment** and **Offset** options now apply to the last annotation selected.

In the example shown in Figure 5–14, the position tolerance is grouped to the toleranced dimension using a bottom alignment and offset of 4mm. The perpendicular tolerance is grouped using a bottom alignment and 0mm offset.

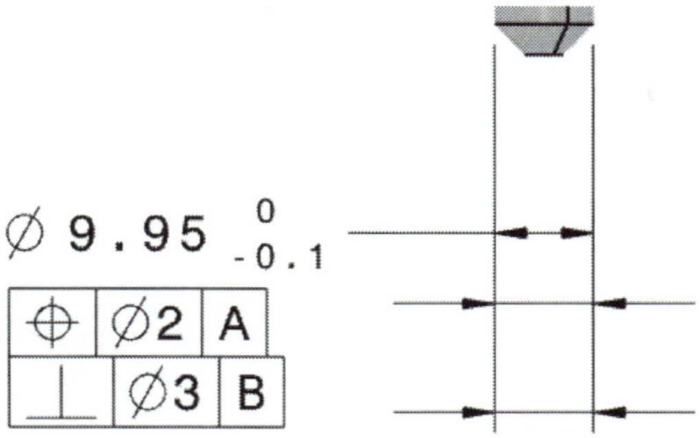

Figure 5–14

Step 5 - Complete the grouping.

Click **OK** to complete the grouping operation.

Once the annotations are successfully grouped, you might have to delete any detached leaders that were left behind when an annotation was grouped. This can be done by selecting the leader lines and pressing <Delete>.

Automatic Grouping

Automatic grouping is very similar to manual grouping, allowing for many different annotations placed on one element to be grouped to act as one. The major difference is you are not given any options for positioning as you are with the manual grouping command.

Hold <Ctrl> and select the annotations on the same element that you wish to group, then select  (Automatic) from the Annotation section of the Action Bar. It is included by default, unlike the Manual grouping tool. The annotations group together into their default locations, as shown in Figure 5–15.

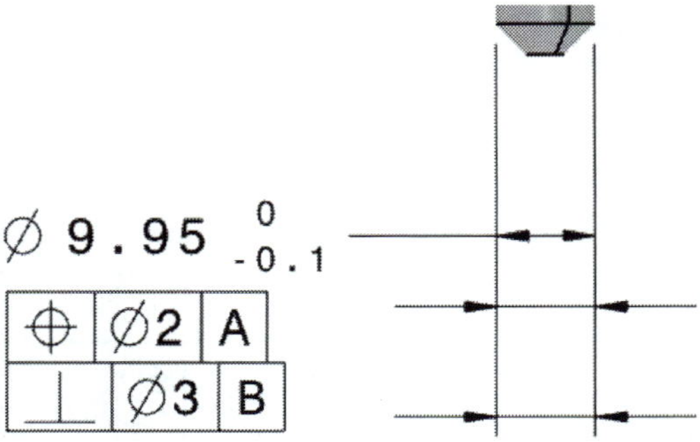

Figure 5–15

5.5 3D Annotation Filters

When viewing a detailed part or product with many annotations, it can be helpful to use a filter to clear up the display. This enables you to hide unwanted annotations and only display those annotations that are applicable to the current model view or application.

General Steps

Use the following general steps to filter annotations:

1. Start the filter operation.
2. Define the filter options.
3. Complete the filter operation.

Step 1 - Start the filter operation.

In the Tools section of the Action Bar, click  (3D Annotation Filter). The 3D Annotation Filter dialog box opens, as shown in Figure 5–16.

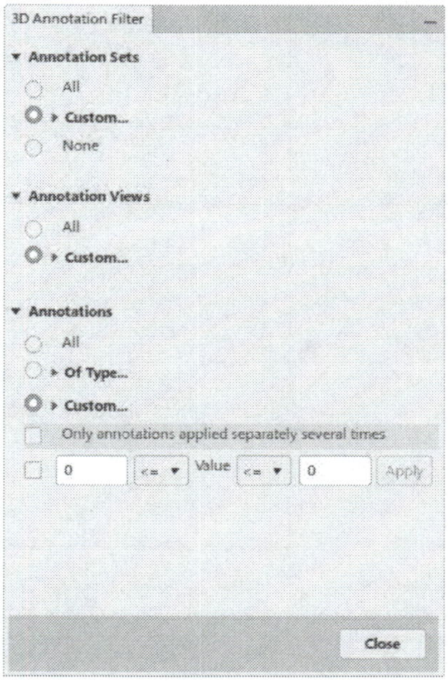

Figure 5–16

Step 2 - Define the filter options.

The 3D Annotation Filter window contains options for three main categories:

- Annotation Sets
- Annotation Views
- Annotations

Annotation Sets

Under the *Annotation Sets* category, you are given three more subcategories: **All**, **Custom**, and **None**. If selecting **All**, CATIA will give you a warning message informing you that displaying all annotation sets can take longer and be more difficult to read. While this is true for parts with many annotations or large products, it can be nice to start with seeing them all and whittle them down as needed.

Selecting **Custom** enables you to include and exclude annotation sets from the filter. Because all annotation views and annotations are sub-elements of annotation sets, if an annotation set is excluded from the filter, its sub-elements will be excluded as well. In other words, to be able to see annotation views and annotations, the annotation set they were created in has to be included. Figure 5–17 shows an example for both a product and a part.

Product ***Part***

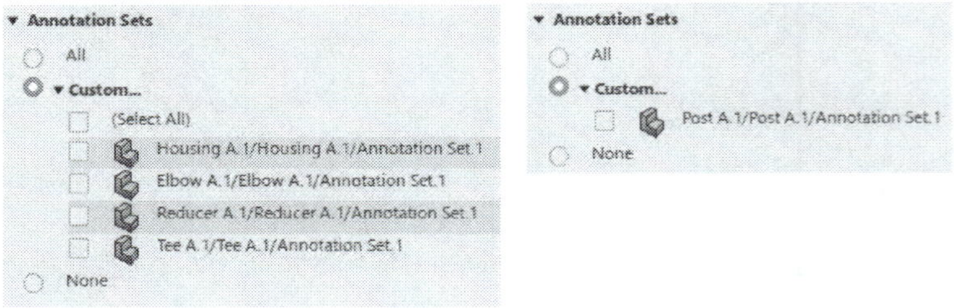

Figure 5–17

Finally, if **None** is selected, all annotation sets are excluded and any annotation views or annotations built within them are excluded as well.

Annotation Views

Under the *Annotation Views* category, you are given two subcategories: **All** and **Custom**. Selecting **All** means every annotation view of the selected annotation sets are included and will be displayed. Selecting **Custom** enables you to include and exclude available annotation views as needed, as shown in Figure 5–18.

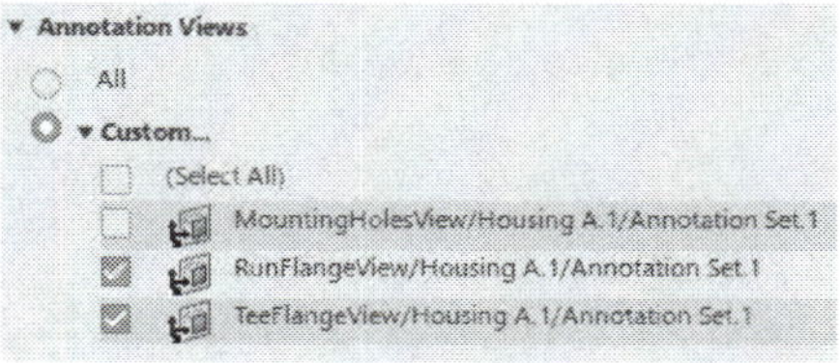

Figure 5–18

Annotations

Under the *Annotations* category, you are given four subcategories: **All**, **Of Type**, **Custom**, and **Value**. These subcategory filter choices are explained below.

Filter Choice	Description
All	The system displays all the annotations of the included annotation views.
Of Type	Enables you to select a specific type of annotation to display. The list is limited to the types of annotations that have been created in the model. Selections can be grouped by a generic type (e.g., Datum) or by a more specific type (e.g., Simple Datum). Some examples are: • Size: Linear Size • Datum: Simple Datum, Datum Reference Frame • Position Orientation and Runout: Position, Perpendicularity
Custom	Enables you to select a specific annotation to display. The list is limited to the types of annotations that have been created in the model. Selections can be grouped by type (e.g., Datums) or by a more specific annotation name (e.g., Datum Feature.1(A)). Some examples are: • Datums: Datum Feature.1(A), Datum Feature.2(B) • Geometrical Tolerances: Perpendicularity.1 • Dimensions: Dimension.1, Dimension.2, Linear Size.1

Value	Enables you to define the limits of the value of the tolerance that is displayed. Non-toleranced annotations are automatically hidden. To define this type of filter, select an operator in the drop-down list and enter a value. The following operators are available: • = equal to • < less than • <= less than or equal to For example, the filter shown below only displays annotations that have a tolerance value greater than or equal to 1, and less than a value of 2. 

An example of the 3D Annotation Filter customized at the *Annotations* level is shown in Figure 5–19.

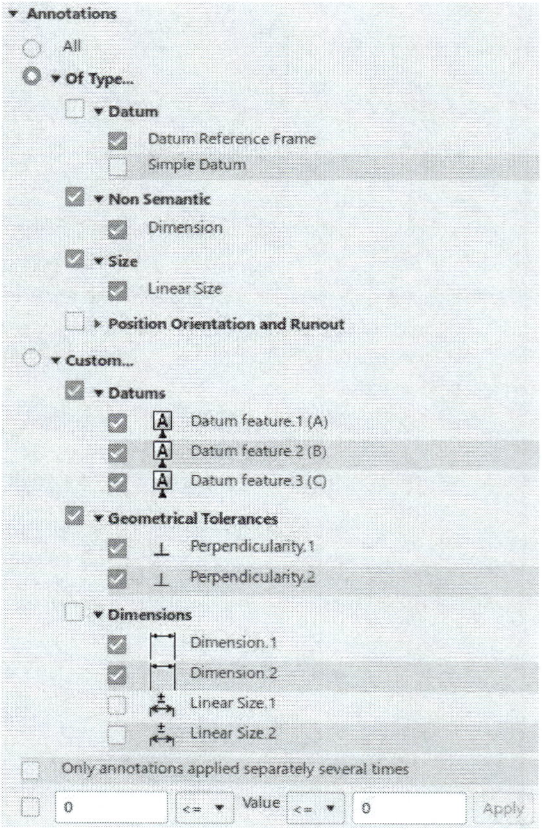

Figure 5–19

The display of the model updates dynamically as you check/uncheck the filter options.

Step 3 - Complete the filter operation.

Once all filter settings have been made, click **Close** to complete the filter operation.

5.6 Cameras

Cameras show a particular viewpoint of the part. They are useful for revealing detail on complex parts by showing a unique view.

How To: Save a Camera View

1. Adjust the orientation and position of the model using the following methods:
   - Dynamically orienting the model using the mouse.
   - Applying an existing named view.
   - Clicking  (Normal View) and then selecting a view.
2. Once the model has been oriented, in the View section of the Action Bar, click  (Views...). The Views dialog box opens, as shown in Figure 5–20.

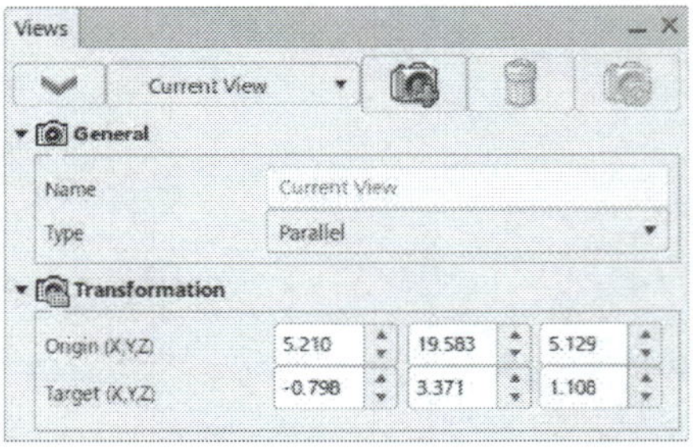

Figure 5–20

Note: The Views window can be expanded or minimized as needed. If minimized, select the  (Expand) icon, as shown in Figure 5–21.

Figure 5–21

3. Click  (Create Camera) to add a new view. The view is named Camera.1 by default.

   Retrieve views by accessing the Views dialog box and selecting the view's name.

5.7 Captures

Captures enable you to save different views of an annotated part. The following parameters can be customized for a capture:

- 3D annotation filters
- Cameras
- Cutting plane
- Mirror annotations

The captures are stored in the specification tree and can be displayed using the shortcut menu, as shown in Figure 5–22.

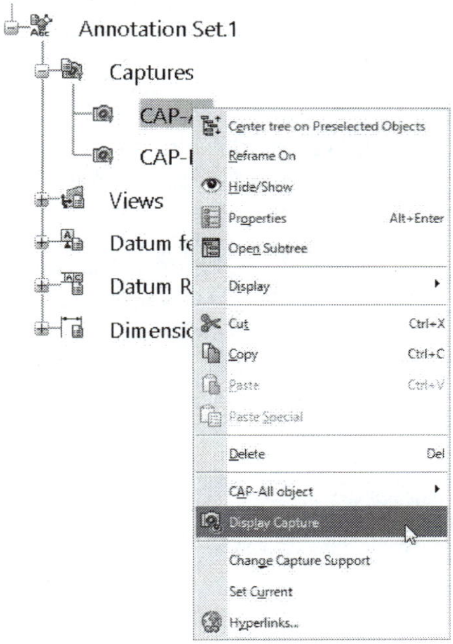

Figure 5–22

Prior to creating a capture, you must customize one or more of the following properties of the annotated model. You use these tools to specify the required display configurations for your capture.

- 3D Annotation Filters
- Cameras
- Cutting Plane
- Mirror Annotations
- Active View State
- Current State

3D Annotation Filters

Click (3D Annotation Filter) to filter out specific annotations from the display. Capture records the annotation display status of the model when it is created, but can be customized after the fact if needed.

Cameras

You can save a camera that has not been saved using (Views). Reorienting the model into a new position without applying a camera does not successfully save the orientation with the capture.

Mirror Annotations

Depending on the model orientation, you might need to click (Mirror annotations) to display the annotations correctly.

Current State

By default, new annotations that are added after a capture has been defined are not shown when the capture displays.

Right-click a capture in the specification tree and select **Set Current**. When the Current State tool is toggled on, the system places a record symbol on the capture icon in the specification tree, as shown in Figure 5–23. Consider this capture to be recording all new annotations made to the model until the Current State mode is disabled.

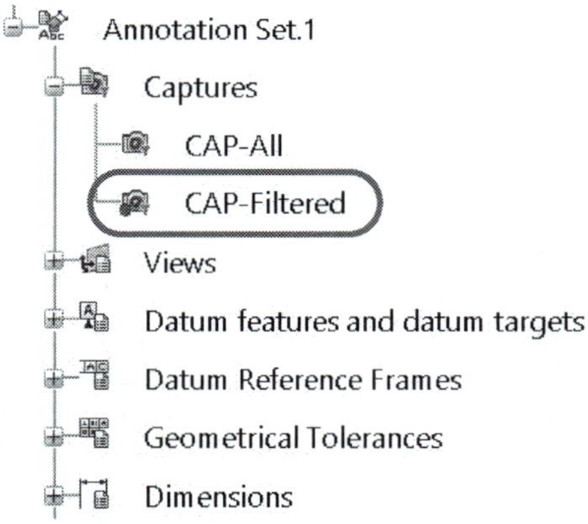

Figure 5–23

You can place more than one capture in Current State mode so that they all display the new annotations added to the model. You can access the **Current State** option by right-clicking on a capture in the specification tree and selecting **Set Current** (enable) or **Unset Current** (disable).

Visibility Status

With Captures, you can use the **Hide/Show** option to control the visibility of bodies and geometrical sets in parts and components in an assembly. By default, the visibility status of a part body, geometrical set, or component is not saved with a capture. However, these settings can be retained by right-clicking on the Capture in the specification tree and selecting **Properties**. In the *Visualizations* tab in the Properties dialog box, select the **Manage the visibility of product components, bodies and geometrical sets** option, as shown in Figure 5–24.

This option can be set for all future captures by selecting ***Me> Preferences>App Preferences>3D Modeling>Mechanical Systems>3D Tolerancing and Annotation****. In the View/Annotation Plane arrow, select the* ***Manage the visibility of product components, bodies and geometrical sets*** *option.*

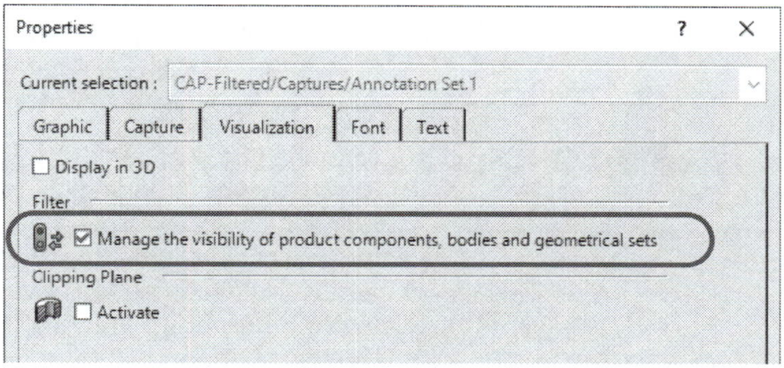

Figure 5–24

Once the view settings are applied, click  (Capture) from the View Layout section of the Action Bar. The Capture Creation dialog box opens, as shown in Figure 5–25.

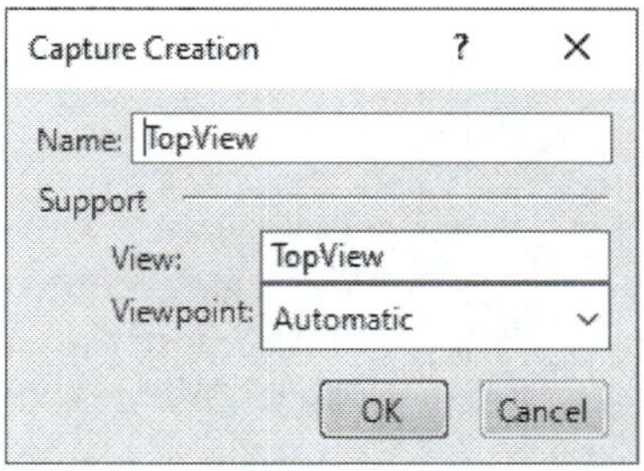

Figure 5–25

A capture is always associated with a view/annotation plane. If your model does not contain any view/annotation plane, a projection view/annotation plane is created parallel to the xy plane, passing through the origin.

When the model contains a view/annotation plane, the active view/annotation plane is selected by default. However, you can select another view/annotation plane by selecting the **View** field and selecting a view/annotation plane from the specification tree or from the model.

By default, the capture name and viewpoint is the same as the associated view/annotation plane, but you can edit the **Name** field and Viewpoint as required. The Viewpoint is selected from the list of existing cameras.

Enter a name for the capture and click **OK**.

Cutting Plane

In order for the system to display a section in a capture, you have to enter Edit Filter mode. After a capture is created, double-click it in the specification tree. Click  (Cutting Plane), then click **OK** to exit Edit Filter mode.

Edit Filter

When a capture has been displayed, it automatically sets the state to **Current**, meaning it is recording changes made to the annotations being displayed. At the same time, the name of the capture is shown in the upper right corner of the screen. If you hover over that name, you have up to three options: **Remove Current Filter**, **Edit Filter**, and **Persist Annotation Set items visibility**, as shown in Figure 5–26.

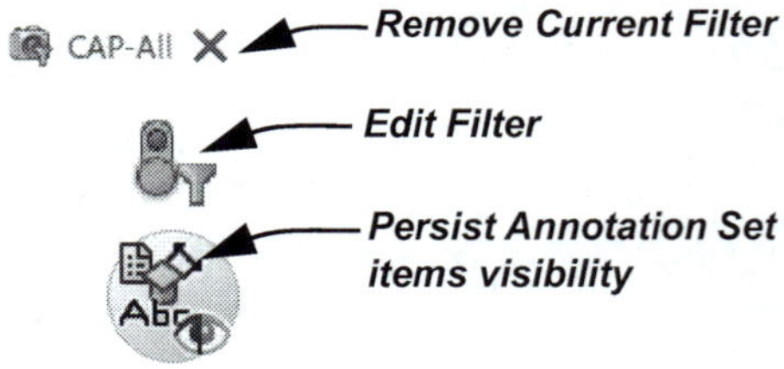

Figure 5–26

Selecting **Remove Current Filter** in this case removes the name in the upper right corner. The display might change depending on what the display looked like before **Display the Capture** was chosen. If the capture was different from what the original display looked like, the display will revert back to its original look. If they were the same then no change is noticed.

When the displayed capture is different from the original displayed model, the **Persist Annotation Set items visibility** option will become available. Selecting this icon will ensure that the display of the current capture will be retained even after **Remove Current Filter** is selected. It sets the current display to that of the current capture.

*Edit Filter can also be selected by right-clicking on a view and selecting **Filter> Edit Filter*** *or by double-clicking on a capture in the tree.*

Selecting **Edit Filter** will open the Edit Filter window, as shown in Figure 5–27.

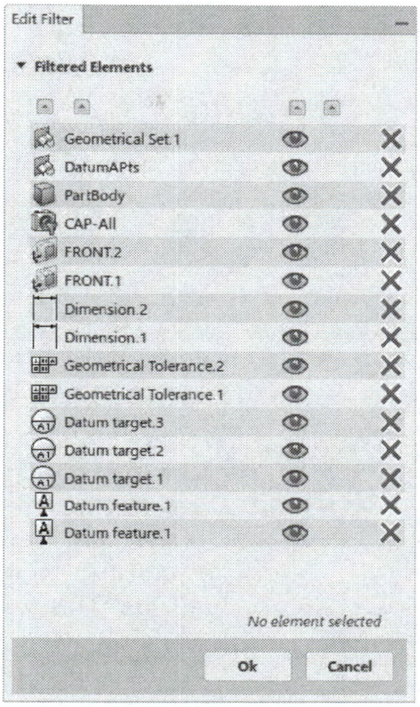

Figure 5–27

All of the currently displayed elements will be listed in this window. These items can be further customized by selecting the  (Activate/Deactivate visibility property) icon to turn on/off the display or by selecting  (Remove Element) to remove the item from the list.

Visualization Chooser

While the Edit Filter window is open, an icon called the Visualization Chooser (shown in Figure 5–28) will be available in the upper right hand corner. Selecting this icon lets you select from three different display options.

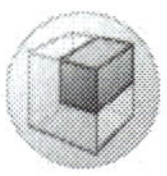

Figure 5–28

Icon	Name	Description
	Standard previsualization mode	Shows the context of the filter.
	Reversed previsualization mode	Shows all the elements that are not contained in the filter.
	Combined previsualization mode	Shows all the elements that are not contained in the filter in standard visualization, and shows the elements that are contained in the filter in half transparent and in specific color.

Select **OK** to complete the Edit Filter.

Hide and Show All Features

While both the 3D Annotation Filter and Edit Filter tools give a great amount of control over what annotations are displayed, if the goal is to simply hide or show all annotations quickly, there is a unique tool for just that. Right-click on the annotation set and select **Annotations/Features>Hide all features/Show all features**. This can be helpful when needing to reset the display back to an original look, especially if a default capture wasn't created. This does create a filter and the **Persist Annotation Set items visibility** icon will need to be chosen if you want this filter to be applied to the current display.

Delete History of Displayed Views and Capture

When a view or a capture is displayed, CATIA will record that those objects have been used by adding a purple highlight over the capture or view that has been used, as shown on the left in Figure 5–29. Functionally this doesn't change anything, but it lets the user know that those objects have been used. To remove this marking and reset the recording of these objects, right-click on the annotation set and select **Delete History Of Displayed Views And Captures**. The purple highlights will be removed, as shown on the right in Figure 5–29.

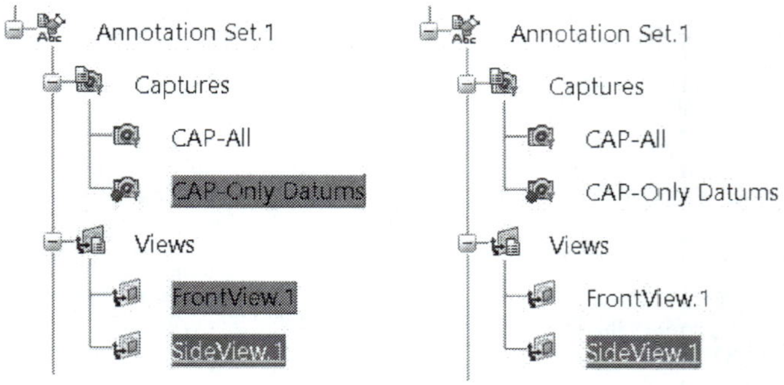

Figure 5–29

Capture Management

By default, annotations are not included if they are created when there is no current capture in the model. You can manually associate or disassociate an annotation from a capture using the Capture Management tool.

You can automatically add new annotations to an existing capture using the Current State tool.

How To: Add Annotations to a Capture(s)

1. Select the annotations to be added the capture(s).
2. Right-click and select **Capture Management**. The Capture Management dialog box opens, as shown in Figure 5–30. The left side of the dialog box displays all captures in the model that do not currently contain the selected annotations. The right side of the dialog box displays any captures that do currently contain the selected annotations.

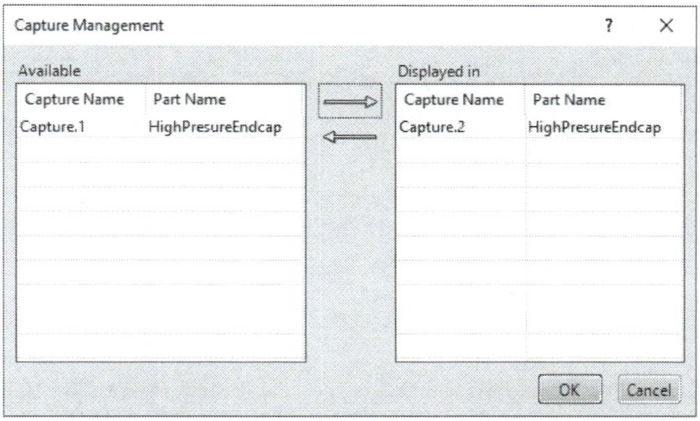

Figure 5–30

3. To add the selected annotations to a capture, select the capture in the Available list, and click . To remove an annotation from a specific capture, select the capture in the Displayed in list, and click 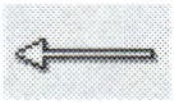.
4. Click **OK** to close the Capture Management dialog box and apply the change.

Default Capture

When a capture is applied to the model, you cannot automatically restore the model to its default display status. Therefore, you should create a default capture (recommended) as the first capture in the model.

1. Ensure that all annotations display.
2. Create a camera with an appropriate orientation.
3. Select  (Capture) from the View Layout section of the Action Bar.

4. Edit the *Name* and set the View Point to the appropriate camera.
5. Click **OK**.

   This creates a capture that shows all annotations and displays the model in a default position.

5.8 Geometry Connection Management

The Geometry Connection Management tool enables you to investigate, change, add, and rename geometric references that have been selected to create an annotation. This is useful when executing design changes, since modifications to the underlying geometry might cause annotations to lose their references and fail.

This section describes how to change a reference using the model shown in Figure 5–31. This model contains a toleranced dimension (Dimension.1) and a simple datum. The hole position is currently dimensioned to the incorrect face and must be modified to reference Datum A.

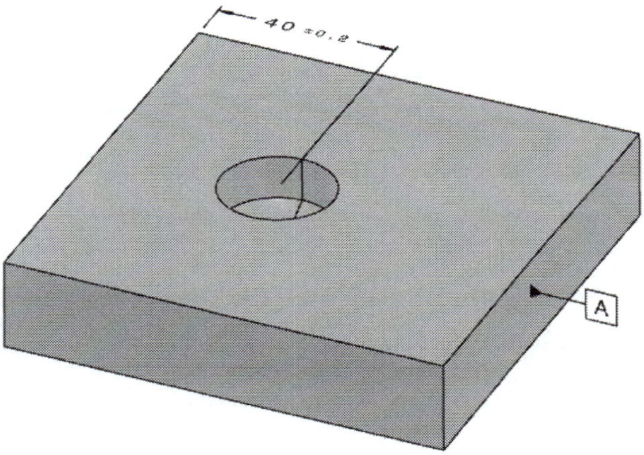

Figure 5–31

General Steps

Use the following general steps to modify an annotation reference:

1. Start the Connection Management operation.
2. Replace the reference.
3. Check the validity and complete the operation.

Step 1 - Start the Connection Management operation.

Right-click on **Dimension.1** in the tree and select **Associated Geometry>Geometry Connection Management**. The Connection Management dialog box opens, as shown in Figure 5–32.

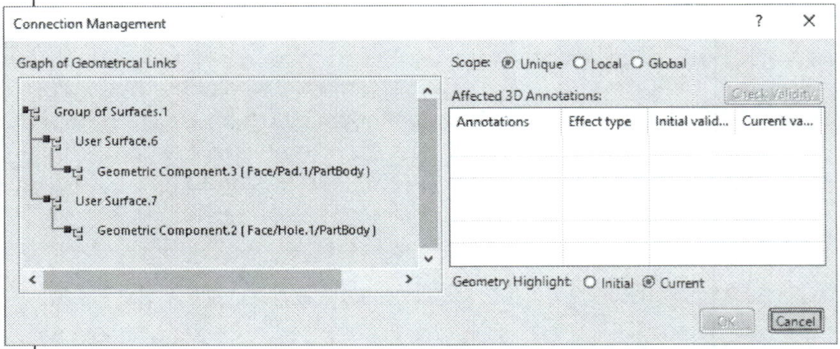

Figure 5–32

The left side of the dialog box displays references that belong to **Dimension.1**. You can highlight these references on the part model by selecting them in the dialog box.

Step 2 - Replace the reference.

Right-click on the reference to be modified and select **Connect**, as shown in Figure 5–33.

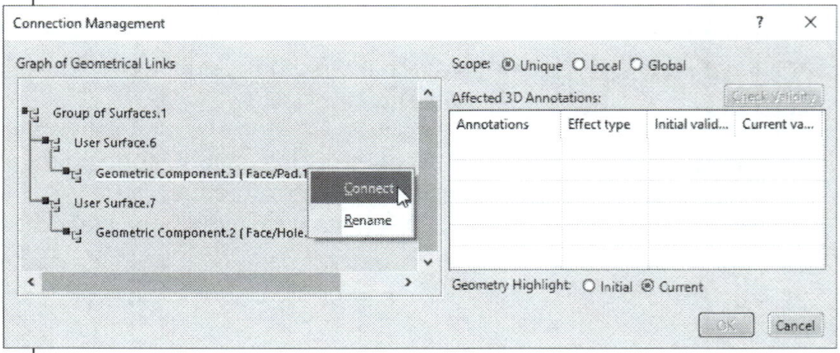

Figure 5–33

When this is done, the icon for the surface changes, as shown in Figure 5–34, indicating that a new reference can be selected.

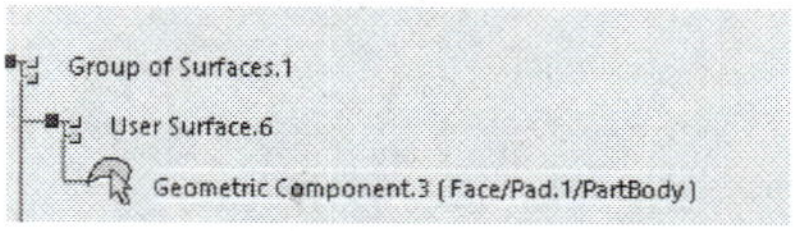

Figure 5–34

Select the new reference in the model. In this example, the Datum A face is selected. The Connection Management dialog box updates as shown in Figure 5–35.

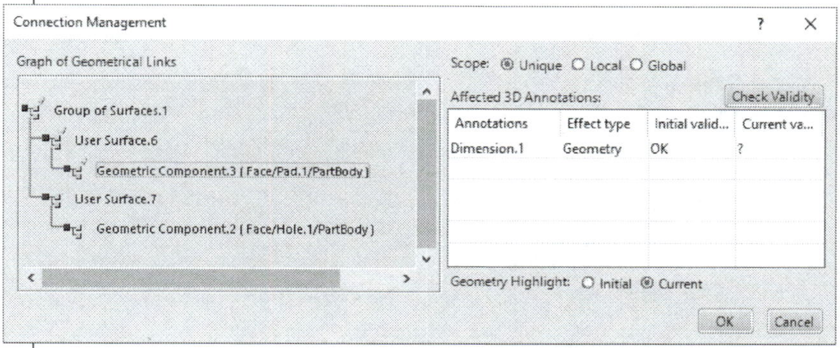

Figure 5–35

Step 3 - Check the validity and complete the operation.

Click **Check Validity** to confirm that the selected reference did not cause a failure in the annotation. If the reference causes a failure, the Current validity column changes to KO. If the reference is successful, the Current validity column changes to OK, as shown in Figure 5–36.

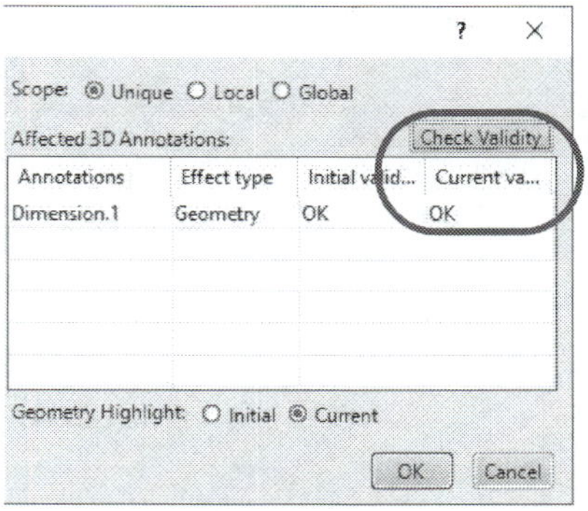

Figure 5–36

Once the reference has been successfully checked, click **OK** to complete the operation. With the new reference for the dimension, the model displays as shown in Figure 5–37.

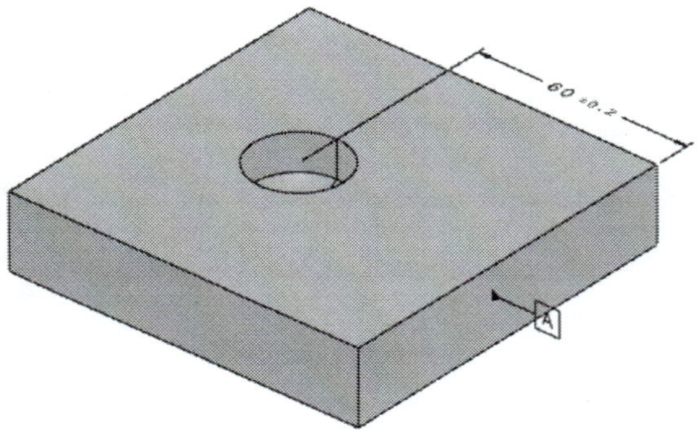

Figure 5–37

Replacing a Datum Reference Frame

You can change the datum reference frame that was used to construct a geometrical tolerance.

How To: Replace a Datum Reference Frame

1. Ensure that the new datum reference frame has been created. For example, the new datum reference frame A|B|C has been created, as shown in Figure 5–38.

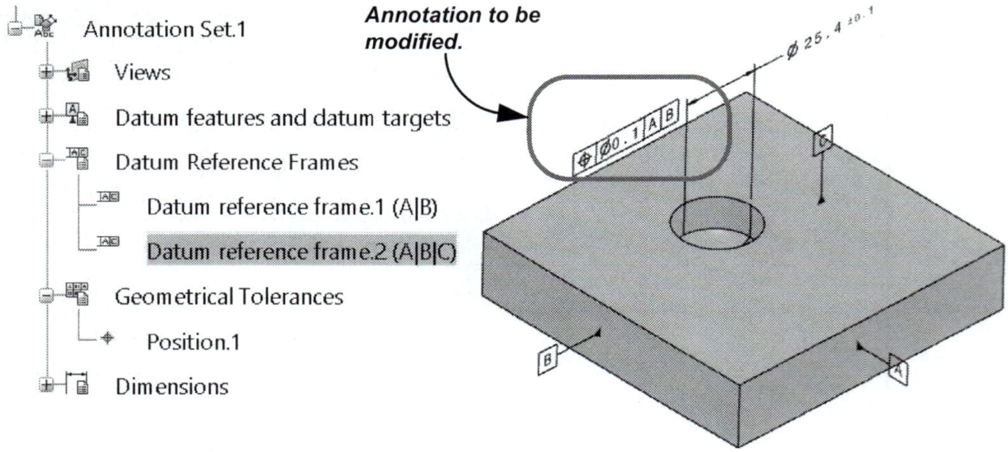

Figure 5–38

2. Right-click on the geometrical tolerance and select **Replace Datum Reference Frame**, as shown in Figure 5–39.

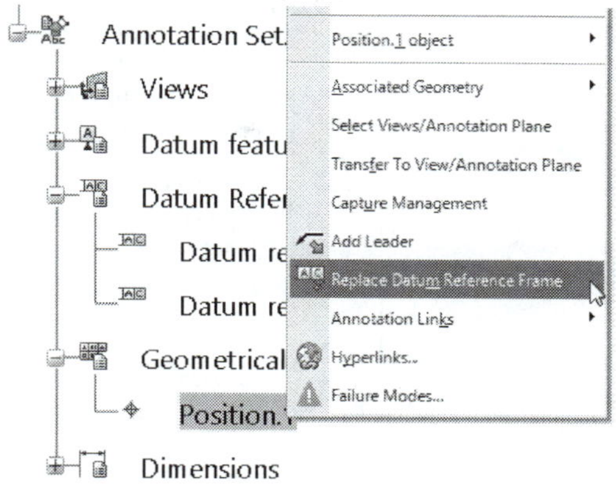

Figure 5–39

3. Select a new datum reference frame. The system updates the tolerance to reference the new datum reference frame, as shown in Figure 5–40.

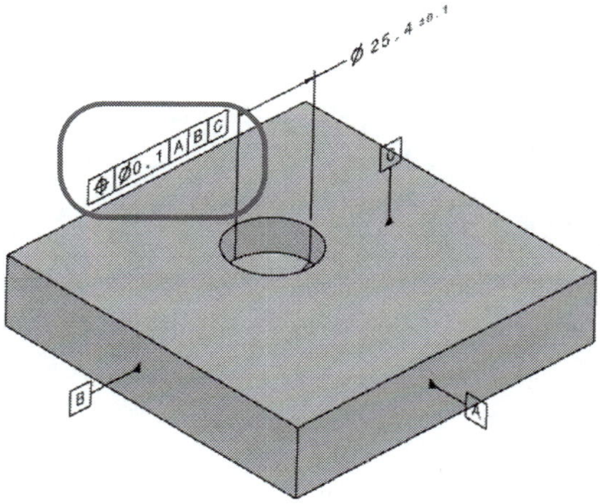

Figure 5–40

Practice 5a Visualization

Practice Objectives

- Create a default capture.
- Create various captures to manage the model display.

In this practice, you will create a variety of captures from the model shown in Figure 5–41. These captures use annotation filters and cameras during their creation.

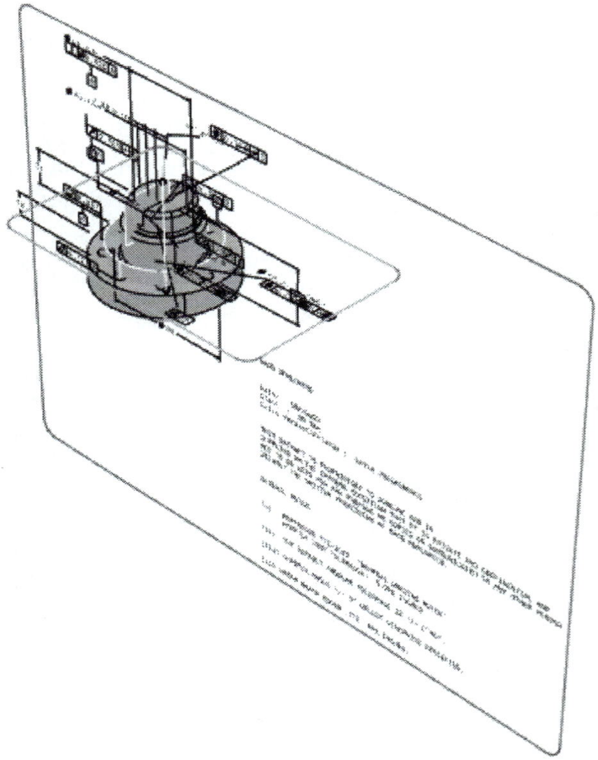

Figure 5–41

Task 1 - Open a part that contains tolerancing and annotations.

1. Import and open **LockingHub_Finished.3dxml**. The part displays as shown in Figure 5–42.

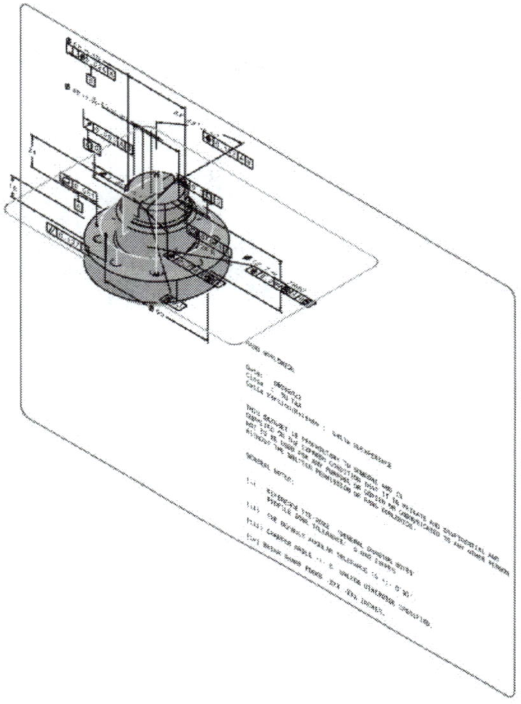

Figure 5–42

Task 2 - Create a default capture.

Design Considerations

In this task, you will use the capture functionality to create a capture of the native state of the model. Since you cannot reset a capture, the default capture enables you to return to the display properties of the original model. In this task, the default capture is called CAP-ALL.

1. In the View section of the Action Bar, select  (Views...).
2. Click  (Create Camera). **Camera.1** is created.
3. Close the Views window by selecting .
4. In the View Layout section of the Action Bar, select  (Capture).
5. Edit the *Name* to **CAP-ALL** in the Capture Creation dialog box.
6. In the Viewpoint drop-down list, select **Camera.1**.

Note: The ability to rename cameras wasn't working as of the time of writing this exercise.

7. Click **OK**. The capture displays in the specification tree, as shown in Figure 5–43.

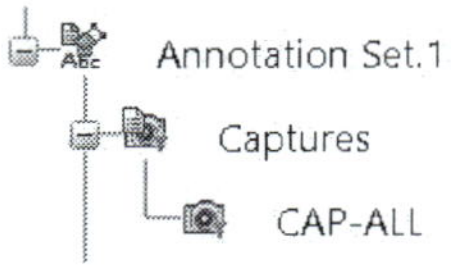

Figure 5–43

Task 3 - Create a filtered capture.

1. In the Tools section of the Action Bar, click  (3D Annotation Filter). The 3D Annotation Filter dialog box opens, as shown in Figure 5–44.

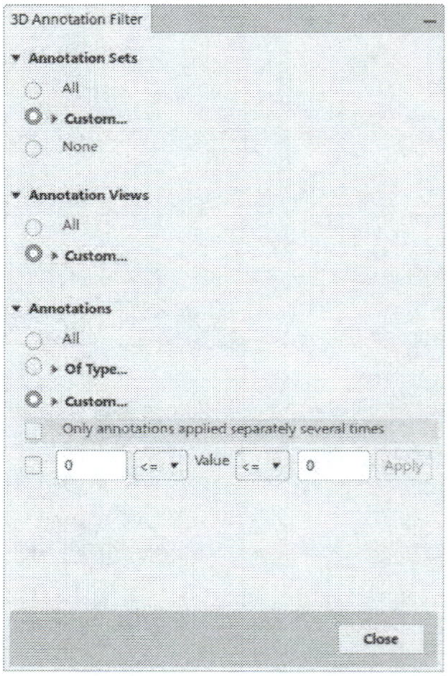

Figure 5–44

2. Under the *Annotation Views* section, expand **Custom...**.

3. Click on **(Select All)** to deselect all of the annotations. The 3D Annotation Filter window updates as shown in Figure 5–45.

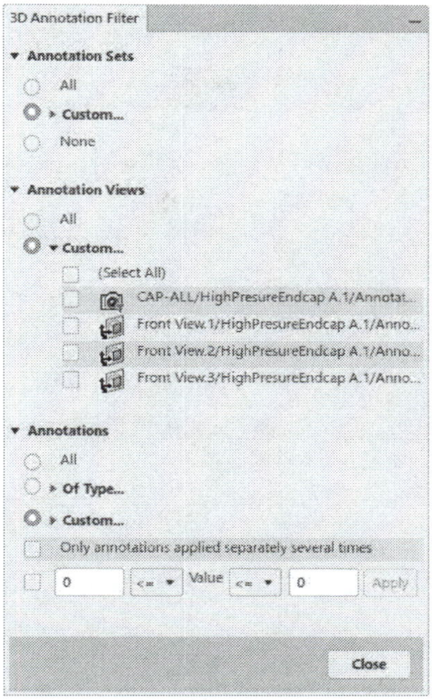

Figure 5–45

4. Under the *Annotations* section, expand both **Custom...** and **Dimensions**.
5. Select the following dimensions, as shown in Figure 5–46:
   - **Linear Size.3**
   - **Linear Size.4**
   - **Linear Size.5**

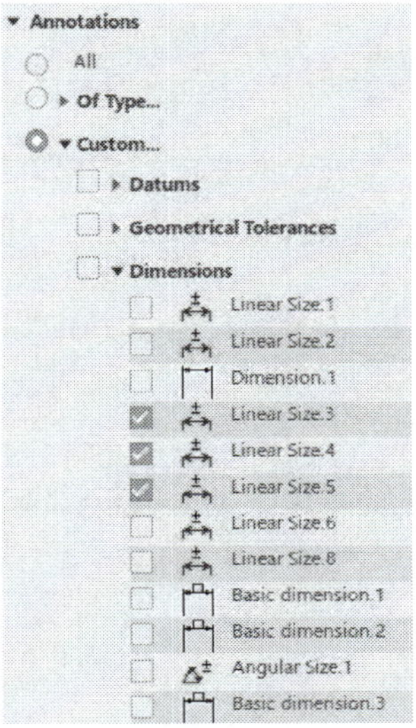

Figure 5–46

- The model updates to display just those three dimensions.

6. Select **Close** to complete the 3D Annotation Filter.
7. In the View Layout section of the Action Bar, select  (Capture).
8. Enter **CAP-FEATURE_001** in the Capture Creation dialog box.
9. Leave the View as **Front.View.1** and the Viewpoint as **Automatic**.
10. Click **OK** to complete the capture. The model displays as shown in Figure 5–47.

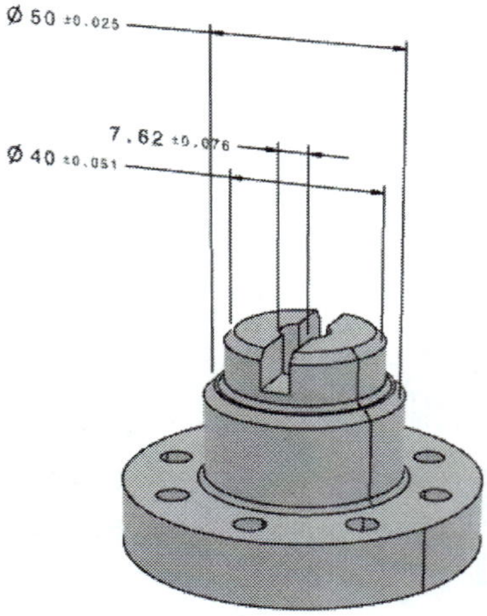

Figure 5–47

Task 4 - Display existing captures.

1. Right-click on **CAP-ALL** and select **Display Capture**, as shown in Figure 5–48, to display all annotations.

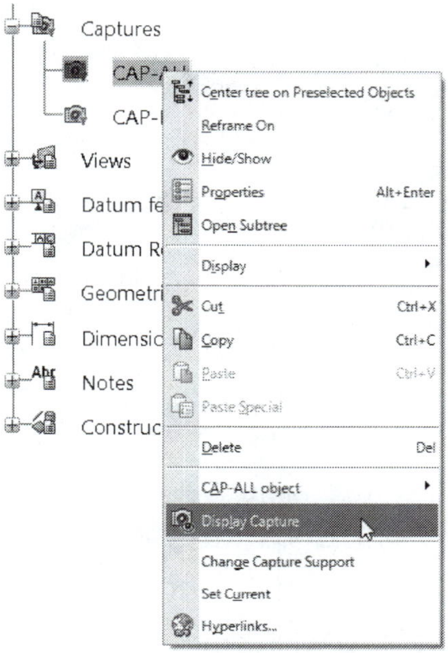

Figure 5–48

The default CAP-ALL capture displays as shown in Figure 5–49.

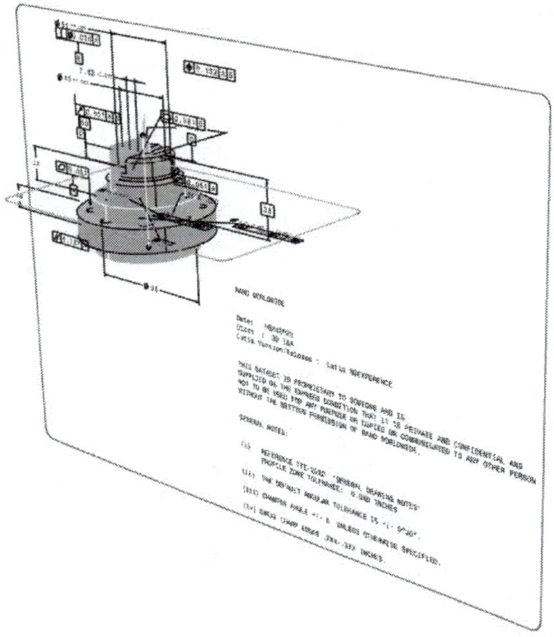

Figure 5–49

*A capture uses the current annotation plane. The **CAP-FEATURE_001** capture orients to the **Front.View.1** annotation plane because you left the Viewpoint as Automatic.*

2. Right-click on **CAP-FEATURE_001** and select **Display Capture**. The model displays as shown in Figure 5–50.

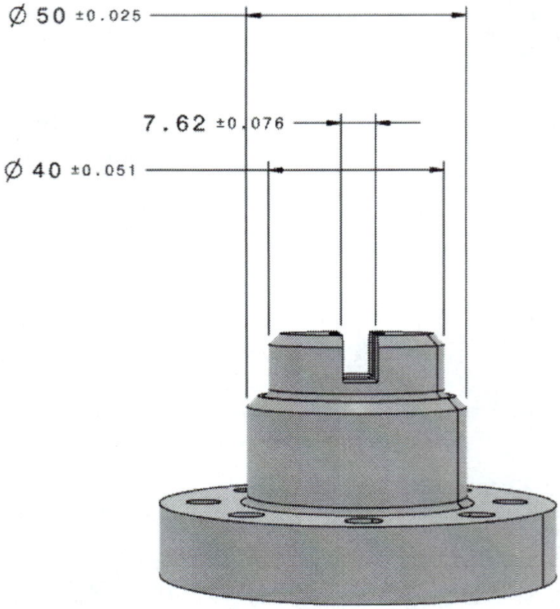

Figure 5–50

3. Right-click on **CAP-ALL** and select **Display Capture**.

4. In the upper right-hand corner, hover over the **CAP-ALL** capture name. Icons will appear underneath it, as shown in Figure 5–51.

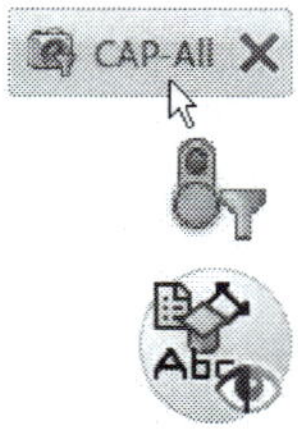

Figure 5–51

5. Select the  (Persist Annotation Set item visibility) icon to apply the capture to a display.

6. In the upper right-hand corner, select the **CAP-ALL** capture name to remove the current filter.

7. Right-click on **Annotation Set.1** in the specification tree and select **Delete History Of Displayed Views And Captures** to clear the purple highlights on the previously displayed captures.

Task 5 - Create a new capture.

1. In the Tools section of the Action Bar, click  (3D Annotation Filter).

2. In the *Annotation Views* node, select **All**.

3. In the *Annotations* node, expand the **Custom...**.

4. Deselect all of the categories except for **Geometrical Tolerances**, as shown in Figure 5–52.

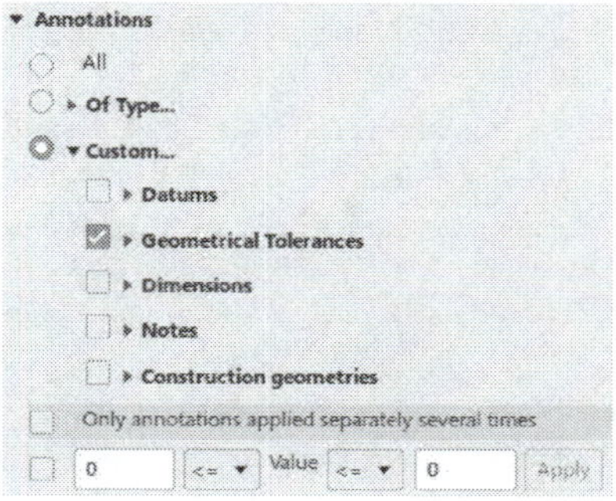

Figure 5–52

5. Click **Close**. Only the geometric tolerances and view borders display, as shown in Figure 5–53.

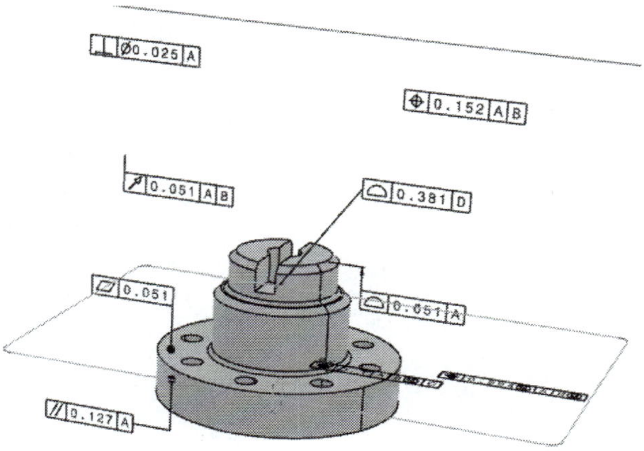

Figure 5–53

6. In the Tools section of the Action Bar, click  (3D Annotation Filter).

7. Expand the **Construction geometries** node under *Annotations* and select the three items shown in Figure 5–54.

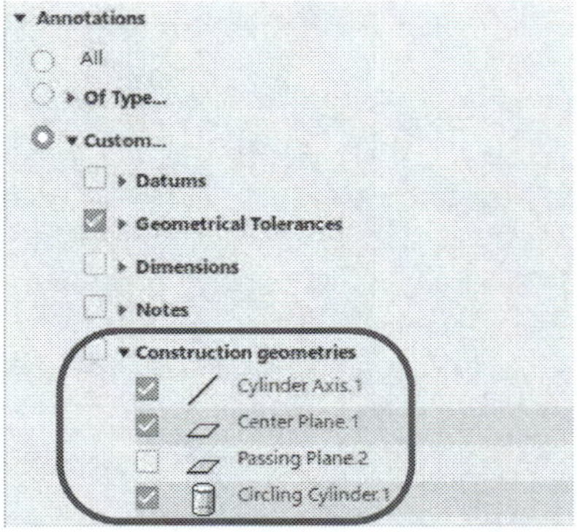

Figure 5–54

8. Click **Close**.

9. Zoom in on the model. The construction geometries display, as shown in Figure 5–55.

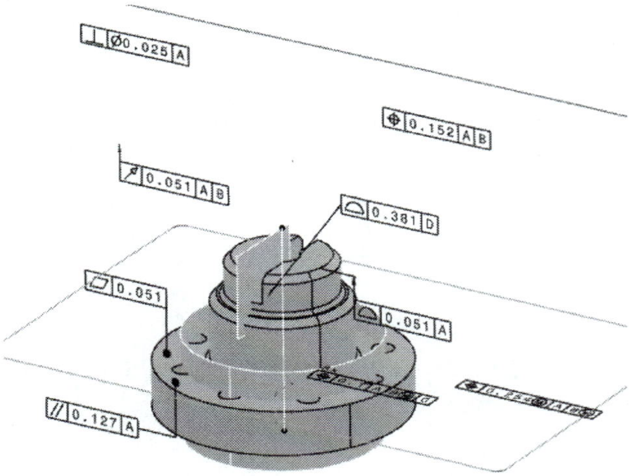

Figure 5–55

10. In the View section of the Action Bar, click  (Views...).

11. Click  (Create Camera). **Camera.2** is created.

12. Close the Views window by selecting .

13. In the View Layout section of the Action Bar, select  (Capture).

14. Edit the *Name* to **CAP-GDT** in the Capture Creation dialog box.

15. In the Viewpoint drop-down list, select **Camera.2**.

16. Click **OK**.

17. Display the **CAP-ALL** capture then display **CAP-GDT** and note that the view is automatically zoomed.

18. Display the **CAP-ALL** capture.

19. In the upper right-hand corner, hover over the **CAP-ALL** capture name. Icons will appear underneath it, as shown in Figure 5–56.

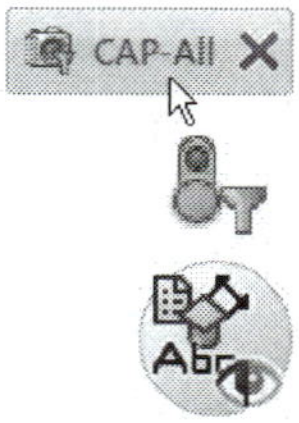

Figure 5–56

20. Select the  (Persist Annotation Set item visibility) icon to apply the capture to a display.

21. In the upper right-hand corner, select the **CAP-ALL** capture name to remove the current filter.

22. Right-click on **Annotation Set.1** in the specification tree and select **Delete History Of Displayed Views And Captures** to clear the purple highlights on the previously displayed captures.

Task 6 - Create a new capture.

1. In the Tools section of the Action Bar, click  (3D Annotation Filter).

2. Under the *Annotation Views* node, expand **Custom...** and select **(Select All)** to clear the selection of all annotation views.

3. Under the *Annotations*>**Custom...** node, select the following as shown in Figure 5–57:

   - **Flatness.1** (Geometrical Tolerances)
   - **Position surfacic profile.1** (Geometrical Tolerances)
   - **Basic dimension.1** (Dimensions)

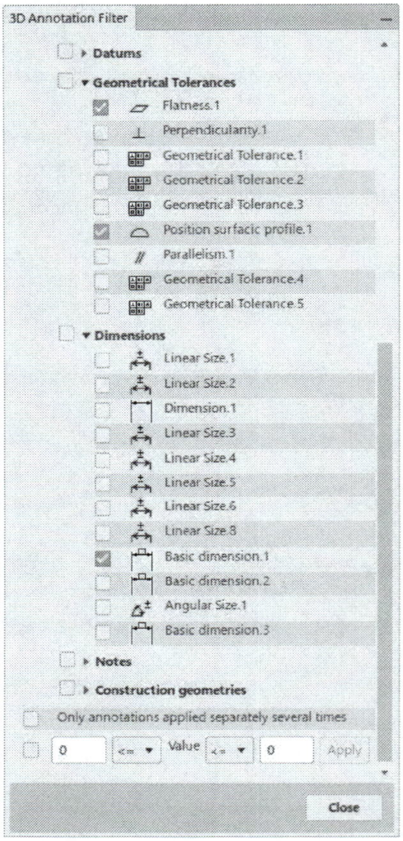

Figure 5–57

4. Click **Close** to apply and complete the filter.

5. Under the View section of the Action Bar, click  (Cutting Plane).

6. Click 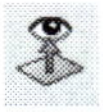 (Normal View) and select **Front View.1** from the specification tree.

   The model displays as shown in Figure 5–58.

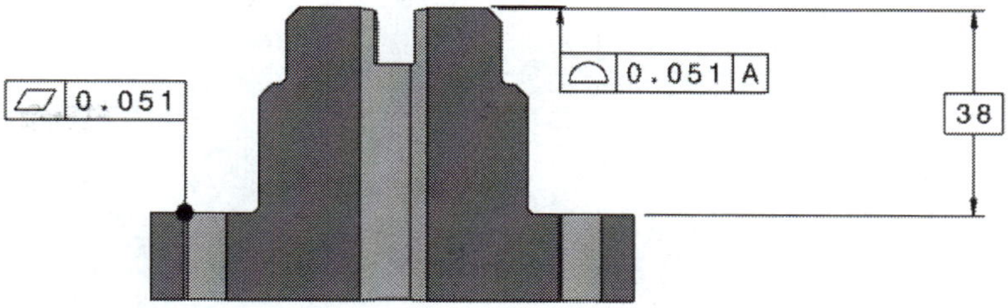

Figure 5–58

7. Click (Views...).

8. Click (Create Camera). **Camera.3** is created.

9. Close the Views window by selecting .

10. In the View Layout section of the Action Bar, select (Capture).

11. Edit the *Name* to **CAP-SECTION** in the Capture Creation dialog box.

12. In the Viewpoint drop-down list, select **Camera.3**.

13. Click **OK**.

14. Display the **CAP-ALL** capture. The model displays as shown in Figure 5–59.

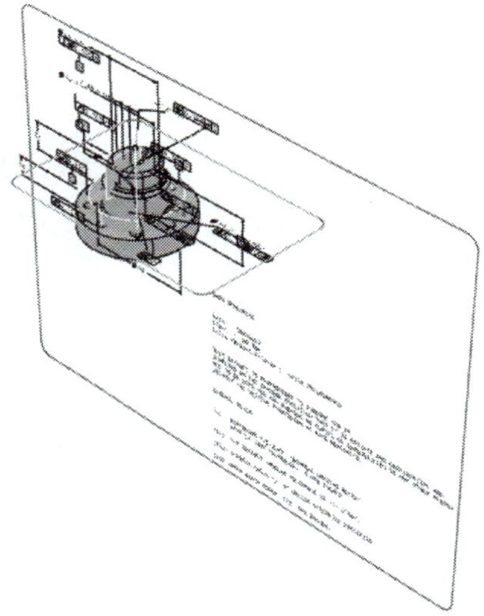

Figure 5–59

15. Display the **CAP-SECTION** capture. The model displays as shown in Figure 5–60.

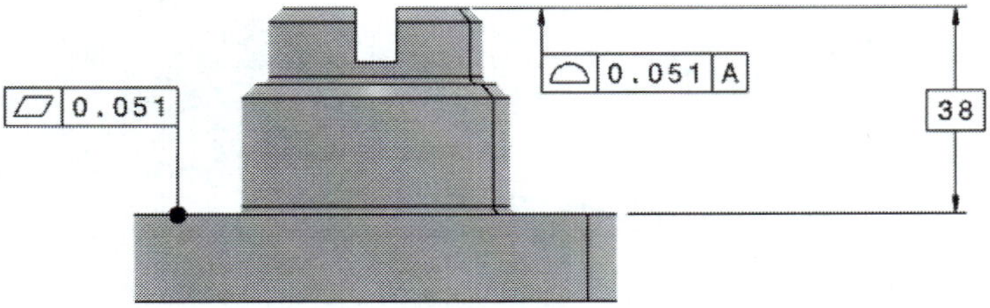

Figure 5–60

Design Considerations

The cutting plane setting does not save with the capture; however, the reason CATIA is not showing the section of the model is not because it wasn't saved, but because by displaying the capture that means the capture is currently selected. When you select a capture or view, the cutting plane won't be shown.

16. Select the background of the model to display the cutting plane.
17. Select **CAP-SECTION** under *Captures* from the tree to see the section disappear again. The only way to turn off the section is to toggle off  (Cutting Plane).
18. Display the **CAP-ALL** capture.
19. In the upper right-hand corner, hover over the **CAP-ALL** filter.
20. Select the  (Persist Annotation Set item visibility) icon to apply the capture to a display.
21. In the upper right-hand corner, select the **CAP-ALL** capture name to remove the current filter.
22. Save the model and close the file.

Practice 5b

Capture

Practice Objectives

- Change the annotation standard.
- Create captures while keeping the Hide/Show status.
- Modify cutting planes.

In this practice, you will create captures that retain the visibility settings of both solid bodies and geometrical sets. You will then modify the appearance of cutting sections in a body by changing its material properties. The model used in this practice is shown in Figure 5–61.

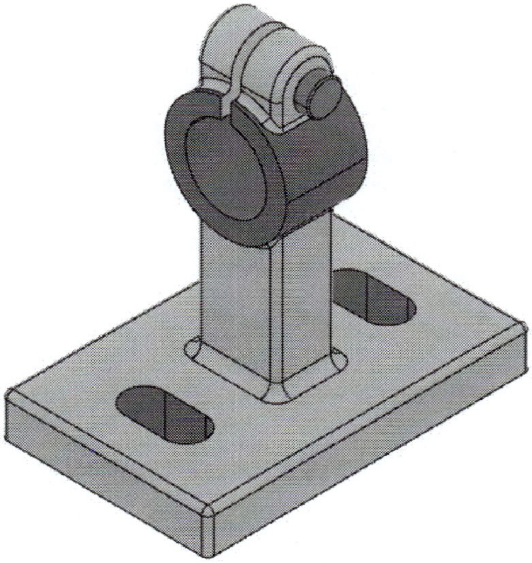

Figure 5–61

Task 1 - Import and open a part containing multiple bodies.

1. Import and open **FlangeLock_Capture.3dxml**. The part displays as shown in Figure 5–62. Note that the part includes geometrical sets, two solid bodies, and an annotation.

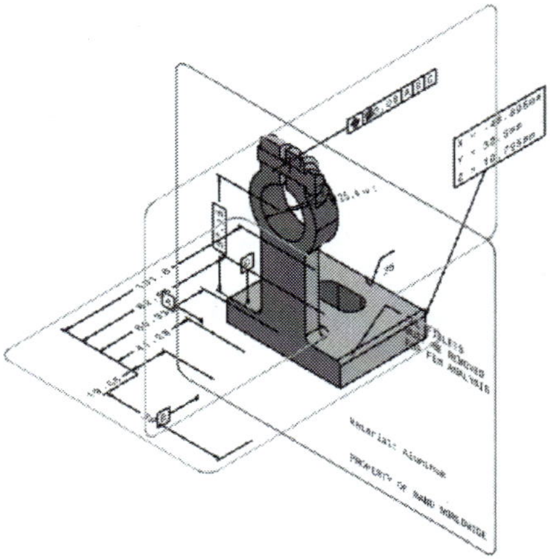

Figure 5–62

2. If the model isn't sectioned as shown in Figure 5–62, turn on  (Cutting Plane) from the View section of the Action Bar.

Task 2 - Change the annotation standard.

In this task, you will change the annotation standard from ASME to ANSI-ASME. This is done to demonstrate the ability to change the annotation standard at any time during the tolerancing process.

1. Right-click on **Annotation Set.1** and select **Properties**.

2. Select the *Standard* tab, then select **ANSI-ASME** in the drop-down list, as shown in Figure 5–63.

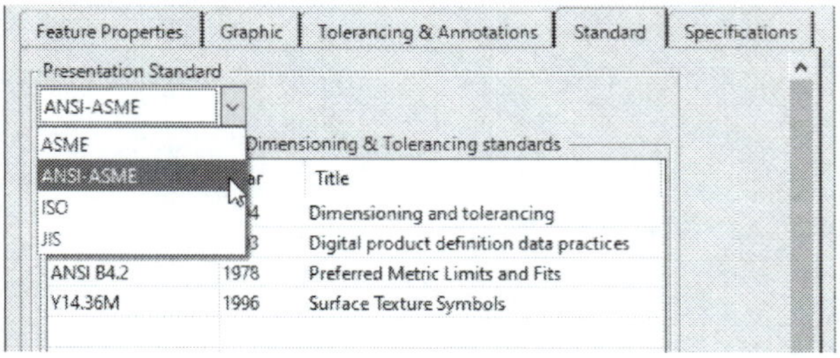

Figure 5–63

3. Click **OK** to change the annotation standard and close the Properties dialog box.
4. Right click **Annotation Set.1** and select **Local Update**.

Task 3 - Create a default capture.

In this task, you will create a default capture that displays all geometry and annotations. This capture is used to return the model to its original display.

1. Select **Me>Preferences>App Preferences>Mechanical Systems>3D Tolerancing and Annotation**.
2. Select the *View/Annotation Plane* arrow and ensure that the **Manage the visibility of Part instances, bodies and geometrical sets** option is selected.
3. In the View section of the Action Bar, select  (Views...).
4. Click  (Create Camera). **Camera.1** is created.
5. Close the Views window by selecting .
6. In the View Layout section of the Action Bar, select  (Capture).
7. Edit the *Name* to **DefaultCap** in the Capture Creation dialog box.
8. In the Viewpoint drop-down list, select **Camera.1**.
9. Click **OK**.

Task 4 - Create a capture with hidden components.

1. Hide the following elements:
   - **LockingPin body**
   - **Geometrical Set.1**

2. Create a second capture and name it **FlangeOnlyCap**. Set the *View Point* to **iso**, and click **OK**.

3. The **Geometrical Set.1** and **LockingPin** elements remain hidden, as shown in Figure 5–64.

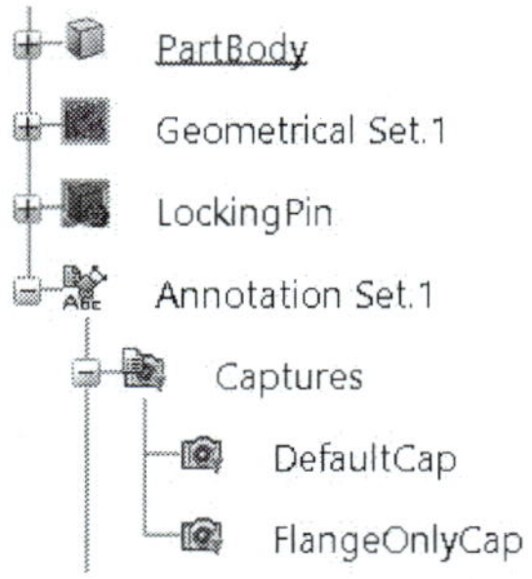

Figure 5–64

4. Display the **DefaultCap** capture by right-clicking on it in the specification tree and selecting **Display Capture**. The model displays with the **LockingPin body** and **Geometrical Set.1** visible.

5. Use the same method to display **FlangeOnlyCap**. The model displays with the **LockingPin body** and **Geometrical Set.1** hidden, as shown in Figure 5–65.

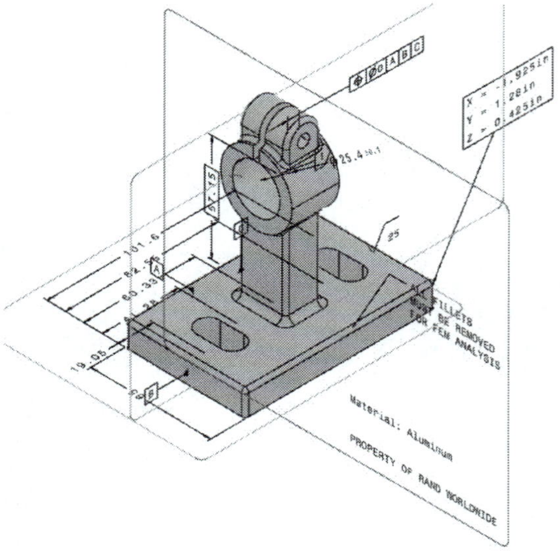

Figure 5–65

6. In the upper right-hand corner, select the **CAP-ALL** capture name to remove the current filter.

Task 5 - Modify and view the cutting plane visualization.

1. Select **Me>Preferences>App Preferences>Mechanical Systems>3D Tolerancing and Annotation** and select the *Display* arrow.
2. In the *Sectioning Properties* area, ensure that the *Background color* is set to **Custom**, and the *Pattern* is set to **Material**, as shown in Figure 5–66.

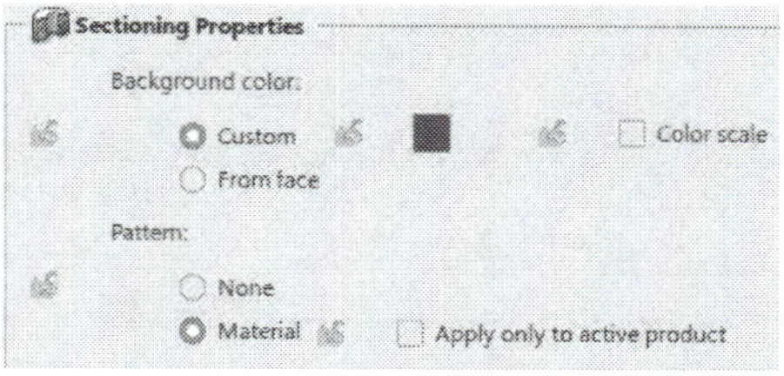

Figure 5–66

3. Click **OK** to close the Options dialog box.
4. Click  (View Modes...) from the View section of the Action Bar.
5. Select  (Shading with Materials) from the View Modes window.

Design Considerations

To display a background color and pattern, the following conditions must be met:

- For *Background Color*, the only requirement is that **Cutting Plane** must be turned on.
- Ensure a capture or view isn't selected so the section can be displayed.
- For *Pattern*, a material must be applied to the part or product.

6. Activate the **RW-100-01 A.1** 3D part at the top of the tree by double-clicking on it.

7. Expand the **Materials** and **Aluminum** branches in the specification tree, then double-click on **Material Drafting Domain**, as shown in Figure 5–67.

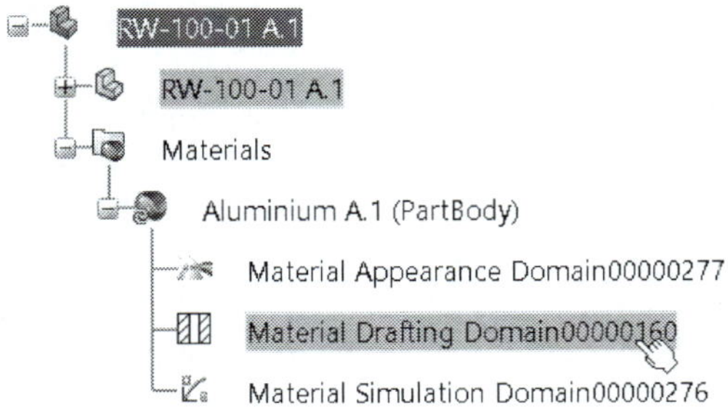

Figure 5–67

8. In the Drafting Material dialog box, in the *Type* field, ensure **Hatching** is selected.

9. In the *Number of hatchings* field, enter **2**.

10. Enter **60 deg** in the *Angle* field of the *Hatching11* tab and **-60 deg** in the *Hatching22* tab.

11. Ensure that the color is set to green and the line type is set to **1** in both tabs, as shown in Figure 5–68.

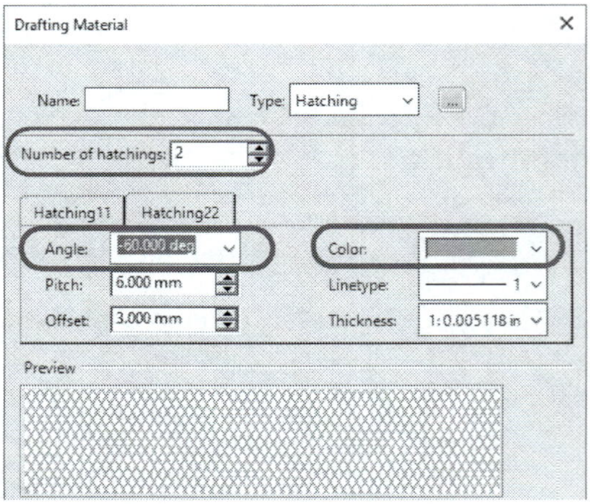

Figure 5–68

12. Click **OK** to close the dialog box.

13. Activate the 3D shape of the part by double-clicking **RW-100-01 A.1**, as shown in Figure 5–69. It will turn blue and the app will switch back to 3D Tolerancing & Annotation.

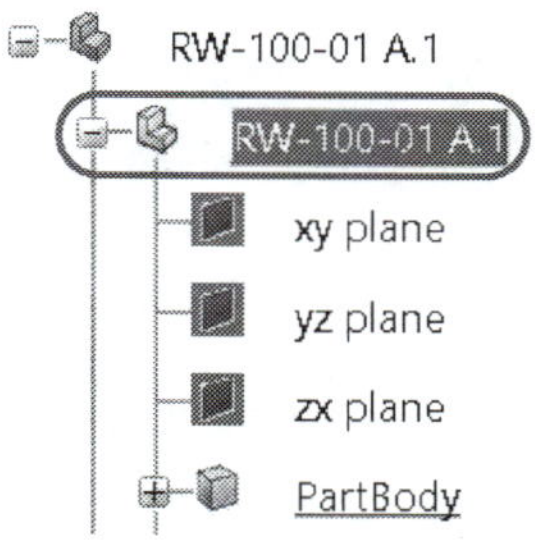

Figure 5–69

14. Activate (Cutting Plane), if needed, then right-click on Annotation Set.1 and select **Hide in 3D**. The model displays as shown in Figure 5–70.

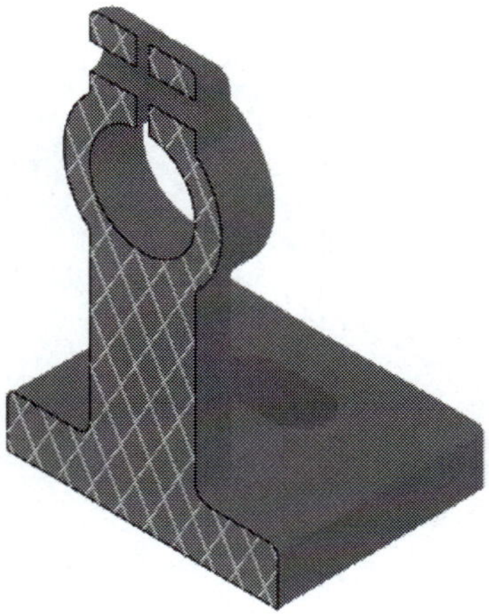

Figure 5–70

15. Display the **DefaultCap** capture.

16. Save the model and close the file.

Practice 5c Geometry Connection Management

Practice Objectives

- Add a datum reference frame.
- Edit a geometrical tolerance.
- Edit a datum.

In this practice, you will modify the references of existing annotations to become familiar with the Geometry Connection Management tool and the **Replace Datum Reference Frame** options. You will use the model shown in Figure 5–71.

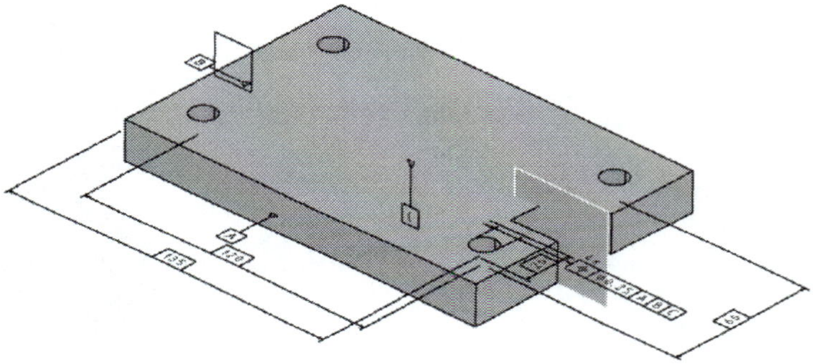

Figure 5–71

Task 1 - Import and open a part file and investigate annotations.

You need to deactivate  (Cutting Plane) to see the model.

1. Import and open **LockingPlate.3dxml**. The model displays as shown in Figure 5–72.

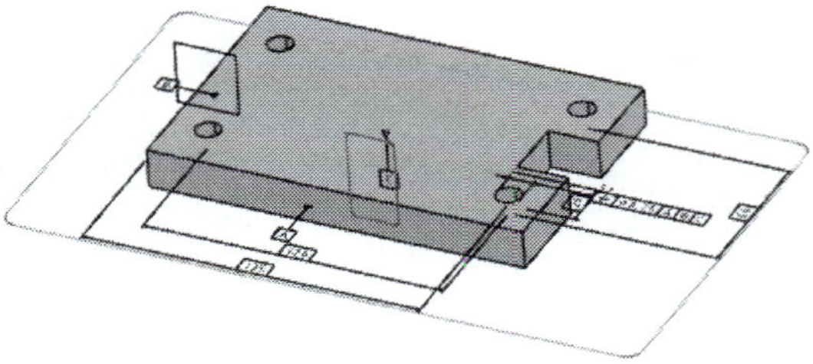

Figure 5–72

2. Click 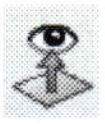 (Normal View) and select **Top View** in the specification tree, as shown in Figure 5–73.

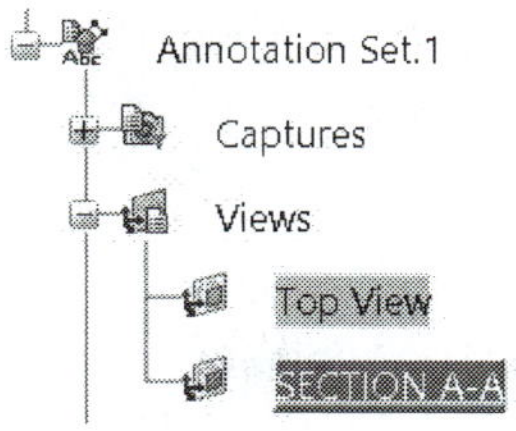

Figure 5–73

The model displays as shown in Figure 5–74. Note the location and reference surface of datum A.

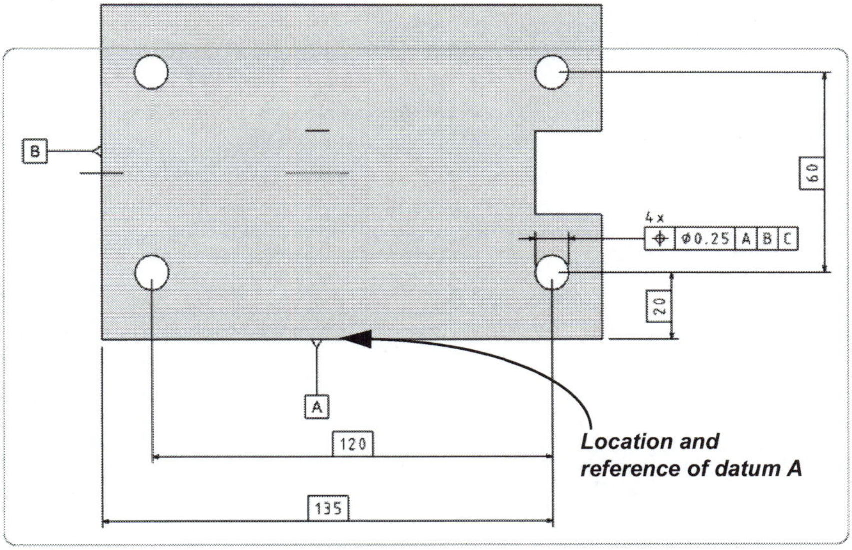

Figure 5–74

3. The positional tolerance (**Position.1**) references the (**A|B|C**) Datum Reference Frame, as shown in Figure 5–75.

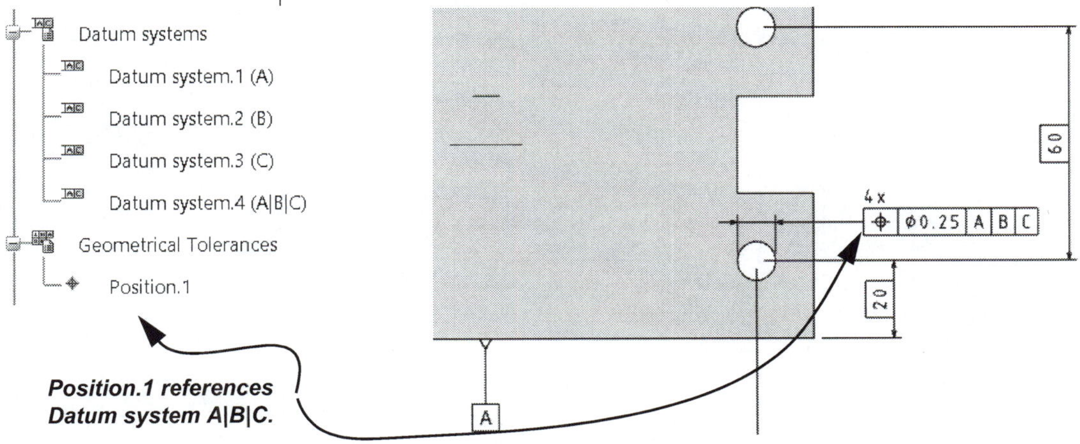

Figure 5–75

Design Considerations

The overall goal of this practice is to change the positional geometrical tolerance that now references datums A|B|C and have it reference a new datum reference frame A|B. The second goal is to change the reference of datum A.

Task 2 - Create a datum reference frame.

In this task, you will create a new datum reference frame that references datums A and B.

1. Click  (Tolerancing Advisor). The Semantic Tolerancing Advisor dialog box opens, listing the current datum reference frames, as shown in Figure 5–76.

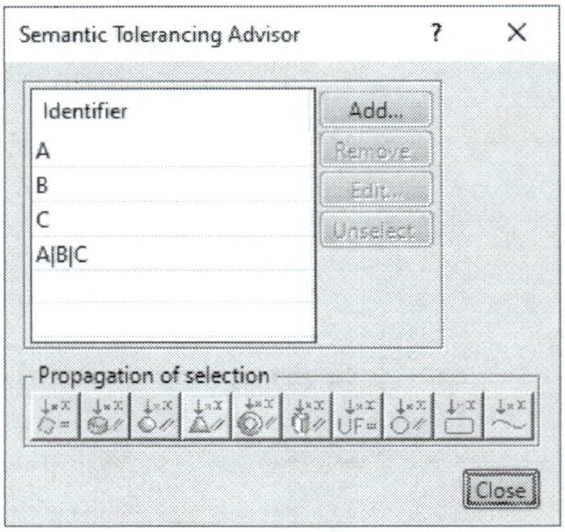

Figure 5–76

2. Click **Add** to open the Datum system dialog box.
3. Select the following datums, as shown in Figure 5–77:
   - **Datum A**
   - **Datum B**

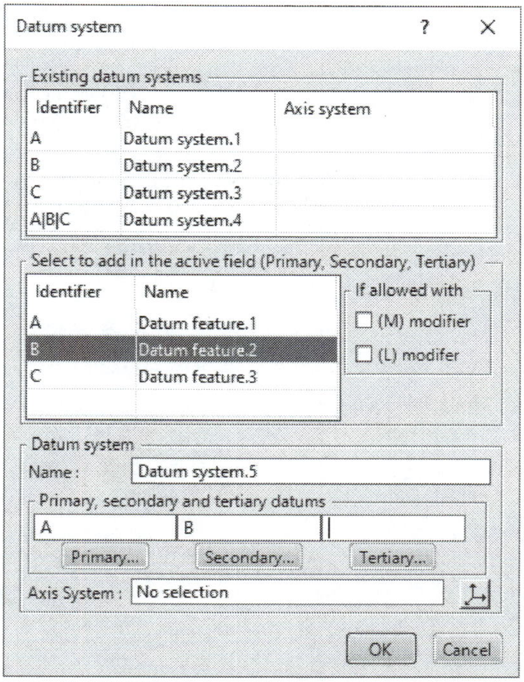

Figure 5–77

4. Click **OK** to complete the datum system. The Semantic Tolerancing Advisor dialog box opens, as shown in Figure 5–78. Note the addition of the **A|B** datum reference frame.

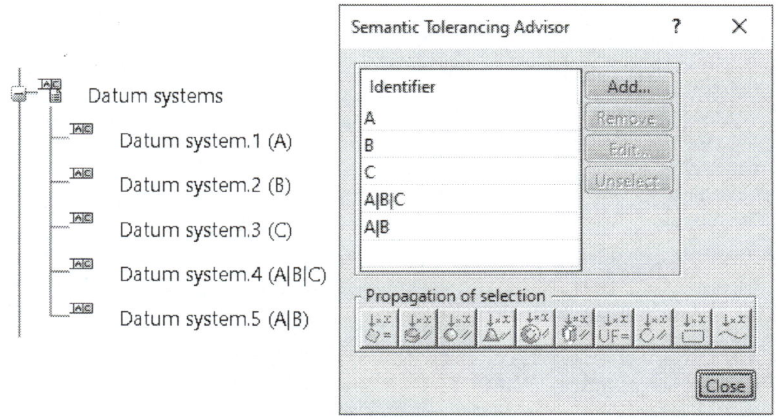

Figure 5–78

5. Click **Close**.

Task 3 - Change the datum reference frame.

In this task, you will change the datum reference frame reference for a geometrical tolerance.

1. Right-click on the **Position.1** tolerance in the specification tree and select **Replace Datum Reference Frame**, as shown in Figure 5–79.

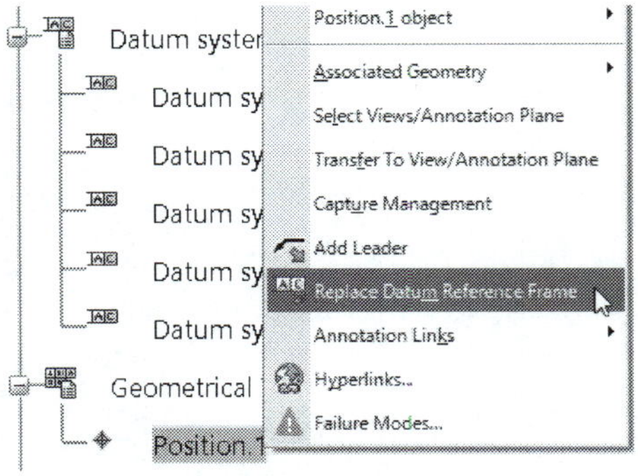

Figure 5–79

2. Select **Datum system.5 (A|B)** in the specification tree, as shown in Figure 5–80.

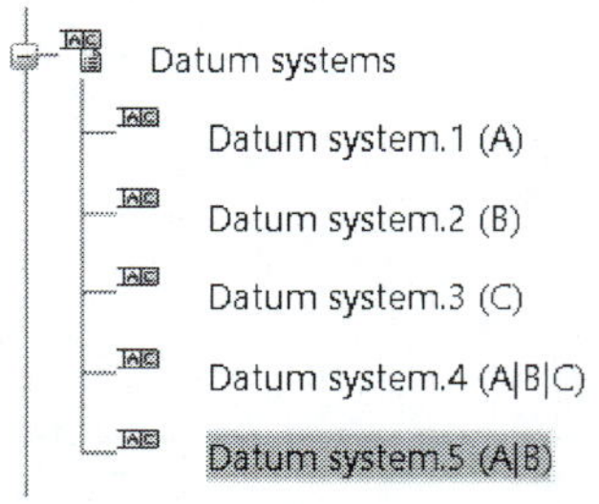

Figure 5–80

The **Positional.1** tolerance now references only datum A|B rather then A|B|C, as shown in Figure 5–81.

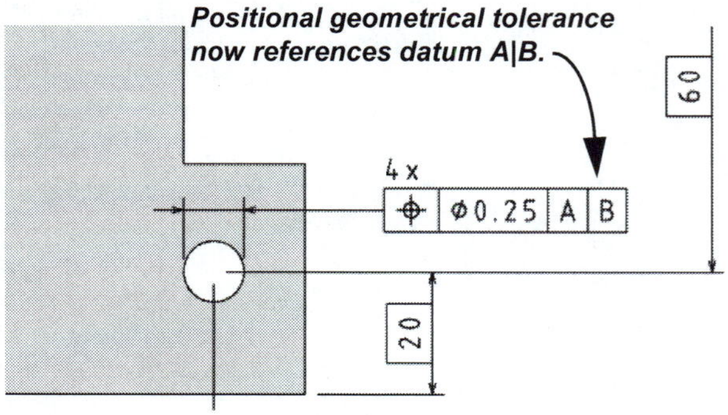

Figure 5–81

Task 4 - Create construction geometry.

In this task, you will create construction geometry that is used to relocate a datum.

1. Preselect the two surfaces shown in Figure 5–82.

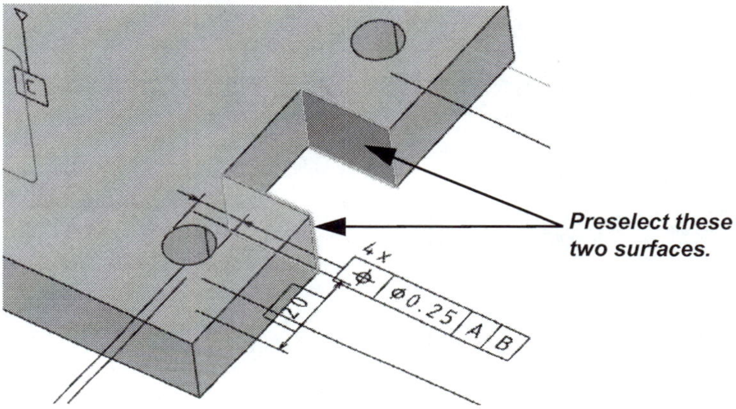

Figure 5–82

2. Click  (Constructed Geometry Creation). Select **Plane**, as shown in Figure 5–83.

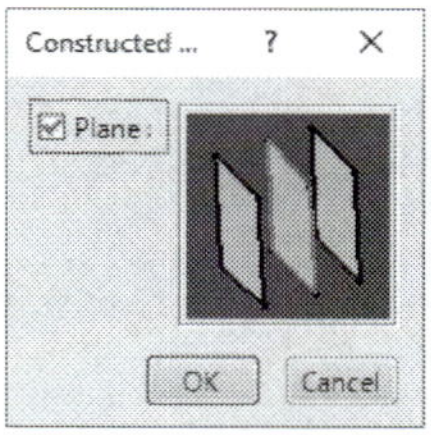

Figure 5–83

3. Click **OK** to complete the geometry. It displays as shown in Figure 5–84.

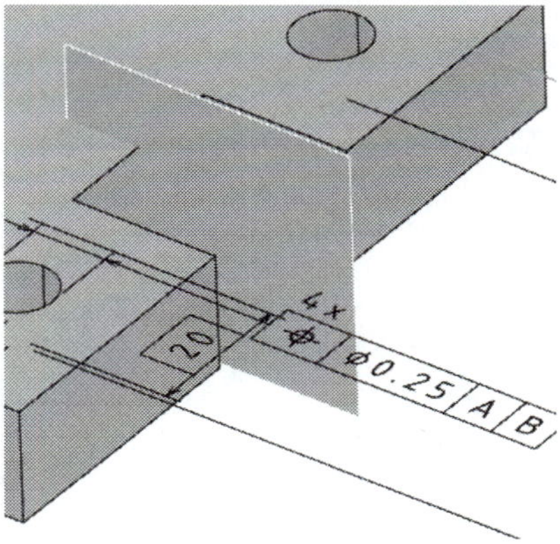

Figure 5–84

Task 5 - Relocate Datum A.

1. Right-click on **Datum feature.1 (A)** in the specification tree, as shown in Figure 5–85.

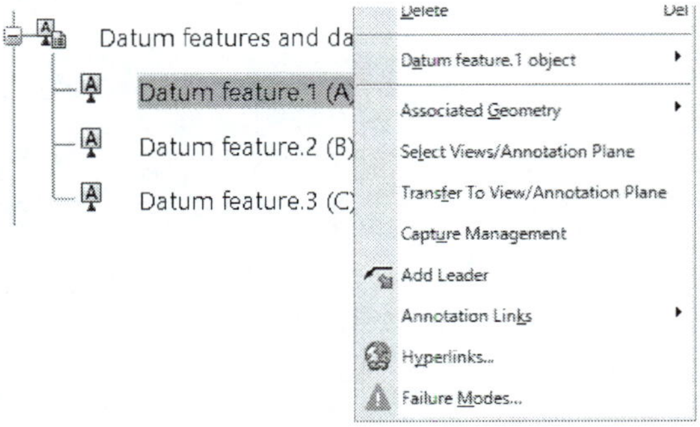

Figure 5–85

2. Select **Associated Geometry>Geometry Connection Management**.The Connection Management dialog box opens.

3. Right-click on **Geometric Component.5** and select **Connect**, as shown in Figure 5–86.

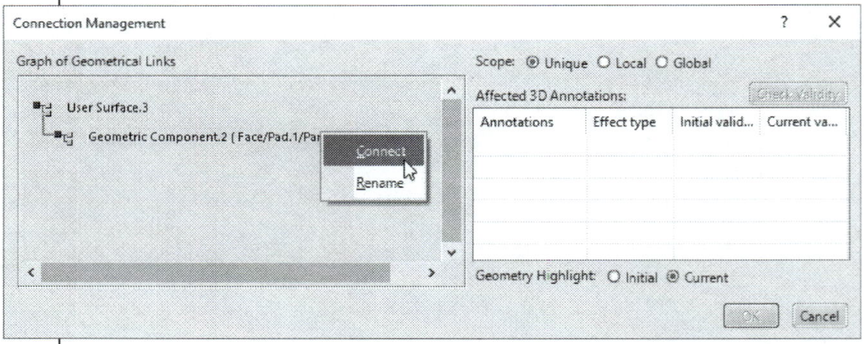

Figure 5–86

4. Select **Center Plane.1** in the specification tree, as shown in Figure 5–87.

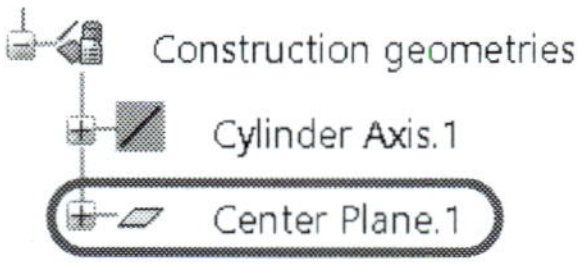

Figure 5–87

5. Click **Check Validity**. The Connection Management dialog box updates, as shown in Figure 5–88.

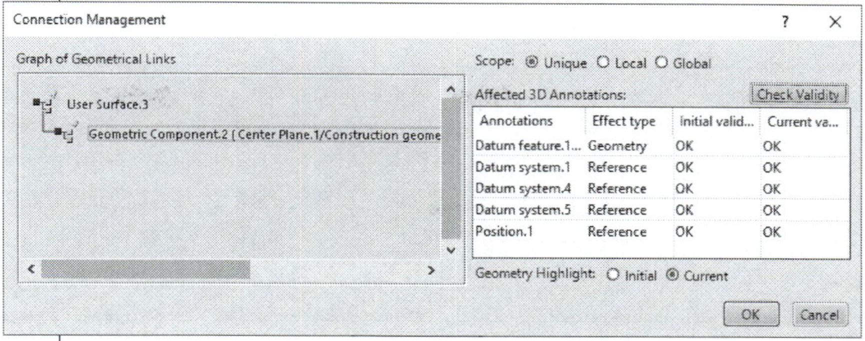

Figure 5–88

Design Considerations

Performing a validity check is important when reconnecting datums to ensure that annotation positions are still valid. You use **Check Validity** in this practice to ensure that the new datum connection is valid for all current annotations. The *Current* column shows that all annotations are valid when referencing the new geometry.

6. Click **OK** to complete the modification.

Task 6 - View the change to Datum A.

1. Click  (Normal View), and select the **Top View** in the specification tree, as shown in Figure 5–89.

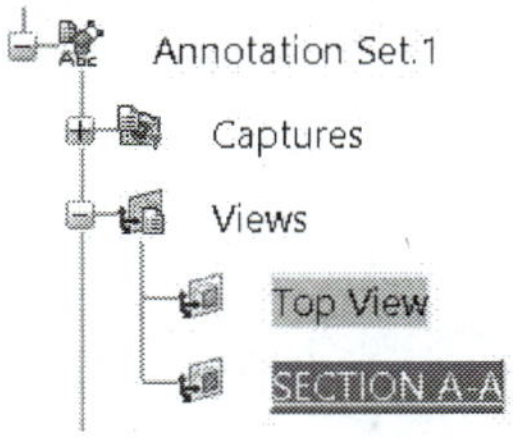

Figure 5–89

2. Modify the attachment of Datum A to switch it to a perpendicular leader. The view displays, as shown in Figure 5–90. Datum A now references the construction geometry that you have created.

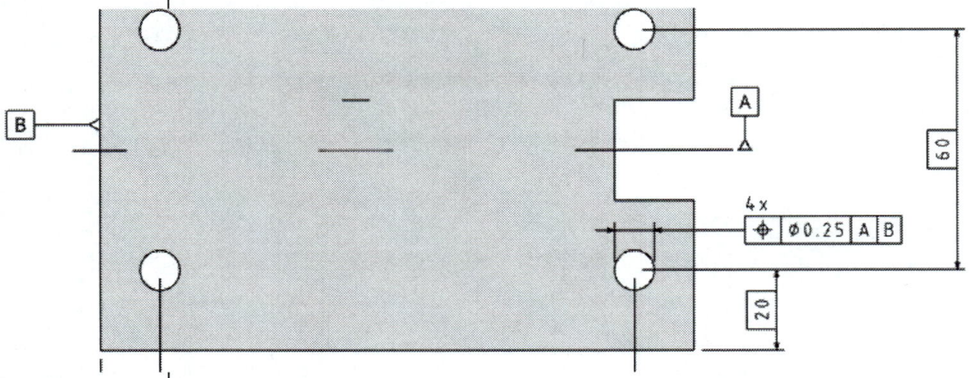

Figure 5–90

3. Save the model and close the file.

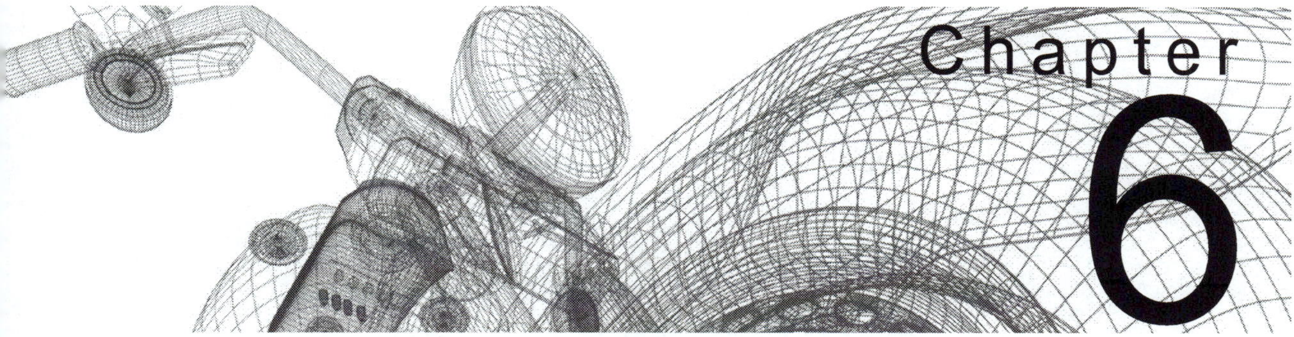

Additional Annotation Tools

This chapter introduces additional tools that are required to develop specialized annotations on your model. Restricted areas are used to divide the face of a model so that two different annotation or tolerance conditions can be defined. The 3D T&A app has the ability to display thread representations and annotations for threaded bosses and holes that have been created in the Part Design app.

Learning Objectives in This Chapter

- Understand how restricted areas are used when a portion of a surface needs to be toleranced differently from the rest of the surface.
- Learn how to use the Thread Representation Creation tool to view the graphical representations of threads.

6.1 Restricted Areas

Restricted areas are used when a portion of a surface needs to be toleranced differently from the rest of the surface, as shown in Figure 6–1.

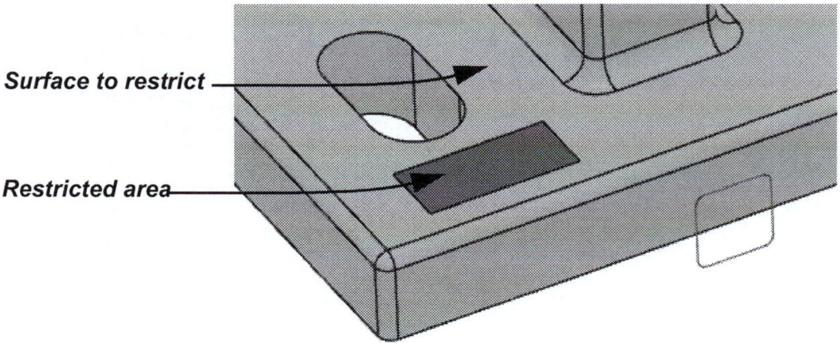

Figure 6–1

How To: Create a Restricted Area

1. Click  (Restricted Area). The Restricted area dialog box opens, as shown in Figure 6–2.

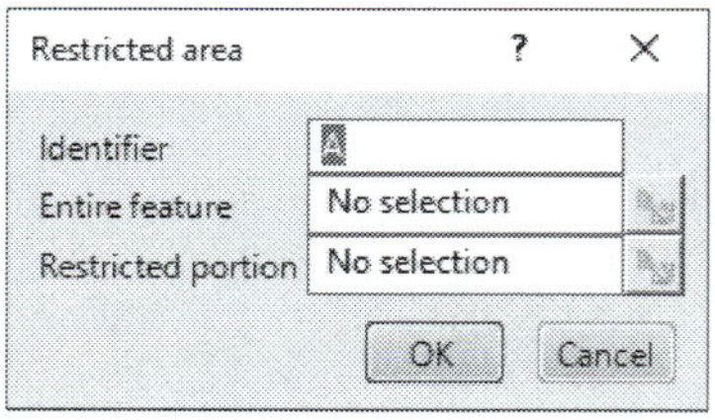

Figure 6–2

2. Select the surface to restrict reference in the model, as shown in Figure 6–1. The surface to restrict is the larger surface that contains the smaller surface. The selected reference displays in the Surface to restrict field.
3. Select the restricted area in the model, as shown in Figure 6–1. The selected reference displays in the restricted area field. The restricted area is a smaller portion of the larger surface, which can be created using the Generative Shape Design app.
4. Click **OK** to complete the feature.

Display Properties

The default display properties of a restricted area can be controlled by selecting **Me>Preferences>App Preferences>3D Modeling>Mechanical Systems>3D Tolerancing and Annotation** and selecting the *Display* arrow.

Select the **Restricted Area** button to expand the *Restricted Area* section, where you can control the color, transparency, and edge properties for the restricted area, as shown in Figure 6–3.

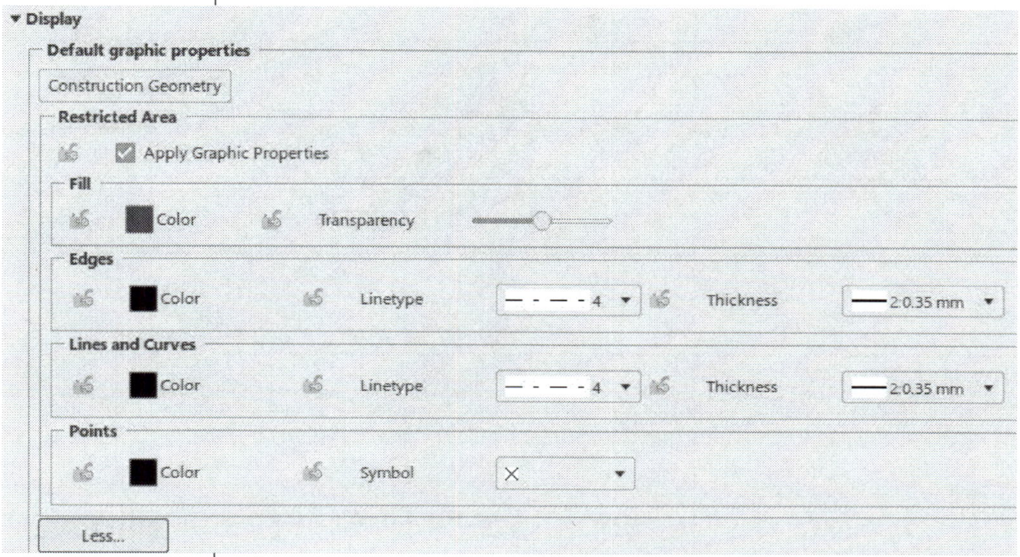

Figure 6–3

When the **Apply Graphic Properties** option is enabled, the referenced geometry in any restricted areas shows the display properties defined in the Options dialog box.

6.2 Threads

When threads are created in the Part Design app, their graphical representations cannot be seen in the model. To view the threads, you need to use the Thread Representation Creation tool. An example is shown in Figure 6–4.

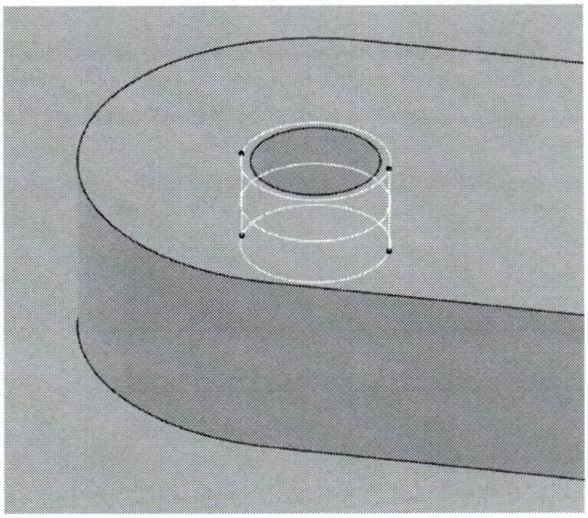

Figure 6–4

How To: Create Thread Representations

Threads need to be defined before a thread representation can be created.

1. Click  (Thread Representation Creation). The Thread Representation Creation dialog box opens, as shown in Figure 6–5.

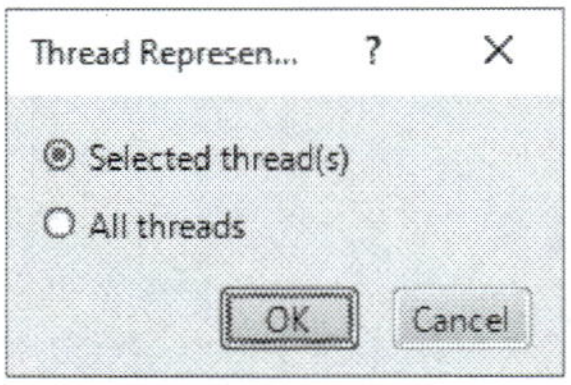

Figure 6–5

2. Select the threaded feature individually or select the **All Threads** option to automatically select all threaded features. A preview of each thread displays in the model, as shown in Figure 6–6.

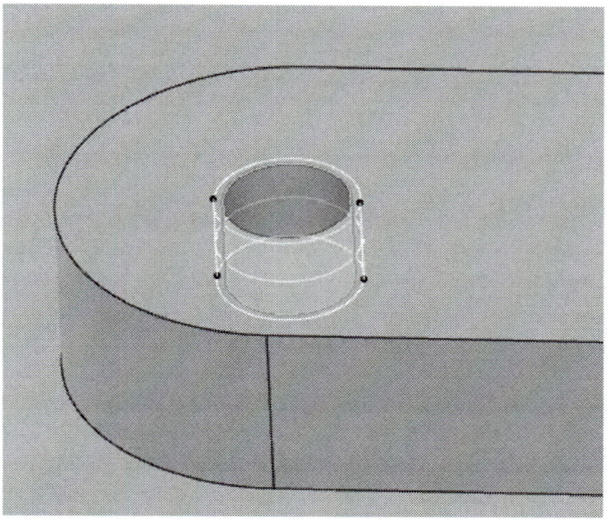

Figure 6–6

3. Click **OK** to complete the feature.

Annotating Thread Representations

How To: Annotate Thread Representations

1. Activate the annotation plane to define the orientation of the thread annotation.
2. Select the middle arc of the thread on which you want to annotate, as shown in Figure 6–7.

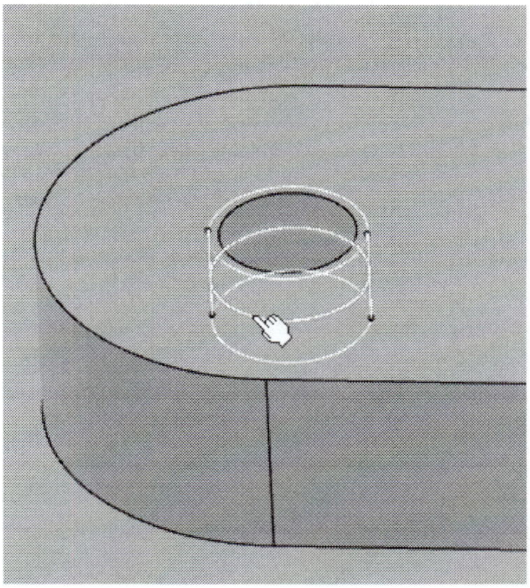

Figure 6–7

3. Click  (Tolerance Advisor).

4. In the Semantic Tolerancing Advisor dialog box, click 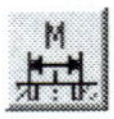 (Thread Diameter), as shown in Figure 6–8.

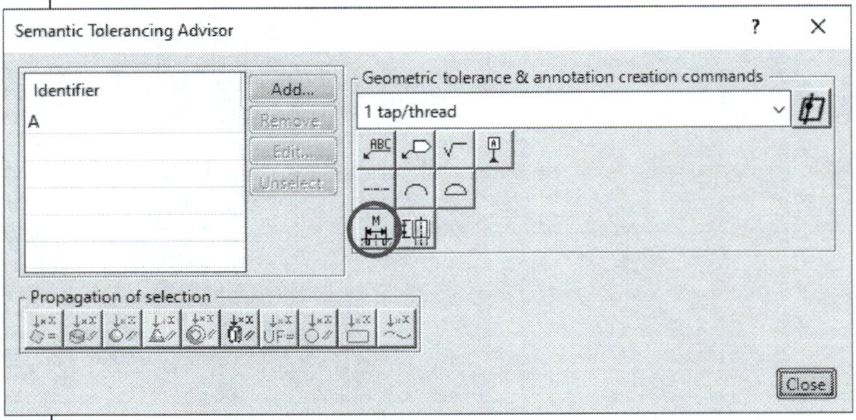

Figure 6–8

5. The Limit of Size Definition dialog box opens, as shown in Figure 6–9.

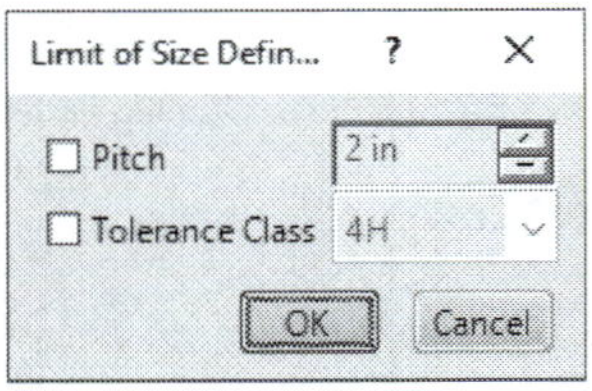

Figure 6–9

6. Activate the option(s) you want to display in the annotation.

7. Click **OK** and then **Close** to complete the feature.

Practice 6a Annotation Tools

Practice Objectives

- Create a restricted area.
- Annotate a restricted area.
- Display threads and thread annotations.

In this practice, you will develop additional annotations for the SimplePad part. These annotations include a parallelism tolerance that varies across the top face of the part. As well, you will display thread representations and annotations. The completed model is shown in Figure 6–10.

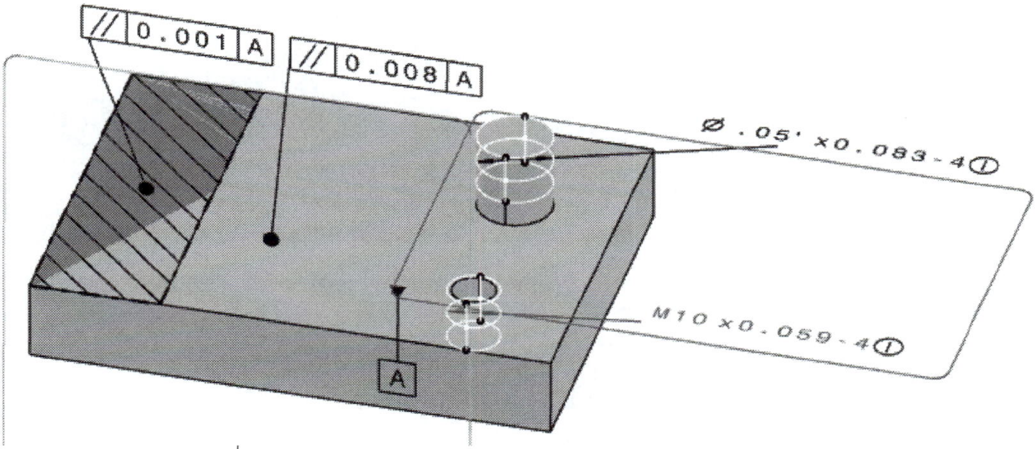

Figure 6–10

Task 1 - Import and open a part file.

1. Open **SimplePad.3dxml**. The model displays as shown in Figure 6–11.

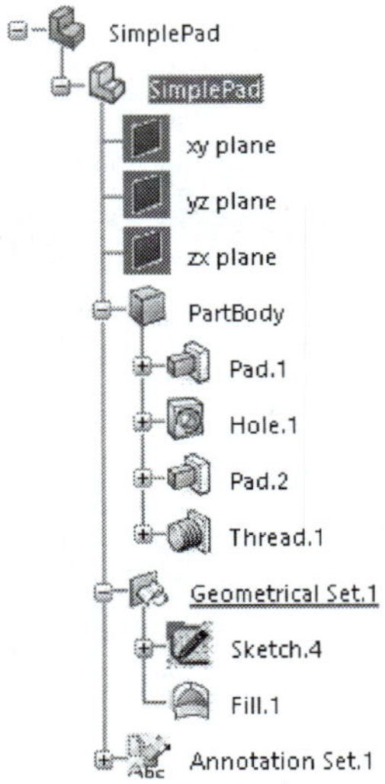

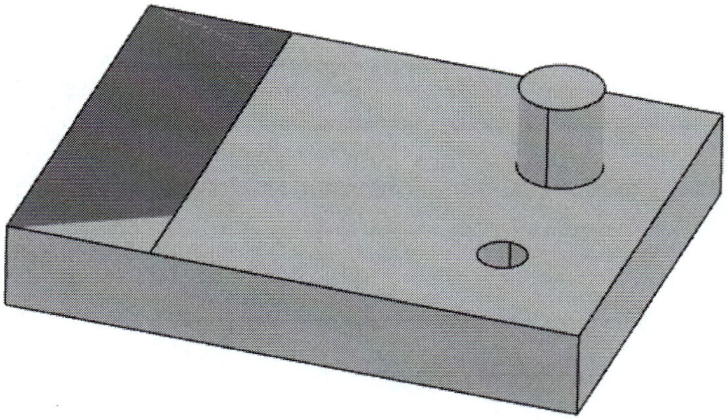

Figure 6–11

2. Investigate the features in the model. The following features are of specific interest during this practice:
   - **Hole.1** - The feature symbol indicates that the hole has been defined as threaded.
   - **Thread.1** - This thread has been added to **Pad.2**.
   - **Fill.1** - This surface has been added to the model to define a restricted area on the top face of the model.

Task 2 - Set options.

1. Select **Me>Preferences**.
2. Select **Common Preferences>Parameters, Measures, and Units** and select the *Units* arrow. Ensure the *Length* units are set to **Inch (in)**.
3. Select **App Preferences>3D Modeling>Mechanical Systems>3D Tolerancing and Annotation** and select the *Tolerances* arrow. Ensure that *Description* is set to **in** and *Precision* is set to **0.001**.
4. Leave the dialog box open for the next task.

Task 3 - Set the partial surface display properties.

1. If required, select **App Preferences>3D Modeling> Mechanical Systems>3D Tolerancing and Annotation**.
2. Select the *Display* arrow.
3. Select the **Restricted Area** button to expand the section.
4. Make the following selections in the *Restricted Area* field:
   - Select **Apply Graphic Properties**.
   - *Fill Color:* **Blue**
   - *Edge Color:* **Black**
5. Click **OK**.

Task 4 - Create a restricted area.

In this task, you will define a restricted area on the top face of the part. You will define the restricted area to enable a variation in a parallelism tolerance between the left and right sides of the part, as shown in Figure 6–12.

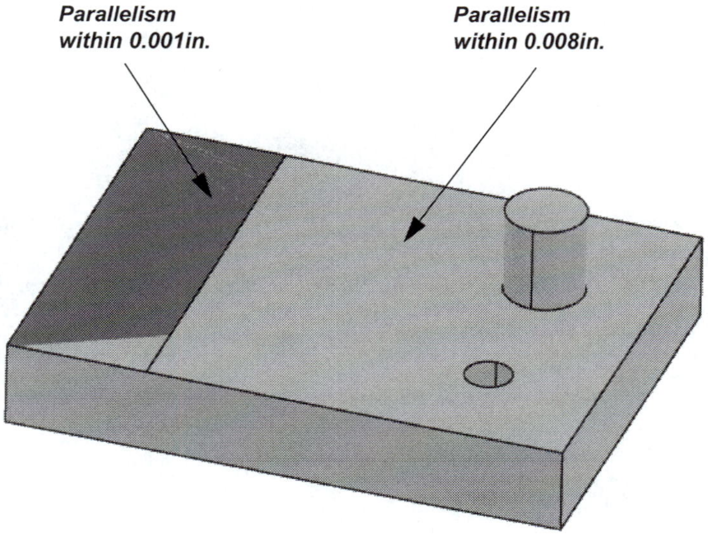

Figure 6–12

1. Right-click on Annotation Set.1 and select **Show in 3D**.

2. In the Annotation section of the Action Bar, click

 (Restricted Area). The Restricted area dialog box opens, as shown in Figure 6–13.

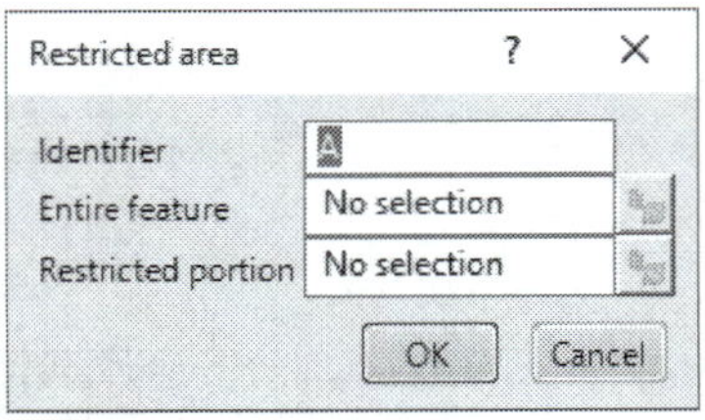

Figure 6–13

3. Select the *top* surface as the *Entire feature* and *Restricted portion* surface, as shown in Figure 6–14.

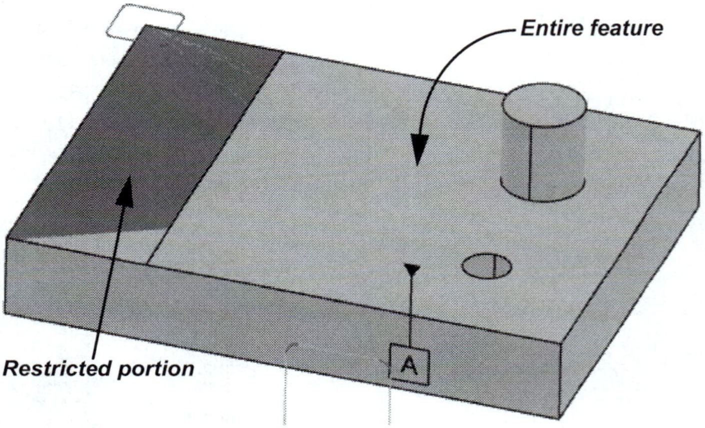

Figure 6–14

4. Click **OK**. The system adds **Restricted Area.1 (A)** to the specification tree and modifies the display properties of **Fill.1** to reflect the settings made in the previous task.

Task 5 - Add a parallelism tolerance to the top face.

1. Activate the Side annotation view.
2. Activate the Tolerance Advisor and make the following selections:
   - Select DRF **A** in the *Datums and datum reference frames* area.
   - Select the top face of the part. The dialog box displays as shown in Figure 6–15.

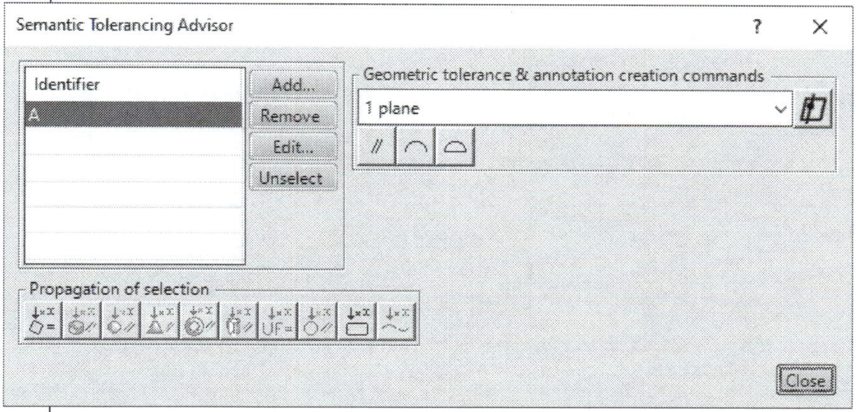

Figure 6–15

3. Click  (Parallelism Specification) to create a parallelism tolerance with a **0.008in** tolerance value, as shown in Figure 6–16.

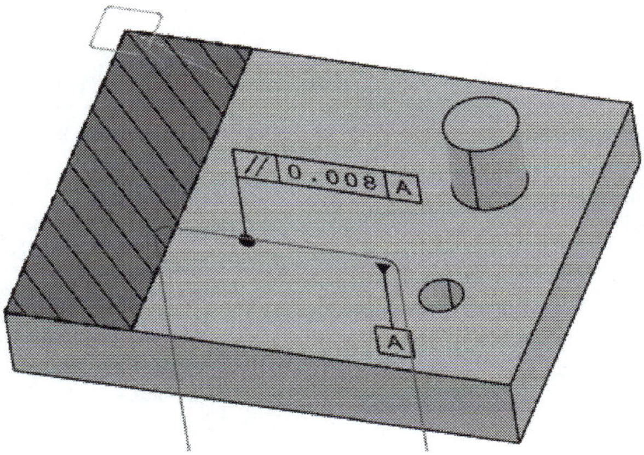

Figure 6–16

4. Complete the tolerance creation.

Task 6 - Create a parallelism tolerance on the restricted area.

1. Activate the Tolerance Advisor and make the following selections:
   - Select DRF **A** in the *Datums and datum reference frames* area.
   - Select **Restricted Area.1** under the **Restricted Areas** branch of the specification tree.

2. Create a parallelism tolerance with a **0.001in** tolerance value, as shown in Figure 6–17.

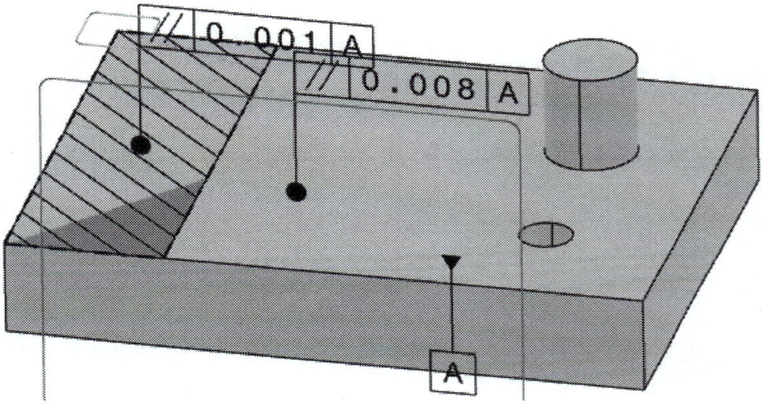

Figure 6–17

3. Apply a 3D Annotation Filter using a *Value* setting of **(0<=Value <=0)** to hide the two geometrical tolerances and the semantic datum.

Task 7 - Display the thread representations.

1. Click  (Thread Representation Creation) in the Annotation section of the Action Bar, as shown in Figure 6–18. The Thread Representation Creation dialog box opens, as shown in Figure 6–18.

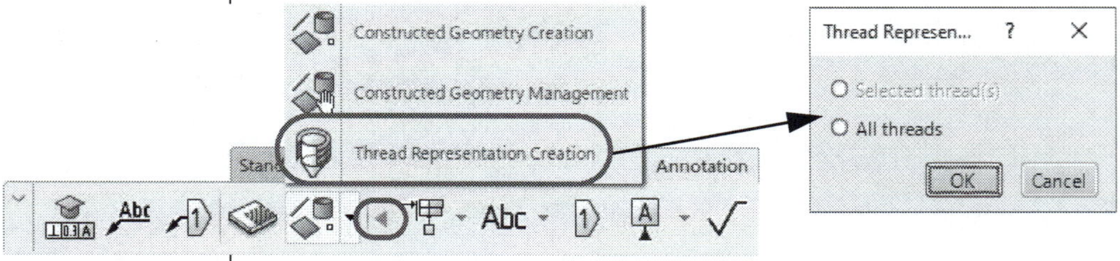

Figure 6–18

2. Select **All threads** and click **OK**. The model displays as shown in Figure 6–19.

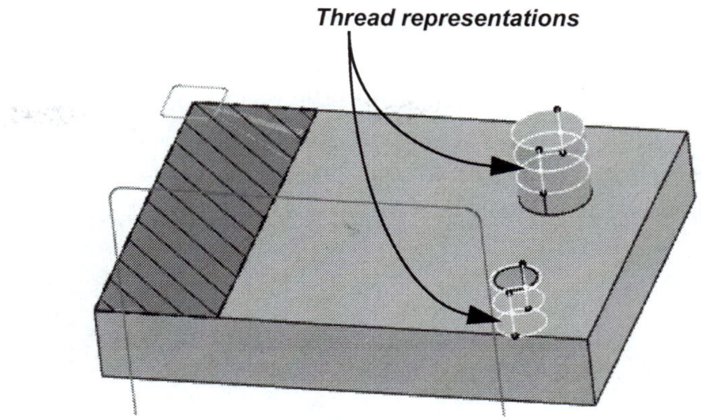

Figure 6–19

Design Considerations

Two thread representation branches have been added under the Construction geometries branch in the specification tree. The thread representation consists of three separate features named Upper Thread Plane, Lower Thread Plane, and Thread Cylinder, as shown in Figure 6–20.

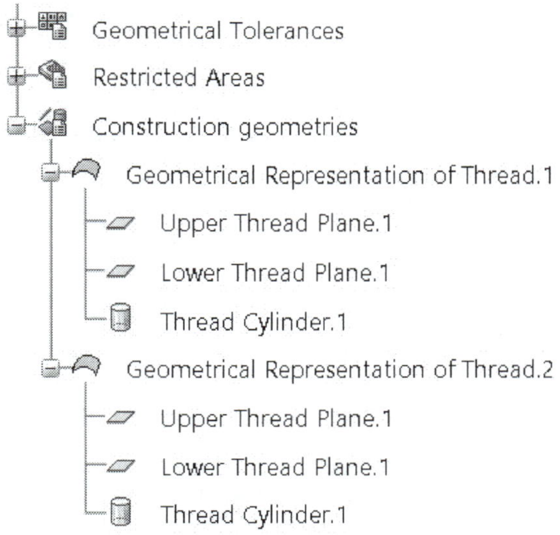

Figure 6–20

Task 8 - Display the thread annotations.

1. Activate the Front view.

2. Preselect the middle curve on the thread for the hole feature, as shown in Figure 6–21.

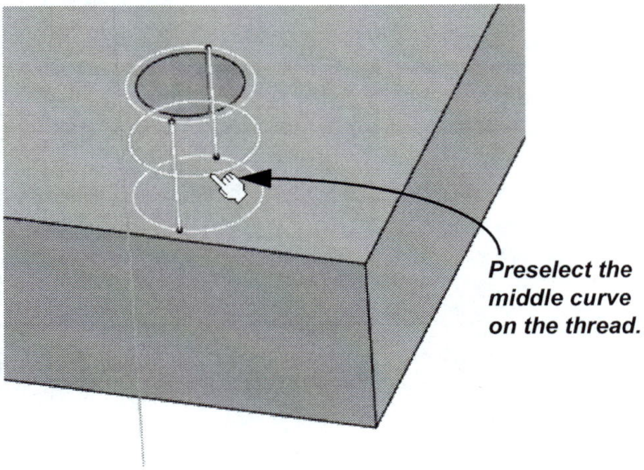

Figure 6–21

3. Activate the Tolerance Advisor.

4. Click (Thread Diameter). The Limit of Size Definition dialog box opens, as shown in Figure 6–22.

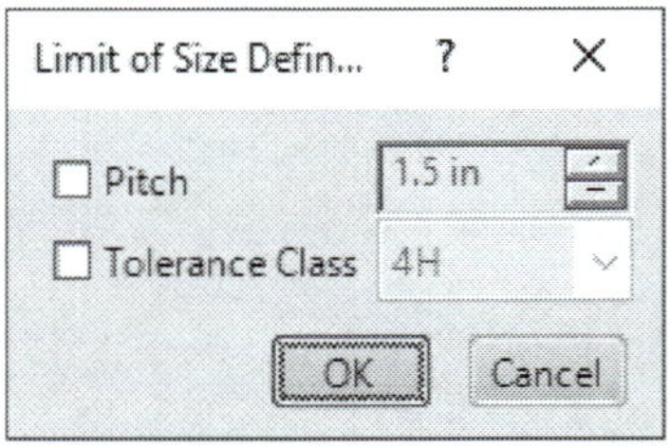

Figure 6–22

5. Accept the default values, and select **Pitch** and **Tolerance Class**.

6. Complete the operation. The model displays as shown in Figure 6–23.

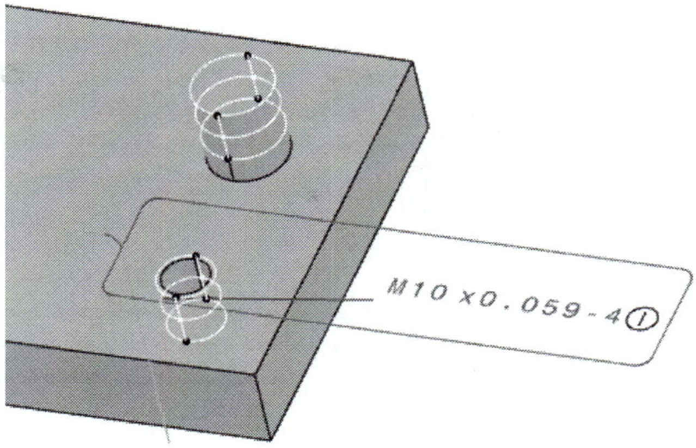

Figure 6–23

7. Repeat this process to display the threaded annotation for the threaded boss. The model displays as shown in Figure 6–24.

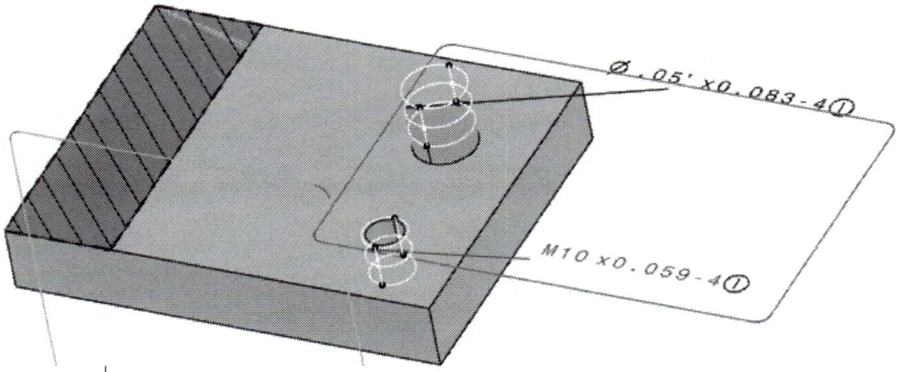

Figure 6–24

8. Save the model and close the window.

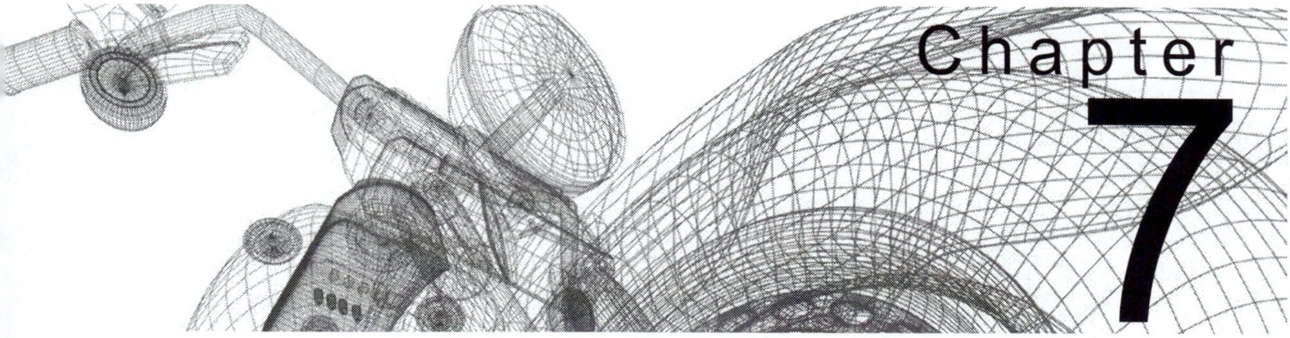

Products and 3D T&A

When dealing with products, there are two apps that will become very useful: the 3D Tolerancing & Annotation (3D T&A) app and a new 3D Annotation Insight app. The 3D T&A app that you have been using for parts is the same one you will use to create annotations in the products. Assemblies are annotated in much the same way as part models. However, the 3D Annotation Insight app is not designed for creating annotations, but rather for reviewing the annotations that already exist with the product, either at the product level or with the parts. This chapter describes similarities and differences between these apps, and the way they are used within a product.

Learning Objectives in This Chapter

- Understand that the 3D Tolerancing & Annotation app enables you to create annotations between different parts in an assembly in a similar way to parts.
- Recognize the various contexts for working with products.
- Unload components from a product.
- Review products using the 3D Annotation Insight app.

7.1 Overview

Just like when creating annotations between features in parts, the 3D Tolerancing & Annotation app enables you to create annotations between different parts in an assembly as well. This ability increases the control over the design as specifications become more precise when dealing with not only the shape and quality of part features, but also the ways in which those features impact the overall assembly.

While the 3D Tolerancing & Annotation app is still used to create annotations when working with products, there is another application that can aid in the reviewing and manipulation of product models as well. This application is called 3D Annotation Insight, as shown in Figure 7–1.

Figure 7–1

This app is only accessible at the product level, meaning only when the product or an instance of a part is active. While the 3D Annotation Insight app won't create new annotations, it can perform the following tasks that can be especially helpful with larger assemblies:

- Visualize mechanical dimensions and tolerances at any level in the product.
- Search for 3D annotations.
- Review the annotations on the product and apply filters to better understand context of information.

7.2 Working Context

Part annotations should be used to their full extent (i.e., to document every aspect of a part to ensure that all standards are met). Product annotations should be used only when the annotation references or refers to more than one assembly component. Keep the design specifications in the individual part to help maintain control of annotation display.

Use product level annotations to define how a product must be assembled. Dimensions in the product level are not intended to drive manufacturing, but to provide valuable information on the maximum allowable deviation when combining deviations from individual parts in an assembly. Annotations can also be used to note assembly instructions, and to point out features, tolerances, and properties common to multiple components in the assembly.

Annotations created at the product level will need to be placed under a 3D shape in the specification tree, as shown in Figure 7–2.

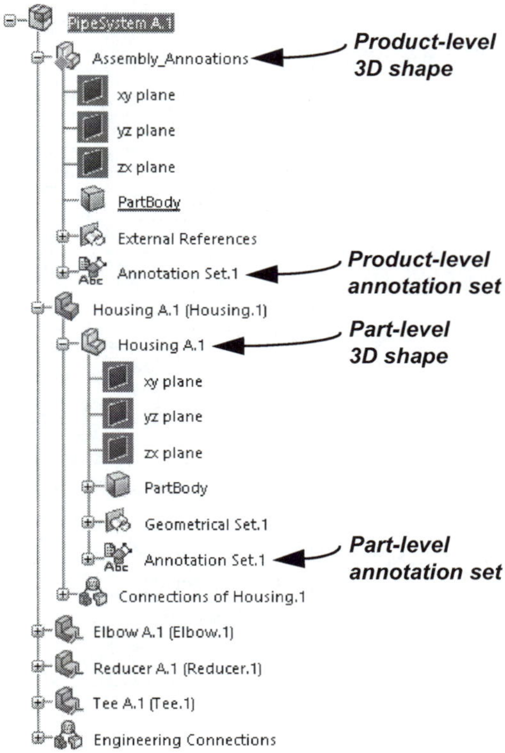

Figure 7–2

This is done by right-clicking on the product in the specification tree and selecting **Insert>3D Shape**, as shown in Figure 7–3. By activating the newly created 3D shape, the 3D Tolerancing & Annotation app can be used to create views, captures, tolerances, and annotations between components within the product.

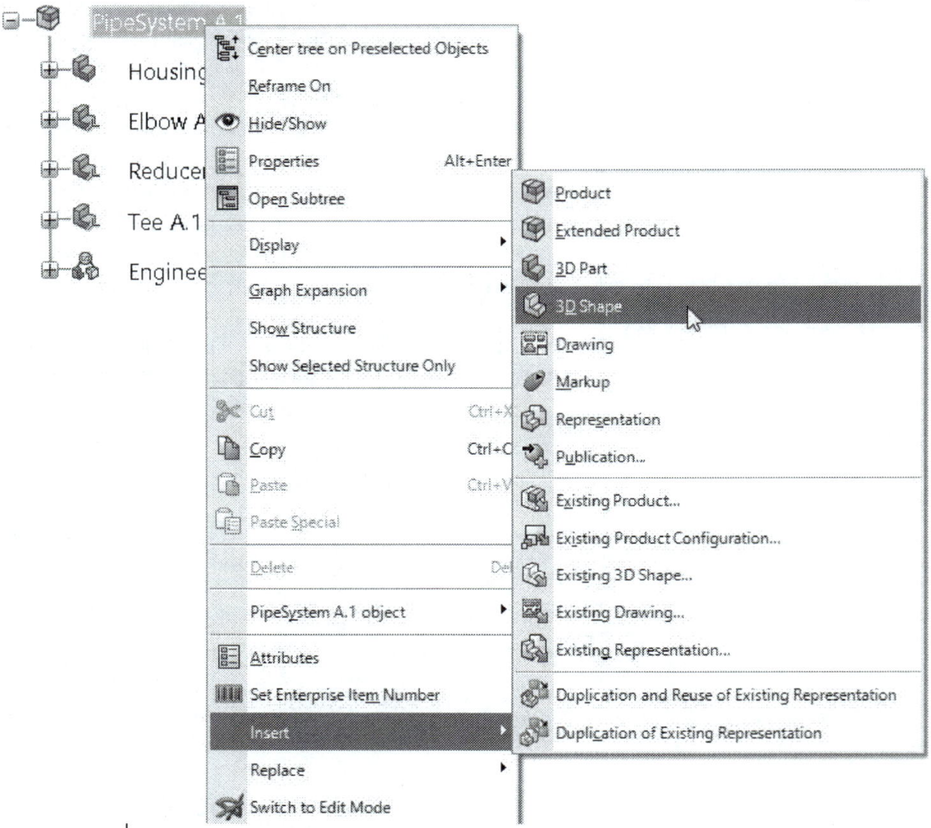

Figure 7–3

When an assembly annotation is placed on components within the product, a corresponding engineering connection is also created. The location of these engineering connections in the specification tree can be customized based on the user's need. Select **Me>Preferences>App Preferences>3D Modeling>Mechanical Systems>3D Tolerancing and Annotation>Administration>Assembly Context**. Once there, you are given the following two options to create engineering connections in the father product of:

- The selected assembly geometries
- The selected assembly geometries and the created annotation

Examples of these two options and their effect on the product are shown in Figure 7–4.

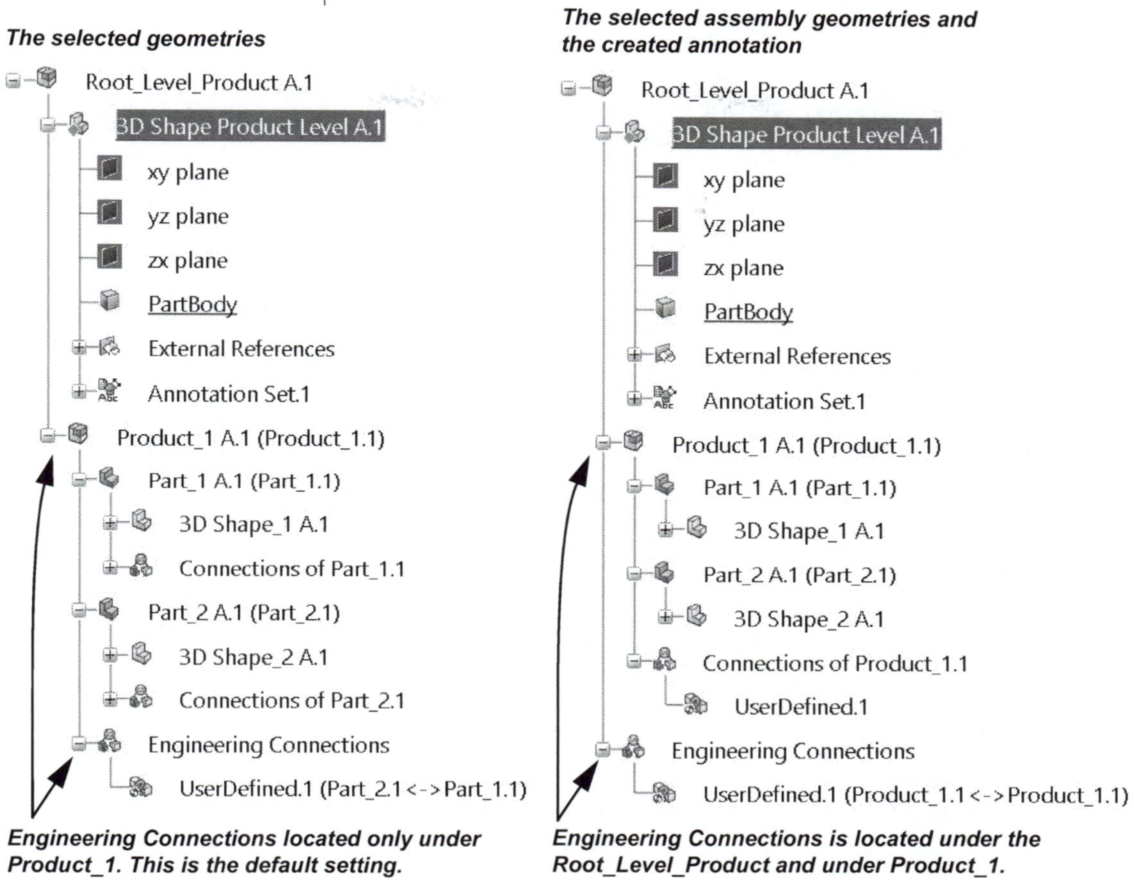

Figure 7–4

Unloading Parts and Products

Controlling the display of larger products and what information is important or irrelevant can become a constant issue. Through the use of 3D annotation filters and captures, one can control the display of many of the 3D Tolerancing & Annotation objects. However, if the product has more components than are needed from the display, and you don't want to permanently delete those unneeded components, a temporary solution is to **Unload** those unneeded parts or products. This will remove the component from memory and from all the widgets that are using that component in session. The product will temporarily display as if the component were deleted; however, once you close and reopen the assembly, the component will reappear again.

How To: Unload Parts and Products

1. In the specification tree, right-click on the component that you wish to remove from the display.
2. Select **Unload**, as shown in Figure 7–5.

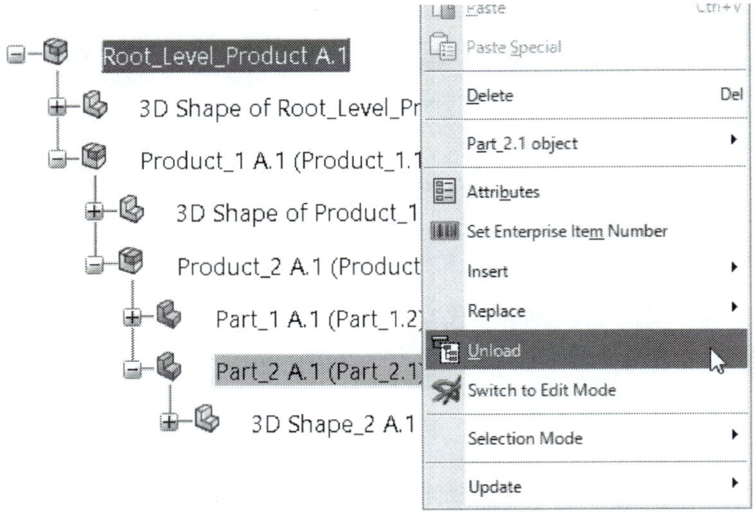

Figure 7–5

3. A warning window will appear, as shown in Figure 7–6. Select **Ok** to confirm you want to unload the component.

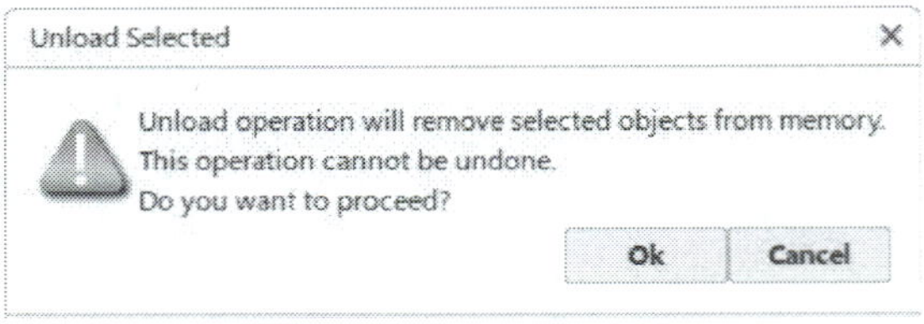

Figure 7–6

4. The component will disappear from the assembly. The only way to display it again is to close the product window and reopen it.

7.3 Product Differences

This section describes the primary differences between working in the part and product 3D T&A apps, which include the following:

- Annotation planes
- Captures

Annotation Planes

Default reference planes exist within the product-level 3D shape and should be used as references for views that are created at the product level whenever possible. While this practice is considered most stable, annotation planes can also reference part-level geometry as well. Caution should be given when creating a part-level reference because it can create an unnecessary link to a part model.

Construction geometry can be created in the assembly annotation set as well. This geometry can be used to define annotation planes.

Carefully consider which references to select for annotation planes. If the part changes and the geometry is modified or deleted, or the assembly constraints are modified, it can affect the annotations. Annotations should be the last step in designing an assembly. If the assembly is still in its design phase, assign annotations to annotation planes that do not change. These annotations can be transferred to more appropriate annotation planes at the end of the design cycle.

Captures

When you create a capture at the product level, it can contain annotations that have been created in either the product or a component (such as a part or subassembly) that has been added to the assembly.

In contrast, when you create a capture at the part level, it displays within the context of an assembly. The system does not display any product-level annotations or annotations that were created in any other parts.

7.4 3D Annotation Insight App

The 3D Annotation Insight app is designed to review and manipulate the display of 3D annotations within a product. While the majority of the material in this guide has focused on the 3D Tolerancing & Annotation app, this section will focus on the key tools that are specific to the 3D Annotation Insight app or that are shared between the two but are important to utilizing the 3D Annotation Insight app correctly.

One of the first things you will notice when you switch to the 3D Annotation Insight app is that it seems like a stripped-down version of the 3D T&A app. Many of the same tools discussed earlier in this guide are available in this app as well. All the tools for viewing and filtering the display are accessible to you but the tools for creating new objects have been removed. The View and Tools sections of the Action Bar are shown in Figure 7–7.

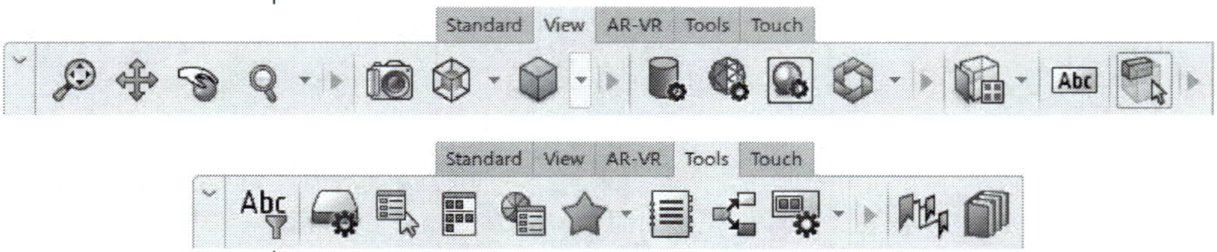

Figure 7–7

Within the 3D Annotation Insight app, there are a number of key functions:

- Enable Display/Disable Display
- Display Selector
- 3D Annotation Filter
- 3D Annotation Browser

Enable Display/ Disable Display

Annotation sets can be hidden or shown individually. The intent is to quickly hide/show all of the views, tolerances, and annotations for any given component. Up until now, the method for doing this for an individual component was to expand the specification tree until you can see the annotation set and then right-click on it and select **Hide in 3D/Show in 3D** as needed. While this does still work, when inside the 3D Annotation Insight app, if you select on a component either from the tree or on the model, a contextual menu will appear, as shown in Figure 7–8.

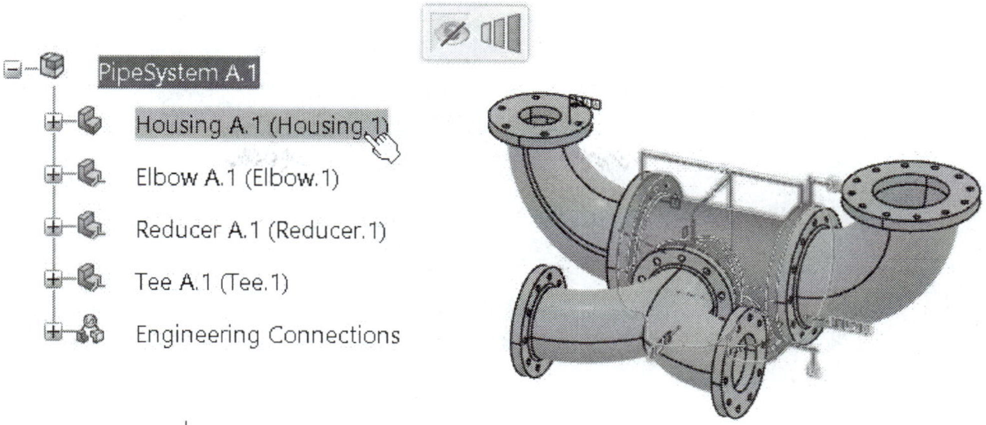

Figure 7–8

In this contextual menu, there will be one of two options, either  (Enable Display) or  (Disable Display), depending on whether the annotation set is visible in the 3D model or not. Selecting these options will quickly toggle on/off the annotation set in the 3D model.

Display Level Selector

Another unique tool to the 3D Annotation Insight app is the  (Display Level Selector). This tool is also displayed in the contextual menu when a component is selected, as shown in Figure 7–9. This command enables you to quickly adjust your selection of a component to the level you want in the product (for example, if you select on something specific like a **Pad.1** that exists within a 3D shape), as shown in Figure 7–9.

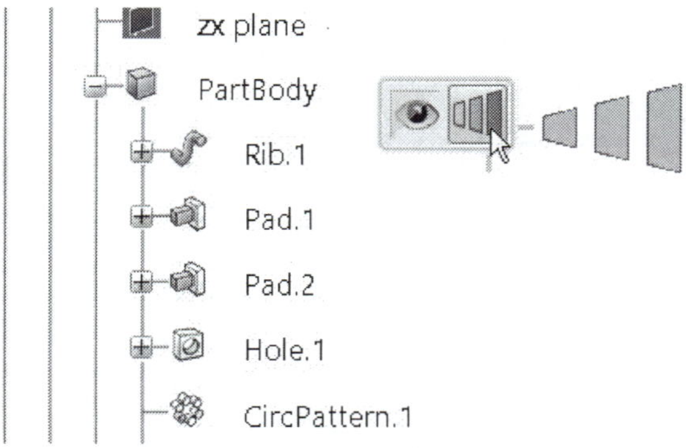

Figure 7–9

When you select the (Display Level Selector) icon, three bars will appear to the right of the icon. By moving your cursor over those bars, it will display either the product, part, or 3D shape, as shown in Figure 7–10.

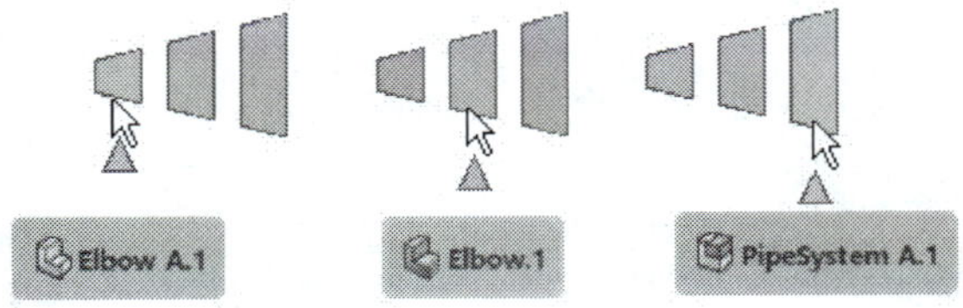

Figure 7–10

Selecting the appropriate bar will change the selection level of the currently selected object. How many levels the product has and the level of the first selection will determine if there are more or less bars to select from.

3D Annotation Filter

The 3D Annotation Filter has exactly the same functionality within 3D Annotation Insight as it does in the 3D Tolerancing & Annotation app, but it is included here because it is a vital tool for controlling the display of a complex product that is filled with views and annotations. Select (3D Annotation Filter) from the Tools section of the Action Bar to open the 3D Annotation Filter window (shown in Figure 7–11).

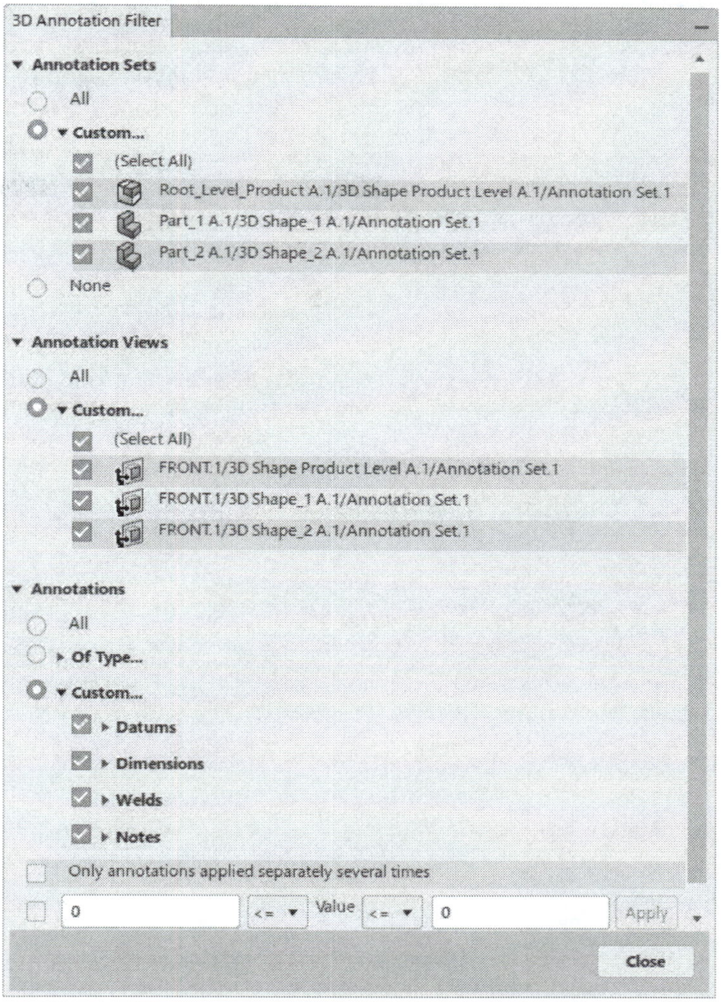

Figure 7–11

Within the 3D Annotation Filter window, you can control the display of *Annotation Sets*, *Annotation Views*, and individual *Annotations* as needed. You can include or exclude all with just a few clicks, or pick and choose which ones to display. Understand that if you want to include a specific annotation, the view and the annotation set it was created in need to be checked as well. If the parent feature is excluded, the children won't be included either.

3D Annotation Browser

The 3D Annotation Browser is available in both the 3D Annotation Insight app and the 3D Tolerancing & Annotation app. This tool is designed for you to easily browse and display the captures of the current activated shape. Found in the View section of the Action Bar, the  (View Browser) command will toggle on/off the display of the Views and Captures window (shown in Figure 7–12).

This window can be resized and relocated as needed, and includes the options  (Thumbnails View) and  (Details View) in the upper right-hand corner to adjust how the views and captures are displayed, as shown in Figure 7–12.

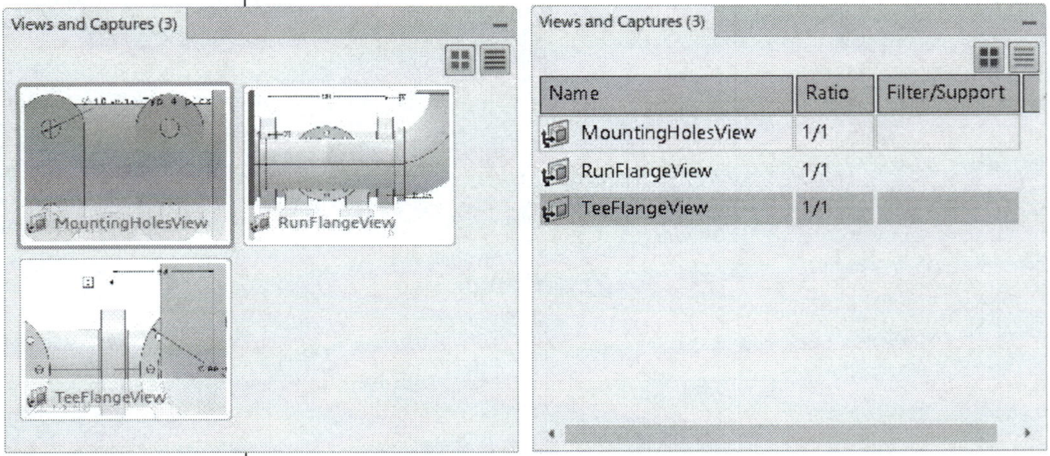

Figure 7–12

Selecting on any of the listed views will display one of the two contextual menus shown in Figure 7–13, depending on whether the view has a capture associated with it or not.

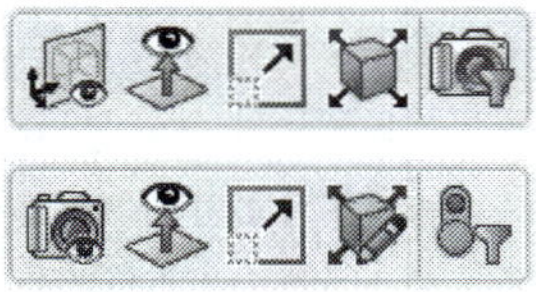

Figure 7–13

Below is a list of these contextual menu options and their descriptions.

Option	Icon	Description
Display View		Activates the selected view and reframes on the view frame.
Display Capture		Displays elements managed by the capture.
Normal View		View objects perpendicular to a selected plane.
Change Ratio		Change the view ratio size.
Capture		Captures the current widget size into the view display area.
Edit		Allows the modification of the view display area.
Capture		Creates a capture.
Edit Filter		Edits the current capture, allowing customization of what is displayed by it.

Practice 7a

Product-Level 3D T&A

Practice Objectives

- Create product-level datums.
- Create product-level geometric tolerances.

In this practice, you will develop a series of annotations for the PipeSystem product model shown in Figure 7–14 using the 3D Tolerancing & Annotation app.

You will dimension and tolerance the flanges on the Elbow, Reducer, and Tee components with respect to the A datum reference frame, which is located at the base of the Housing component. Since all of these annotations reference more than one component, they are stored in the product annotation set. Annotations that only reference geometry from a single part should always be stored in the part annotation set.

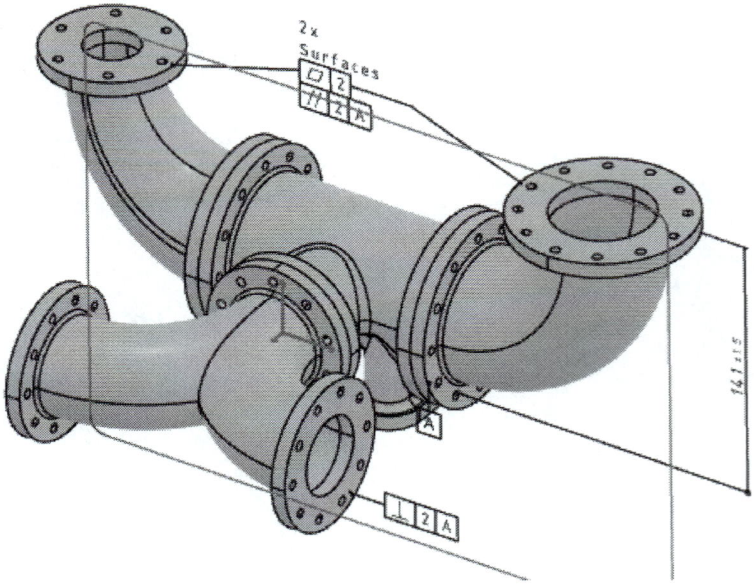

Figure 7–14

Task 1 - Import and open a product file.

1. Import and open **PipeSystem.3dxml** from the *PipeSystem* folder. The assembly displays as shown in Figure 7–15.

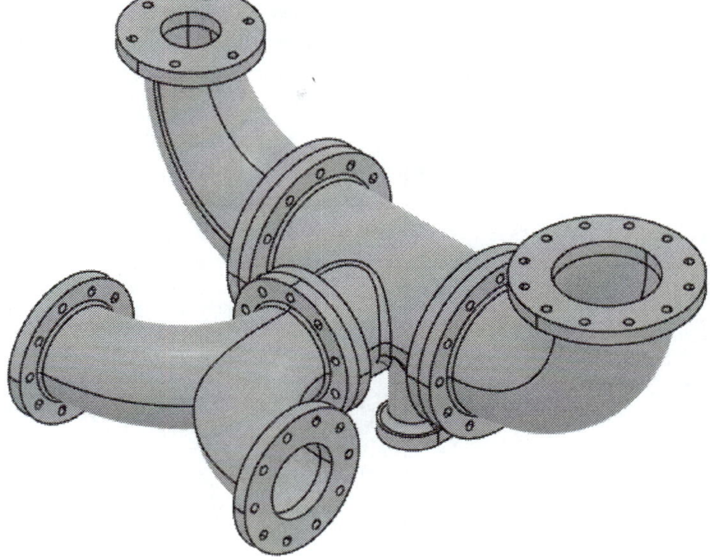

Figure 7–15

Task 2 - Set options.

Review the existing annotations. Note that they are in metric. You will continue to create the annotations and tolerances in metric.

1. Select **Me>Preferences>Common Preferences>Parameters, Measures, and Units>Units** and select the *Units* arrow. Set the *Length* to **Millimeter (mm)**.
2. Select **App Preferences>3D Modeling>Mechanical Systems>3D Tolerancing and Annotation** and select the *Tolerances* arrow.
3. Ensure that the *Geometrical Tolerance Precision* is set to **1**.
4. Click **OK**.

Task 3 - Add a 3D shape to a product.

In this task, you will add a 3D shape to the root-level product so that an annotation set can be created at the assembly level.

1. Expand the **Housing** branch of the specification tree, as shown in Figure 7–16. The annotation sets have been created within the 3D shape of each component of the assembly.

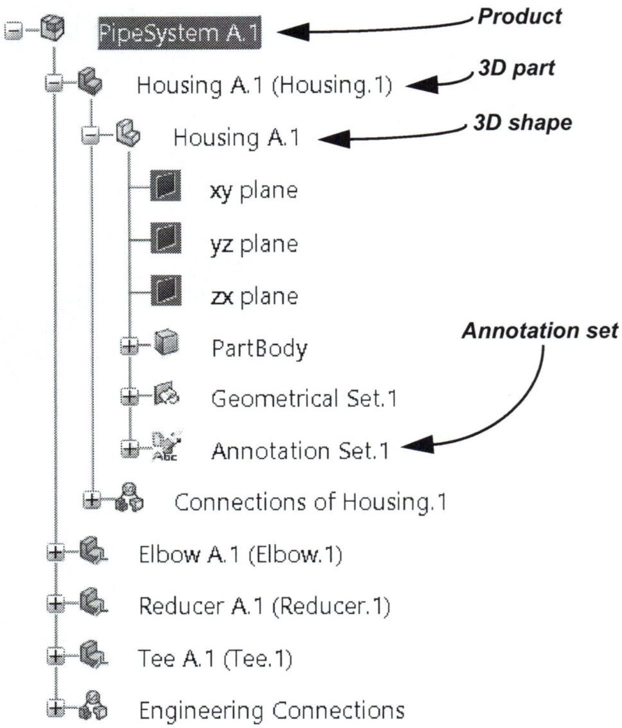

Figure 7–16

Design Considerations

You will notice that, by default, the annotation sets for each component are hidden. You will control the visibility of these using a 3D Annotation Filter later on in the exercise.

To be able to create and control annotations at the product level, a 3D shape needs to be created within the root-level product.

2. Right-click on **PipeSystem** at the top of the specification tree and select **Insert>3D Shape**.The new context window will appear.

3. Select **3D Shape** from under the *Physical Product Structure* node, as shown in Figure 7–17.

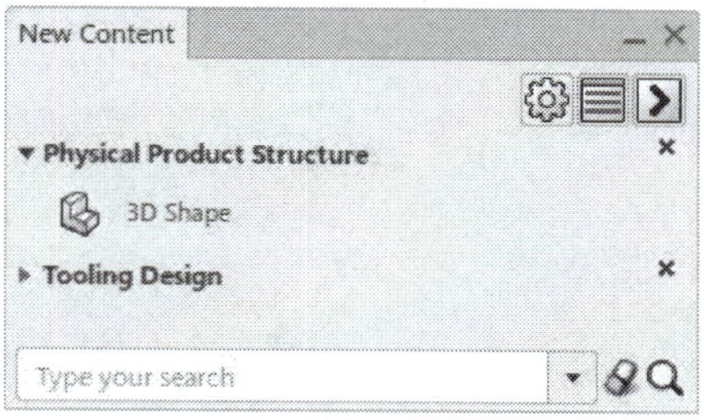

Figure 7–17

4. Within the 3D Shape window, enter **Assembly_Annotations** in the *Title* field.

5. Click **OK** to complete the 3D shape. Assembly_Annotations will be added to the specification tree.

Design Considerations

At this point, the product will still be active. You cannot be in the 3D Tolerancing & Annotation app while being active in a product. This is why you created a 3D shape that will allow you to create tolerances and annotations in it.

6. Activate the **Assembly_Annotations** 3D shape by double-clicking on it in the tree.

7. Hide the **XY,YZ** and **ZX** planes inside the Assembly_Annotations 3D shape.

8. If you are not already in the 3D Tolerancing & Annotation app, select **3D Tolerancing & Annotation** from the outer ring of the compass, as shown in Figure 7–18.

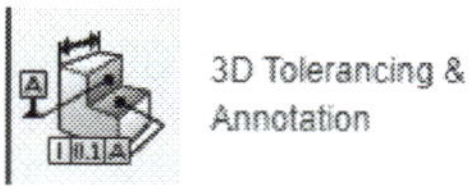

Figure 7–18

Task 4 - Use 3D Annotation Filter to display part-level annotation sets.

In this task, you will control what part-level annotations you want to display.

1. In the Tools section of the Action Bar, select  (3D Annotation Filter). The 3D Annotation Filter window will appear.

2. Under the *Annotation Sets* node, select **All**.

3. A warning window will appear advising that turning on all annotation sets can take a while and be hard to read, so turning on one at a time is advised. While this is true, select **Yes** to continue anyway. The assembly should update as shown in Figure 7–19.

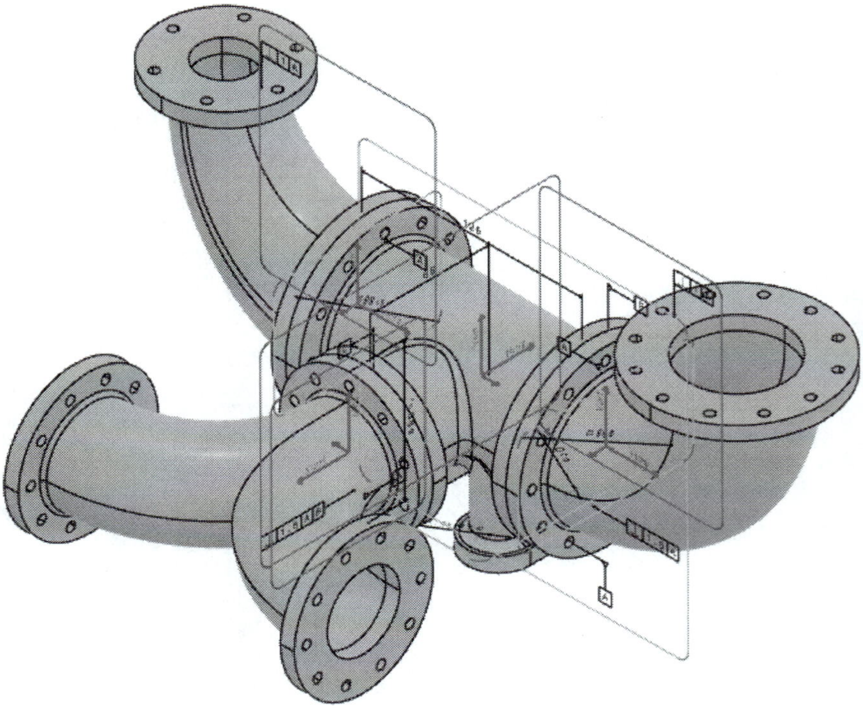

Figure 7–19

4. Using the Annotation Filter is the quickest and easiest way to control the display of annotations at the part or product level, but one can see that displaying everything can get out of hand. Expand the arrow next to **Custom...** in the *Annotation Views* node of the 3D Annotation Filter window.

5. Check and uncheck various annotation sets at this level and watch how the display updates.

6. Select **None** under the *Annotations Sets* node.

7. Click **Close**. The assembly displays as shown in Figure 7–20.

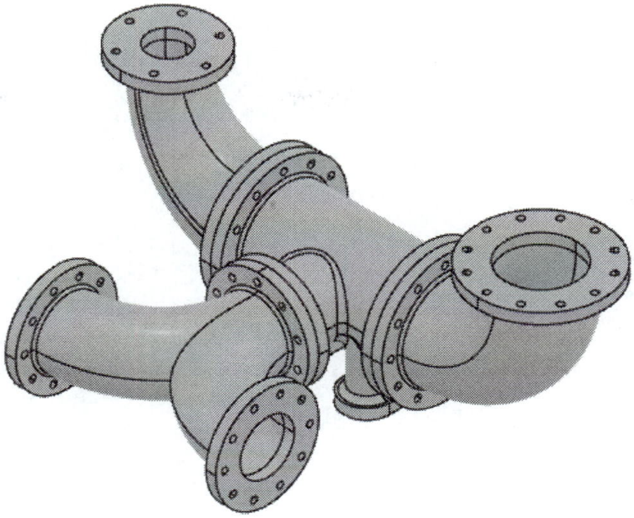

Figure 7–20

8. Hide the Tee component in the specification tree.

Task 5 - Create a view at the product level.

In this task, you will create a view.

1. Select the face, as shown in Figure 7–21.

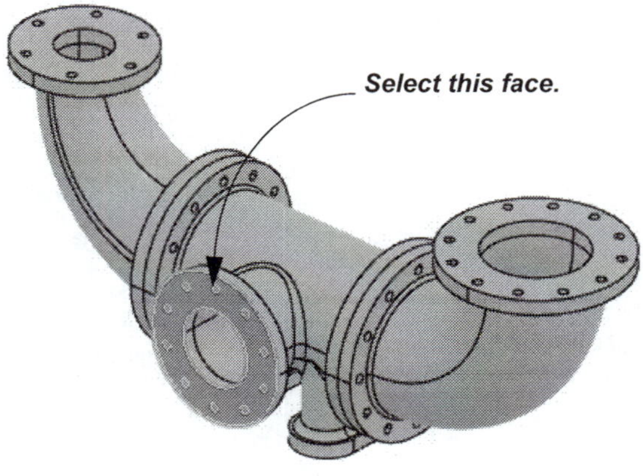

Figure 7–21

2. Create a Projection View view and name it as **TeeFlangeView**. Ensure the view is oriented as shown in Figure 7–22.

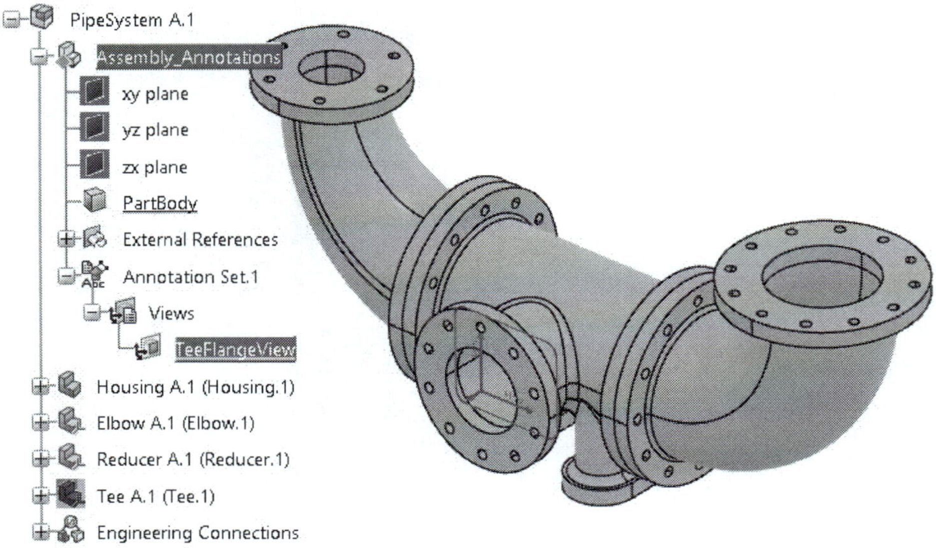

Figure 7–22

Task 6 - Change the tolerancing standard.

1. In the Assembly_Annotations 3D shape, right-click on **Annotation Set.1** and select **Properties**.
2. In the Properties window, select the *Standard* tab.
3. Set the *Presentation Standard* to **ISO**, as shown in Figure 7–23.

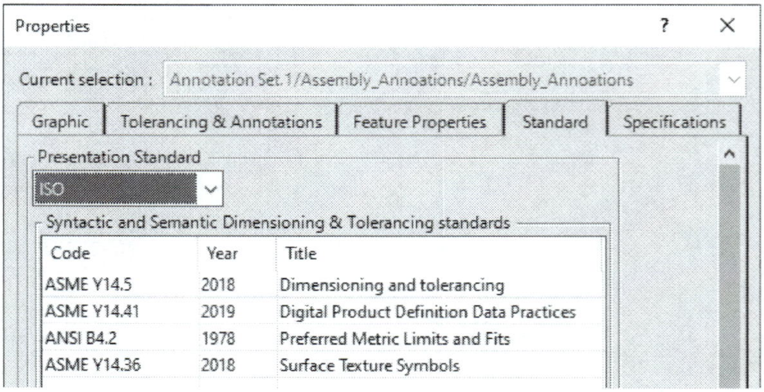

Figure 7–23

4. Select **OK** to close the Properties window.

Task 7 - Create a product-level semantic datum and dimension.

1. Preselect the surface shown in Figure 7–24.

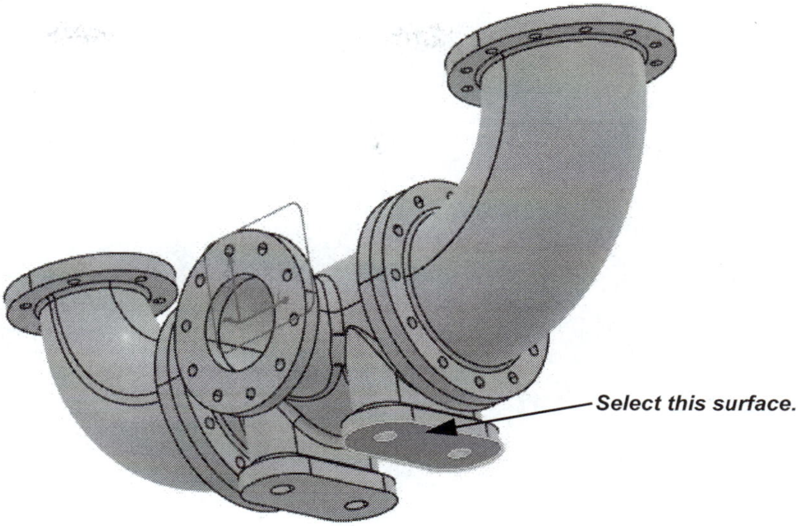

Figure 7–24

2. Use the tolerancing advisor to create the following:
   - **Semantic Datum (A)**
   - **Datum Reference Frame** (enable **Only from this datum feature**)

   The completed datum displays as shown in Figure 7–25 (move the datum to the position shown in the image).

For clarity, annotations have been enlarged to 7.0mm.

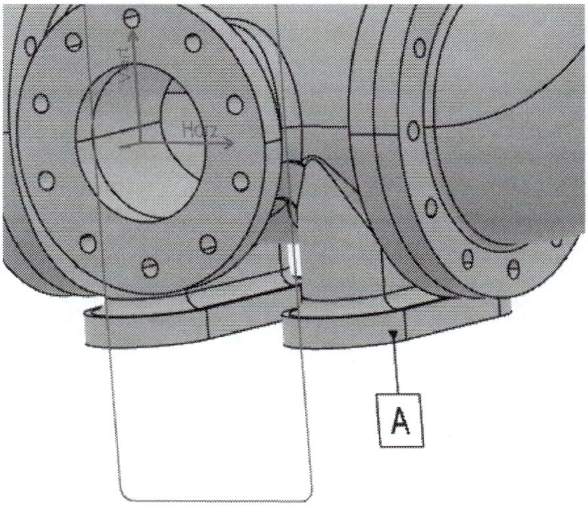

Figure 7–25

Next, you will create a dimension between the surface representing the A datum and the top flange surface.

3. Preselect the two surfaces shown in Figure 7–26.

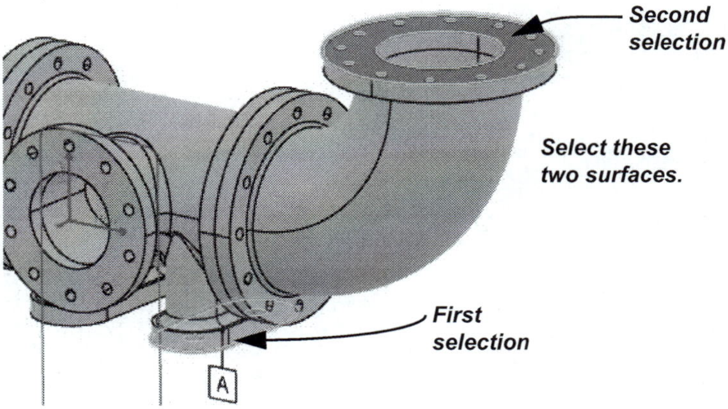

Figure 7–26

4. Use the Tolerance Advisor to create a **Between 2 geometrical features**, (Line Dimension Related to Origin) semantic dimension with a symmetrical tolerance of **1.5mm**, as shown in Figure 7–27.

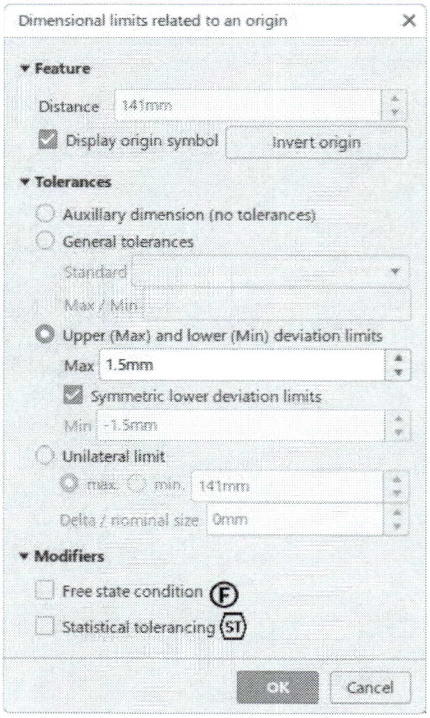

Figure 7–27

5. Use the Object Properties window to change the units to **NUM.DIMM** if needed.

6. Move the completed dimension to the location shown in Figure 7–28.

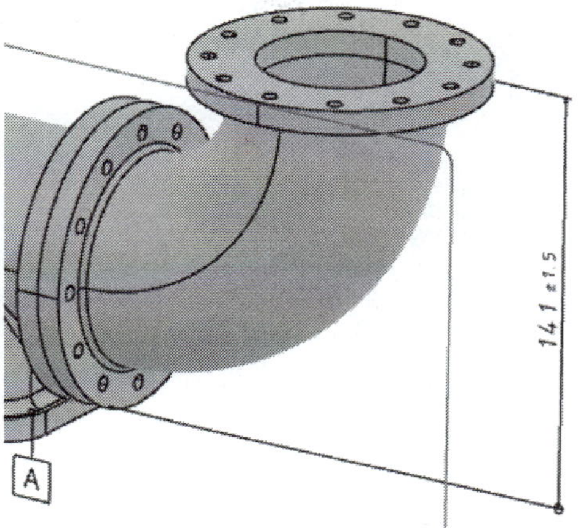

Figure 7–28

Task 8 - Create a product-level semantic tolerance.

In this task, you will create a geometric tolerance that controls the two top flanges relative to datum A.

1. Preselect the two surfaces shown in Figure 7–29.

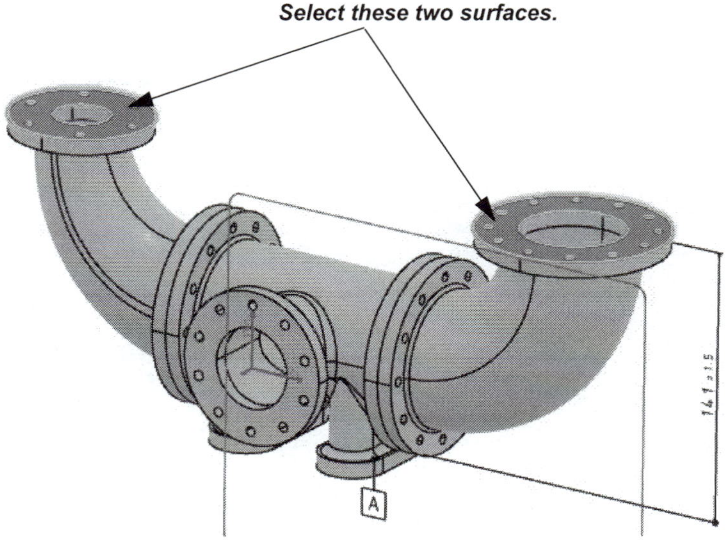

Figure 7–29

2. Use the Tolerance Advisor to create an **N separate planes (Nx)** feature type with Flatness Specification, as shown in Figure 7–30.

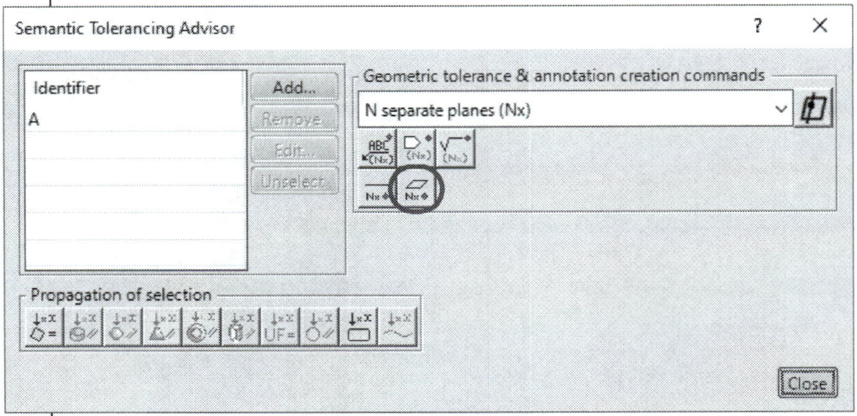

Figure 7–30

3. Enter a tolerance of **2mm**, as shown in Figure 7–31.

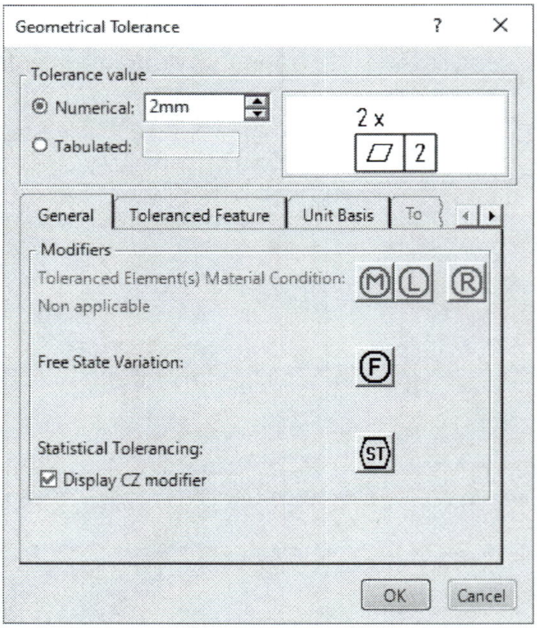

Figure 7–31

4. Click **OK**.

5. Select datum **A** in the *Identifier* section and create an **N separate planes (Nx)** feature with **Parallelism Specification**, as shown in Figure 7–32, to create a parallel geometrical tolerance relative to the datum A.

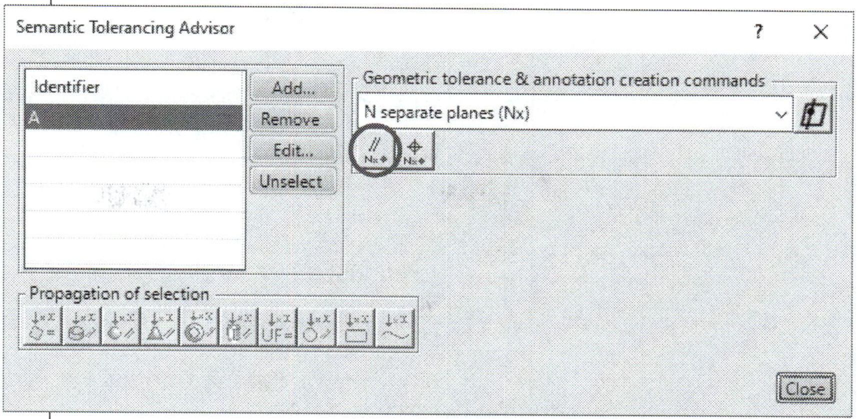

Figure 7–32

6. Enter a tolerance value of **2mm**.
7. Click **OK**.
8. Click **Close**.
9. Move the geometric tolerance as shown in Figure 7–33.

Your geometric tolerance might be located on the other surface. The tolerance will be placed closest to the last selected surface.

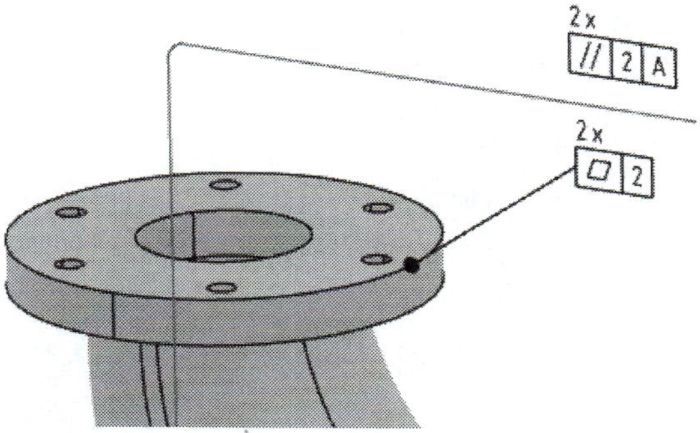

Figure 7–33

Note that the geometric tolerance created points to only one of the selected surfaces. In the following steps, you will add another leader to point to the other surface.

10. Select **Me>Preferences>Customize** and select the *Action Pad* tab.
11. Select **Add Commands** and find  (Manual) in the list.
12. Select **Manual** and click **OK** to add it to the Action Pad if not already there.
13. Click **Close** to close the Customize window.

Note that you could simply select the surface but this is showing you how to reconnect a leader if needed.

14. If the Action Pad window isn't displayed, select  (Action Pad) from the Tools section of the Action Bar.

15. Select 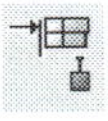 (Manual) from the Action Pad.

16. Select the **Flattness.1** geometrical tolerance first, then select **Parallelism.1** second.

17. Click **OK** in the Positioning window.

18. Right-click on the **Flattness.1** geometric tolerance and select **Add Leader**.

19. Select somewhere close to the other referenced surface in the view frame area.

20. With the leader selected, right-click on the endpoint of the leader that you just added and select **Add Extremity Link**.

21. Select the applicable flange surface to update the leader placement.

22. Right-click again on the endpoint and select **Add a Breakpoint** for the new leader, then place the geometric tolerance as shown in Figure 7–34.

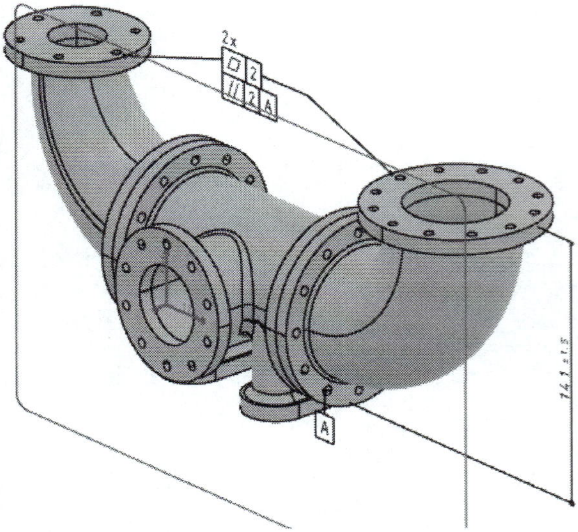

Figure 7–34

23. Double-click on **Flatness.1**. The Geometrical Tolerance window appears.

24. Use the right arrow to select the *Notes* tab.

25. Uncheck the **Automatic display of Nx at** setting, and enter **Surfaces** into the top field, as shown in Figure 7–35.

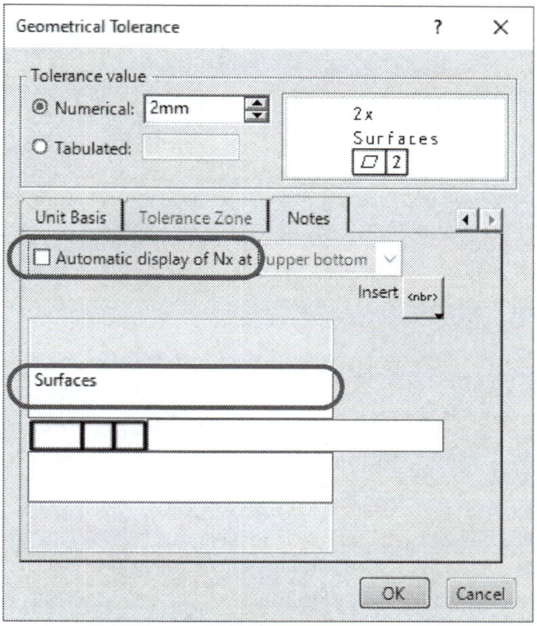

Figure 7–35

26. Click **OK**.

27. Show the Tee component.

28. Preselect the surface shown in Figure 7–36.

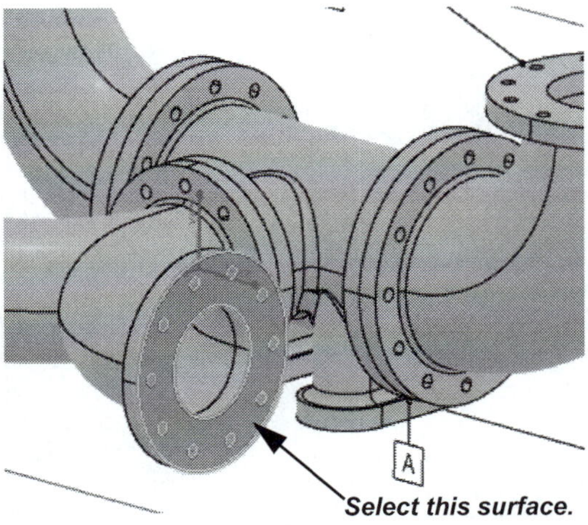

Figure 7–36

29. Use the Tolerance Advisor to create a geometric tolerance that specifies the selected surface be perpendicular to datum A by **2mm**. The completed tolerance displays as shown in Figure 7–37.

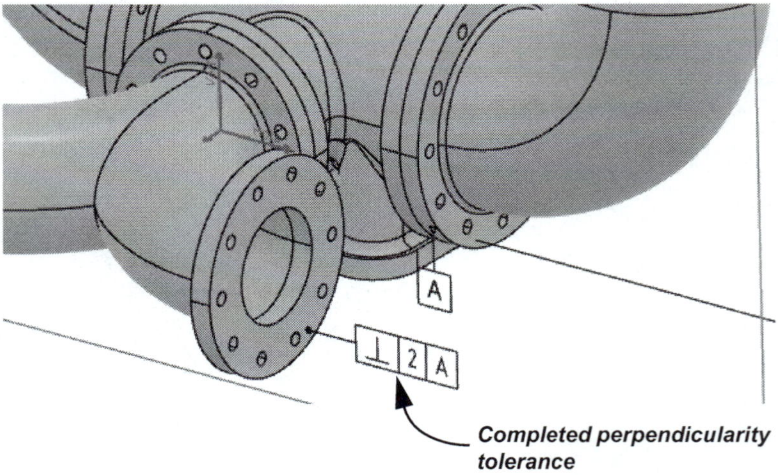

Figure 7–37

30. The completed product annotation displays as shown in Figure 7–38. Save the file.

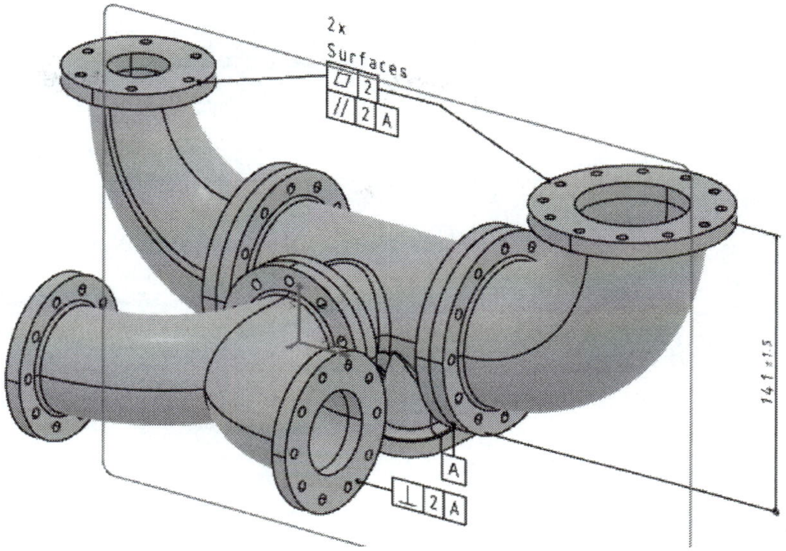

Figure 7–38

Task 9 - Create a drawing.

In this task, you will create a new drawing and add two views using the annotated assembly. The first view uses the TeeFlangeView from the assembly. The second view is created from the Housing component. To do this, you will switch the annotation set for Housing back on.

1. Using the 3D Annotation Filter, enable the annotation set for the **Housing**, as shown in Figure 7–39.

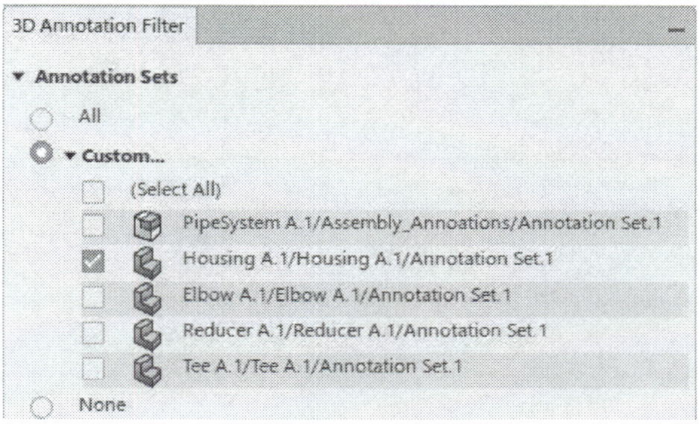

Figure 7–39

2. Click **Close**.

3. Create a new empty drawing using the following parameters:

   - *Standard:* **ISO**
   - *Sheet Style:* **A1 ISO**

4. Click  (View from 3D) and switch to the **PipeSystem A.1** product widget.

5. Select **TeeFlangeView** in the product annotation set.

6. Click somewhere on the background. The new view displays as shown in Figure 7–40.

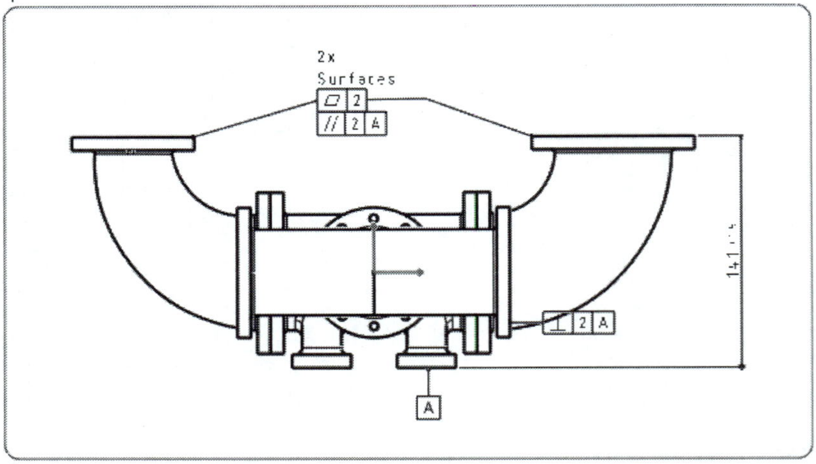

Figure 7–40

7. Create a second view and reference **RunFlangeView** in the **Housing** annotation set. The view displays as shown in Figure 7–41.

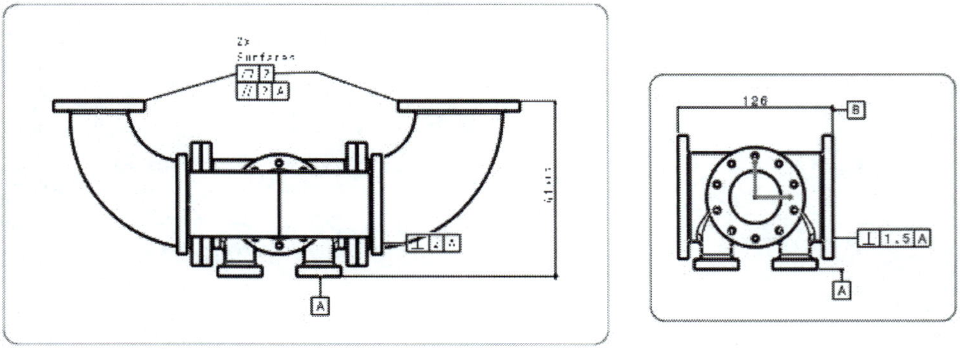

Figure 7–41

8. Add an isometric view of the assembly to the drawing.

9. Right-click on the drawing views in the tree and select **Properties** to toggle off the view frame for all three views. The drawing displays, as shown in Figure 7–42.

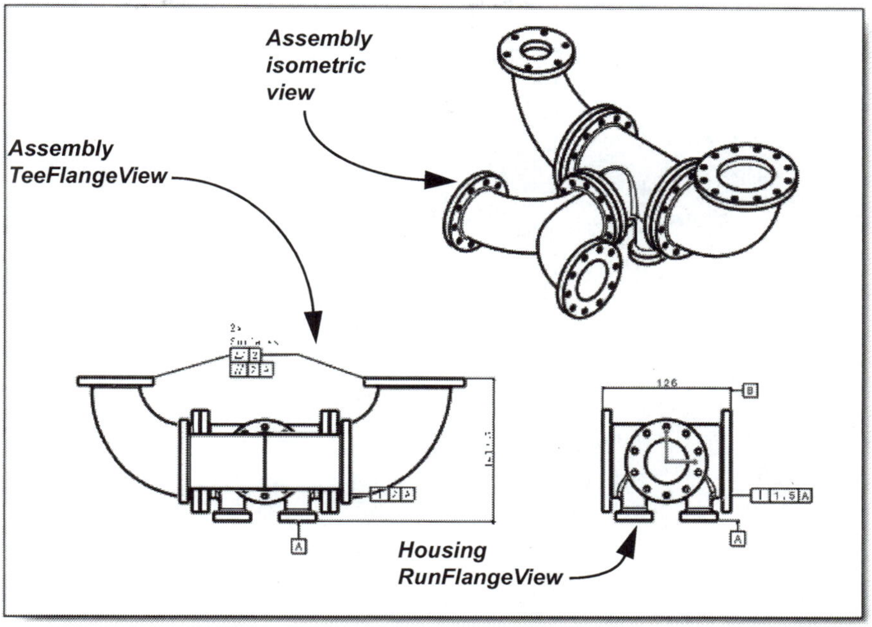

Figure 7–42

10. Save all files and close all windows.

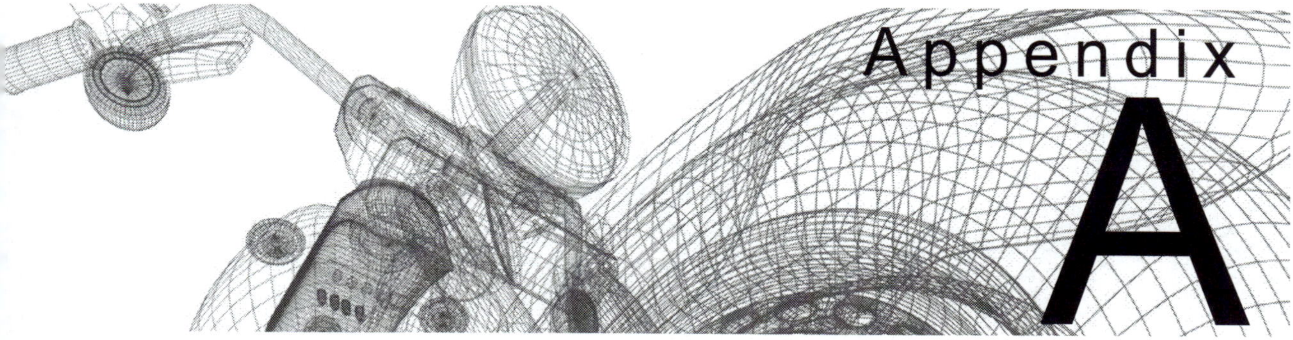

Appendix A

3D T&A Projects

These projects are to be completed with minimal instruction. Complete on your own or as a group, as time permits.

Projects in This Appendix

- Flange Part
- Spindle Part
- Coupling Part
- Threaded Ball
- Pressure Plate
- Coaxial Parts Case

Practice A1

Flange Part

Practice Objective

- Specify runout relative to datum surface and diameter.

In this project, you will add tolerances and annotations to a part and create a drawing view to display them. The completed drawing is shown in Figure A–1.

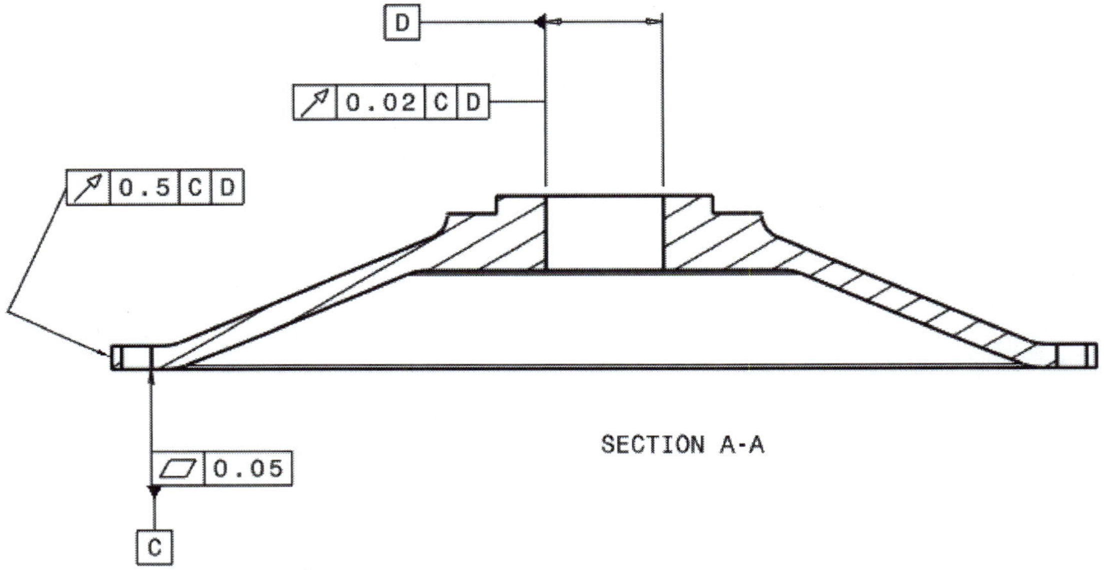

Figure A–1

Task 1 - Import and open a part file.

1. Import and open **Flange.3dxml** from the *Projects* folder. The part displays as shown in Figure A–2.

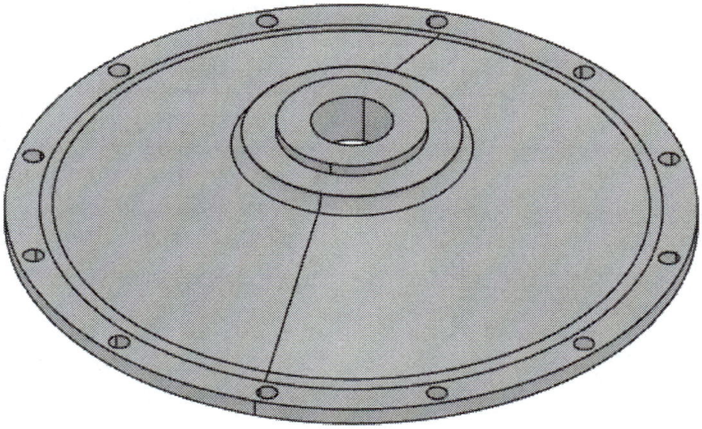

Figure A–2

Task 2 - Create semantic datums and geometrical tolerances.

1. Create semantic datums and geometrical tolerances on a section view plane, as shown in Figure A–3 (you can also reference Figure A–4).

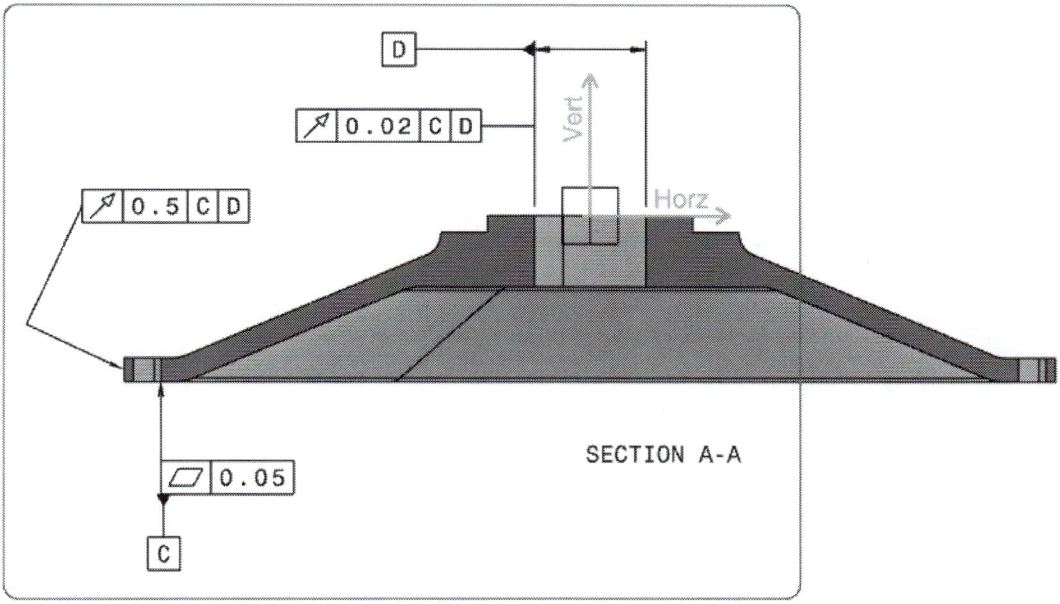

Figure A–3

Task 3 - Create a drawing.

1. Create the following drawing:

   - *Standard:* **ANSI-ASME**
   - *Format:* **C ANSI**

2. Create the view shown in Figure A–4.

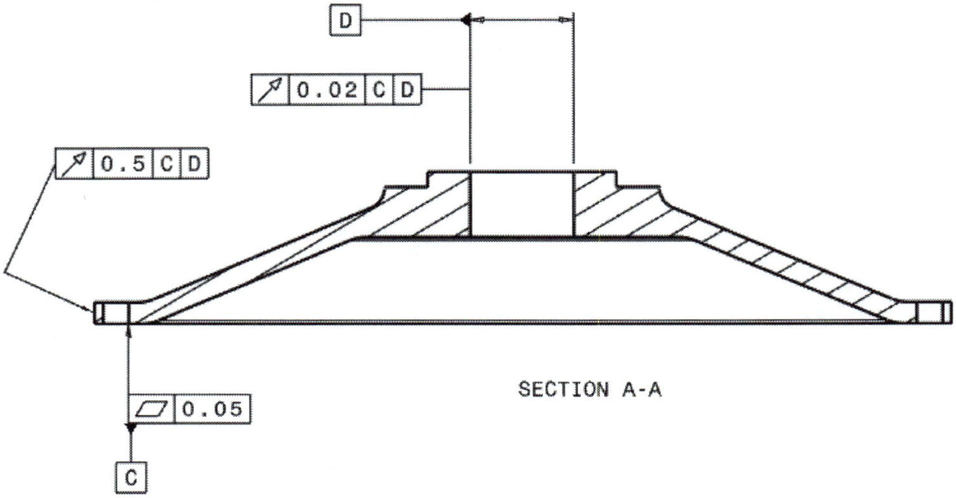

Figure A–4

3. Save the project and close all windows.

Practice A2 Spindle Part

Practice Objective

- Specify runout relative to two datum diameters.

In this project, you will add tolerances and annotations to a part and create a drawing view to display them. The completed drawing is shown in Figure A–5.

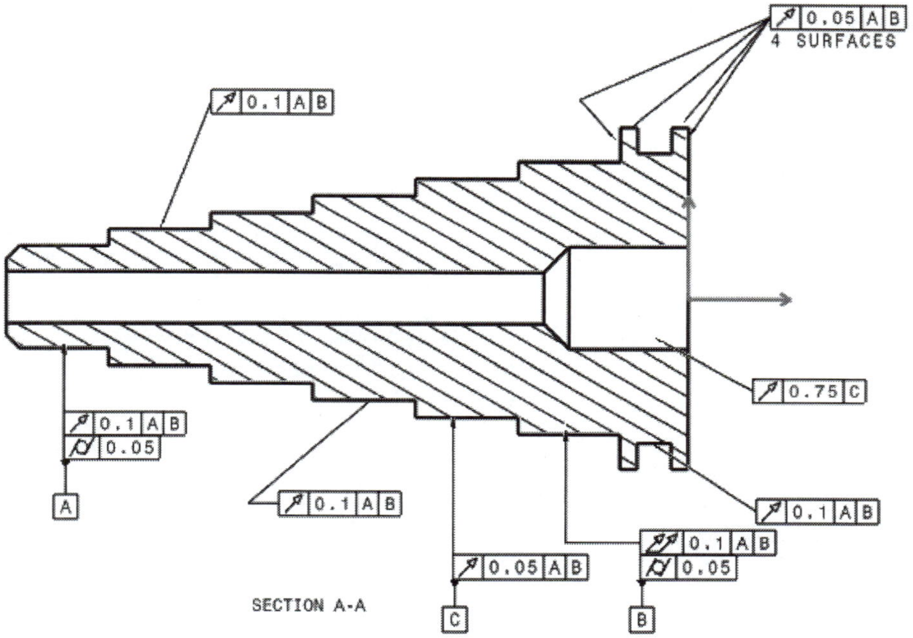

Figure A–5

Task 1 - Import and open a part file.

1. Open **Spindle.3dxml** from the *Projects* folder. The part displays as shown in Figure A–6.

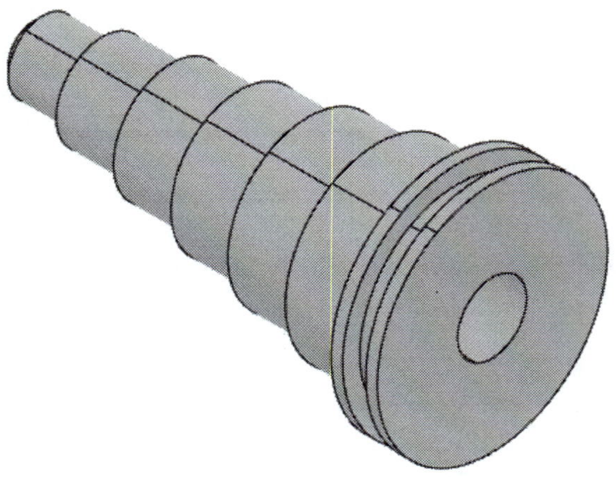

Figure A–6

2. Create semantic datums and tolerances on a section view plane, as shown in Figure A–7 (you can also reference Figure A–8).

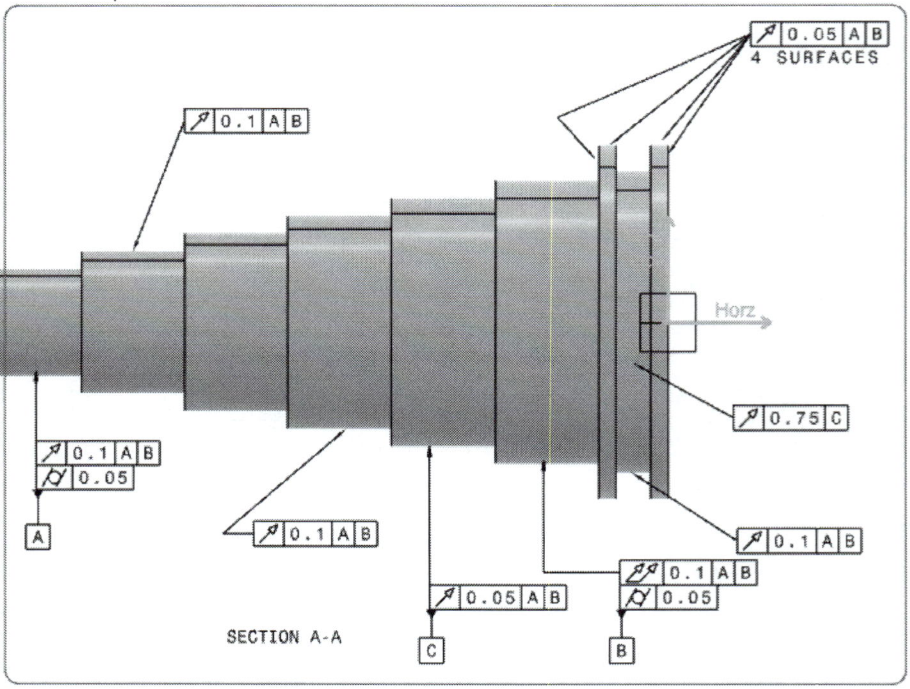

Figure A–7

Task 2 - Create a drawing.

1. Create the following drawing:

    - *Standard:* **ANSI-ASME**
    - *Format:* **C ANSI**

2. Create the view shown in Figure A–8.

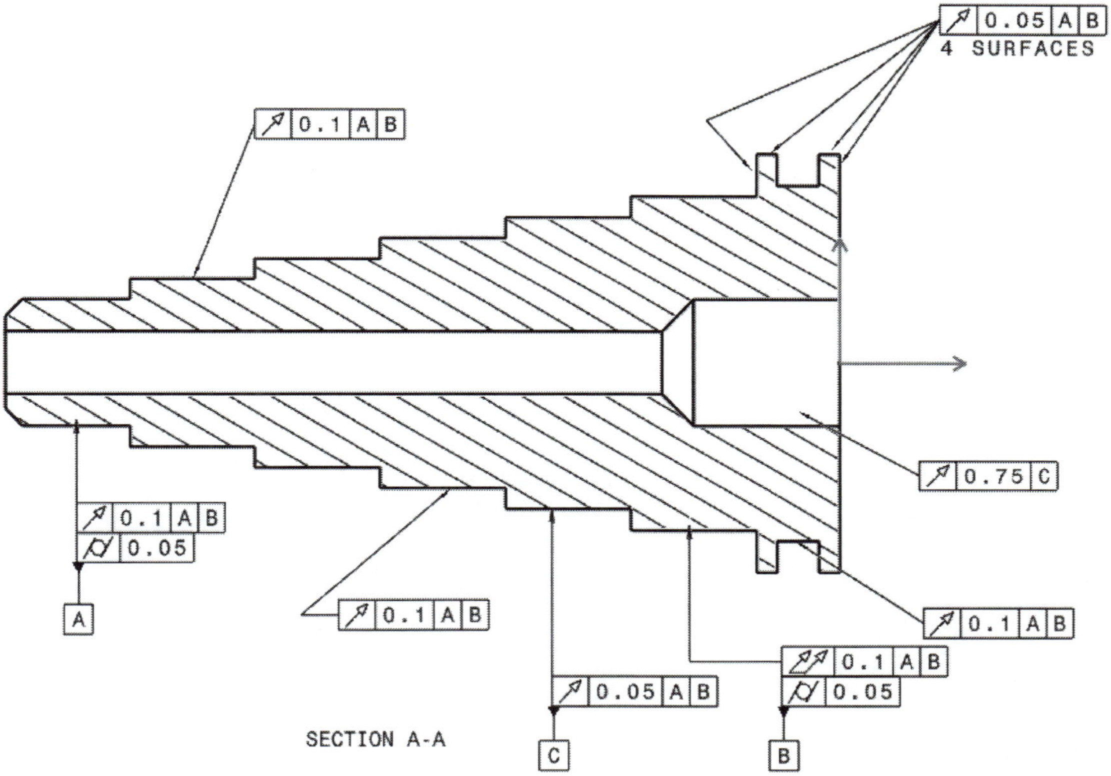

Figure A–8

3. Save the project and close all windows.

Practice A3 Coupling Part

Practice Objective

- Create a radial hole pattern located by composite positional tolerancing.

In this project, you will add tolerances and annotations to a part and create a drawing view to display them.

Task 1 - Open a part file.

1. Open **Coupling.3dxml** from the *Projects* folder. The part displays as shown in Figure A–9.

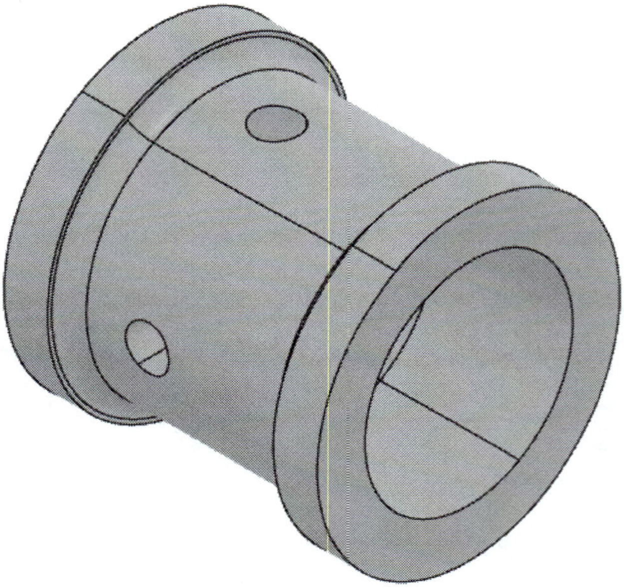

Figure A–9

2. Select **Me>Preferences**.
3. Select **Common Preferences>Parameters, Measures, and Units>Units** and select the *Units* arrow. Verify that the units are set to **Inch (in)**.
4. Select **App Preferences>3D Modeling>Mechanical Systems>3D Tolerancing and Annotation** and select the *Tolerances* arrow. Verify that *Precision* is set to **0.001**.

Task 2 - Create semantic datums, dimensions, and tolerances.

*If a 28mm dimension displays instead of the intended 14mm, right-click on the dimension while placing it and select **Half Dimension**.*

1. Create a section view plane and select the YZ plane as a reference.
2. Create the following:
   - Semantic datums
   - Semantic dimensions
   - A basic dimension
   - Composite positional tolerance

The required dimensions and annotations are shown in Figure A–10 (you can also reference Figure A–11).

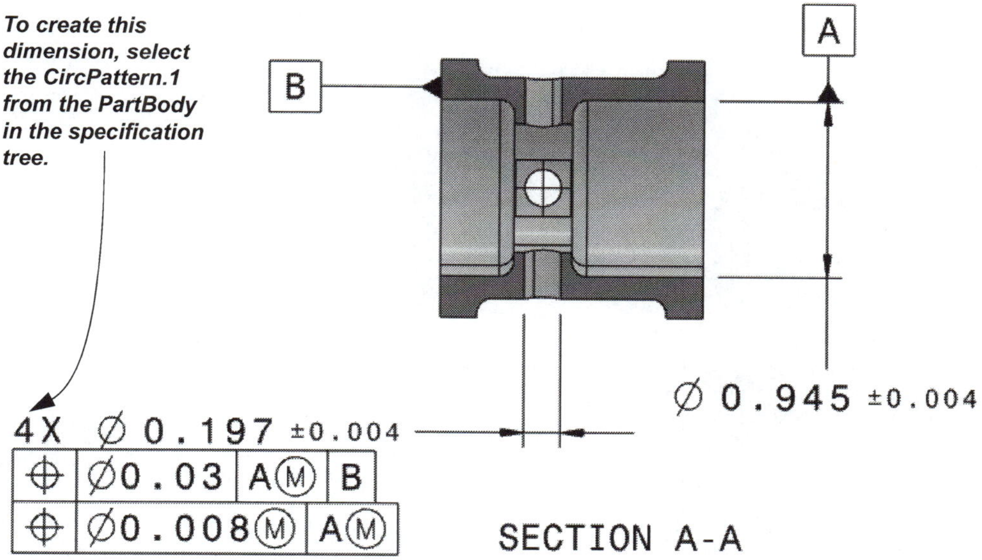

Figure A–10

Task 3 - Create a drawing.

1. Create the following drawing:
   - *Standard:* **ANSI-ASME**
   - *Format:* **A ANSI**
2. Create the view shown in Figure A–11.

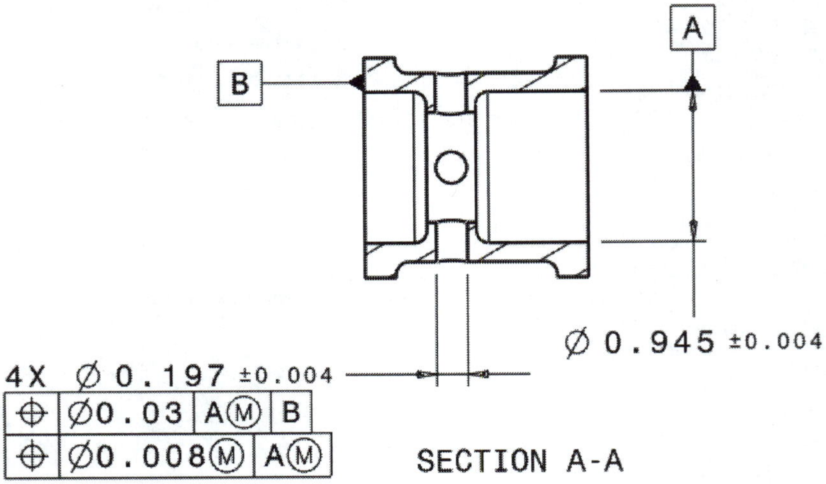

Figure A–11

3. Save the project and close all windows.

Practice A4 Threaded Ball

Practice Objectives

- Display a thread representation.
- Create a thread annotation.

In this project, you add tolerances and annotations to a part, and create a drawing view to display them.

Task 1 - Open a part file.

1. Open **ThreadedBall.3dxml** from the *Projects* folder. The part displays as shown in Figure A–12.

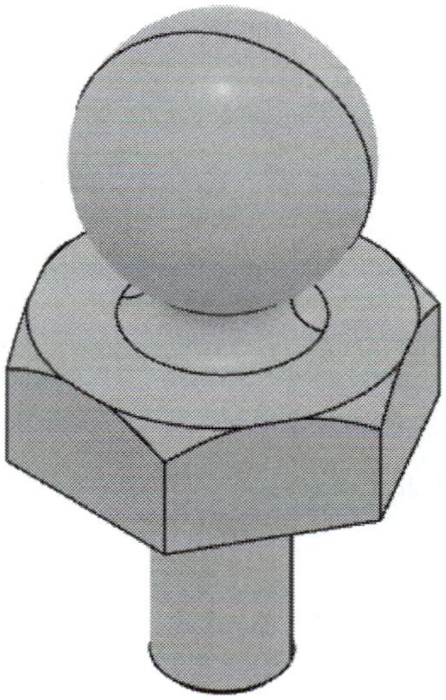

Figure A–12

Task 2 - Create semantic datums, dimensions, and tolerances.

*Note that the units are in metric. Set the global units to **Millimeter (mm)** and use the Object Properties window to convert the dimensions to metric.*

1. Create the following:

   - Front view plane
   - Thread representation
   - Thread diameter annotation
   - Semantic datums
   - A semantic dimension
   - A basic dimension
   - A positional tolerance

   The required dimensions and annotations are shown in Figure A–13 (you can also reference Figure A–14).

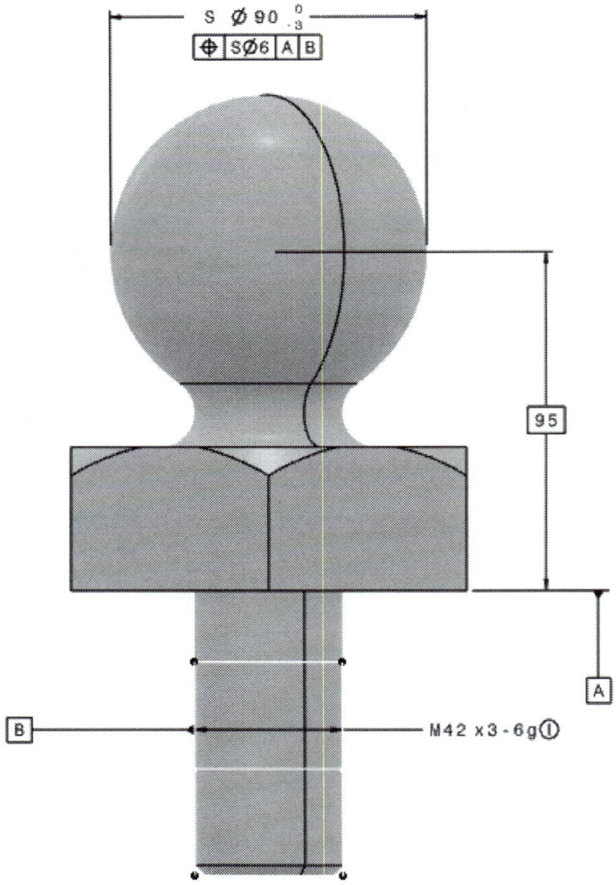

Figure A–13

Task 3 - Create a drawing.

1. Create the following drawing:
   - *Standard:* **ANSI-ASME**
   - *Format:* **B ANSI**
   - *Orientation:* **Portrait**
2. Create the view shown in Figure A–14. Verify that the thread and axes display.

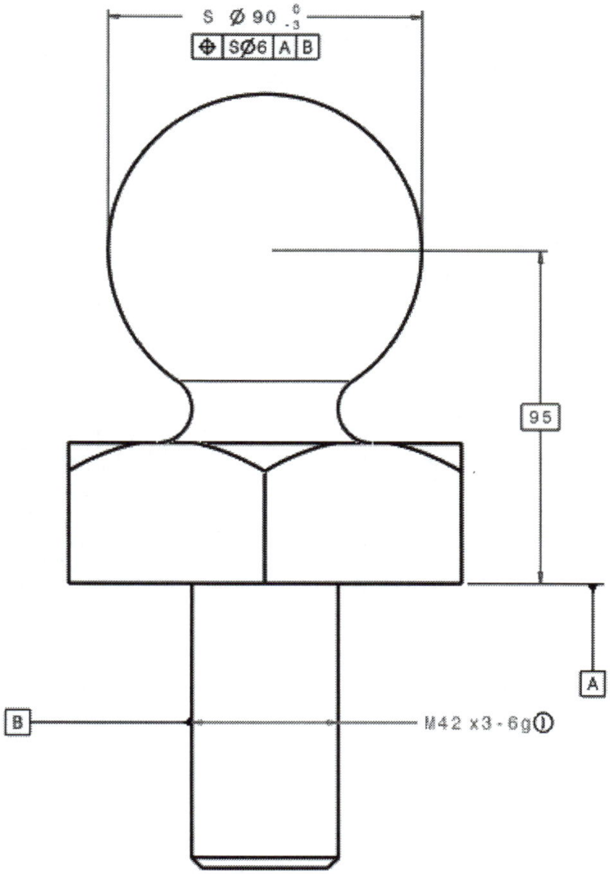

Figure A–14

3. Save the project and close all windows.

Practice A5 Pressure Plate

Practice Objectives

- Annotate a part model.
- Create drawing views of an annotated model.

In this project, you add tolerances and annotations to a part and create a drawing view to display them.

Task 1 - Open a part file.

1. Open **PressurePlate.3dxml** from the *Projects* folder. The part displays as shown in Figure A–15.

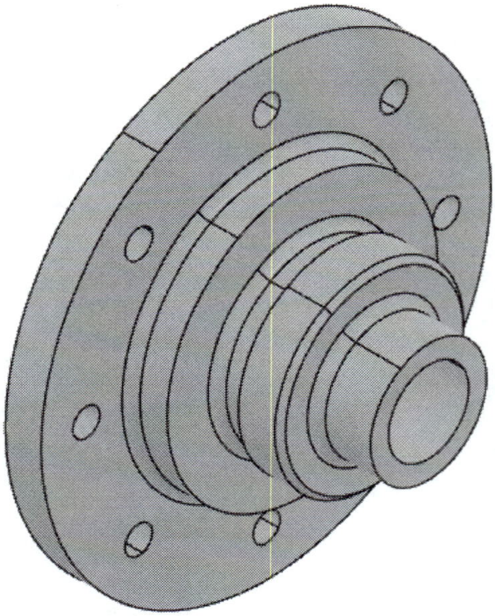

Figure A–15

Note that the units are in metric. Set the global units to ***Millimeter (mm)*** *and use the Object Properties window to convert the dimensions to metric.*

Use the Generative Dimensions tool to create the chamfer dimension.

Task 2 - Create semantic datums, dimensions, and tolerances.

1. Create the following:
   - Section view plane
   - Toleranced dimensions
   - Semantic datums and required datum reference frames
   - Geometrical tolerances
   - Thread representation
   - Thread diameter annotation

The required dimensions and annotations are shown in Figure A–16 (you can also reference Figure A–18).

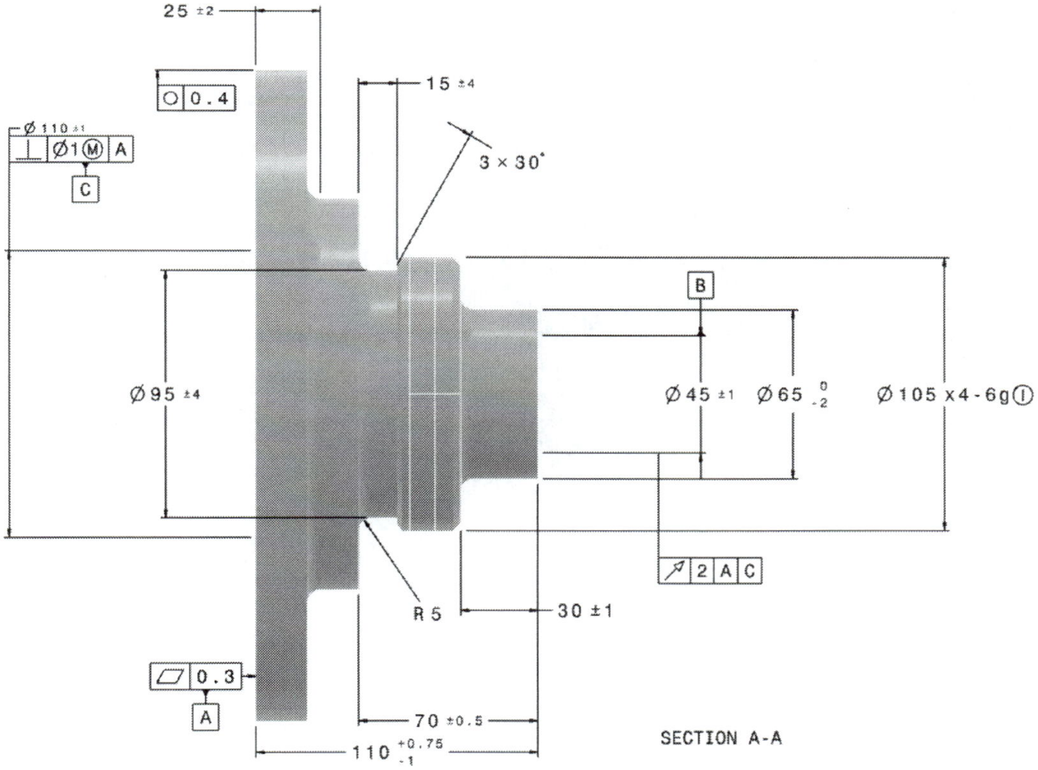

Figure A–16

2. Create the following:

   - Front view plane
   - Construction geometry
   - Semantic dimensions
   - Position geometrical tolerance

   The required dimensions and annotations are shown in Figure A–17 (you can also reference Figure A–19).

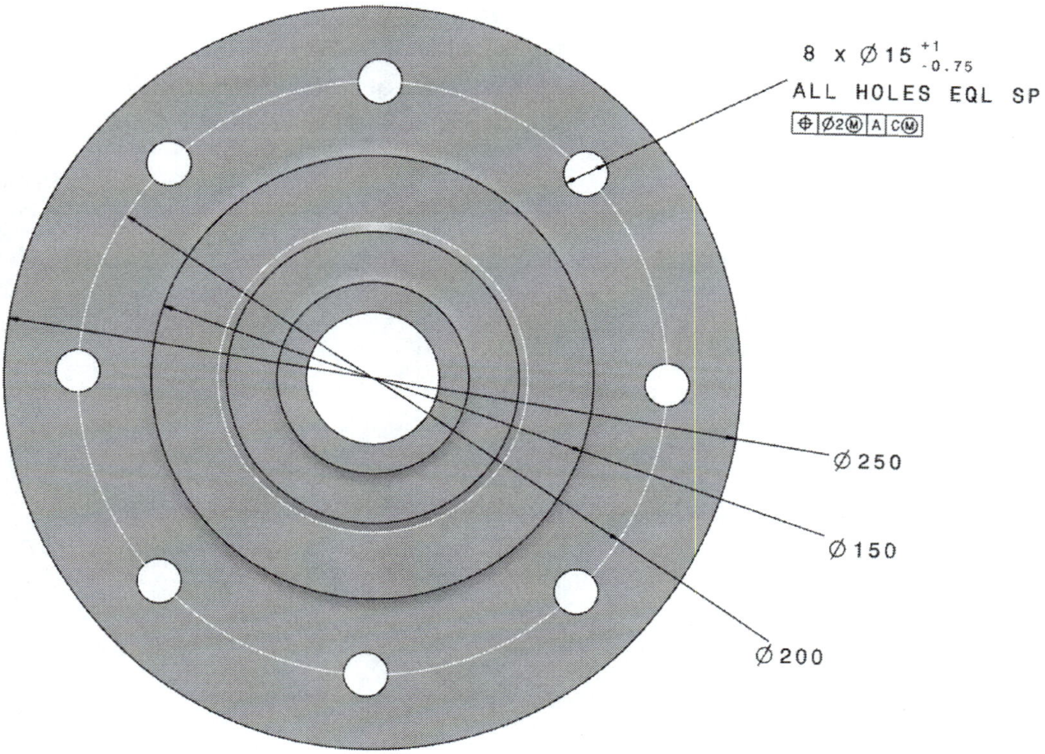

Figure A–17

Task 3 - Create a drawing.

1. Create the following drawing:
   - *Standard:* **ANSI-ASME**
   - *Format:* **E ANSI**
   - *Orientation:* **Landscape**
2. Create the view shown in Figure A–18 and Figure A–19. Verify that the thread and axes display.

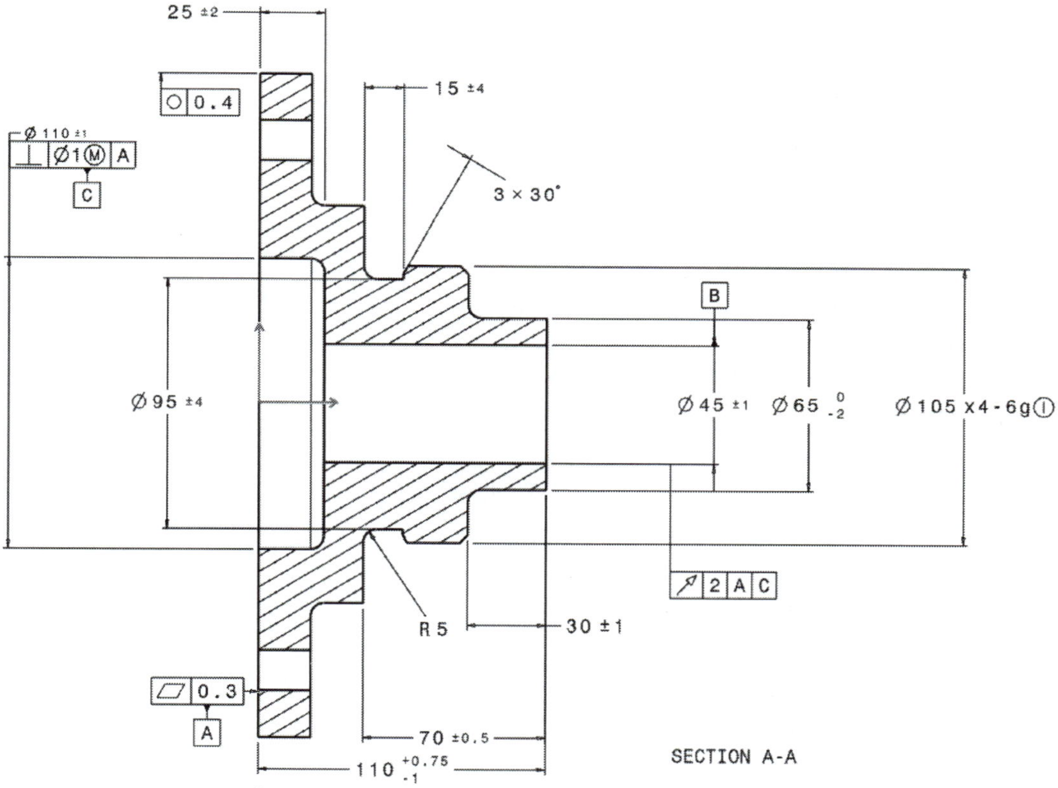

Figure A–18

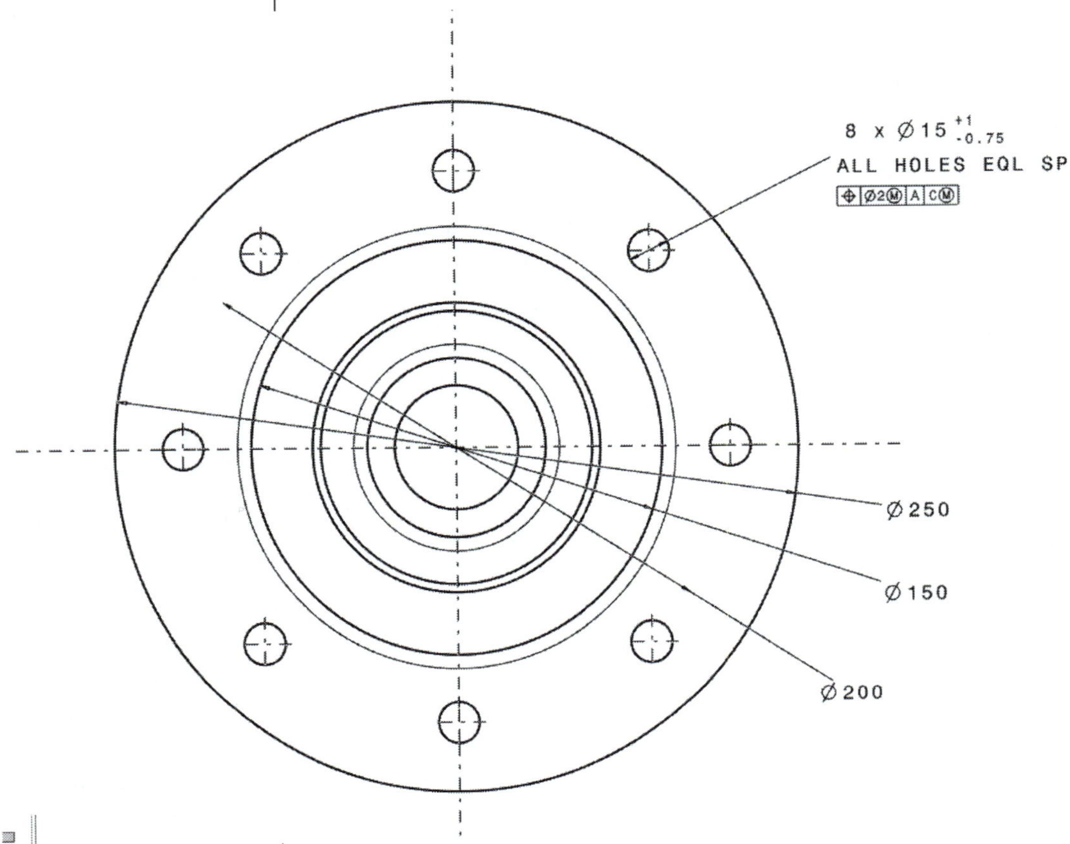

Figure A–19

3. Save the project and close all windows.

Practice A6

Coaxial Parts Case

Practice Objective

- Determine tolerance for two coaxial mating parts.

In this project, you will determine the geometric tolerance for each coaxial mating part. You will use a formula to find the available tolerance and divide it unequally between the two parts. At the end of the practice, you will create a drawing of the assembly and create a view from 3D for the parts of the assembly. The completed drawing displays, as shown in Figure A–20.

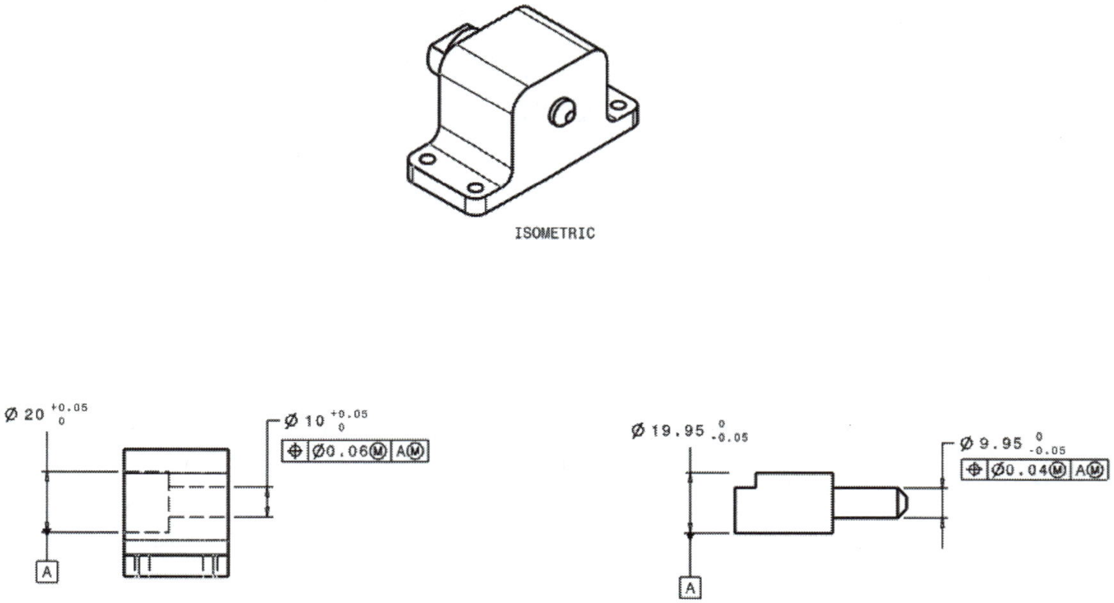

Figure A–20

Task 1 - Import and open a product file.

1. Import and open **CoaxialParts.3dxml** from the *Projects* folder. The two-part assembly displays as shown in Figure A–21.

Figure A–21

This assembly consists of two parts that share an axis (coaxial) and therefore also share the datum that defines that axis. In this project, you will create semantic datums and dimensions for each part. You will then apply a floating fastener case formula to determine the geometric tolerance value in the context of this assembly.

Task 2 - Set options.

1. Select **Me>Preferences**.

2. Select **Common Preferences>Parameters, Measures, and Units>Units** and select the *Units* arrow. Verify that the units are set to **Millimeter (mm)**.

3. Select **App Preferences>3D Modeling>Mechanical Systems>3D Tolerancing and Annotation** and select the *Tolerances* arrow. Verify that *Precision* is set to **0.001**.

4. Click **OK**.

Task 3 - Open a part model.

In this task, you will open one of the parts that belong to the CoaxialParts assembly in a separate window and create a semantic datum and dimensions.

1. Right-click on **Seat A.1** and select **Seat.1 object>Open in new app**. The part displays as shown in Figure A–22.

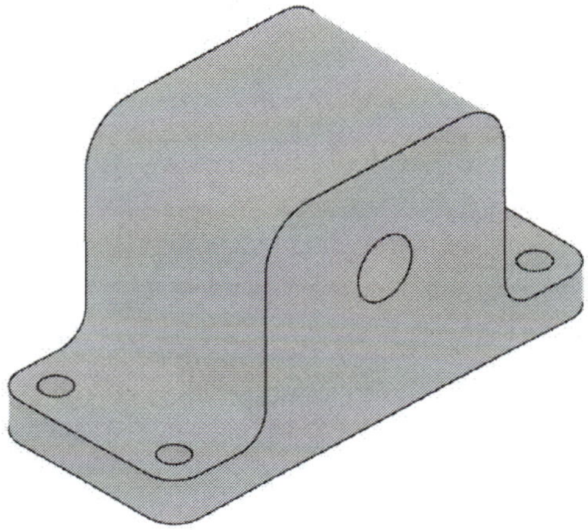

Figure A–22

2. Create a Front View/Annotation Plane by referencing the YZ plane. Verify that the plane is oriented as shown in Figure A–23.

Note: The model will be sectioned temporarily if (3D Master Query) is enabled and the view is selected.

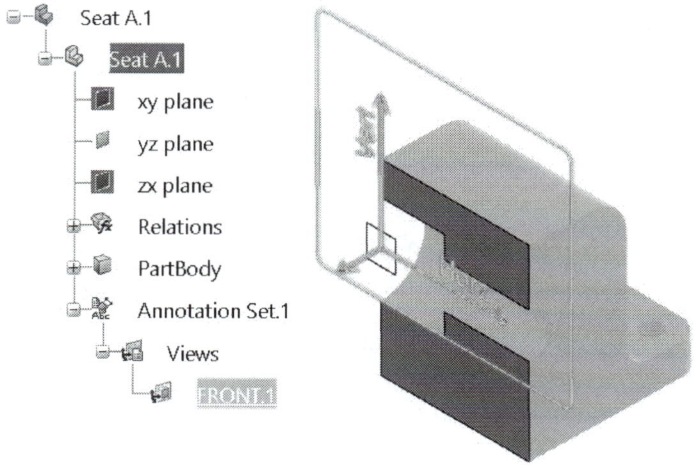

Figure A–23

3. Preselect the larger of the two bores, as shown in Figure A–24.

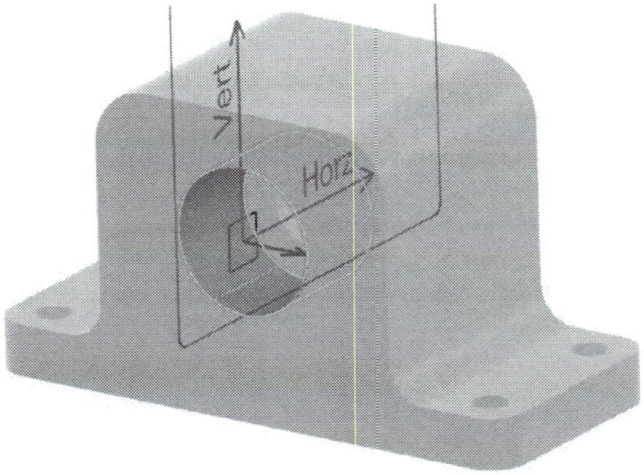

Figure A–24

4. Use the Tolerance Advisor to create semantic datum A with a DRF.

5. Position datum A as shown in Figure A–25.

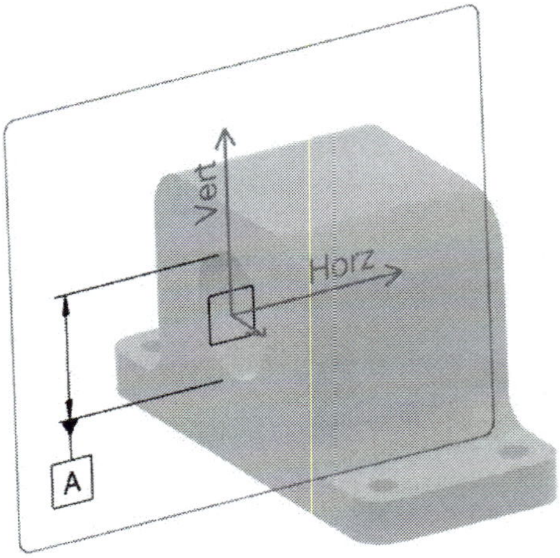

Figure A–25

6. Create a semantic diameter dimension for the same bore. Add the following tolerance:

   - *Upper Limit:* **0.05mm**
   - *Lower Limit:* **0.0mm**

7. Use the Object Properties window to change the units to **NUM.DIMM**.

8. Position the completed diameter dimension as shown in Figure A–26.

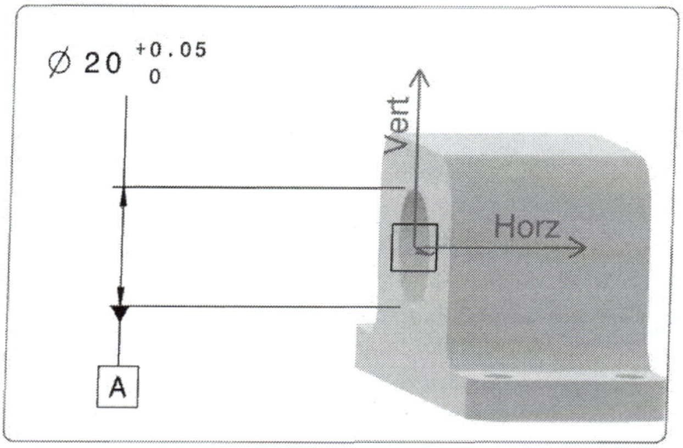

Figure A–26

9. Create a semantic dimension for the smaller bore. Add the following tolerance, as shown in Figure A–27:

   - *Upper Limit:* **0.05mm**
   - *Lower Limit:* **0.00mm**

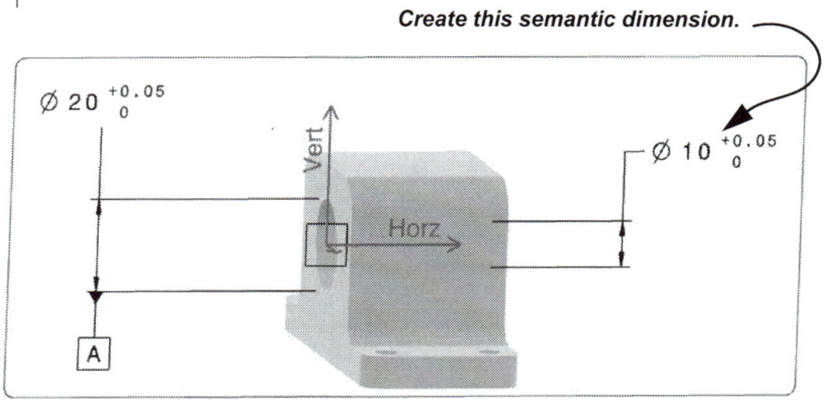

Figure A–27

10. Hide the **YZ** plane.

11. Save the Seat A.1 part.

Task 4 - Open the mating part.

1. Using the tabs at the top of the screen, select the **CoaxialParts A.1** widget. The assembly should be displayed.
2. Right-click on **Post A.1** and select **Post.1 object>Open in new app**. The part displays as shown in Figure A–28.

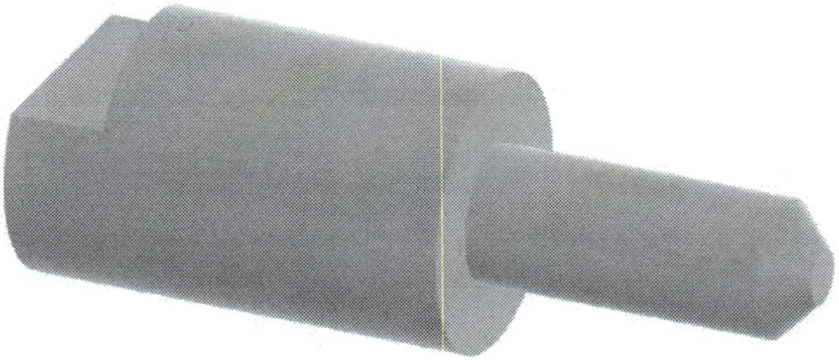

Figure A–28

3. Create a Front View/Annotation Plane by referencing the YZ plane.
4. Create a semantic datum with DRF on the large diameter geometry and position it as shown in Figure A–29.

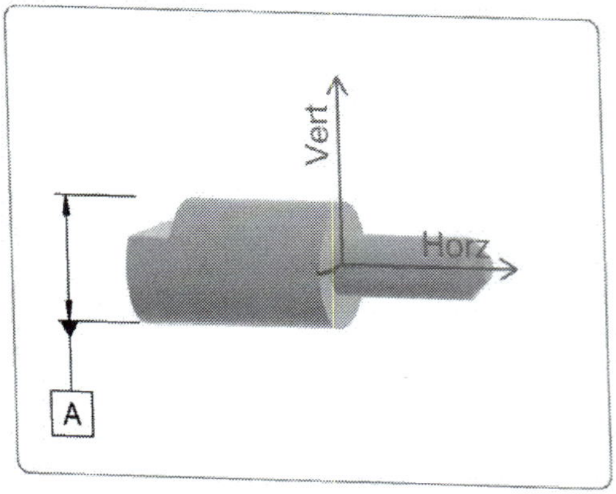

Figure A–29

5. Create the semantic diameter dimension shown in Figure A–30. Add the following tolerance:

   - *Upper Limit:* **0.0mm**
   - *Lower Limit:* **-0.05mm**

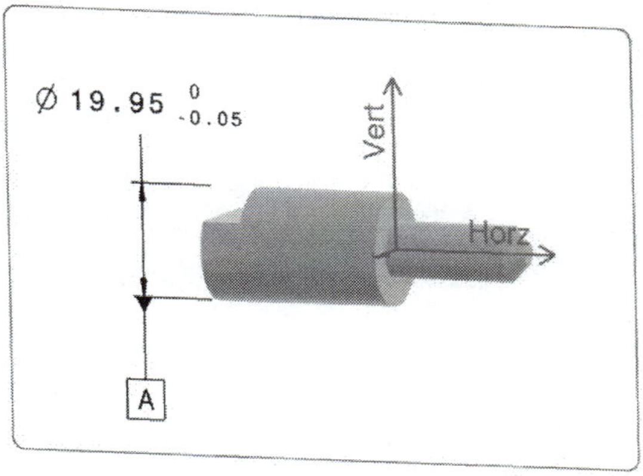

Figure A–30

6. Create the semantic diameter dimension shown in Figure A–31. Add the following tolerance:

   - *Upper Limit:* **0.0in**
   - *Lower Limit:* **-0.05in**

   The completed annotations display as shown in Figure A–31.

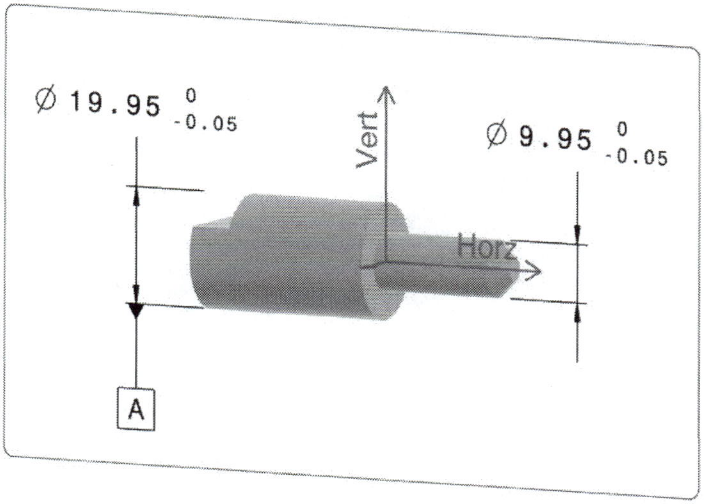

Figure A–31

Task 5 - Determine the tolerance for both parts.

Design Considerations

When two or more parts are assembled (such as bolts and nuts) and all parts have clearance holes, it is termed a *floating fastener case.* Use the following formula to determine the positional tolerance required for a floating fastener case, as shown in Figure A–32 and Figure A–33:

Where:

- F = max. diameter of fastener at MMC
- H = min. diameter of clearance hole at MMC
- T = positional tolerance diameter

$T = H - F$

Therefore:

$T_1 + T_2 = (H_1 + H_2) - (F_1 + F_2)$

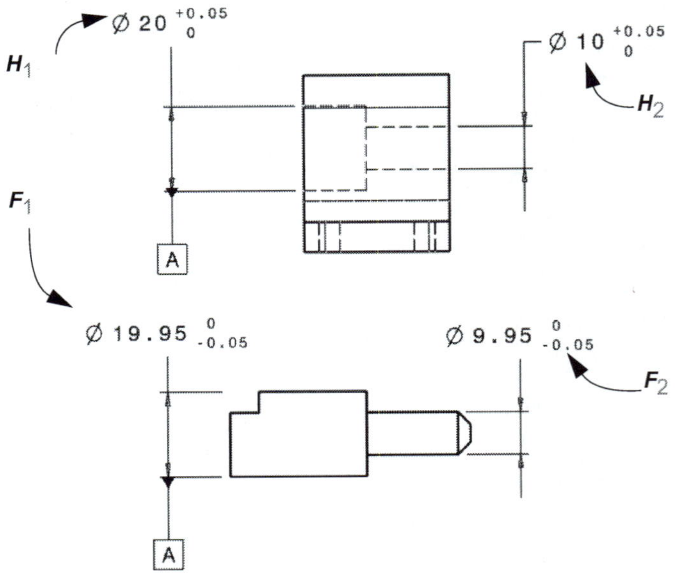

Figure A–32

$T_1 + T_2 = (20 + 10) - (19.95 + 9.95)$

$T_1 + T_2 = 0.1$ total available tolerance

If $T_1 = 0.06$ then $T_2 = 0.04$

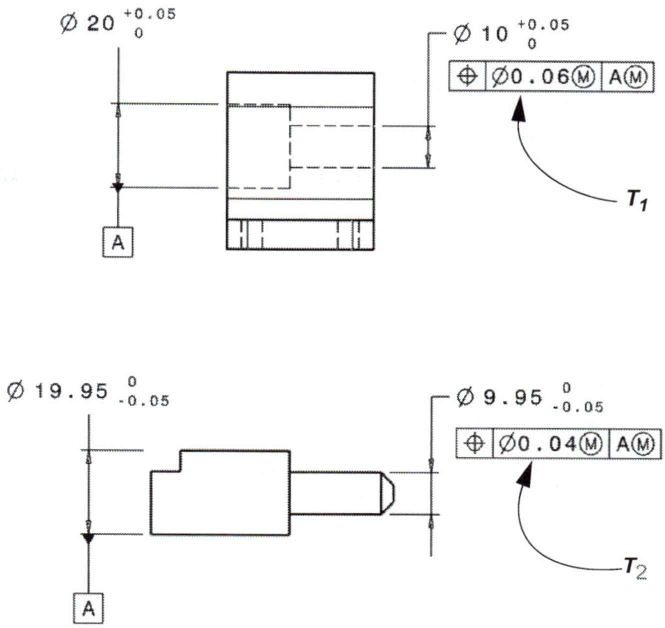

Figure A–33

Task 6 - Create positional tolerances for two mating parts.

1. Activate the **Seat A.1** widget.
2. Create the positional tolerance shown in Figure A–34 for the small bore.

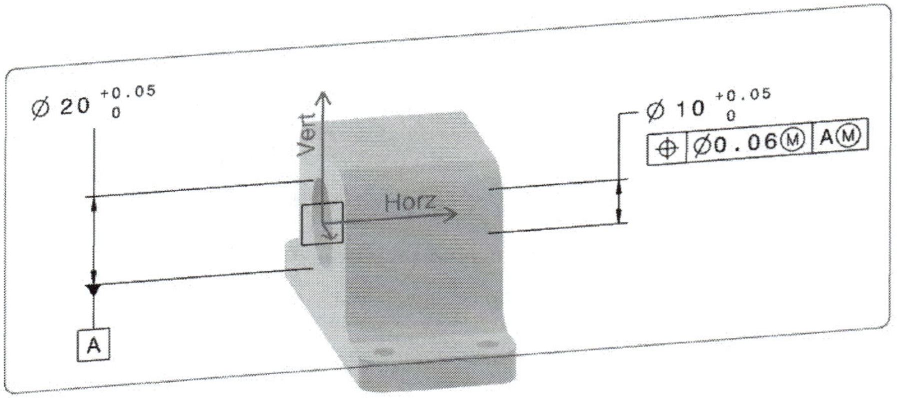

Figure A–34

3. Save the model.
4. Activate the **Post A.1** widget.
5. Create the positional tolerance shown in Figure A–35 for the small bore.

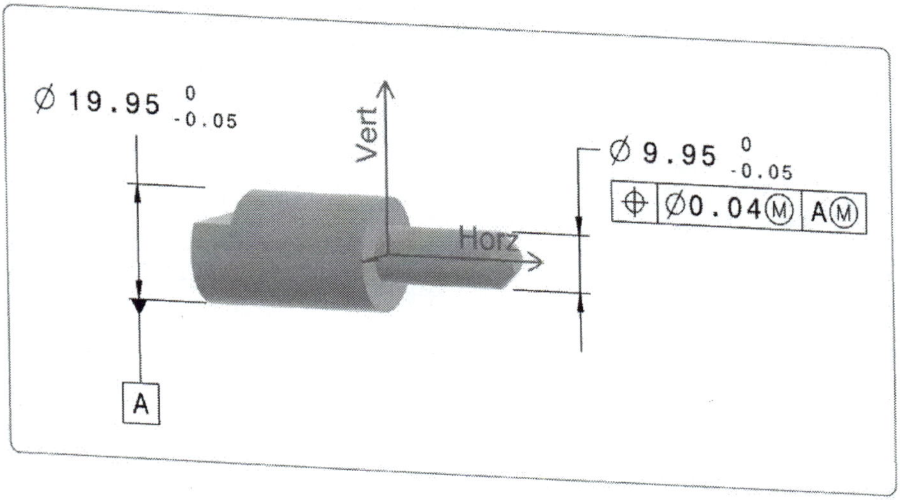

Figure A–35

6. Save the model.

Task 7 - Create a drawing.

In this task, you will create a drawing and show a view of the assembly. You will also show the tolerance information for individual parts of the assembly.

1. Create the following drawing:
   - *Standard:* **ANSI-ASME**
   - *Format:* **B ANSI**

2. Create the three views shown in Figure A–36.

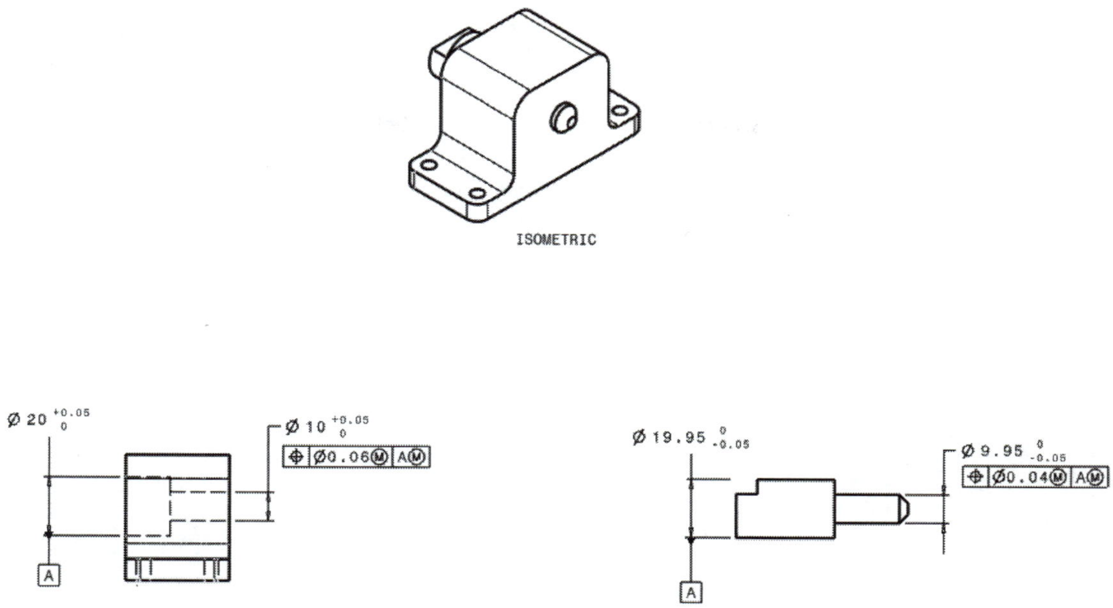

Figure A–36

3. Save the project and exit all windows.

Made in United States
Orlando, FL
04 November 2026

90209253R00192